March of America Facsimile Series

Number 7

The True History of the Conquest of Mexico

Bernal Díaz del Castillo

The True History of
the Conquest of Mexico

by Bernal Díaz del Castillo

ANN ARBOR

UNIVERSITY MICROFILMS, INC.

A Subsidiary of Xerox Corporation

Foreword

Bernal Díaz del Castillo, a veteran of several Spanish expeditions in the New World in the early 16th century, had also accompanied Hernán Cortés for the conquest of Mexico. In the 1550's Bernal Díaz began to write an account of the conquest. Spurred on by the histories of Gomára and of others which he believed to contain serious errors and distortions, he yearned to tell the "true" story of what had happened as he himself had seen it. In 1568 he finished the original draft of *The True History of the Conquest of Mexico.* All of his efforts and those of his family to get the manuscript published were to no avail, however. Not until 1632 did his *History* finally appear in print.

Bernal Díaz had come to the New World in 1514 and served in a number of expeditions before he joined Cortés at the close of 1518. Briefly he described these campaigns. But it was the conquest of Mexico which claimed most of his attention in the book. Disdaining false modesty, Bernal Díaz felt an intense pride in the accomplishments of himself and his fellows. "There never existed in the world men who by bold atchievement have gained more for their Lord and King, than we the brave conquerors." He greatly admired Cortés, but he also believed that Cortés had his share of faults. One shortcoming, in Bernal Díaz' opinion, was Cortés' desire to claim exclusive credit for the success of the Mexican operation. When he wrote to the King, he "made no mention of our valiant actions, nor even our names; but only said, 'this I did; this I ordered to be done.'" Yet, said Bernal Díaz, "we had...in our army many cavaliers equally wise in council as they were brave in the field, with whom Cortés never omitted consulting on important occasions."

Bernal Díaz saw the conquest through the eyes of the soldier. He felt no remorse for the slaughter of the Indians. He was incensed at the charge of cruelty which Las Casas had leveled against him and his comrades. He argued that if they had not dealt severely with the Indians, "our lives would have been in the greatest danger, and had we been destroyed this country of New Spain would not have been so easily gained, or a second expedition attempted." Bernal Díaz had no patience with those who failed to see matters in the same simple terms. After the conquest he and others petitioned the King "not to suffer any scholars, or men of letters to come into this country, to throw us into confusion with their learning, quibbles, and books."

Much of the charm of Bernal Díaz' *History* comes from the touches of color which his firsthand impressions lend to the narrative. He was obviously dazzled by the splendor of the Aztec capital, and he wrote in wonder of "the noise and bustle of the market-place below us." He remarked that "those who had been at Rome and at Constantinople said, that for convenience, regularity, and population, they had never seen the like." The change wrought in the city by the Spanish conquest made an equally strong impression on him as he reflected, "but all is destroyed, and that which was a lake is now a tract of Indian corn, and so entirely altered that the natives themselves could hardly know it."

For more information about Bernal Díaz and his writing, see the recent study by Herbert Cerwin, *Bernal Díaz—Historian of the Conquest* (Norman, Oklahoma, 1963). The Mexican Conquest is examined by Salvador de Madariaga, *Hernán Cortéz, Conqueror of Mexico* (London, 1942).

The True History of the Conquest of Mexico

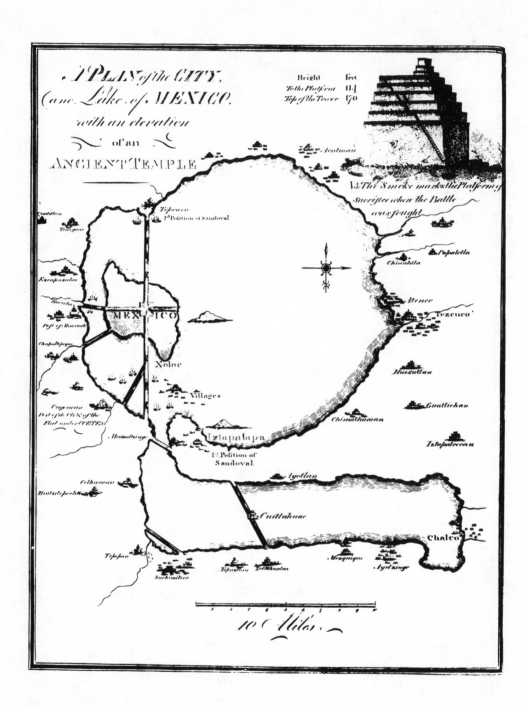

THE

TRUE HISTORY

OF THE

CONQUEST OF MEXICO,

By CAPTAIN BERNAL DIAZ DEL CASTILLO,
One of the Conquerors.

WRITTEN IN THE YEAR 1568.

————*Labore, et expensis, et damno,*
Tempore, veritatis cognitio adquiritur.

Tranflated from the Original SPANISH,
By MAURICE KEATINGE Esq.

————

LONDON,

PRINTED FOR J. WRIGHT, PICCADILLY,
BY JOHN DEAN, HIGH STREET, CONGLETON,
1800.

PREFACE.

I BERNAL DIAZ DEL CASTILLO, regidor of this loyal city of Guatimala, and author of the following moſt true hiſtory, during the time I was writing the ſame, happened to ſee a work compoſed by Franciſco Lopez de Gomara, the elegance of which made me bluſh for the vulgarity of my own, and throw down my pen in deſpair. But when I had read it, I found that the whole was a miſrepreſentation, and alſo that in his extraordinary exaggerations of the numbers of the natives, and of thoſe who were killed in the different battles, his account was utterly unworthy of belief. We never much exceeded four hundred men, and if we had found ſuch numbers bound hand and foot, we could not have put them to death. But the fact was, we had enough to do to protect ourſelves, for I vow to God, and ſay Amen thereto, that we were every day repeating our prayers, and ſupplicating to be delivered from the perils that ſurrounded us. Alaric a moſt brave king, and Attila a proud warrior, never killed ſo many of their foes as we are ſaid by that hiſtorian to have done in New Spain. He alſo ſays we burned many cities and temples; and this he does to aſtoniſh his reader; not ſeeming to recollect that any of the true conquerors exiſted, to contradict him. He alſo enhances the merit of one officer at the expence of another; ſpeaking of ſome as captains who were not with us.

He

He says that Cortes gave orders, secretly, for the destruction of the ships; whereas it was done by the common consent of all, to have the assistance of the mariners. He also depreciates Juan de Grijalva most unjustly; he being a very valiant captain. He omits the discovery of Yucatan by De Cordova, and is in an error again when he speaks of the first expedition of Garray, as if Garray had come with it. In what concerns the defeat of Narvaez, his account is conformable to the relations given; but in that of the wars of Tlascala he is as erroneous as ever. As to the war in Mexico, where we lost above eight hundred and seventy soldiers, this he treats as a matter of little importance; and he makes no mention of our losses in the subsequent siege, but speaks of it as if it had been a festival, or a marriage! but why should I waste paper and ink in the detection of his numerous errors; I will therefore proceed with my relation, for according to what the wise say, the art and beauty of historical composition is, to write the truth; and proceeding upon this rule, with such embellishment and ornament as I shall hereafter judge expedient, I will relate and bring into full light the conquest of New Spain, and the heroic services of us the true conquerors, who with our small numbers, under the adventurous and brave Captain Hernando Cortes, and with great danger and hardships, gained to his Majesty this rich country; for which service his Majesty has frequently issued his orders that we should be amply rewarded. Moreover, as a good pilot sounds, and discovers shoals and sands as he proceeds, by the lead and line, so will I, with my pen in my hand, expose misrepresentations, in my voyage through the history of Gomara, to the haven of truth; but if I were to point out every error, the chaff would outweigh the grain.

My relation will give to historians sufficient whereby to celebrate

our

our general, Cortes, and the brave conquerors by whofe hands this holy and great undertaking fucceeded; for this is no hiftory of diftant nations, nor vain reveries; I relate that of which I was an eye witnefs, and not idle reports and hearfay: for truth is facred. Gomara received and wrote fuch accounts as were intended to enhance the fame and merit of Cortes; no mention being made by him of our valiant captains and foldiers; and the whole tenor of the work fhews how much he was influenced by his attachment to that family by whom he and his are patronifed. He has alfo mifled the Doctor Illefcas, and Bifhop Paulus Jovius.

The following hiftory I have brought to its conclufion, in the loyal city of Guatimala, the refidence of the royal court of audience, on this twenty fixth day of February, in the year of our Lord, one thoufand five hundred and feventy two.

THE CONTENTS.

PART I.

CHAP-

CHAP

THE TRUE HISTORY

OF

THE CONQUEST OF MEXICO.

PART THE FIRST.

CHAPTER I.

Expedition of Hernandez de Cordova. **A.D. 1517.**

IN the year 1514, I left Caſtille in company with Pedro Arias de Avila, who was then appointed governor of Tierra Firma, with whom I arrived at the port of Nombre de Dios. A peſtilence raged at that time, of which many ſoldiers died, and moſt of the ſurvivors were invalids. The governor P. A. De Avila had a jealouſy which terminated fatally, with an Hidalgo who had conquered that province, of which he was Captain: his name was Vaſco Nunez de Balboa, a rich man, and to whom Avila had married his Daughter; but being afterwards ſuſpicious that his Son-in-law had an intention of revolting, he cauſed him to be beheaded.

B

When

When we faw that troubles were likely to enfue, and learned that the Ifland of Cuba had been lately gained under the government of Diego Velafquez, a certain number of us, perfons of quality who had come with Avila, refolved to demand his permiffion to go to Cuba. This he readily granted us; not wanting fo many foldiers as had come with him from Caftille, for the country of which he was appointed to the government, had but few inhabitants, and was already conquered. Permiffion being obtained we failed for Cuba, and arriving there, waited on the governor, who received us kindly, and promifed to give us the firft lands that fhould fall vacant. Three years however elapfed, reckoning from the time we left Caftille, and no fettlements had as yet offered. Confidering this therefore as fo much lofs of time, one hundred and ten of us elected for our Captain a rich Hidalgo of Cuba named Francifco Hernandez de Cordova, and determined to fet out under his command, upon a voyage of difcovery. For this purpofe we bought two veffels of confiderable burthen, and our third was a bark which we obtained on credit from the governor Velafquez; he however propofed as a condition, that we fhould engage the foldiers to make a defcent on certain Iflands between Cuba and Honduras, named Los Guanages, to feize a number of the inhabitants and make flaves of them, in order thereby to pay the coft of the bark; but when the propofal of Velafquez was made known to the foldiers, we to a man refufed it, faying, that it was not juft, nor did God or the King permit, that free men fhould be made flaves.

Velafquez was immediately convinced, and affented to the juftice of what we faid, and he gave us alfo what affiftance he could as to provifions. We laid in a ftore of Hogs, which were then fold at three Crowns each, and Caffava bread, there being in Cuba neither Oxen or Sheep. With fuch poor provifions, and fome trifling Toys and Ornaments for the Indians, we prepared ourfelves for the voyage, having engaged three Pilots, the principal of whom was Anthon de Alaminos, a native of Palos; the other two were named Camacho de Triana, and Juan Alvarez el Manquillo de Huelva. Having provided ourfelves as well as we could with every neceffary, we all affembled at a port on the

North

North of the Ifland, eight leagues from the town of St. Chriftopher, the settlers of which were two years after removed to the Havannah. This port is called in the language of Cuba, Agaruco. That our expedition might be conducted on proper principles, we perfuaded a Clergyman of that town named Alonzo Gonzales, to accompany us, and we alfo chofe for Veedor a foldier named Bernardino Iniguez, that in cafe Gold fhould happen to fall in our way, the proper Officer might be at hand, to take care of his Majefty's rights.

On the eighth of February 1517, having recommended ourfelves to God, and the bleffed Virgin, we failed from the port of Agaruco, and in twelve days paffed St. Anton, otherwife called the land of the Guanatareyes, a tribe of favages. Doubling this Point, we failed at hazard towards that part of the Horizon where the Sun fet, utterly ignorant of fhallows, currents, or prevailing winds. During our voyage a ftorm came on, and for two days and two nights we were in the moft imminent danger; the wind however fubfided, and in twenty-one days from our leaving the Ifland of Cuba, we faw land which had never before been difco-vered. We alfo on approaching perceived a large town, at the diftance of two leagues from the coaft, which from its fize, it exceeding any town in Cuba we named Grand Cairo. The fmalleft Veffel was then ordered to approach and examine the neighbouring coaft.

On the morning of the fourth of March, five Canoes came off to us. Thefe veffels are like troughs, made of one entire tree, and many of them capable of containing fifty men. We made fignals of invitation to thofe on board, with which they readily complied, not fhewing the leaft apprehenfion. Above thirty entered the principal veffel, where they were treated with fuch provifions as we could give them, and each was prefented with a ftring of green beads. After admiring the veffels for fome time their chief defired to return, faying that he would on the enfuing day come again to us with more Canoes, in order to bring us to land. Thefe Indians wore clofe dreffes of cotton, their waifts being girded with a narrow cloth; in which, we obferved that they exhibited

more

more fenfe of decency than the natives of Cuba, with whom this drefs
was ufed by the women only. On the enfuing day, the fame chief
came with twelve large Canoes, and made fignals to our Captain that he
would bring us to land. This he expreffed by faying, " Con-Efcotoch,"
" Con-Efcotoch," which fignifies, come to our town: and it was from this
that we gave it the name of Punta de Cotoche. It was determined by us
to accept the invitation, obferving the proper precaution of going all in a
body, and by one embarkation, as we perceived the fhore to be lined
with Indians. We therefore hoifted out our own boats, and in them,
with twelve Canoes brought to us by the chief, and our fmalleft veffel
we proceeded to the land. On arriving there we halted for a time to
confider what fhould be done, but the Cacique or Chief ftill urging us by
figns to advance, we proceeded in good order, with fifteen crofs-bows and
ten mufquets, the chief guiding us, and accompanied by a number of
the natives. On a fudden, as we paffed by fome thick woods, the
Cacique began to call out loudly to a body of Indians which he had
pofted there in ambufcade; they fallied out upon us at the fignal, and
poured in a difcharge of arrows, whereby they wounded fifteen of our
foldiers.

Thefe warriors were armed with thick coats of cotton, and carried,
befides their bows and arrows, lances, fhields and flings; they alfo
wore ornaments of feathers on their heads. Having difcharged their
arrows they advanced, and attacked us with their lances, but the keen-
nefs of our fwords and the effect of our crofs-bows and mufquetry foon
drove them to a diftance, with the lofs of fifteen left dead upon the fpot.
Near the place of this ambufcade were three buildings of lime and ftone,
wherein were idols of clay with diabolical countenances, and in ftrange
unnatural poftures, and feveral wooden chefts which contained fimilar
idols but fmaller, fome veffels, three diadems, and fome imitations of
birds and fifhes in alloyed gold. The buildings of lime and ftone, and
the gold gave us a high idea of the Country we had difcovered. On
our return to the fhore we had the fatisfaction to find, that while we
were fighting, our chaplain Gonzales had taken care of the chefts and
their

their contents, which he had with the affiftance of two Indians of Cuba brought off fafely to our fhips. In this action we made two natives prifoners, who were afterwards baptized, and called by the names of Melchor, and Julian. Having re-embarked, we proceeded as before, coafting towards the Weft.

After fifteen days cautious failing by an unknown coaft, we difcovered from our fhips a large town with an inlet which was apparently a River. This place we named from the day on which we difcovered it, which was Sunday of Lazarus ; and here we determined to endeavour to procure water, of which we were in want, owing to the badnefs of our cafks, our limited means not enabling us to purchafe proper veffels for that purpofe. As the tides run very far out, we left our large fhips a league's diftance from the fhore, and proceeding thither well armed, came to the water which fupplied the town; for in this Country as far as we could obferve, there are no running ftreams. Here we filled our cafks, and juft as we had finifhed, about fifty Indians dreffed in cotton mantles and to all appearance chiefs, approached us, enquiring by figns what we wanted ; to which we replied in the fame manner, that we came for water, and were returning to our veffels. They then pointed to the Eaft, by way of afking if we came from that quarter, repeating feveral times the word " Caftillan ;" after which they invited us to their town, to which we proceeded with them, and arrived at fome large, and very well conftructed buildings of lime and ftone, with figures of ferpents and of idols painted upon the walls. When we entered thefe temples, for fuch they were, we perceived about one of the altars traces of blood frefh fpilled ; there were alfo feveral idolatrous figures and fymbols, all which contributed to imprefs us with furprife and horror. During this time the Indians behaved peaceably, but collected in great numbers, which put us upon our guard though they appeared only to be attracted by curiofity. A body of natives foon appeared, dreffed in very ragged mantles, and each bearing a bundle of dry reeds, which having depofited together, they retired. After them came two bodies of warriors, each commanded by its captain, who drew them up oppofite to us; immediately

mediately after which, ten priefts rufhed out of an adjoining temple.——
They were dreffed in loofe robes of white cotton, their long hair was clotted with blood, and matted and twifted together fo as to be apparently
impoffible to be feparated; they had in their hands veffels containing fire
and aromatics, with which they fumigated us, making figns at the fame
time, that unlefs we quitted their Country before the fuel lying by us was
confumed, they would put us to death.   They then kindled the faggots,
and retired without doing any thing more.   The warriors however
began to make a noife by whiftling, founding their horns, and drums.
Thefe formidable preparations made us think it moft prudent to retire,
which we accordingly did, and regaining our boats on board of which
the water cafks had been already put, we embarked, and reaching our
veffels, proceeded on our voyage.   We coafted for fix days, during
which time we encountered a violent gale of wind from the North, and
were in imminent danger of being driven on fhore.   We alfo fuffered
from want of water, owing to the badnefs of the veffels, and were conftantly obliged to go on fhore and fink wells, in order to procure a daily
fupply.   Continuing our route, we arrived oppofite a town about a
league from the coaft, which we determined to proceed to, and for that
purpofe caft anchor.

This town the name of which was Pontonchan, contained feveral
buildings of lime and ftone, and was furrounded by fields of maize.——
Having landed and found a fpring of water, while we were engaged in
filling our cafks, large bodies of warriors approached us in filence; they
were armed with their ufual miffile weapons, fhields, and two handed
fwords.   Their bodies were covered by a defenfive armour of cotton
reaching to the knees, their faces painted black, white, and red, and
plumes of feathers ornamented their heads.   They accofted us in the
fame manner that the natives of Campeche had done, pointing to the
Eaft and faying " Caftillan, Caftillan," we replied to them by figns
that we came from the Eaft, but were much perplexed to know the
meaning of this expreffion, or whether to conftrue it favorably or otherwife; and as we meant to remain on fhore, for the night, we formed
ourfelves

ourselves into a body, and kept a good watch in every direction; being also occupied in consulting upon the arrangement of our future movements. During this time we heard a great noise among the Indians, which we considered as portending us no good. Some of us were for embarking, but that was considered too dangerous to attempt in the face of the enemy, others were for attacking them, on the old principle that he who makes the first attack conquers; but we had at least three hundred to encounter, for each one of us, and this was considered too rash. While thus occupied, day broke, and gave us a sight of our danger. We comforted each other with hopes of God's mercy, and each determined to exert himself to the utmost. We soon perceived great bodies of warriors advancing, with colours flying, and joining themselves to those who had assembled on the preceding night. They then enclosed us on all sides, fighting with us foot to foot, and wounded above ten of our soldiers; the execution however of our fire arms and swords made them draw off a little, but it was only to use their arrows to more effect.— They continually cried out, " Al Calachioni," or shoot at the captain; in consequence, he received no less than twelve arrows. I also got three for my share, one of which, in my left side, was very dangerous, and two of our soldiers they carried off alive; one was named Alonzo Bote, the other was an old Portuguese. Our captain seeing that all our exertions to drive them off were ineffectual, that the enemy were continually receiving supplies, while we had above fifty of our number killed, determined to endeavour to cut his way through them. This we effected, being formed into a compact body; but they pursued us at our heels, attacking us with their lances, and with showers of arrows. We however reached our boats, but it was only to encounter new difficulties; the hurry and pressure to embark was such, that the boats were sunk, and we were forced, half wading, and half swimming, to endeavour to reach the small vessel, which came as far as possible to our assistance; our soldiers received many wounds, while in and about the boats, and it was with the utmost difficulty that any of us escaped with our lives. On counting our numbers when we arrived on board the ships, we found that our loss amounted to fifty-seven. This action lasted above half an hour.

hour. In the marine charts this bay is named " De Mala pelea."
Our wounds after a little time became very painful, from the cold and sea
water, and we began to grow very much out of humour with the pilot
Alaminos, and his discoveries. He still however persisted in his original opinion, and in denying that this land was a continent.

One soldier only of those who survived had escaped unwounded;
most of us had three or four wounds, our captain twelve. The mariners
also were many of them disabled; for which reason we burned our
smallest vessel, and divided her crew between the others. But I have
yet to mention the greatest misfortune that attended us. In the hurry
to escape from the natives, we had been forced to leave our casks behind. The thirst we endured in consequence thereof, during the time
that we were at sea was such that our very tongues and lips cracked:
Such cruel hardships attend those who go on voyages of discovery! After
three days sail, we perceived an inlet which we concluded would lead to
a river or some fresh water; fifteen mariners and three soldiers entered to
examine it, but what water they found was all salt, even where they sunk
pits on the shore, and when they returned with it, distressing as our
thirst was we found it undrinkable. We called this the inlet of alligators, from the number of those animals seen there. The reigning
winds of North and North East at this time increased to a storm which
we fortunately weathered, and then, having determined to return to the
Havannah, by the advice of Alaminos we ran for the coast of Florida,
which by his maps, his degrees, and altitudes, he found to be distant
about seventy leagues. With this navigation he was well acquainted, having been in that country in a voyage of discovery with Juan Ponce de Leon,
ten or twelve years before. Accordingly, having sailed for four days
across the gulf, we discovered that part of the coast of America to which
we were bound.

When we approached the coast, the first object with us was to
obtain a supply of water. Our captain, from his wounds and sufferings
by thirst, was sinking hourly; on his account therefore and our own,

twenty

twenty of us, of which number I was one, went on fhore with the cafks. The pilot Alaminos warned us to be prepared againft a fudden attack of the natives, who had in that manner fallen on him, in his former vifit to this coaft. We accordingly put a good guard in an open place near the fhore, and proceeded to make wells, in which to our great fatisfaction we found excellent water. We ftayed about an hour fteeping cloths in it, and wafhing our wounds, and this delay enabled the Indians to fall on us; for at the expiration of that period, one of our out centinels came to give us the alarm of their approach, a few moments only before they appeared. Thefe Indians were very tall of ftature, and were clothed in the fkins of animals. They affailed us with a flight of arrows, with which they wounded fix of us, and myfelf among the reft. We however beat them off, and they then went to fupport another body of their countrymen, who, in their canoes, had attacked and feized our boat, and were dragging it away with them, having wounded the pilot Alaminos, and four of the mariners. We followed them clofe, and wading above our middles in the water, refcued the boat, leaving in all twenty-two of them dead, and three who were flightly wounded, we made prifoners; thefe however died in the voyage. After the natives were beaten off, we enquired of the foldier who brought the report of the enemy, what had become of his companion; he faid that a fhort time before, he faw him go towards the water fide with a hatchet in his hand, to cut a palmita; that he fhortly after heard him cry out as he fuppofed when the enemy were putting him to death, and therefore he gave the alarm, the Indians appearing immediately after. This foldier was named Berrio: he was the only perfon who efcaped without a wound in Pontonchan. We went in fearch of him, and found the plant which he had begun to cut, and the fand much trodden, but no trace of blood: of courfe we concluded that he had been carried off alive. After fearching for the fpace of an hour we gave him up, and returned to the veffels with the water, which, when our companions faw, they knew no moderation in their joy. One man in particular leaped into the boat when it came along-fide the veffel, and feizing a cafk of water, did not ftop drinking until he died.

C

We

We then proceeded on our voyage by fome low Iflands named Los Baxos de los Martires, where the veffel on board which our captain was ftruck ground, and in confequence took in fo much water that fhe was near finking; indeed we feared that our utmoft exertions in pumping could not bring her into port. There were as I recollect two failors of the Levant on board: when we called to them to affift us in pumping they replied, "facetelo vos ! Do it yourfelves !" At this time we were exhaufted by fatigue, and the veffel in the moft imminent danger of finking: however we forced them to give us their affiftance, though unwillingly: and by our exertions, with the bleffing of God, we arrived fafely at Puerto de Carenas, where is now built the city of the Havannah.

On our arrival an exprefs was forwarded to the Governor D. Velafquez, to inform him that we had difcovered a Country where the houfes were built of lime and ftone, and the inhabitants decently clad; that they fowed maize, and poffeffed gold. Our captain went immediately to his eftate near Santi Spiritus, where he died in ten days after his arrival. Three foldiers alfo died of their wounds in the Havannah, and the reft difperfed to their different homes or avocations. The fame of our difcovery was fpread through the Iflands by the veffels on their arrival. When the figures and idols which they brought were produced, it was believed that they were antiques conveyed to thofe countries by a Jewifh colony, after the deftruction of their city by Titus and Vefpafian. Our Indian prifoners on being afked if their country produced gold, replied in the affirmative, which is contrary to fact, as has been fince well afcertained. The name which that part of the continent now acquired, was owing to an equivocal expreffion or miftake of words. Yuca is the Infular name of the plant made ufe of for bread, the heap of earth in which it is planted is called by thefe people, Tale; on being queftioned relative to it, they faying they knew it, and ufing this word with its fignification in their language, the two repeated together made the word Yuca-tal, or Yucatan as it was expreffed by the Spaniards, and ever after remained applied to that part of America. Such was all

that

that the foldiers gained by this difcovery, from which we came back, poor and wounded, and thought thofe fortunate who had reached their homes alive, for our lofs from firft to laft amounted to feventy of our number. Diego Velafquez wrote to his patron the Bifhop of Burgos relating the particulars of his difcovery and the expences he had been at, for all which he obtained fame and credit with his Majefty, but not a fyllable was faid of the poor foldiers who had expended their properties, and loft, or rifqued, their lives in the expedition.

Three foldiers of us whofe object was to reach the town of Trinidad, as foon as our wounds were healed, agreed with an inhabitant of the Havannah who was going thither in a canoe with a cargo of cotton to fell, for our paffage, for which he was to be paid ten crowns in gold. Accordingly we embarked with him, and after coafting for eleven days, we arrived near an Indian town named Canarreon, where we were driven on fhore by a violent gale of wind. The canoe was dafhed to pieces, and we with difficulty reached the land, naked, wounded, and bruifed, by the violence of the waves. We had no refource but in the clothing adopted by the firft pair, and in the fame wood where we procured this, we found a fpecies of tough flexible roots called Bejucos, with which we tied on our feet fandals made of the bark of trees, which we cut out for that purpofe with fharp ftones; and travelling thus for two days, we came to the village of Yaguarrama where Fray Bartholome de las Cafas afterwards bifhop of Chiapa was then parifh prieft. On the next day I went to another town named Chipiona, belonging to Alonzo de Avila, where, at the houfe of a friend named Anthonio de Medina I got clothed, and then purfued my journey to St. Jago, where I found the governor Velafquez bufily employed in fiting out another armament for difcovery. As he was my relation, and alfo as governor, I went to wait upon him, and after paying him my refpects, he afked me if I was able to undertake another expedition to Yucatan. I told him that he fhould fay the land of wounds and calamity; to which he anfwered that he knew we had fuffered much in the former voyage, but that

fuch

ſuch was the fate of thoſe who ſought honour and fame in new diſcoveries; and that his Majeſty ſhould know and reward our merits.
" And now," continued he "my ſon, try your fortune again, and I
" will put you in a ſtation where you ſhall acquire honour."

CHAPTER II.

Expedition of Juan de Grijalva. A. D. 1518.

THE governor Diego Velafquez, encouraged by the accounts of thofe who returned from the laft expedition, now fitted out a fecond armament confifting of four fhips, two of which were employed in the former voyage, and the other two were purchafed by himfelf. Thefe veffels were to be commanded by his relation Juan de Grijalva, (in chief,) Pedro de Alvarado, Francifco de Montejo, and Alonzo de Avila, all perfons of valour, and poffeffed of eftates in the iflands. The charge of the equipment was divided thus; each captain found provifions and failors, the arms and fome trifling neceffaries were provided by the go-vernor. The accounts of the richnefs of the country, efpecially thofe given by the native Melchorejo, created an univerfal difpofition in thofe who were unprovided in the iflands to engage in the expedition. Ac-cordingly, two hundred and forty companions immediately entered them-felves, amongft whom I determined to try my fortune a fecond time.

Each of us depofited a certain fum to provide various neceffary articles, both for the veffels and for ourfelves in the field. The orders and inftructions given by the governor to our chief were, to procure and bring back all the gold and filver that he could, and he gave him difcretionary power to act as he thought beft, in regard to colonization or eftablifhments. The veedor appointed by us was named Penalofa, and our chaplain was named Juan Diaz. We had the fame pilots who had gone the former voyage, and a fourth whofe name I do not recollect. Our rendezvous was at the port of Matanzas, which was convenient for victualling, as the colonifts had their plantations and ftores of hogs in that neighbourhood.

The

The name of Matanzas was given to this place on the following account. Before the island was conquered, a Spanish vessel was wrecked on this coast, in her voyage from St. Domingo to the Lucayan Islands to procure slaves. Thirty men and women escaped to the land, and were met by a number of Indians who offered them an hospitable reception, and proposed to take them in their canoes. Our people being embarked, when they were in the middle of the river the Indians upset the canoes, and killed or drowned them all except three men and one woman who was handsome; she was taken by one of their principal caciques, and the three men were allotted to others. After the conquest of the island was effected, she and the Indian chief parted, and I afterwards knew her married in the city of Trinidad to one Pedro Sanchez Farfan. I was also acquainted with the three men; one was named Gonzalo Mexia, another Juan de St. Estevan, and the third Cascorro. This last mentioned had married the daughter of the cacique to whose lot he fell, and had his ears and nose bored like the Indians.

On the fifth day of April 1518, after having heard mass with great devotion, we set sail, and in ten days passed the point of Guaniguanico, called by the pilots St. Anton. In eight days more we came in sight of the Island of Cozumel, whither we were driven in part by the currents, which forced us farther down than when we came with Cordova. Coasting along the island by the South, we perceived a landing place at which our captain Grijalva went on shore with a considerable body of soldiers. The natives of an adjacent town fled at the sight of the ships, but our people found two old men who could not follow them concealed in some maize. Our interpreters, Julianillo, and Melchorejo, understood these Indians very well, for that island is distant but four leagues from their native country. Grijalva treated them well, and made them some presents, in hopes to be thereby able to induce the inhabitants to return to their town, for which purpose they were then dismissed. Some time after, an Indian girl of a good person and countenance joined us, and addressed us in the language of the Island of Jamaica, which is the same with that of Cuba. The account she gave of herself was, that she had failed from Jamaica two years before in a large canoe with ten of her countrymen, to fish at certain small Islands, and that the current had driven them hither, where the natives had killed and sacrificed her husband and all her companions. Our captain thought that this woman might be serviceable in inducing the natives to return; he therefore sent her on a message to that effect, for which he allowed them a period of two days; but on the ensuing one she came back and informed us that she could not prevail on any of them to do so. We named this place Santa Cruz, having discovered it on the day of that holy festival. In the town we found a quantity of honey in hives, vegetables, such as boniatos and potatoes, and droves of hogs of the species of the country with the navel on the back. There were two smaller towns in the Island which we did not visit, Grijalva perceiving further stay to be loss of time.

Pursuing the route of F. H. de Cordova, in eight days we arrived at Champoton, and casting anchor at the distance of a league from the shore, on account of the height of the tides, we disembarked one half of our soldiers, landing them close to the town. The natives, proud of their former success, attacked us immediately on our landing in great bodies, and with much military parade. Experience had taught us to go well prepared, and accordingly we brought falconets in our boats. Half our number was wounded before we reached the land, but when we formed, and had received a reinforcement by a second embarkation, we soon drove them to the marshes, with the loss however of three of our soldiers, and our captain received three arrows, and had two of his teeth beaten out. When we entered the town after the defeat of the natives, we found that they had removed all their effects. Three of them whom we had taken prisoners we thought by kind usage to have made friends of, and that they would have induced their countrymen to return, but after we had dismissed them they never came back to us, and we suspected that our interpreters had treacherously spoken to them in opposition to our intentions. The field where we fought with these people was very stony, and there was on it a prodigious swarm of locusts. These animals during the action sprang up and struck us in

the

the faces, fo that we hardly knew when to put up our fhields to guard us, or whether they were arrows or locufts which flew round us, they came fo mixed together.

After four days ftay in Champoton we re-embarked, and purfuing our voyage arrived at what appeared to be the entrance of a large river ; but our pilot Alaminos infifted that what we faw before us was an Ifland, and that he faw the termination of it. Thefe circumftances caufed us to name the bay, Boca de Terminos. Captain de Grijalva with many officers and foldiers went to examine the bay and neighbouring country ; on the fhore they found fome adoratories or temples, built of lime and ftone, and containing idols made of clay and wood, fome in the figures of women, others of ferpents, and many horns of deer. Thefe were the occafional offerings of traders or hunters, who frequented thofe parts, for they were entirely uninhabited, but abundantly ftocked with deer and rabbits. We killed ten of the former with one greyhound, and many rabbits. The dog was left behind us on our embarking, but when we returned with Cortes we found him on the fhore, and he feemed to have fared well in our abfence for he was very fat and fleek.

From the harbour of Boca de Terminos we coafted weftward, and in three days arrived at another inlet, which being difcovered by founding to be fhallow, was entered by the veffels of the lighteft burthen, in which, together with the boats, we embarked our whole force, as we perceived numbers of armed Indians in canoes. We therefore judged that we were near fome populous town or diftrict, and the more fo, as we found, and took fifh out of nets, which were laid in the track of our veffels. This River was called Tabafco from a native chieftain; but it was from this time named in honor of our Captain, de Grijalva, and it is fo put down in the maps. When we approached the fhore we heard the noife occafioned by the falling of timber, which was a preparation of defence, for they were very well acquainted with the tranfactions of Pontonchan. We difembarked at a point of land which was diftant about half a

league

league from the town, where was a grove of palm trees, and the natives advanced againſt us here, painted and prepared for battle, in about fifty canoes; but fortunately it was determined on our part, to addreſs them through our interpreters, who declared to them our pacific intentions, and invited their chiefs to an interview. Upon this, about thirty Indians landed, to whom we preſented beads and coloured glaſs. Our captain then cauſed to be explained to them how we had come from a diſtant country, and were the vaſſals of a great prince to whom we recommended them to ſubmit, and further, that in exchange for thoſe beads and glaſſes, we expected that they ſhould give us a ſupply of proviſions. Two of them, a chief and prieſt made anſwer to us by ſaying that they would barter, and give us proviſions: that as to a ſovereign, they already had one, and that our demand was ſo unſeaſonable that they adviſed us to be cautious how we repeated that, or any ſimilar one, leſt they ſhould attack us as in Pontonchan, they having two xiquipils (eight thouſand men each,) of warriors ready for the purpoſe, adding, that though confident of their force, they had come to treat with us amicably, and would repeat to their chiefs our propoſal, and return to us with their deciſion for peace or war. Grijalva embraced them in token of peace, and preſenting them with ſtrings of beads, required their ſpeedy return with an anſwer, which they promiſed and fulfilled, aſſuring us on the part of their chiefs, of the moſt pacific conduct; and as it is the cuſtom of that country in amicable treaties to make preſents, thirty Indians ſhortly afterwards came to us loaded with broiled fiſh, fowls, fruit, bread of maize, and veſſels with lighted coals to fumigate us with incenſe, and ſpreading a mat upon the ground and a mantle over it, they laid thereon ſome toys of gold made in the form of birds, and lizards, and three necklaces of gold caſt like beads, with ſome other trifles not altogether worth two hundred crowns; they alſo produced ſome cotton mantles and other articles of clothing uſed by them, ſaying, that we ſhould receive their preſent kindly, it being the whole of the gold that they were able to collect. But they added, that more to the Weſt there was abundance thereof, repeating ſeveral times, "Mexico," and "Culua," words which we at that time did not underſtand.

D   We

We were satisfied however by this proof that there was gold in the country, and we haftened to quit our ftation, where a gale of wind from the North, fuch as was to be hourly expected, might prove fatal to us.

In two days fail from this place, we arrived oppofite to a town on the coaft, named Aguayaluco, where we obferved the inhabitants parading, armed with fhields of the fhell of the turtle, which being polifhed and fhining in the fun our foldiers infifted were of gold. This place we named La Rambla. We next came to an inlet where the river Farole difcharges itfelf: this we named the river of St. Anthonio. Continuing our route by the mouth of the great river Guacayalco, and the high chain of mountains which are covered with perpetual fnow, as alfo others nearer the fea and which we named the ridge of St. Martin, becaufe they were firft defcribed by one of our foldiers of that name, Alvarado difcovered and entered the river called by the natives Papalohuna, but by us afterwards the river of Alvarado, where the natives of a place named Tlatocalpa prefented him with fome fifh. Our chief was much difpleafed with the conduct of this officer, for whofe return we were obliged to wait during three days, and gave orders that in future no fhip fhould ever feparate from the fquadron, left an accident fhould happen where it might not be poffible to afford affiftance. As foon as Alvarado had rejoined us we proceeded on our voyage until we came to the river Vanderas, fo called by us on account of the white banners which we obferved upon the fhore, and which were borne by numbers of Indians, who waved them as a fignal of invitation to us.

It is now well known through moft of Chriftendom, that Mexico is a city as large as Venice, and built in the fame manner upon the water, alfo that the numerous and extenfive provinces of that empire were ruled by a great monarch named Montezuma, whofe thirft for conqueft induced him to extend his views to the utmoft limits of poffibility. This monarch had received information of our firft expedition under Cordova, of the battle of Champoton, that we were very few in number, and that we came to procure gold in exchange for certain

articles

articles which we brought with us. All thefe particulars had been faithfully reported to him by painted reprefentations tranfmitted by ex-preffes to his court. Montezuma therefore on our arrival coming to his knowledge, iffued orders to his officers to procure from us in exchange for gold, our green glafs beads, on which they fet great value, not knowing them to be artificial, and he had alfo given them inftructions, to endeavour to make particular enquiry, both as to our perfons and in-tentions. We alfo underftood that he was much influenced by an ancient prophecy which is faid to have declared, that men were to come from where the fun rifes to rule that country. In compliance with thefe orders, his officers were now upon the coaft and making figns of invita-tion to us. This induced our general to fend a party to the fhore under the command of Capt. F. de Montejo; the weather was favorable, an unufual circumftance on that coaft; we therefore landed without diffi-culty, and found the governor of that diftrict, under Montezuma, attended by many natives with provifions of fowls, bread, and fruit, fuch as pines, and fapotes. They were repofing upon mats under the fhade of fome trees, and invited us by figns to do the fame, for our In-dians of Cotoche did not underftand their language; they alfo, as on former occafions, prefented us with incenfe. Our reception being re-ported to our chief, Grijalva, he immediately landed with the whole of the foldiers, and as foon as his rank was made known to the Indians, they treated him with the greateft refpect, which he returned with equal courtefy, and ordered beads and cut glafs to be diftributed to them, fignifying his wifh to procure gold in return; in confequence of which, we obtained pieces of gold of various workmanfhip, to the value of fifteen thoufand crowns. It muft be this gold that Gomara and Oviedo mean, when they fay in their hiftories that fo much was obtained in Tabafco, a country in which that metal is not to be found at all, or but in very fmall quantity. We at this time took poffeffion of thefe terri-tories under the Governor of Cuba, and in his Majefty's name; and after diftributing fome fhirts of European manufacture among the na-tives, we re-embarked, taking with us one of them, who was baptized and named Francifco. I faw him after the conqueft of Mexico, fettled

D 2

and

and married at a place called Santa Fe. After ſtaying here ſix days we now re-embarked and failed along the coaſt, paſſing a low Iſland diſtant three leagues from the main, called by us Iſla Blanca. Farther on we came to a large one, diſtant about a league and a half therefrom, where a party commanded by our captain went on ſhore. Our people found on this laſt mentioned Iſland two buildings of lime and ſtone, well conſtructed, each with ſteps, and an altar placed before certain hideous figures, the repreſentations of the Gods of theſe Indians. They found alſo here the bodies of five unfortunate perſons who had been ſacrificed on the preceding night, their hearts cut out, their limbs ſeparated from the bodies, and the walls and altars ſtained with their blood. This Iſland was named Iſla de Los Sacrificios. Oppoſite to it on the continent we landed, and conſtructing huts, remained ſome time time in expectation of trading with the natives for gold. Many Indians came thither, but brought very little of that metal, and appeared ſhy and timorous; in conſequence of which we re-embarked, and proceeded.

On our arrival at that part of the coaſt where the town of St. Juan de Ulua is now built, we lodged ourſelves in huts which we conſtructed upon the ſand hills, and having ſounded the harbour we found good anchorage, and it was ſecure to the North. A party of thirty of us commanded by our captain then proceeded to examine the Iſland, where we found a temple containing a very large and hideous image intended to repreſent a God, the name given to which was Tezcatepuca. Here were four Indians in long black mantles reſembling the habit of the Do-minicans; theſe were prieſts, and they had that day ſacrificed two boys, and offered their hearts to that curſed idol. On our entering they came to us with their pots of incenſe, but we could not endure it, being diſ-guſted and grieved at the ſight, and the horrid cruelty of their ſacrifices. Our interpreter who ſhewed ſome marks of intelligence being queſtioned as to the cauſe of thoſe victims being put to death in that manner, made anſwer as well as he could, that it was done by the Indians of Culva or Culchua, meaning the Mexicans; but he pronounced this word, Ulua, a name which ever after diſtinguiſhed the place. It was called St. John,

partly

partly becaufe this was the day of St. John, and partly in compliment to our chief, Juan de Grijalva. The neighbouring Indians brought us fome gold, but in fo trifling a quantity as not to be worth mentioning, and here we remained feven days defperately annoyed by the mofquitos. Our bread now growing very bad, and our wounded men declining, being alfo convinced that the land where we were was a part of the continent, and our number having been fo reduced as to be infufficient for colonization, it was determined to fend P. de Alvarado to Cuba for a reinforcement, which was accordingly done, for our chief was very anxious to eftablifh a fettlement, and always fhewed himfelf a moft valiant officer, the very reverfe of what would be fuppofed, from the afperfions caft upon him by Gomara.

From the time of our failing the Governor of Cuba had always been penfive and uneafy as to our fate; at length he determined to fend a veffel in fearch of us, commanded by a valiant foldier named Chriftoval de Oli: but after De Oli had failed for fome time in our track, he met with a gale of wind which fo fhattered his veffel that he was obliged to return to Cuba, without having gained in any degree the intelligence he was fent for. This was a great difappointment to Velafquez; however he was foon relieved by the arrival of Alvarado. The difplay of the gold ftruck the governor and all who faw it with aftonifhment; and Velafquez thought he never could fufficiently fhew his favor to one who had brought fuch agreeable intelligence; Alvarado was feafted and honored, and the fame of the newly difcovered and wealthy country was diffufed and enhanced through the Iflands, and foon reached Caftille.

We determined now to extend our difcoveries as far as circumftances would permit, and paffing by the mountains of Tufta and Tufpa, we approached the province of Panuco, thickly fet with populous towns, about three or four leagues from the coaft; and advancing further, arrived at the river de Canoas, fo named by us on account of what I am going to relate. We were here fuddenly attacked while at anchor by ten canoes filled with Indians; they fell violently on the fmalleft fhip

which

which was commanded by Alonzo de Avila, and it seems as if their intention was to have carried her off, for they cut the cable, notwithstanding the gallant defence made by those on board; but we sent them speedy assistance, whereby the enemy were forced to retreat with a considerable loss. We then weighed anchor and pursued our route, until we arrived at a very bold point of land, which the violence of the current, according to the report of our pilot, did not allow us to double; whereupon it was determined in council to return to the Island of Cuba, contrary to the opinion of Grijalva who was anxious to establish a settlement, but was opposed for several reasons, such as the lateness of the season, want of provisions, and hardships already sustained by the troops.

We therefore set sail upon our return, in which, aided by the current, we made way rapidly, and entering the river of Tonala, were obliged to delay, in order to repair one of our ships. This vessel struck three times in crossing the bar, on which the water is shallow. The natives came to us here very amicably, and brought provisions of bread, fish, and fruits. We presented them with beads and cut glass, desiring gold in return, and this being made known in the neighbourhood, the inhabitants of Guacacualco and other places brought to us what gold was in their possession.

It was a custom of the Indians of this province invariably, to carry small hatchets of copper, very bright, and the wooden handles of which were highly painted, as intended both for defence and ornament. These were supposed by us to be gold, and were of course eagerly purchased, insomuch that within three days we had amongst us procured above six hundred, and were while under the mistake as well pleased with our bargain, as the Indians with their green beads. One mariner thought he had made his fortune, having purchased seven of them. I recollect also that a soldier named Bartholome Pardo entered a temple which was on the summit of a high mount, and there found in a chest some diadems and collars of gold, and two figures of idols. The gold

he

he kept for himself, and presented the idols to our commandant. The story however came to the ears of the latter, who insisted on having the gold, but was induced to leave it with the poor man on his paying his Majesty's fifth, and the whole was not worth eighty crowns.

As this country is infested by mosquitos, in order to avoid them I went to sleep in a large temple, near which I at this time sowed seven or eight seeds of oranges, which I had brought from Cuba. They grew very well, for the priests of the temple took care of them when they saw that they were uncommon plants. This I mention, because they were the first trees of the kind that ever grew in New Spain. After the conquest of Mexico, this province being considered as offering the greatest advantages, was chosen by most of the principal persons amongst the conquerors, of which number I was one; and on my arrival there I went in search of, and found my young trees flourishing, and having transplanted them, they all did very well.

We now embarked, leaving the natives very well satisfied with us, and sailed for Cuba, where we arrived after a voyage of forty-five days. The governor was well pleased with the gold, which amounted in value to twenty thousand crowns: but there was much laughter when the six hundred hatchets were produced, and assayed; the governor however was on the whole contented, though he appeared for a time displeased with Grijalva, which was owing to the unjust aspersions of the two captains, Avila and Montejo.

Velasquez now wishing to convey to his Majesty the first account of his voyages of discovery, and the result of them, sent his chaplain Benito Martinez to Castille with letters to his patron the Bishop of Burgos, and to the licentiate Juan Zapata, and secretary Lope Conchillos, both of whom were employed in the affairs of the Spanish settlements in the West Indies. With all these, who were persons in power, Velasquez had created a strong interest for himself, by giving them rich districts in the islands, preferring thereby his own interest

to

to that of his Majefty. Martinez was inftructed to obtain for the governor a patent or commiffion to procure gold, and to make conquefts
and fettlements as he judged expedient, through all the newly difcovered
countries. This he not only completely effected, but fuch was the fatisfaction of thofe in power with the conduct of Velafquez, and the proofs
which he fent of the wealth of thofe countries, that Martinez alfo
brought back with him a commiffion for his employer, of adelantado
of the Ifland of Cuba.

CHAPTER III.

~~~~~

Expedition of H. Cortes. A. D. 1518. 1519

THE Governor of Cuba was anxious to profecute the advantages of which the expedition of Grijalva afforded him fo flattering a profpect. For this purpofe he provided ten fhips at the port of St. Jago, four of which had been on the former voyage, and fupplied them with fuch provifions as that place afforded, but their full complement of neceffaries and appointments was to be taken in at the Havannah. Great difference of opinion exifted as to the appointment of a chief: Vafco Porcallo a man of quality and related to the Count de Feria was propofed, but Velafquez was afraid to truft his armament with one of his bold character, left he fhould revolt, and declare himfelf independent. Auguftin Vermudez, Anthonio Velafquez Borrego, and Bernardino Velafquez, all relations of the governor, were alfo fpoken of, but the foldiers were in general inclined towards Grijalva.

Juft at this time Andres de Duero, fecretary to the governor, and Amador de Lares, the Contador of his Majefty in Cuba, made a private propofal to a refpectable Hidalgo named Hernando Cortes, a native of Medellin in Eftremadura, and fon of Martin Cortes de Monroy, and of Catalina Pizarro Altamirano, both, though poor, Hidalgos, and of the good lineages of that province. Hernando Cortes poffeffed a property in the Ifland of Cuba, had been twice Alcalde there, and had lately from motives of inclination married a lady named Donna Catalina Suarez Pacheco, daughter of Diego Suarez Pacheco of Avila, and of Maria de Mercaida a Bifcayan. This marriage brought much trouble upon Cortes, and he was frequently in confinement by the interference of D. Velafquez. Leaving this to be related more fully by others, I will now however proceed in my narrative of what took place between Cortes and

E   the

the Secretary and Contador. These two officers, the particular confidential friends of Velafquez, agreed with Cortes to procure by their intereft with the governor his appointment to the command of the armament, on condition of his giving them, each, equal parts with himfelf, in the treafure which fhould come to his fhare; for the commiffion was to be extended no farther than barter and obtaining gold, and not to colonization. This being agreed amongft them, the Secretary and Contador took fuch meafures, praifing and recommending Cortes, and vouching for his fidelity, to Velafquez, who had ftood as father to him at his marriage, that they fucceeded in obtaining the commiffion for him, which, it being the office of the fecretary to draw it up, was done as the proverb fays with very good ink, and fully ratified, according to the wifh of Cortes.

As foon as the appointment was made public, to fome it gave fatisfaction, and others were difpleafed at it; and one Sunday, the governor going as ufual to mafs attended by the moft refpectable perfons of the town and neighbourhood, he placed Hernando Cortes by way of diftinction on his right hand; upon which occafion one Cervantes, called the mad, a kind of buffoon, ran before them repeating his abfurdities fuch as, " Huzza for my mafter Diego, what a captain has he " chofen! And how foon he will lofe his fleet!" With much of that kind, but all having a malicious tendency. Andres de Duero who was prefent cuffed him, and bid him be filent, faying he well knew that he repeated what others put in his mouth, but the rogue perfevered, adding, that he would quit his old mafter, and follow the fortunes of Cortes. It was certain that the relations of Velafquez hired him to repeat thofe things under the colour of folly, and to alarm the governor; but all he faid turned out literally true.

Cortes immediately on his appointment proceeded with the greateft activity in making his preparations; he alfo dreffed and appeared in much greater ftate as to his own perfon than before; wearing a plume of feathers, and a gold medal in his cap, which ornaments became him

very

very well. His funds were very inadequate to this expence, for he was much indebted and diftreffed, although he had a good eftate; being very extravagant, both as to himfelf and the drefs and ftate of his wife; but certain merchants, his friends, named Jaime or Jeronymo Tria, and Pedro de Xeres, perceiving that he was rifing in the world, and fortune likely to favor him, advanced him four thoufand crowns in money, and merchandizes alfo, upon his property. With this, he caufed to be made a ftandard of gold and velvet, with the royal arms and a crofs embroidered thereon, and a latin motto, the meaning of which was, " Brothers " follow this holy crofs with true faith, for with it we fhall conquer."

It was proclaimed by beat of drum and found of trumpet, that all fuch as entered the fervice in the prefent expedition, fhould have their fhares of what gold was obtained, aud grants of land, as foon as the conqueft was effected. I muft obferve, that notwithftanding this was announced to be by his Majefty's commiffion and authority, the Chaplain Benito Martinez had not yet returned from Caftille. The proclamation however was no fooner made, than by general inclination, as well as the private influence of Cortes, volunteers offered themfelves every where. Nothing was to be feen or fpoken of but felling lands to purchafe arms and horfes, quilting coats of mail, making bread, and falting pork for fea ftore. Above three hundred of us affembled in the town of St. Jago. The principal perfons in the family of the governor entered with us; Diego de Ordas his firft Major Domo was fent by him as a fpy upon Cortes, whom he already began to fufpect, although he diffimulated: and F. de Morla, Efcobar, Heredia, Ruano, Efcudero, Ramos de Lares, and many others were all adherents of the governor.

The relations of Velafquez ftill continued to be much diffatisfied with him, and envious of the fortune of Cortes upon this occafion; they knew that a bitter enmity had fubfifted between the two on account of certain circumftances attending his late marriage, and they omitted nothing that could be done to induce the governor to revoke his commiffion.

E 2

miffion. Of this Cortes was very well advifed, and for that reafon took care always to be in his company, and to appear entirely devoted to him. Andres de Duero alfo warned Cortes to ufe all poffible expedition, as he perceived that Velafquez was already wavering, from the importunities of his relations. Leaving therefore to his Lady Donna Catalina the care of fupplying him with what was neceffary for his voyage, Cortes warned all his captains, mafters, pilots, and foldiers. to be on board at the given time, which having feen fully complied with, he went, accompanied by his friends the Secretary and Contador, to take his leave of Velafquez, whom he parted from with great politenefs, and many affurances of fervice on both fides. On the enfuing morning he embarked, being accompanied by the governor to his fhip, and fetting fail immediately, our fleet arrived in a few days at the town of Trinidad.

There were in the town of Trinidad at this period very refpectable and opulent Hidalgos, from whom all of us, but Cortes in particular, experienced a moft hofpitable reception. Cortes here planted the royal ftandard in front of his quarters, and caufed a proclamation to be made, inviting volunters, a number of whom, Hidalgos of moft refpectable families, and perfons of wealth, immediately joined us ; amongft thefe were the Alvarados and Alonzo de Avila.

At the call of Cortes, Alonzo Hernandez Puertocarrero, coufin of the Count de Medellin, Gonzalo de Sandoval, Juan Velafquez de Leon a relation of the governor, Rodrigo Rangel, Gonzalo Lopez de Ximena, his brother Juan Lopez, and Juan Sedeno alfo came from the town of Santi Spiritus. They joined us in a body, and were received with rejoicings, difcharge of artillery, and all the marks of refpect and courtefy, due to fuch honorable perfons. Provifions were procured from the eftates of thefe Cavaliers, and the number of our companions was hourly increafing, but it was very difficult to obtain horfes. Cortes ftripped himfelf of fome of his golden ornaments, and therewith purchafed a grey mare for his friend Puertocarrero, whofe means did not permit him

to

to go to that expence, and at this time a veffel arriving with a cargo of provifions, the owner immediately waited on Cortes to kifs his hands, and enrolling himfelf with us, Cortes bought both fhip and lading from him upon credit. His name was Sedeno.

From the time that we quitted the port of St. Jago, the relations of Velafquez had not ceafed to work upon his mind, in order to induce him to fupercede Cortes in the command. In this they were much aided by one Juan Millan, an aftrologer, and confidered to be mad. This old man, to whom the governor gave an ear, was conftantly telling him how Cortes would be revenged for fome former injuries, upon an occafion when Velafquez had thrown him into prifon. Every action of Cortes was alfo explained in the moft unfavorable manner, his fudden failing was dwelt on, and the fecret treaty with the Secretary and Contador furmifed. Velafquez in confequence of thefe reprefentations, fent two confidential perfons, with pofitive orders to his brother-in-law the Alcalde Major of the town of Trinidad, who was named Francifco Verdugo, to take the fleet and troops from uuder the command of Cortes, he having been fuperceded, and Vafco Porcallo appointed in his place. Diego de Ordas, Francifco de Morla, and all the friends and relations of Velafquez alfo received orders to the fame effect.

Cortes who was well aware of thefe proceedings, exerted himfelf to fuch effect, that by promifes and other ways, he contrived to bring over all thofe upon whom Velafquez relied, and efpecially Diego de Ordas, to his own intereft, which the latter fupported moft effectually with the Alcalde Verdugo by his perfuafions and arguments, reprefenting to him the danger that would refult from any violent meafures. Such was the talent of Cortes in making friends, that the very meffengers fent by Velafquez with the orders, came over to him, one of them Pedro Laffo enrolling himfelf under his command. By the other Cortes wrote to the governor, expreffing his attachment to him in the ftrongeft terms, his furprife at the ftep that he had been induced to take, and his requeft to him, not to let himfelf be deceived by the mifreprefentations

fentations of his enemies, and of the old madman Juan Millan. Thus Cortes continued in his command. The twelve enfuing days were paffed in preparations; all the fmiths of the city were employed in making arrow heads for the crofs-bows, and alfo engaged to join the expedition.

Cortes perceiving that nothing more was to be done at the town of Trinidad, gave orders for the fleet to fail for the Havannah, and alfo, that all fuch as chofe to proceed thither by land fhould go under the command of Pedro de Alvarado, who was to receive the volunteers who expected us in fome fettlements upon our road. I and about fifty more marched with Alvarado; and Cortes, having difpatched one veffel to the Havannah under the command of his friend Juan de Efcalante by a northern route, embarked, and fet fail with his whole fleet for that port, by the South. All the fhips except that on board of which Cortes was, arrived at the Havannah without any accident, and our land party having alfo reached that town, we were there for the fpace of feven days, that we could not by any means account for his abfence. We were very apprehenfive that the fhip was loft in fome fhoals called Los Jardines, and it was determined to fail with three veffels in fearch of it, but as there was no one to command, the time was fpent in difputes, and faction began to exift as to the choice of a fubftitute for Cortes, until we fhould know what was become of him. The perfon who was moft particularly bufy on this occafion was Diego de Ordas. At length thefe intrigues were put a ftop to by the appearance of Cortes himfelf. The fhip which he was on board of had ftruck upon a fhoal, but being near the land they had got her off, by lightening her of a part of the cargo.

As foon as Cortes arrived, he took his quarters at the houfe of Pedro Barba, the Lieutenant of Velafquez, where he planted his ftandard before the door, and beat up for volunteers. He was accordingly foon joined by Francifco de Montejo, Diego de Soto, one Angulo, Garci Caro, Sebaftian Rodriquez, Pacheco, Gutierrez, and Rojas, (not Rojas the wealthy)

wealthy) alſo by a lad named Santa Clara, two brothers named Los Martinez de Frexenal, and Juan de Najara, (not the deaf man of the tennis court in Mexico,) all perſons of quality, beſides many other ſoldiers, whoſe names I do not recollect.

Cortes judged it neceſſary to ſend Diego de Ordas to the eſtate of the governor at Guaniguanico, for more proviſions of bread and bacon, and with directions to wait there for further orders. This he did, knowing that during his abſence De Ordas had ſhewn himſelf by no means attached to his intereſt. Cortes now brought his artillery which conſiſted of ten braſs guns and ſome falconets, on ſhore, and gave them in charge to four cannoniers named Meſa, Arbenga, Juan Catalan, and Bartholome de Uſagre. He alſo ordered the croſs-bows to be inſpected, the cords, nuts, and arrows, to be put in proper repair, and their range to be aſcertained by trial at a mark; and as the country about the Havannah produces much cotton, the ſoldiers provided themſelves with good quilted jackets of that material,

Cortes now began to aſſume ſtate in his eſtabliſhment, and to appear in a high character. His ſteward of the houſehold was one Guzman, (not he who took Guatimotzin priſoner,) his chamberlain was one Rodrigo Rangel, and his Major domo Juan de Caceres. He ordered mangers to be fitted up in all the ſhips, and ſtores of maize and hay to be put on board for the horſes, of which I will now deſcribe ſuch as paſſed over with us.

Captain General Cortes, had a cheſnut horſe which died in St. Juan de Ulua: Pedro de Alvarado, and H. Lopez de Avila, (in partnerſhip) an excellent cheſnut mare, for exerciſe, or ſervice; after our arrival in new Spain Alvarado took her entirely to himſelf, either by purchaſe or by force: Alonzo Hernandez Puertocarrero, a grey mare of good ſpeed, bought for him by Cortes: J. Velaſquez de Leon, a very powerful grey mare called La Rabona, (docked tail) well dreſſed, and of great ſpeed: Chriſtoval de Oli, a dark cheſnut horſe, tolerably good:

Franciſco

Francifco de Montejo, Alonzo de Avila, (between them) a dark chefnut, not fit for fervice: Francifco de Morla, a dark chefnut horfe, of
great fpeed and well dreffed: Juan de Efcalante, a light chefnut horfe,
not good for fervice: Diego de Ordas, a tolerable grey mare, but of no
fpeed: Gonzalo Dominguez, an excellent horfeman, a dark chefnut
horfe, very good, and of great fpeed: Pedro Gonzales Truxillo, a good
chefnut horfe, and fpeedy; Moron of Vaimo, a dappled grey, well on
his haunches: Vaena of La Trinidad, a dapple, fomewhat black; this
horfe did not turn out well: Lares the good horfeman, a very good
horfe, bright chefnut, of great fpeed: Ortiz the mufician and Bartholome Garcia who had gold mines, a horfe called El Harriero, one of
the beft that came over with ns: Juan Sedeno of the Havannah, a chefnut mare which foaled in the fhip. Sedeno was the richeft man in our
army, poffeffing alfo a fhip, a negro, bread, and bacon; fome of which
articles were indications of great wealth at that time, for horfes and
negroes were hardly to be procured for any money.

I muft now revert to the proceedings of Velafquez, who was more
determined than ever to deprive Cortes of the command. He was enraged when he found that Verdugo had neglected his orders, and reproached his Secretary and the Contador with having deceived him.
He now therefore fent a confidential perfon named Garnica to his Lieut.
Pedro Barba at the Havannah, with orders to him, and letters to his
friends De Ordas and Velafquez de Leon, earneftly foliciting them by
no means to fuffer the fleet to proceed, but to arreft Cortes, and fend him
a clofe prifoner to St. Jago. The meffenger was no fooner arrived than
Cortes knew his bufinefs, for he brought with him letters from a friar
who was about the governor, to our Chaplain Fray Bartholome de Olmedo, whereby the Secretary and Contador conveyed intelligence of all
the fchemes of Velafquez. Diego de Ordas it has been already mentioned
had been fent out of the way; the other perfon, Velafquez de Leon,
Cortes had now brought over completely to his fide, for he was difpleafed with the governor for not having taken, as he thought, proper
care of him. As to the Alvarados, Puertocarrero, Montejo, De Oli,
Efcalante,

Efcalante, the two Monjarazes, and all the reft of us, the Lieut. Governor not excepted, we would with pleafure have laid down our lives
for him; fo that if the orders of Velafquez were concealed in La Trinidad, they were completely fuppreffed in the Havannah, for Pedro
Barba wrote an anfwer telling him that he dare not put them in execution, fuch was the popularity of Cortes; and that he was fure if he
were to attempt it, the town would be facked, and Cortes would carry
away all the inhabitants with him. Cortes alfo wrote to Velafquez pro-
feffing his eternal devotion to his intereft, and informing him that it
was his intention to fail on the enfuing day.

The whole fleet failed for the Ifland of Cozumel on the tenth
of February 1519. Our fhip, which was commanded by Alvarado, was fent round by the north, under orders to wait for the fleet at
the point of St. Anton; and Cortes alfo fent directions to Diego de Ordas
to do the fame; but our pilot neglected his inftructions, and proceeded
for Cozumel, where we on this account arrived two days before the
reft. As foon as we had caft anchor our whole party went to the town
of Cozumel, which we found abandoned by the inhabitants. We then
proceeded to another place from which the natives fled at our approach,
but not in fufficient time to move their effects, for we found a quantity
of fowls, and fome idols, toys, and ornaments of debafed gold in the
temple of the place, wherewith we returned to the town near which
our fhip was at anchor. At this time Cortes and his fleet arrived, and
the firft thing that he did was to put our pilot Camacho in irons, for
not having obeyed his orders. He then fent for Alvarado, and gravely
reprehended him for his imprudence in feizing the property of the natives, telling him that was by no means the way to effect any good in
the country, and he immediately ordered two men and a woman whom
they had made prifoners to be brought before him, and through our
interpreter Melchorejo, defired them to call back their countrymen to
their habitations, and affured them that they need be under no apprehenfions. He ordered all the articles that had been taken to be returned,
for the fowls which had been eaten he paid in beads and trinkets, and

F

to

to each of the three natives he prefented a fhirt. The people were fo fatisfied with this treatment, that on the enfuing day the chief of the place and all the inhabitants returned, and mixed with us in fo eafy and amicable a manner, that it would have been fuppofed we had paffed our whole lives together.

Cortes now began to take the command upon him in earneft, and our Lord was pleafed to give him grace, that whatever he undertook he fucceeded in.

In the three days which we paffed here, Cortes ordered a review of his troops, which amounted to five hundred and eight, the mariners not included. The number of thefe was one hundred and nine. We had fixteen cavalry, eleven fhips large and fmall, including a brigantine belonging to one Gines Nortes, thirteen mufketeers, ten brafs field pieces, four falconets, and (as well as I recollect) thirty-two crofs-bows with plenty of ammunition. He alfo ordered the artillery-men to put their guns in order, and appointed one Francifco de Orozca, who had been a good foldier in Italy, his captain of artillery. But I know not why I now wafte fo much ink in relating this, for truly he ufed the greateft vigilance and exactnefs in all things relating to the fervice he was upon.

Cortes now fent for me and a Bifcayan named Martin Ramos, in order to queftion us as to our opinions of the meaning of the word " Caftillan," fo frequently repeated by the Indians of Cotoche, when we came with Captain Hernandez de Cordova; adding that he was convinced that it muft allude to fome Spaniards in that country: for which reafon, he queftioned the native chiefs upon the fubject. They all anfwered in the affirmative, and certain indian merchants then in Cozumel affured us that they had fpoken to them a few days before. Cortes was anxious to obtain their releafe, and being informed that compenfation would be expected, he amply provided his meffengers for the purpofe. By thefe perfons he fent letters to them, and he ordered
for

for this service two light veffels, with twenty crofsbow-men and muf-keteers under the command of Diego de Ordas. One fhip was to remain at the point of Cotoche for eight days, while the meffengers went and re-turned, and the fecond was to bring the report to Cortes how the bufinefs proceeded.

The places where the Spaniards were faid to refide, were diftant from the point of Cotoche only about four leagues. The letter which Cortes fent was as follows, " Gentlemen and brothers; here in Co-" zumel I have been informed that you are detained prifoners by a ca-" cique: I requeft as a favour that you will forthwith join me. I fend " a fhip and foldiers, with whatever is neceffary for your ranfom; they " have orders to wait eight days, but come with all difpatch to me, ,, from whom you fhall receive every affiftance and protection. I am " here with eleven fhips and five hundred foldiers, with which I will, " with the affiftance of God, proceed to Tabafco, Pontonchan, &c. &c."

The merchants of Cozumel to whom this bufinefs was intrufted being embarked, the fhips croffed the gulf, and the letters were in two days received by a Spaniard named Jeronimo de Aguilar, together with the beads fent for his ranfom. He immediately waited upon his mafter, who accepted them with fatisfaction, and gave him his liberty. Aguilar then went to his companion Alonfo Guerrero, and having made known his bufinefs, Guerrero replied to him as follows: " Brother Aguilar, I " am married; I have three fons, and am a cacique and captain in the " wars; go you in God's name; my face is marked, and my ears " bored; what would thofe Spaniards think of me if I went among " them? Behold thefe three beautiful boys; I befeech you give me for " them fome of thefe green beads, and fay that my brother fent them " as a prefent to me from our country." The man's wife who was prefent now became greatly enraged and faid in her language, " See this " flave how he comes to feduce my hufband!" Aguilar perfevered in advifing the other not to lofe his precious foul for the fake of an Indian, or at any rate if he could not part from his wife and children, to bring

F 2
them

them with him; but he could not be induced to quit his home. When Aguilar faw that it was impoffible to move him, he came with the Indian meffengers to the part of the coaft where the fhips had been ftationed; but they had already failed, for the eight days to which De Ordas confidered himfelf limited, and one more, were expired; and De Ordas defpairing of the return of his meffengers, had gone back to Cozumel, fo that Aguilar was forced to return with great forrow to his Indian mafter. Cortes was exceedingly difpleafed at De Ordas, for returning without the Spaniards, or even thofe whom he fent in queft of them.

Certain failors named the Penyates of Gibraleon, were at this time accufed of ftealing bacon from one Berrio a foldier, and a general examination and queftions upon oath taking place, they denied it, but upon a fearch, proofs were brought home to them, and notwithftanding much interceffion was made, Cortes ordered feven of them to be feverely whipped.

There was on the Ifland of Cozumel a temple, and fome hideous idols, to which all the Indians of the neighbouring diftricts ufed to go frequently in folemn proceffion. One morning the courts of this temple were filled with Indians, and curiofity having alfo drawn many of us thither, we found them burning odoriferous refins like our incenfe, and fhortly after, an old man in a large loofe mantle afcended to the top of the temple, and harangued or preached to the multitude for a confiderable time. Cortes who was prefent at length called Melchorejo to him, to queftion him in regard to the evil doctrines which the old man was delivering; he then fummoned all the caciques and chief perfons to come to him, and as well as he could, by figns and interpretations, explained to them that the idols which they worfhipped were not gods, but evil things, which would draw their fouls down to hell, and that if they wifhed to remain in a brotherly connection with us, they muft pull them down, and place in their ftead the crucifix of our Lord, by whofe affiftance they would obtain good harvefts, and the falvation of their

fouls;

fouls; with many other good and holy reasons, which he expressed very well. The priests and chiefs replied, that they worshipped these gods as their ancestors had done, because they were kind to them; and that if we attempted to molest them, the gods would convince us of their power, by destroying us in the sea. Cortes then ordered them to be prostrated, which we immediately did, rolling them down some steps. He next sent for lime of which there was abundance in the place, and Indian masons, by whom, under our direction, a very handsome altar was constructed, whereon we placed an image of the Holy Virgin, and the carpenters having made a crucifix which was erected in a small chapel close to the altar, mass was said by the Rev. Father Juan Diaz, and listened to by the priests, chiefs, and the rest of the natives, with great attention.

The regulation of our fleet was now made by Cortes, and the captains appointed. The first or admiral's ship was commanded by Cortes in person, and the rest as follows: The St. Sebastion by P. de Alvarado, the third ship in size by Alonzo H. Puertocarrero, the fourth by F. de Montejo, the fifth by Christoval de Oli. the sixth by Diego de Ordas, the seventh by J. Velasquez de Leon, the eighth by J. de Escalante, the ninth by F. de Morla, the tenth by Escobar, and the eleventh by Gines Nortes. Pilots were appointed, the night signals given, and each captain received his instructions.

In the beginning of the month of March, we set sail, after having taken a friendly leave of the natives, who promised to take care of the holy altar and crucifix; and they presented Cortes on his departure with some fowls and honey. We had sailed but a few hours when a signal gun and cry of alarm informed us that the vessel of Juan de Escalante which contained the bread for the fleet was in danger, having sprung a leak. This forced us to put back to the place from whence we had sailed. On our return there, we were visited by the friendly Indians, and the cause of it being made known to them, they immediately brought their canoes to assist us in taking the lading out of the vessel, and

and we had also the further satisfaction of perceiving on entering the temple, that so far from having done any injury to the holy altar and crucifix, they had taken care of, and placed incense before them.

The Indian messengers and Aguilar hearing of our return, joyfully hired a boat and crossed the gulf to join us. Intelligence of the arrival of a large canoe was given to Cortes, by some soldiers who had gone out to hunt wild swine, whereupon he ordered Andres de Tapia and two others to go and see who and what these Indians were, who came to us thus without apprehension. Aguilar was not in his appearance to be distinguished from a native, and he had hardly the pronunciation of his own language; his only words at first were, " Dios, Santa " Maria," and "Sevilla." His colour was as dark as a native, and he was marked like them; he had a few rags about his shoulders and waist, an oar in his hand, and the remnant of an old book of prayers tied in a bundle on his shoulder. When he came into the presence of Cortes, he like the rest of his companions squatted down upon his hams, and every one was looking for the Spaniard. At length, to the enquiry of Cortes he replied, " Here he is," and then coming forward, he was immediately supplied with proper clothing.

Being questioned concerning himself he informed us that he was a native of Ecija, and had been ordained in the church. That eight years before, he was wrecked with fifteen men and two women, going from Darien to the Island of St. Domingo, at a time of a certain litigation between one Enciso, and Valdivia. That the vessel which they were on board was stranded and went to pieces, and with her were lost ten thousand crowns in gold. Those on board taking to the boat, endeavoured to reach the Island of Cuba or Jamaica, but were forced by the current upon this coast, where the different chiefs had divided and made property of them. Many had been sacrificed, some had died of disease, and the two women had sunk a short time before under hard labour at their mills. He was to have been at one time sacrificed, but he made his escape, and taking refuge with a certain cacique had re-

mained

mained with him ever fince; and of the whole number there were now in exiftence, only himfelf, and Guerrero. As to his knowledge of the country it was very confined, for he was only employed in procuring wood and water, and digging in the maize fields, and had never been farther from the coaft than about four leagues; but he underftood that it was very populous. He defcribed Guerrero as exactly refembling an Indian, adding that he was confidered by the natives as a very brave man, infomuch that when above a year before, three fhips came upon the coaft at the point of Cotoche, (this was the expedition of H. de Cordova,) he planned the attack upon thofe who landed, and led the Indians in perfon. Upon hearing this, Cortes regretted much his not being able to get him into his hands.

Aguilar was well treated by the natives of Cozumel, who fupplied him plentifully with provifions; he in return earneftly exhorted them to continue faithful to our holy religion, the good effects of which they fhould foon perceive; and he alfo advifed them to apply to Cortes for a letter of protection, which would be of fervice to them in cafe of the arrival of other Spaniards on their coaft. This was immediately granted them; and fuch is the true narrative in regard to Aguilar.

On the fourth of March the fleet again put to fea, and was during the night feparated by a gale of wind, but on the next day all the fhips joined company except that of Velafquez de Leon, which not appearing on the enfuing day, Cortes made fail for a certain bay on the coaft, where, according to the furmife of the pilot, they found the fhip, which had put in during the ftorm, and was detained there wind bound. Here feveral of our companions went on fhore, and found in the town hard by, four temples, the idols in which reprefented human female figures of large fize, for which reafon we named this place, Punta de las Mugeres,

Aguilar faid that he had once been fent fo far with a load, and that the town where he refided was about four leagues diftant; he alfo told

us

us that the residence of Guerrero was not far off, and that the country contained gold though in very small quantity, offering to serve as a guide, if Cortes thought proper to send a party on shore; to which the general replied that he did not come for such trifles, but to serve God and his sovereign effectually. Cortes now ordered Capt. de Escobar to examine the bay called Boca de Terminos; and to leave signs on the coast of his having been there, or cruize off the bay, till the arrival of the fleet, for by the description given of the harbour, and the abundance of game, he was inclined to think it an advantageous situation to colonize.

Escobar proceeded thither, and on his landing found the greyhound which had been left behind by Grijalva waiting for him on the shore, and testifying his joy at the sight of our people; he was taken on board, and the vessel then cruized, waiting for the arrival of the fleet; but a strong gale of wind from the South came on, and forced her considerably out to sea, so that when we arrived there, Escobar's ship was no where to be seen. On sending on shore however, a letter was found, wherein he told Cortes of the state of the harbour, and country, both of which he represented in a favorable light. We then stood out, and in the ensuing day his vessel joined us. At this time we were near the point of Pontonchan, the natives of which Cortes and many of us were well inclined to punish for their conduct on former occasions, but it was opposed by the pilots on account of the shallowness of the coast, and height of the tides, whereby vessels are compelled to ride at least two leagues out at sea. We therefore continued our voyage for the river of Grijalva.

On the thirteenth day of March 1519, we arrived with the whole armament at the river of Tabasco or Grijalva. As we knew that it did not admit vessels of great burthen we selected the lighter ones, and in them, together with the boats, our troops proceeded to the shore, and disembarked at the point of Palmares, which was distant from the town of Tabasco about half a league. The borders of the river, which are

covered

covered by mangroves, were filled with canoes containing armed Indians, and above twelve thoufand warriors had affembled in the town of Tabafco which was at that time poffeffed of an extenfive domination over the neighbouring diftricts. This afforded matter of furprife to us who had been at this place before, and the reafon of their prefent hoftility we afterwards found to be, that the neighbouring nations of Pontonchan and Lazarus, (as we named the place,) had reproached them for their daftardly timidity, as they confidered it, in treating amicably with us, inftead of attacking us at our landing as the others had done. For this reafon they were determined to take the prefent opportunity of retrieving their character with their neighbours.

As foon as Cortes perceived what kind of reception he was to expect, he directed Aguilar to addrefs himfelf to fome of the natives who appeared to be chiefs, and who were in a canoe which was then paffing very near us, and afk them the reafon of thefe hoftile appearances when we came to them as friends and brothers, adding, that if they were fo rafh as to recur to hoftilities they fhould certainly have caufe to repent it. This, and more to the fame purpofe being explained to them, only feemed to render them more violent againft us, and they replied by threatening us all with inftant death if we ventured to approach their town, which they had fortified with parapets aud palifades. Aguilar then requefted permiffion to procure wood and water, and an interview with their caciques, to whom our general had matters of the greateft importance and of a holy nature to communicate, but to this they only replied in the fame manner as before.

Cortes hereupon ordered three guns to be placed in each veffel, and alfo divided the mufketeers and crofs-bowmen through them. It was recollected by us who had been there before, that a narrow road went from the point of Palmares, by fome brooks and marfhes, to the town of Tabafco. Cortes ordered three foldiers to watch the motions of the enemy, and report to him if they retired to their town; which they fhortly did.

G

On

On the next morning, after mass, our general detached Captain Alonzo de Avila with one hundred soldiers, to march by the narrow road already mentioned, with instructions, that as soon as he heard the discharge of the artillery, he should attack the town on one side, while the main body did the same upon another. This being arranged, Cortes with his troops proceeded in the vessels towards the shore near the town As soon as those of the enemy who were in canoes amongst the mangroves perceived that we were proceeding to the attack, they all sallied out, and such a prodigious number of them collected at our point of disembarkation, that nothing was to be seen around us but armed hosts, nor heard except their trumpets, horns, and timbrels.

Cortes observing this, ordered a halt, and that the firing should not commence, for he wished to proceed in a strictly justifiable manner. He therefore ordered Diego de Godoy a royal notary, formally to require them to permit us to supply ourselves with wood and water, and speak to them as we were in duty bound upon what concerned the service of our God and King, warning them, that in case of violence they were answerable for all the mischief that resulted. All this, being duly explained to them produced no effect, they seemed as determined to oppose us as they were before. They made with their drums the signals for a general attack, and to close upon us, and these were immediately followed by discharges of arrows. Their canoes then proceeded to surround us, and we were compelled to fight them up to our middles in water. We were detained a considerable time here, partly owing to the attacks of the enemy with their lances and arrows, partly to the depth of the mud on the shore, from which we could not extricate ourselves but with great difficulty; and Cortes in particular, was obliged to leave one of his buskins behind him in it, and come to land barefooted. We were just at that time in very great difficulty, but as soon as we got to the dry land, with our general at our head, calling upon St. Jago, we fell upon the enemy, and forced them to give a little ground. They then fell back behind some circular works constructed of large timber, until we also drove them from thence, and entered by certain small gateways
into

into the town. We then drove them before us up the ftreet to a fecond barricade, behind which they pofted themfelves, fronting us valiantly, whiftling, and fhouting, " Al calachioni," or " kill the captain." While we were thus engaged, the party commanded by Captain De Avila and which had marched from the point of Palmares arrived, and joined us moft opportunely. He had been retarded on his route, in croffing marfhes and breaking down barricades, whereby he arrived at the moft convenient moment, for we had been detained longer than we expected in making the fummons which I have related. We now drove the enemy before us, though they fought manfully and never could be made to turn their backs, until they arrived at a great enclofed court, where were fome large apartments and halls, and three houfes containing idols. Here they had collected all their effects, but as they were forced to evacuate this laft poft, our general ordered a halt, and that they fhould be purfued no farther.

Cortes took poffeffion of the country for his Majefty and in his royal name in the following manner. Drawing his fword, he gave three cuts with it into a great ceiba tree which ftood in the area of this enclofure, and faid, that againft any who denied his Majefty's claim, he was ready to defend and maintain it, with the fword and fhield which he then held. This ftep was generally approved of, and it was formally witneffed by a royal notary. It gave caufe for fecret murmurs however amongft the party of Velafquez. In thefe actions fourteen of our foldiers were wounded; I received a flight one, and eighteen of the enemy were left dead upon the field. Here we pofted ftrong guards, and halted for the night.

On the next day Cortes detached Captain P. de Alvarado with one hundred men, to march through and reconnoitre the country for the diftance of two leagues round our poft. On this occafion the interpreter Melchorejo being ordered to attend, it was found that he had deferted on the preceding night, leaving his clothes behind him. This vexed Cortes much, as it was to be apprehended that he could convey

to

to his countrymen intelligence very injurious to us. Our general detached a second party of equal strength and upon the same duty under Captain Francisco de Lugo. This last mentioned detachment had not marched far, when it fell in with several large bodies of the enemy's warriors, who attacked our people on all sides, insomuch that all the valour of De Lugo and his soldiers could not repulse them and he was obliged to fall back, which he however did with great regularity, to our quarters, sending before him a swift Indian of Cuba to call for succour. Alvarado with his detachment had advanced somewhat farther, to the distance of above a league from the town, when his progress was intercepted by an arm of the sea, or river. Being obliged thereby to march in another direction, it was the will of God that he should come within hearing of the musketry, and the instruments and shouts of the Indians with whom De Lugo was engaged. He immediately flew to his relief, and the two bodies joining repelled the enemy and retreated towards the town, in which we who occupied it had at the same time been attacked by great bodies of the enemy, whom however we soon made retreat by the effect of our musketry and cross-bows, and our good swords. As soon as Cortes received intelligence that his detachments were engaged, he sallied out at the head of all of us who could carry arms, and we met our companions in their retreat, at about half a leagues distance. They had lost in the engagement two soldiers of the company of Captain de Lugo, and had in all eleven wounded. We returned with them to the town, bringing with us three prisoners, one of whom appeared to be a chief. We were informed by them that Melchorejo had advised them to attack us by day and by night, whereby they would, he said, destroy us, being so few. The native who told us this we released and sent to his countrymen with an amicable message, but he never returned, and Aguilar was informed by the others, that we were to expect to be attacked by the whole force of the warriors of that country.

When Cortes understood the formidable preparations which were making against us, he ordered the horses to be landed, and all the wounded men who were able to march to turn out. The horses when first brought to land were very dull and torpid, but in the course of a day they recovered their spirit. Several of our best and most alert young men were at this time taken so ill and weak by an ailment in the reins, that they could not stand on their feet, or help themselves: we could only account for it from their good living in Cuba, and the heat of the weather, and weight of their arms. Cortes ordered them to be put on board the ships, and assigning the horses to the best horsemen, he furnished each with a breastplate with bells hanging to it, and gave his cavalry general instructions not to halt, or make thrusts with the lance, until the enemy were put to flight, but in their attack to point at their faces. He selected the following officers and soldiers to serve in the cavalry. Christoval de Oli, P. de Alvarado, A. H. Puertocarrero, J. de Escalante, F. de Montejo, Alonzo de Avila, J. V. de Leon, Francisco de Morla, Lares (called by way of distinction the good horseman,) Gonzalo Dominguez another excellent horseman, Moron del Bayamo, and P. Gonzales de Truxillo. This body was commanded by Cortes in person. The artillery he put under the command of Mesa, the infantry under that of Diego de Ordas, and the colours were borne by Anthonio de Villaroel. Being thus arranged and appointed, our whole force took the field early on the morning of the day of our lady in the month of March, after hearing mass, and proceeded to the plain of Cintia, our cavalry making a circuit in order to avoid some marshy ground.

Having marched about a league we saw the enemy in the plain in our front, advancing against us, sounding their trumpets, horns, and drums, with plumes of feathers on their heads, their faces painted black, red, and white, all of them bearing defensive armour of quilted cotton, and shields, and their offensive arms consisting of large bows and arrows, lances, two handed swords, darts, and slings. Their numbers covered the whole plain, and they fell upon us furiously, wounding above seventy of our soldiers by the first discharge of their missile weapons. One soldier fell instantly dead by an arrow which pierced his ear: his name was Saldana. The enemy then closed upon and

fought

fought with us foot to foot, while we with our cannon, mufketry, crofs-bows, and fwords, maintained our ground firmly. When they had pretty well experienced the fharpnefs of our fwords, they drew off a little, but it was only to fhoot at us with more advantage; our artillery now however made great havoc amongft them from the manner in which they were crowded together, and they were at that diftance which enabled us to fire at them with the greateft advantage; but all could not make them give way.

I advifed Captain de Ordas to clofe with them, becaufe they feemed to be fhy of our fwords, and had the advantage of their miffile weapons when at a little diftance; but he objected to this, obferving that they were three hundred for every one of us. However we did advance upon them, and as they were unwilling to come within the reach of our fwords they yielded ground, and inclined towards a marfh. During all this time we were anxioufly looking out for Cortes, and very apprehenfive that he had met with fome difafter.

I recollect that in this battle, every time that the cannon were fired, the Indians fhouted, whiftled, and founded their inftruments, throwing up ftraw and duft in the air, and crying, " Ala, lala;" this they did to prevent our perceiving the mifchief done by our artillery in their crowded bodies. While we were engaged as I have now defcribed, we were rejoiced at the fight of Cortes approaching to our fupport. As the cavalry came round by the rear of the Indians, who were entirely occupied in their attacks upon us, the latter did not perceive them until they made their charge. The ground being very level, moft of the horfes active, and the men expert, they now rode through the bodies of the enemy as they chofe, and we, encouraged by this fupport, reiterated our efforts on our fide. The Indians ftruck with furprife thought that the horfe and his rider were one; they were terrified at the fight, and in an inftant fled to the adjacent woods and marfhes, leaving the field and victory to us.

Being

Being thus masters of the field, after taking breath Cortes related to us how he had been retarded in his march by bad ground, and the attacks of some bodies of the enemy who had wounded five of his men and eight horses. The cavalry then difmounted, and under a grove of trees on the field of battle, we gave thanks to God and our Lady his bleffed mother with uplifted hands, for the victory which they had given to us; in confequence whereof, and on account of the day on which the battle was fought, a town was afterwards founded on that fpot named Santa Maria de La Vitoria. We next proceeded to take care of our wounds, which we bound up, and thofe of the horfes we dreffed with the fat of the Indians whom we found dead thereabout. We then walked over the field to examine the lofs of the enemy, which we found to amount to upwards of eight hundred, dead or dying of their wounds by cannon fhots, and thofe of our fmall arms or fwords; alfo where the cavalry had charged we found them to lie very thick. For the firft hour of this battle we could not force the enemy to yield us an inch of ground, nor did they until they faw the cavalry coming on them.

We made five Indians prifoners, two of whom appeared to be chiefs; the day was growing late, and we were fatigued; we therefore retreated to our quarters, firft burying two of our foldiers, who were killed, one by a wound in the ear, and the other by one in the throat, and then, after dreffing our wounds with the fat of Indians, and having placed good guards round our poft, we eat our fuppers, and went to our repofe.

In his account of this action Gomara fays, that previous to the arrival of the main body of the cavalry under Cortes, Francifco de Morla appeared in the field upon a grey dappled horfe, and that it was one of the holy apoftles, St. Peter or St. Jago, difguifed under his perfon. I fay, that all our works and victories are guided by the hand of our Lord Jefus Chrift, and that in this battle, there were fo many enemies to every one of us, that they could have buried us under the duft they could have held in their hands, but that the great mercy of God aided

us

us throughout. What Gomara afferts might be the cafe, and I, finner as I am, was not worthy to be permitted to fee it. What I did fee was, Francifco de Morla riding in company with Cortes and the reft upon a chefnut horfe, and that circumftance, and all the others of that day appear to me at this moment that I am writing, as if actually paffing in the view of thefe finful eyes. But although I, unworthy finner that I am, was unfit to behold either of thofe holy apoftles, upwards of four hundred of us were prefent, let their teftimony be taken. Let enquiry alfo be made how it happened, that when the town was founded on that fpot, it was not named after one or other of thofe holy apoftles, and called St. Jago de la Vitoria, or St. Pedro de la Vitoria, as it was Santa Maria, and a church erected and dedicated to one of thofe holy faints. Very bad chriftians were we indeed, according to the account of Gomara, who when God fent us his apoftles to fight at our head, did not every day after acknowledge and return thanks for fo great a mercy! Would to heaven that it were fo, but until I read the chronicle of Gomara I never heard of it, nor was it ever mentioned amongft the conquerors who were then prefent.

I have related how we made two chiefs prifoners in the late battle; having been kindly treated by Cortes, and exhorted to induce their countrymen to come into amicable terms, they were difmiffed for that purpofe, after having been prefented with a number of beads, and artificial diamonds. Thefe Indians faithfully executed their miffion; and to fuch an effect, that the chiefs of the province immediately fent fifteen of their flaves with their faces befmeared with black, and in wretched habits, in fign of contrition for what had paffed, and bearing fowls, roafted fifh, and maize, as a prefent. Cortes received them with kindnefs, but the interpreter fpeaking fomewhat angrily to them faid, that it was with chiefs, and not with flaves that we were to treat.

On the enfuing day thirty Indians of rank came in good dreffes with another prefent, and to requeft permiffion to inter their dead that they fhould not be eaten by lions and tygers. This being granted
them

them, they proceeded to burn and inter the bodies. They also informed us that on the next day we fhould receive an embaffy to treat conclufively of peace. Accordingly, at the time mentioned, ten chiefs richly dreffed arrived with much ceremony, and faluted Cortes and the reft of us; they brought with them veffels of incenfe which they offered to us, demanding pardon for the paft, and declaring their good intentions in future. Cortes affuming a grave countenance told them they deferved death for their neglect of our former offers of peace; but that our great Monarch Don Carlos had enjoined us to favour them fo far as they fhould deferve it, and in cafe of their adopting a bad line of conduct, they fhould again feel the effect of our vengeance. He then caufed a cannon to be fired, the noife of which terrified them, whofe imaginations were under the impreffion of its being a living creature; and the noife of the ball in the neighbouring woods confirmed them in their way of thinking. One of the moft fpirited of the horfes was then brought into the apartment, and it being fo contrived that he fhould fhow himfelf to the greateft advantage, his apparent fiercenefs, and his action, ftruck the natives with awe. Shortly after this twenty Indians of burthen arrived bearing provifions for our ufe. Cortes converfed a long time with the chiefs, who at length took their leave, highly contented with the refult of their vifit.

On the enfuing day we were vifited by many chiefs of the neighbouring diftricts, who brought with them prefents of gold wrought into various forms, fome refembling the human face, others of animals, birds, and beafts, fuch as lizards, dogs, and ducks. Alfo three diadems, and two pieces in form like the fole of a fandal, with fome other articles of little value, nor do I recollect the amount of the whole. They alfo brought fome mantles of very large fize, but that part of the prefent which we held in the higheft eftimation was twenty women, among whom was the excellent Donna Marina, for fo fhe was called after her baptifm. Cortes thanked the chiefs for their vifit, but caufed it to be intimated to them, that the certain indication of peace was, the return of the inhabitants to their town, which by their authority he expected to fee done within two days, and this was accordingly com-

H   plied

plied with in the time prefcribed. They alfo on being called on to renounce their idolatrous worfhip, declared a ready affent upon that point.
Cortes explained to them the myfteries of our true faith, and thofe parts
of it which are reprefented in the crucifix, and the image of our Holy
Virgin. To this the caciques replied that they admired the " Tecle-
" ciguata," which in their language fignifies a great princefs.

When thefe people were queftioned as to their hoftilities againft
us they excufed themfelves by faying, that they had been inftigated
thereto by the cacique of Champoton, and alfo by our Indian interpreter who deferted from us. This man Cortes was very anxious to
lay hands on, but to his enquiries concerning him the anfwer was, that
he had fled: it came to our knowledge however afterwards, that he had
been facrificed. Being queftioned as to the place where they obtained
their gold they replied, that it was on the weft, and they frequently
repeated, " Culchua," and ': Mexico," words, the fignification of
which was at this time unknown to us. We had here an interpreter
named Francifco, who had alfo been with Grijalva; he did not underftand the language of Tabafco in the leaft, but knew perfectly what
they meant by the word Culchua, which country, he endeavoured to
explain to Cortes, lay far within the land.

On the enfuing day, an altar being built and the crucifix erected,
the town of Tabafco changed its name for that of Santa Maria de la
Vitoria. The twenty Indian women who had been brought to us,
were upon this occafion baptized, the Rev. Father Bartholome de Olmedo preaching to them many good things touching our holy faith.
Donna Marina, the principal of them, was a woman of high rank,
which indeed fhe fhewed in her appearance; and thefe were the firft
chriftian women in New Spain; Cortes gave one to each of his captains,
and we remained here five days longer, taking care of our fick and
wounded. This time Cortes employed in conciliating the natives, recommending to them to preferve their allegiance to his Majefty our
Emperor, whereby they fhould enfure our protection to them: this they
                                                            promifed

promifed faithfully to perform, and thefe were the firft of the natives of this country who became vaffals to the Spanifh monarchy.

On the next day, (Palm Sunday) with the affiftance of the natives a crofs was made in a large ceiba tree on the fpot where the battle was fought, in order to afford a long memorial thereof, for this tree has the quality of reproducing its bark. The natives attended at the adoration of the holy image and crofs, which we went in proceffion to pay our devotions to, on this feftival. They then at our requifition affifted us to make our preparations to re-embark, our pilots wifhing to get far off that coaft, which the wind at this time blew ftrongly upon; and all things being prepared, and Cortes having taken leave of the natives, in the evening of this day the troops went on board, and on the enfuing morning failed for St. Juan de Ulua.

As we proceeded along the coaft, thofe of us who had been there before with Grijalva pointed out to Cortes the different places we faw on the land, faying, here Sir is La Rambla, and there Tonala or St. Anton: more forward we fhewed him the great river of Guacacualco, the lofty mountains covered with fnow, thofe of St. Martin, and Roca Partida. We then fhewed him the rivers of Alvarado, and Vanderas, Ifla Blanca, and Ifla Verde, and clofe to the land Ifla de Los Sacrificios, and early in the evening of holy Thurfday we thus arrived at the port of St. Juan de Ulua. I recollect that while we were pointing out thefe places to Cortes, a cavalier named Puertocarrero came up to him and faid, " It feems to me Sir as if thefe gentlemen who have been here be-
" fore are making their exhibition, as it were, here you fee Montefinos
" of France, and here you fee the great city of Paris, and here the
" waters of the Duero where they run to the fea. But I fay fee the rich
" lands, and look to your meafures!" Cortes very well underftood the purport to which this was fpoken, and replied, " God give us fortune
" in arms like the Paladin Roldan, and for the reft, having you gentle-
" men for foldiers, I fhall know very well how to act to good effect."

H 2

The

The young native who was baptized by the name of Donna Marina, and who rendered such essential services in the sequel, was the daughter of the chief or Prince of Painala, a powerful lord who had several districts subject to him, eight leagues from Guacacualco. He dying while this lady was an infant, his widow married another chief, a young man, by whom she had a son whom they determined to place in succession after them. They therefore gave this girl to certain Indians of Xicalango to carry off secretly, and caused it to be rumoured that she was dead; which report they corroborated by taking the advantage of the death of a child about her age, the daughter of a slave. The people of Xicalango gave her to those of Tabasco, and the latter to Cortes, by whom she was presented to a cavalier named Alonzo Hernandez Puertocarrero: when he went to Old Castille, Cortes took her to himself, and had by her a son who was named Don Martin Cortes, and who was a commander of the order of St. Jago. She afterwards on our expedition to Higueras married a cavalier named Juan Xaramillo.

Donna Marina had by her birth an universal influence and consequence through these countries; she was of a fine figure, frank manners, prompt genius, and intrepid spirit; an excellent linguist, and of most essential service to Cortes whom she always accompanied. I was acquainted with her mother, and her half brother, who was at the time I knew him grown up; they governed their territory conjointly, the second husband being also dead. They were afterwards baptized, the mother by the name of Marta, the son by the name of Lazarus; this I know, for in the expedition to Higueras, when Cortes passed through Guacacualco, he summoned all the neighbouring chiefs to meet him in that settlement; and amongst many others came the mother, and half brother of this lady. She had told me before that she was of that province, and in truth she much resembled her mother who immediately recognised her. Both the old lady and her son were terrified, thinking that they were sent for to be put to death, and cried bitterly, but Donna Marina dried their tears, saying, that she forgave them, that at the time they sent her from them they were ignorant of what they did; and

that

that fhe thanked God, who had taken her from the worfhip of idols to the true church, and was happier in having a fon by her lord and mafter Cortes, and in being married to a cavalier like her hufband, than if fhe had been fovereign of all the provinces of New Spain. All this I heard with my own ears, and fwear to the truth thereof. Amen. At parting fhe gave them a very handfome prefent of gold, and thus difmiffed them. This ftory brings to my mind that of Jofeph in Egypt, when his brothers were in his power. Donna Marina underftood the language of Guacacualco and Mexico which is one and the fame, and as fhe alfo could converfe with Aguilar in that of Tabafco and Yucatan, we thus acquired a medium of communication with the Mexican language, which was an object of great importance to us.

CHAPTER IV.

Arrival of the Armament commanded by H. Cortes, at St. Juan de Ulua. Tranſactions and Occurrences there.

ON Holy Thurſday of the year 1519, we arrived at the port of St. Juan de Ulua, and Cortes hoiſted the royal ſtandard. In about half an hour, two large canoes called piraguas full of Mexicans ſet off from the ſhore to viſit the ſhip which bore the flag. When theſe people came on board, they enquired for the lord, or as they expreſs it Tlatoan, who was pointed out to them by Donna Marina. They then advanced to Cortes with great reſpect, and informed him that a ſervant of their ſovereign Montezuma had ſent them to wait upon him, to know who we were, what our buſineſs was, and if we were in want of any thing, in which caſe they had orders to ſupply us. Cortes thanked them, and having made them a preſent of ſome cut glaſs, ordered an entertainment to be ſerved up, after which he declared that the object of his viſit was, to ſee and treat with the people of thoſe countries; that no one ſhould ſuſtain any injury by him, and that he hoped they would have cauſe to be ſatisfied with his arrival there.

On Good Friday we diſembarked the cavalry, infantry, and artillery, on the ſand hills of which that coaſt is compoſed; and having poſted our artillery, and raiſed an altar, we conſtructed temporary barracks. On the enſuing day we were viſited by many of the natives, who brought hatchets wherewith they proceeded to work in making the huts, that of Cortes eſpecially, more convenient; they alſo brought mantles to guard us from the ſun, and a preſent of gold, fowls, bread, and plumbs. Thoſe who brought them informed Cortes, that on the next day the governor of the province intended to wait upon him.

At

At the appointed time, on the day of the feaſt of the reſurrection, a nobleman named Tendile who was the governor ſpoken of, accompanied by Pitalpitoque afterwards called Ovandillo, and attended by a great train of followers bearing various articles of proviſion, with much reſpect and ceremony, advanced, and made three reverences to Cortes and the ſoldiers who were about him. Cortes went to meet and bid the two chiefs welcome: he then cauſed maſs to be ſaid, after which the tables were placed, and he together with certain of his captains and the two Mexican lords, ſat down to dinner. Their repaſt ended, and having withdrawn together he informed them, that he was the vaſſal of the greateſt prince in the world, who had ſent us thither, to wait upon the king of thoſe countries, whoſe fame had reached him, in order to contract a treaty of peace and amity, and to tell many things to him of the greateſt import to be known. To this Tendile ſomewhat haughtily replied, ſaying, " How is this? You are but juſt arrived, and you talk " of ſeeing our monarch: receive this preſent which he ſends you, and " it is time enough to think of other things afterwards." He then took out of a cheſt many pieces of gold well wrought, which he preſented to Cortes, together with ten loads of fine mantles of white cotton adorned with plumage; and many other things, which, it being ſo long ago, I do not recollect. After theſe followed an abundant ſupply of proviſions, ſuch as fowls, fruit, and roaſted fiſh. Cortes in return preſented them with artificial diamonds, and requeſted that they would encourage the natives to come and barter with us, which they promiſed to do. We afterwards learned that theſe noble Mexicans were the governors of the provinces named Cotaſtlan, Tuſtepeque, Guazpaltepeque, Tlatalteclo, and other diſtricts which had been lately reduced to ſubjection under their monarch. Cortes then produced as a preſent for the great Montezuma, an arm-chair elegantly carved and painted, ſome artificial jewels called margajitas envelloped in perfumed cotton, a ſtring of artificial diamonds, and a crimſon cap with a gold medal whereon was repreſented St. George killing the dragon. Theſe he deſired Tendile to preſent to his maſter in the name of our ſovereign, and to ſignify to him at the ſame time, his requeſt to know when he might he permitted to

wait

wait upon him. To this the Mexican nobleman replied, that his monarch would be happy to hold an intercourfe with our emperor, and that the application fhould be immediately made, and an anfwer tranf-mitted.

With this embaffy fome of the ableft painters of Mexico had been fent, who drew reprefentations to the life, of the countenance of Cortes, the other captains and foldiers, Donna Marina, Aguilar, and even the greyhounds, guns, and balls. Cortes perceiving this, in order to im-prefs the people and their monarch with a formidable idea of our power, caufed the guns to be loaded with a high charge of powder, and mount-ing his horfe, ordered the cavalry down to the wet fands, which were hard, to exercife under the command of P. de Alvarado. He took care to call the attention, as it were by accident, of the ambaffadors at the moment that the guns were fired, and as the air was calm, the explo-fion, and noife of the balls through the trees, ftruck the natives with aftonifhment, and thefe circumftances were immediately reprefented in the painted cloths.

Tendile who was the moft acute of the two in appearance, re-marked at this time a partly gilt helmet with one of our foldiers, and obferved that it refembled one which had belonged to their anceftors, and which was placed on the head of their god Huitzilopochtli; he there-fore expreffed a wifh to carry it to Montezuma. Cortes immediately prefented it to him, faying at the fame time, that in order to afcertain what refemblance exifted between the gold of the two countries, it would not be amifs to return it filled with grains of that metal, as a fit prefent for our Emperor. Tendile now took his leave, affuring Cortes that he would fpeedily return with the anfwer to his requeft. The in-telligence of what had paffed, together with our prefents, was rapidly conveyed to Montezuma by this officer, who was as eminent for his fwiftnefs of foot, as for his rank. That Monarch was moft particularly ftruck with the fight of the helmet; and it impreffed ftrongly on his mind the idea, that we were the men deftined by heaven to rule thofe countries.

The

The other lord, Pitalpitoque, eſtabliſhed his reſidence in a temporary building, at a little diſtance from our camp, his people ſupplying the table of Cortes with proviſions, and the ſoldiers ſubſiſting by barter. Thus ſix or ſeven days paſſed, at the expiration of which time, we one morning perceived Tendile approaching, followed by upwards of a hundred men bearing preſents. With him came alſo a great Mexican lord, who in countenance, feature, and perſon, ſtrongly reſembled Cortes; and the reaſon of his being joined in the embaſſy was, that when the paintings were exhibited at the court, every one was immediately ſtruck with the reſemblance which the portrait of Cortes bore to this lord, who was named Quintalbor. The likeneſs was ſo ſtrong, that whilſt he remained among us in camp, we in ſpeaking of them uſed to ſay, this, and the other Cortes.

On the arrival of the ambaſſadors in the preſence of Cortes, they touched the ground with their hands and kiſſed them, and with their veſſels of incenſe fumigated him and the reſt. After ſome converſation, mats and mantles being ſpread out, the preſents were diſplayed upon them. The firſt was a plate of gold of the ſize of the wheel of a carriage, repreſenting the ſun, admirably wrought, and ſaid to be worth upwards of twenty thouſand crowns; a larger one, equally wrought, of ſilver, repreſenting the moon; the helmet already mentioned filled with gold in its native ſtate to the amount of three thouſand crowns, but the information we hereby obtained of the value of the mines we eſtimated at more than thirty thouſand; thirty pieces of wrought gold repreſenting ducks, very well executed, others in the forms of deer, dogs, lions, tygers, and apes; twelve arrows; a bow with the cord; two rods like thoſe borne by officers of juſtice, five palms long; ten collars, and many other ornaments, all of fine gold, and caſt, or moulded work. After theſe were produced plumes of feathers repreſented in gold, others of ſilver, together with fans of the ſame materials, beautiful penaches of green feathers, thirty loads of the fineſt cotton cloth, with many other things which I cannot now recollect.

I

All

All thefe being laid before Cortes, the ambaffadors made a fpeech, wherein they told him that with the fame good will that their monarch fent the prefent, it was hoped he would receive it, and divide it as he thought beft among the Teules with him. They alfo communicated to him a meffage from the great Montezuma to this effect; " That he re-" joiced in the arrival of fuch brave men in his country as the accounts " he had received proved us to be; that he much wifhed to fee our " great emperor, and to communicate by a reciprocation of prefents " with him; and that he was ready to render us any fervices; but that " as to vifits to his court, they were attended with many difficulties, " and he did not wifh for them." Cortes received this meffage with apparent good humour, and prefented each of the ambaffadors with holland fhirts and other articles of fmall value, but replied by obferving, that after having croffed fuch a vaft fpace of fea, he could not return without executing the miffion which he had been fent upon, which was, to fee and fpeak to the Emperor Montezuma in perfon, fuch be-ing the orders of our great monarch, which he was compelled and de-termined to obey. The ambaffadors replied that they would convey his meffage, but gave no hopes of a favorable anfwer. Out of our poor means Cortes contrived to fend by them a fecond prefent; it confifted of a glafs cup of Venetian manufacture, curioufly gilt and wrought with figures, three holland fhirts, and fome other articles. With thefe the two ambaffadors returned to Mexico, leaving Pitalpitoque to take the charge of provifioning our camp.

Cortes feeing that thefe uninhabited fand banks infefted by mof-quitos were difadvantageous for a fettlement, ordered Francifco de Mon-tejo, with two fmall fhips, to proceed along the coaft for the fpace of ten days fail, in fearch of a port in a better fituation. Montejo ad-vanced as far as the great river of Panuco, which he could not pafs on account of the violence of the currents. He accordingly returned with-out being able to report any information, except that twelve leagues from this place, he had feen a town or fortrefs named Quiabuiftlan, and near it a harbour which appeared to the pilot to be fecure to the north.

It

It was afterwards called Puerto del Nombre Feo from its resemblance to one of that name in Old Spain. In this expedition Montejo employed ten or twelve days, during which time the Mexican lord who was intrusted with the care of our provisions, relaxed so much, that we began to experience great distress; our bread grew rotten, and unless we were successful in fishing we might starve, for the few Indians who occasionally brought fowls valued them much higher than they had done at first.

After waiting for some time very impatiently, the Mexican ambassador Tendile returned, with a present of ten loads of the finest mantles of cotton and feathers. Montezuma also sent four jewels called calchihuis, resembling emeralds, most highly valued by the Mexicans, and various articles of gold, to the amount of three thousand crowns. The two noblemen, Tendile and Pitalpitoque, for the third who resembled Cortes had fallen ill on the road, informed our general that the great Montezuma had received his present with much satisfaction, but that as to the interview, he could not permit any more to be said on the subject. That these rich jewels each of which exceeded in value a load of gold were intended for our emperor, and that herewith all farther intercourse with Mexico was precluded. Cortes, though greatly mortified, thanked them politely, and turning to some of us who were present said, " Truly " this is a great monarch, and rich: with the permission of God we " must see him." To which all the soldiers replied, that they were ready to march. At this moment the bell tolled for the Ave Maria, and all of us fell on our knees, before the holy cross.

The Mexican noblemen being very inquisitive to know the meaning of this, Cortes hinted to the Rev. Father Bartholome the the propriety of a sermon, such as should convey to them the truths of our holy faith. Fra. Bartholome accordingly preached, like an excellent theologian which he was, explaining the mysteries of the cross, at the sight of which the evil beings they worshipped as gods fled away. These subjects and much more he dilated upon, and it was perfectly ex-

plained

plained to, and underſtood by the Mexicans, who promiſed that they would relate all they had ſeen and heard to their ſovereign. He alſo declared to them, that amongſt the principal objects of our miſſion thither, were, thoſe of putting a ſtop to human ſacrifices, injuſtices, and idolatrous worſhip; and then, preſenting them with an image of our Holy Virgin with her ſon in her arms, he deſired them to take it with them, to venerate it, and to plant croſſes ſimilar to that before them in their temples.

A number of articles of gold were now brought in order to barter by the natives, and with this we paid for the proviſions, principally fiſh, which we could procure; this was our only preſent reſource againſt abſolute want; we were moſtly provided with thoſe toys which were in requeſt among the Indians, and with them we procured the gold, which as ſoon as obtained was paid to our fiſhermen, who were chiefly the mariners of the fleet. Cortes well knew of this private trade, nor did it afford him diſſatisfaction, as he conſidered it a furtherance of his views, though he concealed his mind upon the ſubject.

The partizans of Velaſquez however began now to grow jealous at this practice, and demanded Cortes to make ſuch regulations as ſhould bring all the gold which had been, or was in future to be purchaſed, into one common ſtock, under the care of a treaſurer. To this Cortes conſented, and named for the purpoſe one Gonzalo Mexia. He then turned to thoſe who had made the application and with an angry countenance ſaid, " Look you gentlemen! Our companions ſuffer under " want; I therefore thought it prudent to connive at what was doing; " all they obtained amounts to a mere trifle, with the bleſſing of God " we have great and ſplendid proſpects before us; it is now proclaimed, " as you have deſired; ſee if the ſoldiers will in future be able to pro- " cure food." It is upon this tranſaction that Gomara relates, that it was done as a piece of art by Cortes, to induce Montezuma to think that gold was no object with the Spaniards; but the application for the

caſque

cafque to be returned filled with gold, and other previous circumſtances muſt have fully convinced him to the contrary.

One morning at this time, we were diſagreeably ſurpriſed by perceiving that all our Mexican neighbours had quitted us without taking leave. This we afterwards learned was done by the order of Montezuma, who was determined to permit no more conferences. It ſeems this monarch was greatly bigotted to the worſhip of his idols, to which he every day ſacrificed boys, in order to obtain directions how to act. Their commands were, that he ſhould hold no farther intercourſe with us, and they forbid the reception of the crucifix in Mexico. This was the cauſe of the flight of our former neighbours, which gave us an alarm and we prepared for hoſtilities.

One day whilſt I and another ſoldier were centinels upon the ſands at ſome diſtance from our poſt, we remarked the approach of five natives, whom, in order not to create an unneceſſary alarm in the camp, we ſuffered to come up cloſe to us. Theſe men ſaluted us in a friendly manner, and by ſigns deſired to be brought to our camp. I therefore left my comrade at the out-poſt, and attended them thither, for I then had the full uſe of my limbs, far otherwiſe than at preſent that I am worn down and old. When I had brought them to Cortes they ſaluted him with great reverence, addreſſing him with the title of Lopelucio, or lord, which is the ſignification of the word in the Totonaquean language. Theſe Indians were very different in their appearance from the Mexicans, and they wore in their ears large rings of ſtone painted blue, and very fine leaves of gold in their lips. As their language was unintelligible to our interpreters, Donna Marina aſked in the Mexican if any of them could ſpeak in that dialect; to which two of them anſwered in the affirmative, and immediately proceeded to ſay, that their lord had ſent them to congratulate us on our arrival; that he would be proud to ſerve ſuch brave men as he had heard we were, and would have waited upon us before, but from dread of the people of Culchua, who were with us. In the courſe of converſation Cortes was pleaſed to find

that

that Montezuma had enemies in the country; he difmiffed thefe men with prefents, and defired them to affure their chief, that he would fhortly pay him an amicable vifit. Thefe people were ever after named the Lopelucios.

The fands we had remained on during this time, were infefted by the fmall mofquito, which is much the moft troublefome of all, and under whofe attacks it is impoffibe to fleep; our bread was rotten, and we had hardly any thing elfe to eat. The faction of Velafquez, and thofe who had good plantations in Cuba therefore began to be very tired of our prefent fituation, which indeed required fome change, and Cortes prepared to proceed to the fortified town named Quiabuiftlan. Upon this the perfons I have alluded to grew more querulous than before; they complained that they fhould be worn down by the attacks of the natives of this vaft country, having already loft above thirty-five of our number, and that it was preferable to return and report to Velafquez what we had done. To thefe remonftrances Cortes replied, that hitherto we had no caufe to complain of fortune; that death was the fate of war, and it was our faults if we wanted while we lived in a plentiful land; that it was impoffible to quit this country without feeing more of it, and he trufted in God's affiftance. This in fome degree calmed, but by no means extinguifhed the fpirit of the party which had formed itfelf.

Cortes had now obtained from Puertocarrero, Alvarado and his four brothers, De Oli, De Avila, Efcalante, De Lugo, and myfelf, together with other officers and cavaliers, promifes of our fupport in appointing him to an independent command, and this was fufpected by Montejo who clofely watched all our motions. One night very late, Puertocarrero, Efcalante, and De Lugo who was a diftant relation of mine came to my hut, and faid to me, " Senior del Caftillo get your arms and join us to attend Cortes who is going his rounds." I accordingly did fo, and as foon as we had quitted the hut, they told that they wanted fome converfation with me, which it was not proper for my comrades, who were of the faction of Velafquez, to hear. One of
them

them then addreffed me as follows; " Senior del Caftillo it is now the
" third time that you have vifited this country to your coft and lofs;
" Cortes has deceived us; he faid in Cuba that he had powers to
" eftablifh a colony, whereas they went no farther as at prefent appears
" than to traffic, and now we are to return to Cuba and affign all our
" wealth over to Velafquez. Here are many of us determined to take
" poffeffion of this country under Cortes in his Majefty's name, and
" until his royal pleafure is known: Cortes fhall be elected our general,
" and we expect you will give him your vote." To all this I moft
heartily and immediately affented, and we went through the different
huts thus canvaffing for Cortes. The affair was foon known to the
party of Velafquez which was much more numerous than ours; they
immediately went to Cortes, and haughtily defired him to defift from
thefe underhand proceedings; they told him that it was his duty now
to return to Velafquez who had fent him, and that we were not by any
means provided for the eftablifhment of a colony. To this Cortes
mildly replied, that as in duty bound he would inftantly return; but
we who were of the other party now exclaimed againft him for having
deceived us in afferting that he had a commiffion to colonize, whereas
it appeared that it went no farther than barter; adding, that we demanded a fulfilment of his original engagement with us, as neceffary
for the fervice of God and his Majefty. That once we were fettled
more foldiers would join us, and that Velafquez had drawn us to our
ruin, by inducing us to come here in hopes of a fettlement, and difap-
pointing us; and we concluded by faying, that thofe who chofe to return to Cuba were welcome to do fo.

We then infifted on Cortes accepting the command of us who were
determined to try our fortunes in this new country, for the fervice of
God and his Majefty: he for fome time refufed, but at length acceded,
for as the proverb fays, " You afk me that, to which I have already got
my own confent," and thus he was appointed our captain general, and
fupreme magiftrate. The worft part of the bufinefs was, the power
which we gave him, to draw for himfelf, one fifth of all the gold after
that

that of his Majesty was deducted. However with all these authorities
and privileges he was formally invested, before a royal notary, Diego de
Godoy. It was now determined to proceed immediately to the foundation of a settlement and town, which we named De la Vera Cruz, because we arrived here on Holy Thursday, and disembarked on Good
Friday, and we called it Villa Rica, from the words of a cavalier, who
said, " Behold the rich lands." We also appointed civil magistrates,
the two first alcaldes being A. H. Puertocarrero, the cavalier I have
just alluded to, and Francisco de Montejo; the latter was no friend to
Cortes, and it was for that reason he was from policy appointed to this
situation. A gallows was erected in the square of the town, and another at some distance out of it. Pedro de Alvarado was appointed captain of the expeditions, Christoval de Oli maestre de campo, Juan de
Escalante Alguazil mayor, Gonzalo Mexia treasurer, Alonzo de Avila
contador, and one Corral standard bearer, for Villaroel who had held
that situation was displaced, on account of some umbrage Cortes had
taken against him about an Indian woman of Cuba. Ochoa Viscaino,
and Alonzo Romero, were appointed military alguazils. If it is asked
now, why I do not name Gonzalo de Sandoval that valiant captain,
who was noticed by our great monarch the emperor, I reply, that he
was at this time a stripling, and had not acquired the fame in arms he
afterwards obtained.

The steps which we had taken enraged the faction of Velasquez
beyond all measure; they were almost ready to break out into acts of
violence, and uttered the most mutinous expressions. Juan de Escalante now, having previously concerted the measure with Cortes, demanded in the name of us all, a sight of the instructions given by Velasquez. The tenor of them was as follows; " As soon as you shall
" have procured the utmost quantity of gold that is to be had, return."
We requested this instrument, in order that the whole of the proceedings should be laid before his Majesty; a necessary precaution as afterwards appeared, from the steps which were taken against us by the
Bishop of Burgos and Archbishop of Rossano, Don Juan Rodriguez

de

de Fonseca, for so he was named, who wished, throughout, to destroy us all.

The adherents of Velasquez now declared, that they would not remain under the command of Cortes, but, would return to the Island of Cuba; to which Cortes replied, that it was not his wish to detain any one contrary to his inclination, even though he should remain alone. This pacified many, but Juan Velasquez de Leon a relation of the Governor of Cuba, Diego de Ordas, Escobar who had been his page, Escudero, and others were not to be reconciled; so that Cortes was obliged to arrest them, and keep them for a time in irons.

K

CHAPTER V.

The Spanish Army advances into the Country.

THE wants we experienced now required some relief, and Alvarado was accordingly sent with a hundred soldiers principally of the party of Velasquez, to search the country, and procure maize, and other provisions; for it was thought most politic, that the whole of those who were friends to Cortes should remain with him. It must be observed that this neighbourhood where the language of Culva was spoken, was dependent upon Mexico. Alvarado proceeding on his expedition, marched to some small villages, dependencies of the district, named Costitlan, which the inhabitants had quitted a short time before his arrival. In their temples he found the bodies of men and boys lately sacrificed, the stones on which the horrid ceremony was performed, and the knives yet smoking; the limbs were severed from the bodies, and taken away, as our people were informed, to be eaten. These shocking scenes astonished our soldiers, but we every where as we proceeded through the country found similar ones. In these villages they obtained abundance of provisions, of which they stripped them, without doing further damage, by the strict orders of Cortes, and returned with two prisoners to our quarters, where we rejoiced in the novelty of good fare: for, as the saying is, all hardships and misfortunes are supported with a hearty meal.

The address and activity of Cortes made him daily acquire an interest amongst the former adherents of Velasquez, some with gold which breaks the solid rocks, and more with promises were successively drawn over to him. He first brought his prisoners from the ships where they had been in confinement, and in a few days released them

entirely,

entirely, attaching them sincerely to his interest, and all by the softening effects of gold.

We now proceeded to the fortress of Quiabuistlan, and on our march thither along the coast, I recollect that we passed a great fish which was left behind by the tide. We then arrived at a river where the present town of Vera Cruz is built, and crossed it to a village on the opposite side. The district was subject to the great town of Cempoal, to which the five Indians belonged who visited us with golden ornaments in their under lips. In some temples we found the instruments and remains of human sacrifices, much plumage of parrots, and books of the paper of the country, folded in the manner of cloth of Castille; but the natives had all fled, and no provisions were to be found.

We now quitted the coast, and struck into the country towards the west, where, in some large plains without any beaten track, we saw herds of deer feeding. Alvarado with his swift chesnut mare gave chace to one of them, which he wounded with his lance, but the animal escaped from him into the woods. Just at this time twelve Indians came to us, bearing provisions; they had been sent by their chief with an invitation to go to his town, which was distant one day's journey. Cortes thanked them, and we proceeded on, to a town where we halted for the night. We found here the remains of human sacrifices, both of men and women, with the repetition of the further details of which, I will not tire the reader.

Early in the morning we proceeded under the conduct of our friendly Indians, and sent forward to the chief of Cempoal to inform him of our approach. When we came within a league of the place, we were met by twenty principal persons, who presenting Cortes and the cavalry with very odoriferous flowers tied in bunches, told him, that they came with an excuse on the part of their chief, who was so fat and unwieldy that he was not able to come out, but had sent them to invite us to his town. Cortes thanked them, and we proceeded.

K 2

When

When we entered, we were surprised with the beauty of the buildings and situation, and the various plantations of trees. All the streets as we passed were filled with men and women, attracted by curiosity. Our advanced guard having gone to the great square, the buildings of which had been lately whitewashed and plaistered, in which art these people are very expert, one of our horsemen was so struck with the splendor of their appearance in the sun, that he came back in full speed to Cortes, to tell him that the walls of the houses were of silver. When we came to know the reality we all laughed heartily at him, and used in future to say that every thing that was white, was silver in his eyes. These buildings were appointed for our lodgings, and large apartments assigned to us, which contained the whole; and here the fat cacique, for so I am in future to call him, came to pay his respects to Cortes. They had provided an entertainment for us, with baskets of plums, and bread of maize. We were well pleased with our situation, and named the town Villa Viciosa; though some called it Seville. Cortes ordered that the soldiers should give no umbrage to the inhabitants, and that we should for that reason remain in our quarters.

As soon as the fat cacique understood that we had dined, he signified to Cortes his intention of waiting on him, which he shortly after did, attended by many of the principal inhabitants, dressed in rich mantles, and ornamented with gold. Cortes went out to meet them with great ceremony, and having embraced the fat cacique, the latter ordered a present to be brought, composed of gold and mantles, but of little value, which he offered to Cortes, saying, " Great lord, receive " this present kindly, for if I had more it should be yours." Cortes answered that he would repay it with good works, and desired to know what services he could render him, having been sent by the emperor whose vassal he was, to redress wrongs, punish the wicked, and prevent the sacrifice of human souls. He then said many things to him concerning our holy faith. As soon as the fat cacique had heard them out, giving a deep sigh, he complained bitterly of Montezuma and his officers, saying, that having lately been compelled to submit to the

yoke

yoke of that monarch, he had feized all his gold, and now held him completely enthralled.

Cortes promifed that he would foon take fuch meafures as fhould free him from the tyranny he complained of. The cacique then made a very difcreet anfwer, and they parted for the prefent. On the enfuing day we quitted this place attended by above four hundred Indians to carry our baggage. Thefe perfons are called Tamenes: they carry a burthen of about fifty pounds for the fpace of five leagues, where they are relieved; and we underftood that in peaceable and orderly times, in thefe countries, each cacique was obliged, on demand, to provide them through his diftrict. At night we arrived at a village hard by the town of Quiaviftlan, where we found a good fupper provided for us by the care of the fat cacique.

At ten o'clock in the forenoon of the enfuing day, we entered the fortified town of Quiaviftlan, fituated upon a rock of very difficult afcent, with our artillery in the front. Though I may be charged with breaking in upon my narrative to relate old ftories, I muft mention, that as we were marching up to this place, Captain A. de Avila, an ill-tempered man, being angry with a foldier named Villanueva for breaking his rank, gave him a thruft of his lance in the arm which lamed him ever after; he was therefore in future called Villa nueva el Manquillo. We advanced to the middle of the city without any refiftance, or even meeting an individual; but on approaching the temples, which were upon the principal fquare, we faw fifteen perfons dreffed in rich mantles, who approaching Cortes prefented him with incenfe, and apologizing for the abfence of the people, through fear, invited us to repofe ourfelves, and promifed that before night the inhabitants fhould return. Cortes informed them of that which related to our miffion, in the fervice of our great emperor, and holy faith, and prefenting them with fome trinkets, defired that they would fend us a fupply of provifions, which they inftantly did.

Cortes

Cortes was now informed of the approach of the fat cacique, who shortly appeared, borne in a litter by his principal nobility; and on his arrival, he immediately joined with the chiefs of this place, in bitter complaints of the tyranny of Montezuma; one of the heaviest articles of which was, his demand of their children for the purposes of sacrifice, or slavery; and they asserted that this was the practice, with many other acts of outrage committed by his officers, through the whole of the country where the language of Totonaque was spoken; a tract which contained above thirty towns. Cortes consoled them, promising redress, and whilst they were thus conversing a person came to inform the chiefs, that there were just then arrived five Mexican officers, or collectors of tribute. This intelligence drove the colour from the cheeks of all the natives, and they went trembling, to receive them, leaving Cortes quite alone.

For these officers lodgings were prepared with the greatest dispatch, and chocolate got ready for their refreshment. As they went to their apartments they passed us by with great state, not deigning to cast a look upon Cortes. They were dressed in mantles elegantly wrought, and drawers of the same; their hair shining, and as it were tied at the top of the head, and each of them had in his hand a bunch of roses, which he occasionally smelt to. They were attended by servants who fanned them, and each of whom carried a cord and a hooked stick. They were also attended by a numerous company of the principal persons, who did not quit them until they had taken their refreshment, after which they sent for the fat cacique, and those of this place, and gave them a severe reprimand for receiving and entertaining us, contrary to the will of their sovereign, Montezuma; and having used many threats of punishment, they concluded with a demand of twenty men and women to sacrifice to their gods, in order to expiate the offence.

This being made known to our general he acquainted the caciques, that in conformity to his duty, he deemed it proper to seize the persons of these officers, until their lord, Montezuma, should be informed of the

tyrannies

tyrannies they committed on his subjects. This proposal terrified and astonished the chiefs, and they at first refused to lay hands on them, but Cortes was determined, and caused them to be seized and fastened by the neck in a kind of pillory made of large staves and collars. They were so fixed as not to be able to stir, and one of them also being refractory was beaten soundly. Cortes then proclaimed that neither tribute nor obedience should be paid to Montezuma, and this he ordered to be made universally known through these districts, and also, that wherever he should hear of any officers of Montezuma coming, he would send for and arrest them. The intelligence of these measures soon spread through the country, which the natives said were to be attempted only by superior beings, or Teules, the name which they give to their idols, and by which they henceforward distinguished the Spaniards.

The chiefs were now violent to sacrifice the officers, whom before their arrest they hardly dared to look at; and this they said was in order to prevent them from conveying intelligence to Mexico; but when it came to the knowledge of Cortes, he prevented it by taking them into his own custody, and putting them under a guard of soldiers. At midnight he caused two of them to be untied, and brought secretly into his presence; when they came before him, he asked them, as if ignorant of what had happened, what country they belonged to, and why they were kept prisoners. They answered, " That they had been seized by " the caciques and people of that town, who were favored and encou- " raged in it by him and us." To this Cortes replied, " That he " knew nothing of it, and was very sorry for what had happened." He then caused food to be brought to them, and treating them with great kindness, desired that they would go and inform their sovereign how much he wished to be his friend and servant. He also promised that he would release their companions, and reprimand the caciques for what they had done. He then desired them to go away as fast as they could, but they informing him that it would be their destruction to at- empt to pass through the country, he sent them by a boat with six

sailors,

failors, who had orders to put them on fhore beyond the territory of Cempoal.

In the morning, when the caciques found that two of their prifoners were flown, they were very determined on facrificing the reft, but Cortes affuming the appearance of great difpleafure at the lofs, ordered a chain to be brought, in which he fent the remainder of the Mexicans to the fhips, and this he did to get them out of the power of the others, for as foon as they were on board he releafed them, with a promife that they fhould foon be permitted to return to Mexico. The caciques now reverted to Cortes for advice how they fhould act, as Montezuma muft inevitably know the manner in which his officers had been treated, and would in confequence overwhelm them with his great armies; to which Cortes with a cheerful countenance replied, that he and his brothers there would guard them againft all attacks. The caciques on their part offered to fupport us with all their powers, and they at this time entered under allegiance to his Majefty before Diego de Godoy the royal notary, and caufed proclamation thereof to be made through the province, the people of which rejoiced in the exemption from the vexatious demands of Montezuma's officers.

The ftrong alliance which we had now made, induced us to lofe no time in eftablifhing our fettlement in fo advantageous a fituation. For the fcite of our town we chofe a plain, half a league from the fortrefs where we now were; and tracing out the foundations of the church, fquare, arfenal, and fort, we raifed all the buildings to the firft ftory, and alfo the walls and parapets of the fort, with loop holes and barbacans. Cortes was the firft to carry earth, or ftones, or dig in the foundations; and his example was followed by all the officers and foldiers, fome digging, and others making the walls of clay, bringing water, and at the kilns making bricks and tiles; others feeking provifions or timber, and the fmiths preparing the iron work. In this manner we continued, until, with the affiftance of the natives, we had nearly completed the church, houfes, and fortreffes.

At

At this time, it appears, the great Montezuma received intelligence of the manner in which his officers had been treated, and of the rebellion of the provinces. He was much enraged with Cortes, and had ordered two armies to march, one to punish his refractory subjects, the other against us, but when they were ready to set out, the arrival of the two officers whom Cortes had released, and the account of the manner in which they had been treated while in our power, assuaged his anger, and induced him to send us a peaceable message. For this purpose he selected two of his nephews, whom he sent to us under the care of four old noblemen of the first rank about his court, with a present of gold, and mantles, worth two thousand crowns, and also to return his thanks to Cortes, for the civility shewn to his officers; but adding a complaint of his having instigated these people to throw off their allegiance, for which he would at a future opportunity punish them, though he refrained from doing so at the present, on account of our being amongst them; because he was convinced that we were those of whom the ancient prophecies had spoken, and that we were of the same ancestors with himself. Cortes informed the ambassadors, that he and all of us were the most humble servants of the great Montezuma, for whom we had taken care of those officers, three of whom were now on board of our ships, and these he ordered to be immediately brought and delivered to their friends.

Cortes then complained of Montezuma, and the uncivil flight of his officer the governor, saying, that was the reason of his now coming to this country, where he had received much kindness; hoping what had passed would be pardoned, and that as to tribute, it was not possible to serve two masters, and the people of these provinces were now the vassals of our lord the emperor; but that he expected soon to wait on the great Montezuma, and then every thing should be done to his satisfaction by us. He presented the young princes with glass diamonds and beads, and treated them with much honor, ordering the cavalry out to exercise in their presence, a sight which afforded them great sa-

L   tisfaction;

tisfaction; after which they returned to Mexico, very well contented with their visit.

Cortes at this time lost his horse, whose place he supplied by that called El Harriero: he was a dark chesnut and one of the best that were brought to New Spain. The embassy sent by Montezuma had the greatest effect on the people of those countries, for said they how formidable must those Teules be, whom even the great Montezuma fears!!

The fat cacique now waited on Cortes, to complain of the outrages committed by a garrison of Mexican troops which occupied a town called Cingapacinga, nine leagues distant from the place where we were. After some consideration, Cortes laughing said to those about him, " Gentlemen you see that these people esteem us to be a superior " race of beings, let us encourage the prejudice, and impress them " with the idea that one of us is enough to drive an army before him. " For this purpose I will send old Heredia the Biscayan musketeer, " whose fierce and scarred face, great beard, one eye, and lame leg, " will terrify them." This man had been a soldier in Italy. Cortes told him when he had got as far as the river to fire a musket as a signal, for he did this only to try how far the credulity of the Indians in our favor would carry them. Heredia being present, he called to the caciques saying, " Go with this Teule, whom I send to kill or make pri- " soners all your enemies." The caciques set out with their party accordingly, being headed by the old soldier, who went firing his musket before them out of the town. As soon as he arrived at the river he gave the signal, and Cortes sent to stop them, having sufficiently tried their faith, and when they returned he informed them that it was his intention to proceed against their enemies with his whole force.

When the soldiers were warned for this duty, those of the party of Velasquez refused to obey orders, saying, that they would go on no expedition, but insisted on returning to the Island of Cuba. The number of mutineers who openly declared themselves was seven; when these were

were brought before Cortes and asked by him how they could behave so ill, they insolently replied, that they wondered at his idea of colonizing amongst such numbers of the natives; that for their parts they were tired of being dragged about, and would go to their plantations in Cuba. Cortes replied that he would not oppose their going, though he disapproved of their conduct; accordingly they embarked, and brought their provisions of bread, oil, and vegetables, on board, and one of them named Moron sold a good horse to one Juan Ruano, who was to pay for it by an assignment of certain articles of his property in Cuba.

Just as the vessel was ready to sail, the soldiers, headed by the alcaldes, and other civil officers of the settlement, waited on Cortes with a request that he would permit no persons whatever to quit their colours, a crime for which those who committed it deserved to suffer death. Cortes for some time appeared to be unwilling to withdraw the permission, but at length suffered himself to be persuaded, and the seven malcontents were obliged to come back to us and sustain the ridicule their conduct brought on them; Moron also lost his horse, which the other kept, referring him for the payment, to his assignment on his property in the Island of Cuba.

Our internal troubles being appeased for the present, Cortes set out upon his expedition with four hundred soldiers, being joined at Cempoal by a thousand of our allies divided into four companies. The first days march was five leagues, and on the ensuing day we reached the outskirts of the town of Cingapacinga, which was built among steep and difficult rocks. When the inhabitants heard of our approach, a deputation of eight of their chieftains was sent to Cortes, and being brought into his presence, these persons with tears in their eyes asked him why he came to destroy them, who had given no occasion for such an aggression, adding that this surprised them the more from the celebrity of our justice, which had reached them; and as to our allies of Cempoal, their malevolence against them was founded upon an old dispute about boundaries, and now they took advantage of our support

to

to rob and murder them. They admitted that a Mexican garrison had been in their town, but it had retired on the arrest of the officers of Montezuma. They therefore prayed that we would grant them our favor.

As soon as this was explained to Cortes, he gave orders to his troops not to suffer any of the allies to advance. This order was speedily communicated, but they were already plundering the people in the suburbs, at which Cortes was greatly enraged, and ordering the captains into his presence, he commanded them to return what had been taken, adding, that they deserved the punishment of death for their misrepresentations, when their real and evident intention was, to rob and sacrifice their neighbours: an injustice which we were bound to prevent or redress. The chiefs of Cempoal, duly impressed by these menaces, instantly surrendered their prisoners and plunder. Cortes then, with an enraged countenance commanded them to quit the place for the night, which they accordingly did. This conduct won the hearts of the people of the district, and both chiefs and priests listened attentively to, and were convinced by, the truths which Cortes told them relative to our holy faith, and his exhortation to quit their abominable worship and customs, insomuch that, calling in the people of the neighbouring districts, the whole engaged under allegiance to his Majesty; after having done which, they made heavy complaints of the tyranny of Montezuma.

On the ensuing morning, Cortes called for the chiefs of Cempoal, and effected a permanent reconciliation between them and his people. We then departed by a different route, and being much fatigued, we halted in a town which was in the district of the place we had left. It happened here that a certain soldier named De Mora, took two fowls from the house of one of the inhabitants, and Cortes on hearing of it was so incensed at such an outrage being committed in a peaceable country, that he immediately hung him up, but Captain de Alvarado drawing his sword, cut the rope just in time to save the poor man's life;

life; this foldier was afterwards killed in an action at a rock in Guatimala. I mention the circumftance as a proof of the ftrictnefs with
which Cortes enforced difcipline.

Proceeding from the place where this happened, we arrived at
fome huts where we found the fat cacique waiting for us with refrefhments and provifions. Our conduct on this expedition made the natives hold us in higher eftimation than before; for although untaught,
they could fee that juftice is holy and good, and that the behaviour of
Cortes was conformable to what he profeffed, when he declared that he
came to redrefs and prevent tyranny. Here we refted for the night, and
on the enfuing day all the caciques attended us to our lodgings in
their town.

They were doubly interefted now to retain us amongft them, for
they were in great dread of the vengeance of Montezuma; they therefore in order to fix us propofed an intermarriage, and for that purpofe
offered to us eight ladies, all of the firft families, who were intro-
duced richly dreffed, and ornamented with gold collars and ear rings,
and attended by a number of female flaves. The fat cacique then faid
to Cortes, " Tecle or lord, thefe feven young women are for the cap-
" tains of your army, and this my niece who is proprietor of towns
" and vaffals, I beg leave to prefent to you." Cortes received the offer
as it merited, but took the opportunity to obferve, that in order to
ftrengthen the friendfhip with us, it was neceffary that they fhould firft
renounce their idolatrous worfhip, the abominable cuftom of male
youths appearing in women's drefs, and their human facrifices; for
every day our fight was offended by the repetition of four or five of thefe
horrid murders, the unfortunate victims being cut up and their limbs
fold in the public markets, as beef is in the towns of Old Caftille. He
alfo added, that before we could accept their propofal relative to thefe
ladies, it was neceffary that they fhould undergo the ceremony of baptifm.

The chiefs and priefts replied, that they could not think of re-
nouncing

nouncing the worſhip of their gods in any reſpect : but as to the other evil practice a ſtop ſhould be put to it. This anſwer however did not by any means ſatisfy us, and-Cortes ſtrongly repreſented the neceſſity of ſuppreſſing by force their idolatrous worſhip, and his determination, though it coſt the lives of all, on that very day to proſtrate their falſe gods. For this purpoſe we therefore immediately got under arms, and then Cortes declared his intention to the chiefs. As ſoon as the fat cacique heard it, he ordered the people to arm and aſſemble in defence of their temple, and they all appeared greatly agitated; but when they ſaw that we were preparing to aſcend the great flight of ſteps, the chief abovementioned came up to Cortes and expoſtulated with him, aſking him why he proceeded upon a meaſure whereby he would bring deſtruction upon them and us alſo. Cortes anſwered that he was determined ſince they paid no regard to what he ſaid, to hurl their pretended gods down the ſteps. The chiefs replied, that they were unworthy to approach them, but if we were reſolved on doing what we ſaid, they could not help themſelves. Accordingly, they had hardly ſaid this, when fifty of us going up for the purpoſe, threw down and broke to pieces the enormous idols which we found within the temple, ſome in the form of dragons, others of half human ſhape, and others like dogs. At this ſight the chiefs and prieſts wept and prayed for pardon, but the warriors prepared to attack us with their arrows. Perceiving their intention, we immediately ſeized the fat cacique and ſix more chiefs and prieſts, Cortes exclaiming, that if any outrage was attempted, they ſhould every man die that moment. The fat cacique then called to his warriors to deſiſt, and matters being ſoon brought to a ſtate of quiet, Cortes took an opportunity of haranguing the people upon the ſubject of religion.

He next ordered that the fragments of the idols ſhould be burned, and immediately eight prieſts who uſed to have the care of them came, and collecting them together, brought them into the temple, where they were conſumed.

Theſe

Thefe priefts were dreffed in long black mantles like fheets with hoods refembling thofe of our canons hanging to the fhoulders, their robes reached to the feet, and they had a fmaller hood like the dominicans. Their long hair was matted together with clotted blood; with fome it reached to the waift, and with others to the feet, their ears were torn and cut, and they fmelt horribly, as it were of fulphur, and putrid flefh. They were faid to be all of noble families, and they were addicted to the evil practice of the country. On certain days they fafted: I have feen them make food of the feeds or kernels of the cotton plant, what elfe they might have ufed at other times I cannot fay.

Cortes then harangued the people, faying that now we were really brothers, Montezuma fhould no longer opprefs them, and he would place them under the protection of the great Lady whom we adore, the mother of Chrift, with many other good and holy reafons and arguments, which could not be better expreffed by any one, and all which the people liftened to with great attention. He then caufed a number of Indian mafons to be collected, with lime, which abounded in that place, and had the walls cleared of blood, and new plaiftered. He alfo conftructed an altar which he hung round with rich mantles, and adorned with wreaths of rofes. The temple being thus purified and cleaned, he commanded four priefts to cut off their hair, and change their black garments for white ones, and entrufted them with the care of the altar, and he placed an old foldier named Juan de Torres de Cordova, who was lame, as a hermit to refide in the temple. He alfo planted a crofs againft a column of timber, and on the next day mafs was faid there by F. Bart. de Olmedo. We likewife taught the natives to make candles of wax, and they were enjoined to keep them always burning before the holy altar.

The principal perfons of this and the neighbouring diftricts attended at divine fervice, and the eight ladies were at this time baptized and inftructed in our holy faith. The niece of the fat cacique was named Donna Catalina; fhe was as ugly as poffible, but the general received

ceived

ceived her by the hand affectionately. Puertocarrero was more fortunate; his lady was for an Indian very handsome; she was the daughter
of a great cacique named Cuefco, and was called Donna Francifca.
The alliance confolidated the friendfhip between us and this people, of
whom we now took our leave, and returned to Villa Rica.

On our arrival we found a veffel from Cuba in the harbour, commanded by one Francifco Saucedo, called el Pulido on account of his
affectation of finery and manners. Luis Marin a very able officer, and
ten foldiers with two horfes were on board. We learned by thefe
people that Velafquez had received from Old Spain his authority to
barter and colonize. This, with his appointment to the commiffion of
adelantado of Cuba, put his friends in our army in very great fpirits.

The works of our town were nearly finifhed, and many of us now
grew anxious to pay a vifit to the great Montezuma, and expreffed to
Cortes our wifh to try our fortune. Confultations being held hereon,
it was determined in the firft place to fend a deputation to his Majefty,
with an account of what we had done, and also with the gold and other
articles of value which had been obtained. This determination was
agreed to by Cortes, and was immediately carried into effect, and Diego
de Ordas, and Francifco de Montejo, two men of bufinefs, going
through the whole of the officers and foldiers, and reprefenting to
them, that, although to fuch as claimed their fhare it fhould not be
denied, yet it was for the general intereft that the whole of the treafure
fhould be fent to his Majefty, all our companions gave their confent, and renounced their claim to a partition. Alonzo Hernandez
Puertocarrero, and Francifco de Montejo were named as our agents,
the laft mentioned of whom Cortes had already fecured in his own intereft by a gift of two thoufand crowns. By thefe gentlemen Cortes
wrote his private letters, the contents of which we never knew. The
council alfo wrote conjointly with thofe of the foldiers who were moft
folicitous for the eftablifhment of the colony, and the election of Cortes
as captain general. In this letter nothing was omitted that could ferve
our

our cause; my hand was to it with the reft: and besides these, a letter to the following purport was written in the name of the whole army.

Beginning with the expreffions of refpect due to fo great a monarch, it proceeded to inform him of the events which had occurred during our expedition, to the period of our election of Cortes, until his Majefty's pleafure on the fubject fhould be known; with our engagement to yield him a fifth of all treafure, after the deduction for his Majefty. It alfo contained an account of our difcovery of the two Spaniards in this country, and our war in Tabafco, until we brought thofe people to fubmiffion to his Majefty, and to embrace our holy faith, of our obtaining two excellent linguifts, of our arrival at St. Juan de Ulua, and our interviews with the ambaffadors of Montezuma; our fubfequent march into the country, and our alliance with the people here, who had in confequence renounced obedience to the Mexican monarch, of the expedition to Cingapacinga, the conftruction of our fortrefs, and our prefent determination to advance into the country, to the court of the great Montezuma. The letter alfo gave an account of the military and religious cuftoms of the inhabitants, of the former expeditions of our countrymen, and an enumeration of the various articles of treafure which we fent by our agents, and how we alfo fent by the fame opportunity, four natives, whom we refcued out of the cages of Cempoal, where they were fattening for victims. After thefe accounts we further ftated, how we were at prefent four hundred and fifty foldiers, furrounded by hofts of enemies, and ready to lay down our lives for the fervice of God, and his Majefty, and we fupplicated, that his Majefty would be pleafed not to beftow the government of fo great and rich a country, which deferved to be ruled by a great prince or lord, on any unworthy perfon. We alfo ftated to his Majefty our apprehenfion, that the Governor of Cuba might be attempted to be put in upon us, through the intereft of his patron the Bifhop of Burgos, whom he had attached to him by the affignment of valuable eftates in that Ifland, in which he failed in his duty to his Majefty, who was by right entitled to them. That thefe things we were bound to reprefent, and await the

M   return

return of his gracious anfwer proftrate on the ground; and that if the Bifhop of Burgos fent any perfon over us, we fhould fufpend our obedience, until his Majefty's pleafure was known, and that in the mean time, we remained under the command of his Majefty's faithful fervant Cortes, whofe merits we exalted to the fkies.

This being all drawn up in due form, our general defired to be permitted to read it, and on the perufal he expreffed his higheft fatisfaction thereat. The only two articles he excepted to were, the mention of his fhare of the treafure, and of the names of the preceding difcoverers; for it feems that he had in his private letter afcribed all the honor and merit to himfelf. Thefe parts he defired to fuppreſs, but there were not wanting thofe who told him, that his Majefty was to know, not only the truth, but the whole truth. This bufinefs completed, the letters were intrufted to our agents, with ftrict injunctions by no means to touch at the Havannah, nor at the port of El Marien, as we wifhed to keep the affair from the knowledge of Velafquez.

After mafs on the twenty-fixth of July 1519 our agents failed, and arrived fafely at the Havannah, in direct oppofition to our inftructions, for, Puertocarrero being fick, Montejo compelled the pilot Alaminos into his views, on the pretence of getting provifions from his eftate at El Marien. As foon as the fhip caft anchor, Montejo fent a failor on fhore with letters and advices to the Governor Velafquez, and this man as he went through the Ifland proclaimed the news of all that had happened in the army under Cortes.

Velafquez on receiving the intelligence communicated by Montejo, as is faid, heartily curfed Cortes, his fecretary, and the contador, by whofe advice he had chofen him. He immediately fent two veffels armed in fearch of our fhip, of which the unwelcome intelligence was foon received, that fhe was by that time confiderably advanced towards Europe; and with this news his veffels returned to St. Jago, making Velafquez more difconfolate than ever. He lodged a complaint before
the

the Bishop of Burgos, and the court of royal audience in St. Domingo, but the reverend fathers sent him back an answer highly favorable to us, whose services they were by this time made acquainted with. This answer, which was brought by a licentiate named Zuazo, or arrived about the same time with him, vexed the governor so much, that from being very fat, he grew quite lean. He now made the utmost exertions to collect a powerful armament in order to overwhelm us, on which business he went in person, and by the fury and determination he exhibited, he induced most of the settlers of Cuba to take part in the expedition, and prepared a fleet of eighteen sail great and small, under the command of Pamphilo de Narvaez.

Our agents passing the canal of Bahama, under the guidance of Alaminos, the first pilot who ever navigated through it, proceeded to the Islands of Terceras, and from thence to Seville; and in a few days arrived at the court, which was then at Valladolid; the Bishop of Burgos being president of the royal council of the Indies. Our agents went to wait on him in great spirits, expecting a gracious reception, but having presented their letters and requested a speedy transmission of them and their present, to his Majesty, who was then in Flanders, the bishop returned a very repulsive and haughty answer, saying, that he would make his own representations of our conduct, in having thrown off our obedience to the governor of Cuba. The arrival of Benito Martinez the chaplain of Velasquez at this time, contributed much to set our affairs in an unfavorable situation, and the bishop in consequence of a remonstrance which was made to him by A. H. Puertocarrero, one of those employed by us, and a cavalier of rank, caused him to be thrown into prison, on a pretended misdemeanor, in carrying away with him to the Indies a woman of Medellin, named Maria Rodriquez. All this it was necessary, according to the dictates of prudence, to keep silence upon, until the proper time and place.

The bishop now wrote to his Majesty, representing the transactions in the most favorable light for Velasquez, and the most opposite

one

one for us, and entirely suppressed all mention of our letters, or presents, of which he appropriated a great part to his own use. Our agents then, in concert with Martin Cortes father to the general, and the licentiate Nunez, relator of his Majesty's royal council and a near relation to Cortes, with the countenance of some noblemen their friends, and others who were jealous of the haughty manners of the bishop, resolved to send the duplicates of our letters to his Majesty, and also others, complaining of the partiality of this prelate. It was the will of God that the said accounts should reach his Majesty's hands, and that he should be well pleased with them, insomuch that, for many days, nothing was talked of but the services of Cortes, and us his soldiers. The Emperor was ever after dissatisfied with the Bishop of Burgos for the part he had acted. When he heard the turn our affairs had taken at court he was more furious against Cortes and the rest of us than ever, but it was the will of God that by the time two years more had elapsed, his courage should be cooled, for he was censured, while we continued to be held in estimation as loyal subjects to his Majesty, and the Emperor was pleased to say, that he would shortly come to Castille, and there attend to our memorials, and reward our services.

In four days after the departure of our agents, a plot was formed by certain persons who were enemies to Cortes on various accounts, such as the return to Cuba being precluded to them, and their being deprived of a share of the gold. Amongst these conspirators were one Escudero, and one Cermeno, Gonzalo de Umbria a pilot, Bernaldino de Coria, a clergyman named Juan Diaz, and certain sailors who had been whipped in Cozumel. It was determined amongst them to seize a vessel and sail for Cuba, there to give information to Velasquez of the departure of our agents, and this plan was suggested by some persons of consequence. Their scheme was frustrated a few hours before they were to have sailed, by the repentance and discovery of De Coria, who revealed it to Cortes. They were in consequence seized, and being examined confessed the whole, and accused several others; but of these no farther notice was taken. The prisoners were all condemned except the priest, whose

orders

orders protected him, but he got a great fright. Escudero and Cermeno were hanged, the pilot Umbria had his feet cut off, and each of the mariners received two hundred lashes. I remember when Cortes was ratifying this sentence, he gave a deep sigh and exclaimed, " How " happy is he who is not able to write, and is thereby prevented from " signing the death warrants of men." It seems to me that this expression is very frequently affected amongst judges, and that it was borrowed from the cruel Nero at the time he counterfeited the appearance of being a good emperor. As soon as the sentences were executed, Cortes posted off at full speed to Cempoal, commanding two hundred soldiers, and all the cavalry, as also a detachment which was out under Alvarado, to follow him.

In the consultations which we held at Cempoal upon our intended expedition to Mexico, the friends of Cortes advised him to destroy the fleet, in order to prevent attempts similar to that related in the last chapter, and also to obtain so considerable a reinforcement as the whole body of mariners, who amounted to above a hundred. It appeared to me that Cortes had already determined this in his own mind, but he preferred that it should come as an application from us, in order that if damages were sued for on account of the loss incurred, we should be all responsible as himself. Cortes therefore ordered his friend Juan de Escalante who bore a bitter enmity to Velasquez on account of not being given a good district in Cuba, to dismantle the ships, and then sink them, retaining only the boats for the purpose of fishing. Escalante executed this service, and returned to Cempoal with a company formed of the mariners, many of whom turned out very good soldiers. Cortes now summoned the chiefs of these people who had renounced their allegiance to Montezuma, and enjoined them to render all services in their power to the party he left in Villa Rica, and to assist them in completing the town. Then taking Escalante by the hand he said, " This is my brother: obey him in whatever he desires you to do, and " if you require assistance or protection against your enemies, recur to " him, and he will give it to you." This the caciques all promised

to

to perform, and I recollect they immediately hereupon began, much against his will and endeavours, to fumigate Escalante with their incense. This officer was placed here in order to repel any attempts which might be made by Velasquez, as he was thoroughly attached to the interest of Cortes. Gomara here asserts that Cortes dared not publish to the soldiers his intention of marching to Mexico. I beg to be informed what is the disposition of a Spaniard? Or when it ever happened that he was not ready to march forward? He also errs where he says Pedro de Ircio remained commandant in Vera Cruz. I say again that Juan de Escalante was captain, and also alguazil major. Pedro de Ircio was not fit to be a corporal, nor is it just to take from one what belongs to him, and give it to another.

After having rendered the vessels unserviceable, but not privately as Gomara asserts, being one morning assembled after mass, and conversing on military affairs with Cortes, he desired our attention, and addressed us, saying, " We now knew the business which was before " us; that with the aid of our Lord we should conquer, and it was " necessary to do so, for in case of a defeat there was no escape; nor " had we any support but in our valour, and the mercy of God." To this he added many comparisons of our situation with those drawn from the history of the ancient Romans. We one and all replied, " That we " were prepared to obey him; that the lot was now cast, let fortune " take what turn she would, as Cæsar said in passing the Rubicon, for " that all our services were devoted to God and his Majesty." Cortes then addressed us again in a very eloquent and impressive speech, which having concluded, he called for the fat cacique, and having informed him of our determination, he injoined him to take care of our church, and holy cross.

When we were just ready to depart, a soldier arrived with a letter to Cortes from Juan de Escalante, whereby he was informed that a strange ship was then at anchor in a river three leagues distant from Villa Rica, and that he could not obtain any answer to his signals

from

from thofe on board. Upon this, Cortes appointed Alvarado, and Sandoval who already began to fhew himfelf the officer he afterwards was, to take the command of the army in his abfence; (Avila being paffed by, and Sandoval preferred on this occafion, firft caufed a certain jealoufy on the part of the former;) he then fet out with four of the cavalry to Villa Rica, ordering thirty of the lighteft infantry to follow him thither, which number accordingly arrived there that night.

When we arrived at Villa Rica, Efcalante offered to Cortes to go with twenty men to the veffel, left fhe fhould make her efcape, and that Cortes might take fome repofe; but Cortes replied, that he could not think of that, for " A lame goat took no afternoon's nap." Accordingly, without eating a morfel, we proceeded along the coaft, and on our road fell in with four Spaniards, who were fent to take poffeffion of the country, by Captain Alonzo Alvarez de Pineda. One of thefe, who was named Guillen de la Loa, was a notary, and the reft attended him as witneffes. Cortes having queftioned thefe men as to what brought them there they replied, that Francifco de Garay, governor of Jamaica, had obtained from the court, a commiffion of adelantado and governor of fuch diftricts as he fhould difcover on that coaft, northward, from the river of St. Peter and St. Paul, by virtue of which, he had fent three fhips, with two hundred and feventy foldiers, under the captain already named, who was then in the river Panuco. Cortes treated them with much kindnefs, and afked them if they thought that we could get poffeffion of their fhip; to which Guillen de la Loa replied that they would do their utmoft to affift us, but no figns nor invitations that they made could induce thofe on board to approach, and we were told by them that their captain was aware of our being on the coaft, and they fuppofed, when the boat did not come off, that we had been difcovered. Cortes now bethought himfelf of a ftratagem, and it was this; he dreffed four of his foldiers in the clothes of thefe men, and left them there upon the fpot, tracing back the way that he had come along the fhore, fo that we might be obferved from the fhip. Thus we proceeded, until we were out of fight of it, when we ftruck

into

into the woods and made a ftolen march back, reaching about midnight the rivulet where we had left our four companions. Here we concealed ourfelves, and early in the morning our foldiers who were in difguife went down upon the fhore, and made figns to thofe on board the veffel, in confequence of which a boat put off with fix failors, two of whom landed with cafks for water. Our four men pretended that they were wafhing their hands, and holding down their faces endeavoured to avoid being obferved, but thofe in the boat calling to them, one of ours replied, defiring them to come on fhore. The ftrange voice gave an alarm, and fufpecting a trick they made off: we were going to fire upon them, but Cortes would not let us. Thus we obtained fix men, and returned to Villa Rica, without having eaten a morfel during two entire nights and a day.

CHAPTER VI.

March of the Spanish Army for the City of Mexico. Wars in Tlascala. Submission of that Nation.

BEING now ready to proceed to Mexico, our allies of Cempoal proposed to us to march by the province of Tlascala, the people of which were their friends, and bitter enemies to the Mexicans. In compliance with our requisition, fifty of their principal warriors attended us, and also two hundred men to draw our guns, and thus we set out from Cempoal, in the month of August 1519, our army in good order, and patroles of cavalry, and light infantry in front.

Our first day's march was to a town named Xalapa, and the second was to Socochima, a place of difficult approach, abounding with vines. The people here were harangued through our interpreters, who informed them that we were vassals of the Emperor Don Carlos, who had sent us to put a stop to human sacrifices, and other abuses. They also explained to them many things concerning our religion, and as these people were allies of Cempoal and independent of Montezuma, we found them very well disposed to us. We here erected a cross, explaining what it signified, and that it should be held in veneration. Proceeding from this place, by a pass among lofty mountains, we arrived at another named Texutla, the people of which we found equally well disposed to us, and they also paid no tribute to the Mexican monarch. Continuing our march through desert mountains, we that night experienced great cold and storms of hail. On the next day we reached another pass, where were some houses and large temples, with great piles of wood for the service of the idols. Provisions were scarce with us for these two days, and we now approached the territory of

N   Mexico,

Mexico, at a place called Cocotlan, sending forwards to inform the cacique.

Appearances demonstrated that we had entered into a new country, for the temples were very lofty, and together with the terraced dwellings, and the house of the cacique, being plaistered and whitewashed, appeared very well, and resembled some of our towns in Spain. We named this place Castel Blanco. In consequence of our message, the chief, and other principal persons of the town came out to meet us, and took us to our quarters, where they gave us paltry and cold entertainment. After supper Cortes made enquiry relative to the military power of Montezuma. He was informed, how that monarch had under him great armies, and that the city of Mexico was of uncommon strength, being founded in the water, and no passage from one house to another except by bridges or boats; that each house was terraced, and only required a parapet to be converted into a fortress; that the entrance to the city was by three causeways, in each of which were four or five apertures for the passage of the waters, and that on each of these apertures was a bridge of wood, which being raised, precluded the entrance into Mexico. We were also informed of the great wealth of Montezuma, in gold, silver, and jewels, the hearing of which filled us with astonishment, and such is the nature of Spanish soldiers, that we were anxious to try our fortunes, although the accounts we had been given, made our hopes appear almost visionary; and truly we found Mexico stronger than what it was now described to us. The cacique launched out also in the praises of his great lord, Montezuma, saying, that he ruled where ever it was his will to do so, and that he was apprehensive of his dissatisfaction at our being entertained in that place, without his licence. To all this Cortes replied saying, " That we came from a " distant country, by the orders of our sovereign, to warn the great " Montezuma to desist from human sacrifices, and all outrages either " upon his own vassals, or his neighbours, and to require from him " submission to our monarch. And, " added Cortes, " I now require " you all who hear me, to renounce your human sacrifices, cannibal

" feasts,

" feasts, and other abominable practices, for such is the command of
" our Lord God, whom we adore and believe, who gives us life and
" death, and who is to raise us up to heaven." All this the natives
heard with a profound silence, and Cortes then turning to the soldiers,
proposed to them immediately to plant the holy cross; but the Rev.
Father Olmedo objected, upon the grounds of the ill will and ignorance of the people, which might induce them to commit some outrage
or indignity against that holy symbol; he therefore recommended that
it should be deferred until a better opportunity.

We had with us a very large dog, the property of Francisco de
Lugo, which during the night used to bark, a thing that greatly surprised the natives, who asked our allies if that fierce animal was a lion
or tyger which we brought to kill them; they answered that he fell on,
and tore to pieces any who offended us; they also told them that our
guns sent forth stones, which killed our enemies as we pleased to direct
them, and that our horses caught whoever we pursued: to which the
others replied, that with such powers we were really Teules. Our
allies also warned them to take special care, for that we knew their most
secret thoughts, and advised them to conciliate us by a present. Shortly
after we received from them some gold in different articles but very
much debased, four Indian women to make bread, and a load of mantles.

I remember a particular circumstance of this place. Near some
temples were laid numbers of human skeletons, so arranged that they
could be counted with ease and certainty; I am convinced from my own
observation that there were above a hundred thousand; I repeat it, I am
sure there were more than a hundred thousand. In another part of the
square, human bones were heaped up in such quantities that they could
not be counted. Numbers of skulls were also suspended from beams,
and all these were watched by three priests. The same thing was seen
every where in some degree, as we passed through this country and that
of Tlascala.

The

The cacique of the place where we were, being asked by us relative to the road to Mexico, recommended that by Cholula; but our allies strongly advised us against going that way, on account of the treacherous disposition of the people, and that the town had always a Mexican garrison in it. Cortes demanding twenty of the principal persons to attend him from this place, we now quitted it in order to go to Tlascala, by advice of our allies, who promised us every advantage from that nation, and we proceeded thither, sending messengers before us with a letter and also a present of a crimson velvet cap. I must observe that although our letters were not legible to these people, they knew that such a thing was as it were an authority, or sanction of the message that was to be delivered, and of the office of those who brought it, and as such it was sent upon all occasions.

Proceeding with our accustomed order, we arrived at a village in the country of Xalacingo, and from thence sent two of our allies, with the letter, to Tlascala. At this place we received intelligence, that the whole nation was already in arms against us, on the supposition, from the number of persons who attended us, of those nations which were subject to Montezuma, that we were in alliance with the Mexican power, whose inveterate enemies they were. Having suspicion of treachery from the Mexicans by these appearances, they instantly on their arrival seized our messengers, whose return we impatiently waited for during two days, which Cortes employed in exertions for the conversion of the Indians to our holy church, by his advice and exhortations. He also demanded the attendance of twenty principal inhabitants, who readily joined him, and we at the expiration of that time continued our march, during which we met the messengers whom we had sent to Tlascala, and who had made their escape, owing to the negligence or connivance of their guards.

These Indians had not yet recovered from the terror into which they were put by what they had seen and heard, for the people of Tlascala vowed destruction to us, and all our adherents. The standard

was

was now advanced to the front, and we all said, " If it muſt be ſo, " forward in God's name." Our general then inſtructed the cavalry how to charge by threes in front, not halting to give thruſts with their lances, but pointing them at the height of the face; and he taught them how, if the enemy ſeized the lance, to wreſt it out of their hands by the action of the horſe, and holding the butt-end of the lance under the arm.

Having advanced about two leagues, we arrived at a kind of fortification built of lime and ſtone, and ſome cement of ſo ſtrong a nature that nothing but tools of iron could have any effect on it. It was alſo extremely well conſtructed for defence. We halted to examine this work, which the people informed us was built by the Tlaſcalans, on whoſe territory it ſtood, as a defence againſt the incurſions of the Mexicans. After pauſing ſome time in ſerious contemplation of this object, Cortes ordered us to march on, ſaying, " Gentlemen follow your ſtan- " dard the holy croſs, wherewith we ſhall conquer;" to which we one and all replied " That we were ready, for God was our true " ſupport."

After we had proceeded ſome diſtance, our advanced guard ſaw about thirty of the enemy, ſent out to obſerve us. Cortes ordered ſome of the cavalry to endeavour to take them priſoners, while we advanced at a quick ſtep to ſupport the advanced party. Our cavalry attacked them, but the enemy defended themſelves ſo well with their ſwords, wounding the horſes ſeverely, that our people were obliged to kill five, it being impoſſible to make them priſoners. A body of three thouſand warriors which had been placed in ambuſcade now ſallied out with great fury, and began to ſhoot at the cavalry, who were aſſembled in a body; but as we at this time brought our artillery and muſketry to bear upon them, they were after a time compelled to fall back, though regularly, and fighting during their retreat. They left ſeventeen dead on the field, and one of our ſoldiers died a few days after of his wounds. Evening was now drawing on, and we did not follow them, but pur-

ſuing

ſning our march, quitted the hills for a flat country thickly ſet with farm houſes, in fields of maize and the maguey plant. We halted for the night near a brook, and dreſſed our wounds with the greaſe we took out of a fat Indian who was left on the field; and although the people had removed all their effects and proviſions, their dogs, which we caught when they returned to their habitations at night, afforded us a very good ſupper.

On the enſuing day, after having recommended ourſelves to our God, we marched out to meet the enemy. Both cavalry and infantry had been duly prepared with inſtructions how to act in the attack, the former to charge, and then clear themſelves of the enemy, the latter not to ſuffer their ranks to be broken. Proceeding on our march, we ſhortly met two bodies of Tlaſcalan warriors amounting to about ſix thouſand in number, who attacked us valiantly with their miſſile weapons, ſhouting, and ſounding their inſtruments. Cortes ordered a halt, and ſent to them three Indians whom we had made priſoners on the preceding day, directing them to require of their countrymen a peaceable and amicable intercourſe with us, who wiſhed to conſider them as brothers, and this notice and invitation he deſired Diego de Godoy a royal notary to witneſs officially. As ſoon as our meſſage was delivered, they attacked us more violently than before, inſomuch that it was impoſſible to endure it any longer, and Cortes therefore cried out, " St. Jago, and at them." We accordingly attacked, and made a conſiderable ſlaughter of them by the firſt diſcharges of our artillery, killing, amongſt others, three of their chiefs.

They now retreated towards ſome broken ground, where the whole army of Xicotenga the general in chief, amounting to upwards of forty thouſand men, was poſted under cover. In this ground the cavalry could not act, and we were forced to paſs it as well as we could in a compact column, much annoyed by the enemy, who ſtarted up, and taking the due diſtance, availed themſelves of the expertneſs of their archers. Theſe troops were all clad, and bore devices of white and red,

which

which was the uniform of their general. Thofe who were armed with lances clofed upon us while we were embarraffed in the broken ground, but as foon as we arrived on the plain with our cavalry and artillery, we made them fmart for it. Notwithftanding this they clofed upon us on every fide, infomuch that we could not venture to move, and we were in the greateft danger but that the hand of God affifted us. Whilft we were engaged as I have already related, a number of the ftouteft of thofe warriors who carried the tremendous two-handed fwords, affociated themfelves in order to feize one of our horfes; accordingly, as Pedro de Moron, an exceeding good horfeman, was charging amongft them in company with three more, thefe warriors firft feized his lance, and then wounding him dangeroufly, one of them with a blow of a two-handed fword, cut through the neck of the mare he rode, fo that fhe fell inftantly dead, and Moron was brought off with the greateft difficulty; for it was utterly out of the power of us who formed the battalion to quit it, from fear that the enemy fhould break into us completely. However on this occafion we fucceeded in refcuing him out of the hands of the enemy, and we alfo cut the girths and brought off the faddle, but in fo doing we had ten of our number wounded, and I believe that we then killed ten chiefs of the enemy, for we were fairly engaged with them foot to foot, and we ufed our fwords to fuch effect that they began to retire, taking with them the body of the mare, which they cut in pieces, and fent all through the diftricts of Tlafcala. This mare was the property of Juan Sedeno, who was at that time ill of three wounds which he had received on the preceding day Moron died of his wounds, at leaft I do not recollect having ever feen him afterwards. After being engaged with the enemy for above an hour, during which the artillery made great havoc in their thick and numerous bodies, all of us alfo fighting as we were compelled to do for our lives and his Majefty's fervice, they drew off regularly, and left the field to us, who were too much fatigued to follow them. We therefore remained in the next village, for that country was thickly inhabited, and they had fubterraneous dwellings, in which numbers of

people

people lived. The name of this place is Tehuacingo, or Tehuacacingo, and the battle was fought on the second day of September 1519.

The lofs of the enemy on this occafion was very confiderable, eight of their principal chiefs being amongft the number. As foon as we found ourfelves clear of them we returned thanks to God for his mercy, and entering a ftrong and fpacious temple, we dreffed our wounds with the fat of Indians. Of fifteen wounded men, only one died. We obtained a plentiful fupper of the fowls and dogs which we found in the village, and refted for the night under the protection of ftrong guards. In this and all other battles, as foon as we wounded an enemy he was immediately carried off by his companions, fo that we never could afcertain the number of the dead. Fifteen of them were made prifoners by us, of whom two were chiefs.

After the fatigues fuffered in the late battle we repofed for one day, which was employed in repairing our crofs-bows, and making arrows. On the next, Cortes, not to give the enemy time to arrange new attacks, fent out as many of the foldiers as were fit for fervice, to fcour the country, which is there very flat and well adapted for cavalry. Accordingly, feven of the cavalry, and two hundred infantry, attended by our allies, went out, and made prifoners twenty men and women, but without any harm whatever being done by the Spaniards. The fame cannot be faid of our allies, who being cruel, made great deftruction, and returned loaded with fowls and dogs. As foon as we returned Cortes releafed the prifoners, and having given them food, and treated them kindly, he expoftulated with them upon their madnefs in attempting to refift us. He alfo at this time releafed two of the chiefs whom we had taken in the late battle, and fent them with a letter, and to inform their countrymen, that we only required an unmolefted paffage to Mexico. Thefe chiefs waited upon their General Xicotenga, who was pofted with his army at the diftance of two leagues, at a place named to the beft of my recollection Tehuacinpacingo, and delivering the meffage with which they were intrufted, the reply of Xicotenga was,

was, " That we fhould go to the head town of Tlafcala, where peace
" fhould be made with us by devouring our bodies, and offering our
" hearts and blood to their gods; and that on the next morning, he
" would give us his anfwer in perfon." This language, after what we
had experienced, it muft be confeffed founded moft terribly in our ears.
Cortes however did not fuffer his apprehenfions to appear, and treated
the meffengers even more kindly than before, in order to induce them
to go again. He then enquired relative to the power of Xicotenga and
the nature of his command. They informed him, that the army now
affembled confifted of the quotas brought by five chiefs, each of which
was ten thoufand men. Thefe chiefs were, Xicotenga the elder, father
of the general, Maxicatzin, Chichimecatecle, Tecapaneca cacique of
Topeyanco, and a cacique named Guaxobcin. Thus fifty thoufand
warriors were now ranged under the banner of Xicotenga, which was,
a white bird with the wings fpread refembling an oftrich. Each divifion of the troops had alfo its own marks of diftinction: this we found
to be the cafe, and that each cacique bore them in the manner of our
nobility in Caftille, although when we were firft informed of it by our
prifoners we difbelieved it. When all this was communicated to us,
being but mortals, and like all others fearing death, we prepared for
battle by confeffing to our reverend fathers, who were occupied during
the whole night in that holy office.

On the fifth of September 1519, having brought out our whole
force not excepting the wounded, the crofs-bowmen and mufketeers
being directed to fire alternately, fo that there fhould always be fome of
each loaded, the foldiers with fword and buckler being ordered to ufe
the points, paffing them clear through the bodies of their opponents,
and the cavalry being inftructed to keep their ranks, and charge at half
fpeed, pointing their lances at the eyes of the enemy, and riding through
them without halting to give thrufts, with our colours flying, and four
of our companions as a guard upon them, we fet out upon our march.
We had not proceeded half a quarter of a league, when we faw the
troops of the enemy covering the plains. Each body difplayed its re-

O   fpective

spective device, and they advanced, sounding all their warlike instruments.

Much might be written on the subject of this great, and long doubtful battle, where four hundred men stood opposed to hosts, which surrounding them from all parts, filled these plains, extending in every direction for the space of two leagues. Many of our small number were sick and wounded, and we knew that the enemy came upon us in a determination to sweep us from the earth, and sacrifice us to their idols. Their first discharges of arrows, stones, and two-headed darts which pierce any armour, and through the body where unprotected, covered the ground; and they continued advancing until they closed upon, and attacked us with their lances, and two-handed swords, fighting foot to foot, and encouraging each other by their cries and shouts. Our artillery, musketry, and cross-bows played on them, and the home thrusts our infantry made with their swords, prevented their closing upon us as much as they had done on the former occasion. Our cavalry also charged with such effect, that, next to God, it was to them we owed the victory. At one period I saw our battalion completely broken, nor could all the exertions of Cortes for a time rally it, such was the pressure of the enemy upon us. By the sole effect of our swords, however, we at length forced them off from us, and were then enabled to close and form. One circumstance that preserved us was the thickness of the enemy, whereby full play was given to our artillery. Another was, that they did not know how to bring up their forces upon us without confusion, and some of the divisions could not come to the attack at all. The one composed of the warriors of Guaxocingo, was prevented from engaging by Chichimecatecle, whom Xicotenga, the commander in chief, had provoked by some insulting observation relative to the preceding battle. This circumstance we were informed of afterwards. They were also apprehensive by experience of our cavalry, our cannon, and other arms; but above all was the great mercy of God, who gave us force to sustain their attacks. Two divisions as I have observed stood aloof, from disgust at what Xicotenga had said

relative

relative to the conduct of the fon of Chichimeatecle on the former occafion: this being obferved by the others, flackened their ardour, and
the lofs of one of their greateft chiefs killed, at length caufed them to
draw off their forces and retire, purfued by our cavalry, though but for
a very little diftance, owing to their exceffive fatigue. Thus being
again mafters of the field, we returned our thanks to God for his mercy.
One of our foldiers was killed, above feventy and all the horfes were
wounded. I received two wounds, one by a ftone, the other by an
arrow; but they were not fuch as to prevent my doing duty; indeed if
wounds had exempted us, few would have been fit for it.

We now returned to our former poft, having buried our dead in
one of the fubterraneous dwellings already mentioned, filling and level-
ling it, that our lofs fhould not be perceived by the enemy. How
wretched and comfortlefs was our fituation after our hardfhips and
dangers! We could not procure even oil and falt; and the cutting winds
of the Sierra Nevada, made us fhiver again.

Cortes now fent three of his prifoners, together with thofe who
had carried the former meffage, to repeat his demand of a free paffage
to Mexico, with threats of deftruction in cafe it was refufed. When
our meffengers arrived at Tlafcala, they found the chiefs of that nation
much difgufted with their misfortunes and loffes; ftill they heard our
propofals with a very unwilling ear, and fent for their priefts, and certain wizards who divine and foretell by cafting lots, in order to learn
from them, if we were vincible, and which were the moft likely means
of fucceeding againft us; alfo, if we were fupernatural beings, and what
our food confifted of. It feems their wizards informed them, that we
were human beings, and fubfifted as fuch, not eating the hearts of thofe
we killed, as they had been told, and that though invincible by day,
we were to be conquered by night, for that all our force was derived
from the prefence of the fun. This being believed, orders were immediately fent to their General Xicotenga to make an attack upon us during
the night. Accordingly, he marched againft us with a force of ten

thoufand

thoufand warriors, who attacked our poft in three different bodies, but our out parties had kept too good a look out to be furprifed, and a moment was fufficient to put us under arms. They therefore met with fuch a reception as foon caufed them to turn their backs, being, as it was moonlight, purfued by our cavalry with a confiderable lofs; and they returned to their poft heartily fick of a nocturnal attack. I have heard it faid, that finding themfelves deceived by their priefts and wizards, they in revenge facrificed two of them. We had but one of our allies killed, and two Spaniards wounded in this action, and we made four prifoners; but on the enfuing day when we came to look into the fituation of our army, it was far from confolatory; we were dreadfully harraffed, had loft above fifty-five foldiers by battle, ficknefs, and feverity of weather, and had feveral fick; our general was ill of a fever, as was our Rev. Father Olmedo, and the expectation of reaching Mexico was now confidered as a vifionary idea, after what we had experienced of the refiftance of the Tlafcalans.

We had however in our army many cavaliers equally wife in council as they were brave in the field, with whom Cortes never omitted confulting on important occafions, notwithftanding Gomara fays that Cortes did this and that, as if he was the fole actor, infomuch that even if he had been made of iron, he could not have executed all which that hiftorian afcribes to him. Let it fuffice that he did in every refpect like a good captain which he was, and this I fay, that in addition to his other mercies God was pleafed to give us wifdom to counfel and advife Cortes, upon all important occafions, for the beft, as the refult proved. But to have done with praifes, we waited on Cortes, and reprefented to him the favors which heaven had fhewn to us, and how evidently they pointed out that we were referved for fome great end, and now we advifed him to releafe his prifoners, and by them to make a fecond offer of amity to thefe people. Donna Marina, whofe fpirit fupported her in all dangers, and when fhe knew that we were upon the brink of deftruction, and were in momentary apprehenfion of being devoured, was at this time of moft effential fervice, for fhe explained to

thofe

thofe we fent, that it was our determination, if their countrymen did not immediately treat, to march againft and deftroy them and their town. With this refolute meffage they went once more to Tlafcala.

Our meffengers having arrived at Tlafcala, waited on the chiefs, the principal of them bearing in one hand our letter, and in the other a dart. It was the will of heaven that the Tlafcalans fhould be now inclined to enter into terms of accommodation. The two chiefs named Maxicatzin, and Xicotenga the elder, immediately fent to invite the reft, and alfo the cacique of Guaxocingo their ally, and being all affembled, they reprefented to them, that their attacks had been ineffectual on us, and deftructive to them, and that we were in hoftility to their inveterate enemies the Mexicans, who had made war on them for upwards of a hundred years, by which they were now deprived of falt and cotton. They therefore propofed, that their nation fhould accept our alliance, and that, in order to perpetuate it, the daughters of their firft families fhould be offered to us as wives. To thefe propofals they all agreed, and fent notice thereof to their general. This chief was highly offended at it, and infifted on making another night attack upon us. The council of Tlafcala being informed of this, fent orders to fuperfede him, but the captains and warriors refufed to obey, and in confequence of his violent conduct, four of their principal and moft venerable chiefs, who were appointed to wait on, and invite us to their town, were intimidated, and prevented from executing their miffion.

Having remained two days without doing any thing, we now propofed to Cortes to march to a place called Zumpacingo, the chief town of the diftrict, the people of which had been fummoned, but had treated our meffage with neglect. Accordingly, early in the morning we fet out, under the command of Cortes who was not yet quite recovered. The morning was extremely cold, the wind affecting two of our horfes fo much that we were afraid they would have died. Proceeding on our march, we arrived at the town before daybreak. The inftant the natives heard of our approach, they fled from their houfes, crying, that
the

the Teules were coming to kill them.   We halted in a walled inclofure, until it was light, when certain priefts and old men came from the temples, and apologized for not having attended to our fummons, afcribing their conduct to the threats of Xicotenga.   Cortes ordered thefe people to go to their head town and defire the chiefs to attend him, in order to bring about a peace; for we were as yet ignorant of what had paffed.   We obtained here a good fupply of provifions, and the farther advantage, that the Indians formed a favorable opinion of us, which daily gained ground.   The chiefs and old men went to Tlafcala, and their reprefentations had fuch an effect, that orders were given to all the neighbouring people, to fend in provifions to us.

Some of our foldiers began now to hold very querulous language; more efpecially thofe who had left good houfes and plantations in the Ifland of Cuba.   Seven of them waited at this time upon Cortes, and their fpokefman addreffed him in a prepared oration in the manner of advice, wherein he reprefented to him, that above fifty-five of our companions were dead, and that we were ignorant of the fituation of thofe in Villa Rica.   That notwithftanding the mercies which had been fhewn us, it was imprudent to tempt God too often, and it was neceffary to avoid being brought into a worfe fituation than that of Pedro Carbonero, for at prefent there was hardly a hope of efcaping being facrificed to the idols of the natives.   But that though it fhould pleafe God to preferve us, ftill it was expedient to return to Villa Rica, and conftruct a veffel to fend to Cuba for affiftance; and they lamented the imprudence of having totally deftroyed our fhipping, a deed the rafhnefs of which could not be parallelled in hiftory.   They added, that though our fituation was worfe than that of beafts of burthen, who if forced to labour have at leaft food and reft, yet they had hitherto defifted from remonftrating, as not thinking the time admitted of it, but that now the enemy were withdrawn and the country feemed peaceable, the prefent opportunity fhould not be omitted to be taken.

Cortes replied mildly, that he believed there never exifted Spanifh
foldiers

foldiers who had exhibited more valour and perfeverance than ourfelves, and that it was neceffary to continue to do fo in order to fave our lives. That with our courage he was well acquainted, as he alfo was with many other circumftances which they had then mentioned. But, that as God had delivered us from thofe great perils, he hoped the fame mercy would be continued to us in future. He then appealed to them if he had ever fhewn himfelf unwilling to fhare dangers with us, which indeed he well might, for he was ever forward on thofe occasions, and continued his reply, adding, that as we had wherever we went preached to the ignorant natives the doctrines of our holy faith, he trufted we fhould ftill receive the divine affiftance, and that of his patron St. Peter. That as to deftroying our fhips, it was done by good advice; " And," continued he, " Gentlemen, our fame will exceed
" far that of the moft illuftrious of our predeceffors, who never, as you
" obferve, dared to take fuch a meafure; and therefore it is better, in-
" ftead of repining, to look forward, and leave all to be guided by the
" hand of God. As to our return, it is true the natives we had left
" behind are now friendly, but if we feemed to retreat, the very ftones
" would rife againft us. Therefore gentlemen, thus it is; bad there,
" worfe elfewhere, better ftay as you are, here in a plentiful country,
" and as to what you fay of loffes, deaths, and fatigues, fuch is the
" fortune of war, and we did not come here in fearch of paftimes and
" amufements. Therefore I beg of you, who are all cavaliers by your
" ftation authorized to fet an example, that you no longer will think
" of returning, but do your duty like the valiant foldiers I have always
" found you to be."

The others replied deprecating ftill the march to Mexico; he then cut them fhort by faying, that according to the fong, it was better to die at once than live difhonored; and Cortes being fupported in thefe fentiments by all his friends, the complaints of thefe people were ftifled for the prefent, for we all cried out that no more fhould be faid upon the fubject.

After

After four meffages from the chiefs of Tlafcala to their general, to fend a peaceable embaffy to us, that chief was obliged to comply. Accordingly forty Indians arrived at our quarters, fent by him with fowls, bread, and fruit; they alfo brought with them four old women in wretched clothing, fome incenfe, and a quantity of parrots feathers.

Having offered their incenfe to Cortes, one of the men addreffed him as follows. " This prefent our General Xicotenga fends you. If " you are, as it is faid, Teules, and defire human facrifices, here are " thefe four women; take their hearts and blood for food; as we " knew not your pleafure, we have not hitherto facrificed them to you, " now do as you chufe with them. If you are men, here are fowls, " bread, and fruit; if you are benignant Teules, we offer to you this " incenfe and thefe parrots feathers." Cortes replied that he had already fent to them requiring peace, as our object in coming was to make manifeft the truths of our holy religion, and in the names of our God and Emperor, to prohibit human facrifices; that we were men like themfelves, but not accuftomed to put any to death except in our own defence, and that they fhould no longer continue their mad refiftance, but embrace peace when it was offered to them.

Thefe men it feems were fpies; we were warned of this by our friends of Cempoal, who informed us likewife that the people of Cimpacingo had faid that Xicotenga meant to attack us. Cortes now made immediate inveftigation, and caufing four of thefe Indians to be feized, they confeffed the whole, and that their general was waiting only for their report, to attack us on that very night. Cortes then caufing feventeen of the Tlafcalans to be arrefted, made their hands be ftruck off, and alfo the thumbs of others, and in that condition fent them to their chief, with an invitation to him to come and attack us; faying, that we would wait, for the fpace of two days, and at the expiration of that time, if he heard no farther, would come and feek for him in his poft. Xicotenga was prepared to march againft us, when his fpies rejoined him in that lamentable ftate; but from the moment he faw them,

he

he loft his courage and haughtinefs. Alfo one of thofe divifions with the chiefs of which he had quarrelled, at this time quitted his army, as we were informed.

A vedette now, unexpectedly, announced the approach of a numerous train of Indians by the road of Tlafcala, and his companion who had ftayed to obferve them, fhortly after galloped in and informed us that they were hard by; we therefore conceived hopes of that which it turned out to be, an embaffy of peace. Cortes ordered us all to our quarters, and on the arrival of the embaffy, the four old men deputed for the purpofe, advancing from the reft, went to the place where our general was, and bowing their heads, touched the ground with their hands, and kiffed them; making three more bows they then advanced, and having prefented their incenfe they faid, that they were fent on the part of the people of Tlafcala, to put themfelves under our protection; declaring that they never would have made war upon us, but for their belief that we were the allies of Montezuma, their mortal and ancient enemy. They added, that the firft attack made upon us was by the Chontales Eftomies, or mountaineers, (without their approbation,) who thought that they could eafily bring our fmall number to their lords the Tlafcalans; they then faid, that they were come to folicit pardon for the offence, and that the general of their army and other chiefs fhould fhortly wait upon us. Having finifhed, they bowed, touching the ground, and kiffing their hands. Cortes, affuming a fevere look, reproached them for the violence they had committed, but in confideration of their wifh to expiate their offences he told them, that he was now willing to accept their prefents and receive them into favor. He bid them immediately fend their chiefs to him, as in cafe they failed to come he was determined to proceed in hoftility againft them, but that his wifh was for peace; in token of which he made them a prefent of fome artificial diamonds. The four ambaffadors returned with this meffage, leaving thofe who had attended them with provifions, in our quarters. We now were convinced of the fincerity of their profeffions,

P

which

which came in very good time, for we were heartily tired of this severe and hopeless war.

The historian Gomara says, that Cortes ascended a rock, in order to get a view of Zumpacingo. I say it was close to our station, and the man must have been blind indeed who could not have seen it from thence. He also talks of mutinies, and other things, of which he says that he was informed. I say that never was a captain in the world better obeyed than Cortes, and that no such thought ever entered the mind of any of us, nor any thing that could be so construed, except the affair of the sands, and what I have lately related, which was only by way of advice, for the whole of our soldiers followed him most zealously, and it is no strange thing that good soldiers should occasionally counsel their chief.

The news of the great victory which it had been the will of God to give to us flew through all parts, and soon reached the ears of the great Montezuma; insomuch that this monarch, awed by the fame of our valour, sent five of the principal noblemen of his court, to congratulate us upon our successes. By them he sent a present of various articles of wrought gold, to the amount of a thousand crowns, and twenty loads of the richest mantles, with a declaration of his wish to become a vassal of our great monarch, to whom he offered to pay an annual tribute; adding, that from the esteem in which he held our general, he much wished to see him at his court in Mexico, but that he was obliged to deprive himself of that satisfaction, in consequence of the poverty of the country and badness of the roads by which he was to pass. Cortes expressed his obligation to this great monarch for the present, and his offer to pay tribute to our sovereign; he requested the ambassadors to stay and accompany him to Tlascala, with which government he had not yet made his conclusive arrangements, and desired that they would allow him to defer giving any farther answer on that day. He was now convalescent, and had taken as a medicine certain apples of great virtue, the produce of the Island of Cuba.

While

While Cortes was conversing with the ambassadors of Montezuma, Xicotenga and fifty of his principal warriors, all clothed in uniform habits of white and red, arrived and waited on him with great respect. Cortes received him with no less, and made him sit down at his side. The chief then told him, that he came in the name of his father, and the rest of the principal persons of his nation, to solicit our friendship, to submit to our monarch, and to apologize for having taken up arms against us, the reason of which was, the apprehension of the wiles of Montezuma. He added, that their country was very poor, producing neither gold, silver, jewels, cotton, nor even salt, which last article Montezuma prevented them from obtaining. He said also, that what gold their ancestors had collected, he had deprived them of, and that if they did not now bring satisfactory presents, their poverty must plead their excuse. He made many other complaints of Montezuma, and concluded by earnestly soliciting our alliance. This chief was of tall stature, strong, and well proportioned; his face broad, and somewhat wrinkled; of a grave aspect, and aged about thirty-five years. Cortes treated him with every mark of friendship, and expressed his satisfaction at having been the means of inducing so respectable a nation to become vassals to our sovereign, and allies to us. The Tlascalan chief then invited him to his city, which Cortes promised to visit as soon as he had dispatched his business with the ambassadors of Montezuma. At the conclusion of the conversation however, Cortes addressed a few words to them of a more serious nature, in respect to the offences which they had committed against us, warning them to take care of their conduct in future. They all promised the utmost fidelity, and this conversation having passed in the presence of the ambassadors of Montezuma, they attempted to ridicule the credit which we gave to the assurances of the Tlascalans, which they asserted were so many deceptions, their intention being to fall on and murder us in their city. Cortes replied, that any such attempt would bring with it its own punishment, and that he was determined to march to Tlascala, if it were only in order to ascertain the sincerity of the people. The ambassadors of Montezuma then requested a delay of six days, to obtain far-

ther

farther inftructions. This Cortes acceded to; for which he had two motives, firft, his ftate of health, fecondly, becaufe the obfervations of
the Mexican ambaffadors afforded grounds for ferious reflections. He
now alfo fent to Juan de Efcalante, informing him of what had happened, and requiring fome veffels of facramental wine, which had
been buried in a certain place, and alfo fome confecrated bread, that
which we had brought with us being ufed. We at this time erected
a fumptuous and lofty crofs in our quarters, and Cortes ordered the
people of Zumpacingo to purify and whitewafh a temple, which they
accordingly did.

Our friends of Tlafcala brought us continually ample fupplies of
provifions, fuch as fowls, and tunas or Indian figs, and they repeated
their invitations, which we could not as yet accede to, confiftently with
the engagement which we had made to the Mexican ambaffadors. At
the expiration of the time which Cortes had given, fix noblemen fent
by the great Montezuma arrived, with a prefent of various articles in
gold to the value of three thoufand crowns, and two hundred rich
mantles. They alfo brought a meffage of a congratulatory nature, and
containing the moft earneft requeft and advice, by no means to go to,
or truft the people of Tlafcala. Cortes received the prefent with every
expreffion of gratitude, affuring them that he would repay it in good
works to their monarch, adding, that, as to the Tlafcalans, he was
thankful for the warning, and if they attempted any treachery, would
make them pay for it with their lives. At this moment he received intelligence of the arrival of the Tlafcalan chiefs; he therefore requefted
of the ambaffadors a delay of three days, before he gave his anfwer to
them.

The ancient chiefs of Tlafcala, named Maxicatzin, and Xicotenga
the elder, a blind man, together with Guaxolacima, Chichimecatecle,
and Tecapaneca of Topeyanco, now arrived at our ftation, borne on
hammocks, in litters, and on men's backs, attended by a great train.
Saluting Cortes with great refpect, Xicotenga the blind chief addreffed
him

him faying, that they had often fent to him, to requeft pardon for their hoftilities, which they afcribed to the fufpicion they entertained of our being allied to Montezuma. But now we know, faid he, who, and what you are, we would go down to the coaft to invite you from your fhips, and fweep the roads before you; at prefent the utmoft we can do is, to requeft your company in our city, where you fhall be ferved in every manner that is in our power. We at the fame time warn you, not to give credit to the mifreprefentations of thefe Mexicans, who are influenced by the malice which they bear to us. Cortes returning many thanks to them, faid, he would have vifited them before that time, but that he wanted men to draw his cannon; upon which, in lefs than half an hour, above five hundred of the natives were affembled for the purpofe, and early in the morning we fet out upon our march, attended by the Mexican ambaffadors, by the requeft of Cortes, who kept them near him, left they fhould meet with any infult. Before I proceed, I muft mention, that from this time the natives always addreffed Cortes by the name of Malintzin; the reafon of which was, that Donna Marina being our linguift, and interpreting to Cortes, they gave him the name of Marina's captain, which in their pronunciation was perverted to Malintzin. We entered the territory of Tlafcala twenty-four days before our arrival at the chief city, which was on the twenty-third of September 1519.

As foon as the chiefs perceived that we were on our march, they went before us to provide our lodgings, and when we approached their city they came out to meet us, bringing their daughters and female relations; but each tribe, or divifion of inhabitants, diftinct and feparate; for it feems that of thefe there were four, exclufive of that under the government of Tecapaneca, lord of Topeyanco. Each of thefe tribes was diftinguifhed by a different uniform, of cloth made of nequen, for cotton was a luxury not within their reach. The priefts came with their incenfe pots, in loofe white garments, with their long hair matted and clotted with blood which flowed from recent cuts in their ears, and the nails upon their fingers were remarkably long. They faluted

Cortes

Cortes with reverence, and the people, when we entered the town, crowded upon us in such numbers as to make the streets hardly passable, presenting to Cortes and the cavalry, garlands of beautiful and odoriferous flowers. When we arrived at some large courts, in the apartments about which we were to be lodged, the two chiefs taking Cortes by the hand, brought him to that which was intended for him, and every Spanish soldier was accommodated with a bed, composed of a mat, and clothes made of nequen. Our allies were lodged near us, and the ambassadors of Montezuma, by the desire of Cortes, in the apartment next to his own. Although we had every confidence in the sincerity of the Tlascalans, yet Cortes never permitted the least relaxation in military duty; when the chiefs observed this, it gave them a jealousy, as they thought it to indicate that we harboured suspicions of them, and they spoke to Cortes on the subject in such terms as convinced us all of their sincerity. Cortes replied by assurances of his perfect reliance upon their truth, and also informed them, that it was merely a compliance with the custom of our country.

As soon as an altar could be erected, Cortes ordered mass to be said by Fra. Juan Diaz, the Rev. Father Olmedo being ill of a fever. At this many of the native chiefs were present, and after it was ended Cortes took them with him to his apartment, attended by those soldiers who usually accompanied him. Xicotenga the elder then told him, that they had prepared a present of which they requested his acceptance. Accordingly, some pieces of gold, and of cloth were produced, not altogether worth twenty crowns. The chief then addressed him, expressing his fear that he would despise such a paltry offer, but that their poverty, and the extortions of Montezuma, of whom they were obliged to purchase peace at the expence of all they possessed, were the causes of it. Cortes received their present with thanks, saying, that little as it was, he valued it more from them, as a testimony of friendship, than if others had given him a house full of gold. Xicotenga then proposed to him an alliance between our two nations, and that we should accept their daughters in marriage, making the offer of his own

to

to Cortes. Our general thanked him for these marks of good will, and the chiefs remained with him a whole day. Xicotenga who shewed particular attachment to Cortes, was blind; he was curious to examine with his hands, his head, features, and beard, which the general permitted him to do.

On the next day the chiefs brought five daughters of caciques, handsome in comparison to the other women of the country, well dressed, and each attended by a female slave. Xicotenga then presented his own daughter to Cortes, desiring him to assign the rest to his officers. Cortes thanked him, but observed, that for the present the ladies must remain with their parents. The chief asking the reason why he would not receive them he replied, that it was necessary first to obey the mandates of our Lord God, and the will of our monarch who had sent us thither, to put a stop to human sacrifices, and other evil practices, and bring them to the true faith in the adoration of one God. He then shewed them a beauteous image of our Lady, with her precious son in her arms, and explained to them that it was the representation of the holy Mary, who is in the heavens, and mother to our Lord, by the grace of the Holy Ghost, " Sine peccato concepta," and that she is our mediatrix with her precious son, who is our Lord God; then, said he, if you wish to be our brethren, and that we should intermarry with you, renounce your idolatrous worship, and adore our God; the good effects of which you will soon perceive in your temporal concerns, and thereby, after this life, your souls shall be taken into heaven, there to enjoy eternal happiness. Whereas, by persisting in the worship of your idols, which are devils, you will be drawn by them to their infernal pit, there to burn eternally in flames of fire. Cortes after an excellent harangue containing much more matter to the same effect, which was perfectly well explained by our interpreters, here ceased and waited their answer, which was given by the chiefs as follows. That they readily believed all that they had heard now, and before, of the excellence of our God, and his saints, and that they hoped in time to understand more upon the subject; that in regard to the renunciation of their ancient religion,

if

if they were to do it in their old age, in order to please us, what would their priests and the rising generation think of them? They would raise an insurrection; the more so, as the priests had already consulted their gods, who had commanded them by no means to omit their human sacrifices, and other ancient customs; as in case of failure in the observance of them, they would punish the country with famine, pestilence, and war. They therefore requested to be no more spoken to on the subject, as they could not renounce their gods but with their lives.

When the Rev. Father Olmedo, who was a wise man and good theologian, heard this, he advised Cortes to urge it no farther at present, being adverse to forced conversions, notwithstanding it had been done in Cempoal. He also observed, that the destruction of their idols was a fruitless violence, if the principle was not eradicated from their minds by arguments, as they would find other idols to continue their worship to, elsewhere. Three other cavaliers, Alvarado, De Leon, and De Lugo, also spoke to Cortes to the same effect. We however got one of the temples cleared out, and erecting an altar, converted it into a christian church, and here the ladies destined to be the brides of our officers were baptized. The daughter of Xicotenga received the name of Donna Louisa, and was taken by the hand by Cortes, who presented her to Alvarado, telling her father, that officer was his brother: at which the old chief expressed his entire satisfaction. The niece or daughter of Maxicatzin was given to Velasquez de Leon, to the best of my recollection: she was very handsome, and took the name of Donna Elvina; and the rest whose names I do not now remember, but they were all Donnas, were assigned to De Oli, Sandoval, and Avila. After the ceremony, the reason of the erection of crosses was explained to the natives, as being done in order to terrify and expel the evil spirits they worshipped, to all which they listened with proper attention. Before I proceed farther I must mention, that almost the whole province of Tlascala paid homage and made presents to Donna Louisa: Alvarado had by her a son named Don Pedro, and a daughter named Donna Leonora, wife at present to D. Fra. de la Cueva, a good cavalier, cousin

to

to the Duke of Albuquerque, by whom she has four or five sons all worthy cavaliers; Donna Leonora herself being an excellent lady, the true descendant of such a father, who was in right of Donna Louisa, great lord, or as it were sovereign, in Tlascala.

Cortes now obtained in a conversation with Xicotenga the elder and Maxicatzin, considerable information relative to Mexico. They told him, that Montezuma had an army of a hundred thousand warriors; that the enmity between the Mexicans and Tlascalans had subsisted above a hundred years, the latter having formed an alliance for mutual protection with the people of Guaxocingo, and that all the districts which Montezuma had brought under his subjection were dissatisfied with his tyranny, and inclined to favor his enemies. They said that the people from whom the Tlascalans had suffered most, were those of Cholula, from which city, the troops of Montezuma could come by surprise upon the Tlascalan territory; that the Mexican garrisons occupied all the cities of the neighbouring states, who were obliged to pay tribute to their monarch, in gold, manufactures, and victims for sacrifice; and in short, that his wealth and power were immense. They informed him also of the great strength of the city of Mexico, of the lake, and the causeways with their wooden drawbridges. They farther described that city as built principally in the water, so that there was no passing from one house to another except by drawbridges or in canoes, and that all the houses were terraced at top, and defended by parapets. The arms of the Mexicans they described as consisting of double-headed darts thrown by a kind of sling, lances with double-edged blades of an ell in length, made of stone, and sharper than a razor, two-handed swords of the same material and construction, and shields. The Tlascalan chiefs then produced for our inspection large cloths of nequen, whereon were painted representations of their various battles. The discourse afterwards turned upon themselves and their nation. They said that their ancestors had told them, that in former times the country was inhabited by men and women of great stature, and wicked manners, whom their ancestors had at length extirpated; and in order that we

Q

might

might judge of the bulk of thefe people, they brought us a bone which had belonged to one of them, fo large, that when placed upright it was as high as a middling fized man; it was the bone between the knee and the hip; I ftood by it, and it was of my height, though I am as tall as the generality of men. They brought alfo pieces of other bones of great fize, but much confumed by time; but the one I have mentioned was entire; we were aftonifhed at thefe remains, and thought that they certainly demonftrated the former exiftence of giants. This bone we fent to Caftille for his Majefty's infpection, by the firft perfons who went on our affairs from hence. The chiefs alfo told us how their idols had predicted, that men fhould come from diftant parts where the fun rifes, to fubjugate the country, and that they believed us to be thofe of whom their gods had fpoken. Cortes replied that it certainly was the cafe, that we were fent by our monarch to cultivate friendfhip with them, and that he hoped we fhould be the inftruments of their falvation, to which we one and all faid, Amen.

By this time the cavaliers my readers, are I fear tired of the converfation with the Tlafcalans; I muft however mention fome other things which occurred here. There was a volcano near Guaxocingo, which at this time threw up great quantities of flames. Captain Diego de Ordas went to examine it, attended by two foldiers and fome principal Indians. The natives were afraid to approach nearer to it than the temples of Popocatepeque, but De Ordas with his two companions proceeding, reached the fummit, and looked down into the crater, which forms a circle of about a quarter of a league in diameter; from hence they alfo had the firft view of the city of Mexico, at the diftance of twelve or thirteen leagues. This was thought at the time a great achievement. When De Ordas went to Caftille, he obtained permiffion from his Majefty, to bear the volcano of Guaxocingo in his coat of arms, and it is fo borne by his nephew who lives in La Puebla. This mountain for feveral years, until 1530, did not throw out flames; but at that period it raged again violently.

In

In this town of Tlaſcala we found wooden cages, where they confined and fattened their victims. Theſe we deſtroyed, releaſing the unfortunate priſoners, who remained with us, not daring to venture to their
homes. Cortes ſpoke in very angry terms to the chiefs of Tlaſcala
upon their perſeverance in this horrid cuſtom; they promiſed amend-
ment, but what availed that, when, on our backs being turned, they
immediately reverted to their old abominations !

CHAPTER VII.

The Spanish Army proceeds on its march to Mexico.

AFTER a repose of seventeen days in Tlascala, it was determined to prosecute our march to Mexico. Upon this subject much difference of opinion existed, the rich settlers of Cuba being very adverse to it. The resolution which we had taken grieved our friends of Tlascala, who earnestly advised us by no means to trust Montezuma or his people, nor their smooth and courteous words and manners; for that they were treacherous in the extreme, and would either retain us to breed men for Montezuma's service, or in a favorable hour, would fall upon, and destroy us. But, in case of our having hostilities with them, they advised us to kill all, neither sparing the rising youth, nor the aged counsellor. Cortes thanked, and proposed to them, an amicable treaty with their neighbours the Mexicans; but they would not hear of this, saying, they could not trust those, who would only under the veil of peace, better execute their treacherous designs. In regard to our road, the Mexican ambassadors earnestly recommended that by Cholula; but our friends of Tlascala as strongly advised us by no means to go that way, but by Guaxocingo. Nevertheless we determined to go by Cholula, intending to remain there, until we could by negociation obtain a peaceable entry into Mexico. Cortes therefore sent messengers to that place, to inform the chiefs of his intention, and expressing his dissatisfaction that they had not come to wait upon him.

At this time arrived four of the principal nobility of Mexico, with a rich present. It consisted of gold to the value of ten thousand crowns, and ten bales of the finest mantles of feathers. Having saluted Cortes with the profoundest respect, the ambassadors delivered the message of
their

their monarch, which was to this effect. That he wondered at our stay amongst a people so poor and base as the Tlascalans, who were robbers, and unfit even for slaves; and he earnestly requested that we would immediately visit his capital. Cortes replied assuring them that he would shortly pay his respects to the great Montezuma, requesting their stay with him during the interval. He also determined to send two cavaliers as ambassadors, to wait on Montezuma, and view the city of Mexico. The persons he pitched on were Pedro de Alvarado, and B. Vasquez de Tapia. They set out on their journey, accompanying the former Mexican ambassadors who had hitherto continued with us. I was at this time ill of my wounds, and of a fever; and therefore incapable of observing exactly all that passed, but I know, that their going thither appeared to us a very unwise measure, and in consequence of our remonstrances, they were recalled.

The chiefs of Cholula now sent us four men of low condition, with a very dry and uncourteous answer to our message, and without any present whatever. This evidently appeared to be done in contempt, and Cortes sent notice to them, that if their chiefs did not wait upon him in three days, they should be considered as rebels; but that in case of their compliance, he would be happy to esteem them as brothers, and had much to tell them of great importance. They then sent word that they dared not to come amongst their enemies the Tlascalans, who they knew had misrepresented them and the great Montezuma to us; but they requested that we would visit their city, where they would give us an honorable reception. When the Tlascalans saw our determination to accept this proposal they told us, that since we were resolved to neglect their advice, they expected that we would take with us ten thousand of their best warriors. This was thought two great a number for a peaceable visit; we however agreed to take two thousand, who were immediately ready to attend us.

Being well prepared against whatever might happen, we now set out on our march, and arrived in the evening at a river, distant a short
league

league from Cholula, where a ſtone bridge is now built acroſs it. Here ſome of the chiefs of the city came to congratulate us on our arrival. Continuing our march on the next day, when we came near the city, we were met by the chiefs and prieſts in a body, all dreſſed in caſſocks of cotton, reſembling thoſe of the Zapotecans. The chiefs preſented their incenſe to Cortes, and after apologizing for not having gone to Tlaſcala, requeſted that he would not permit ſo large a body of their enemies to enter the city. This appearing reaſonable, Cortes ſent Alvarado and De Oli, to deſire our allies to hut themſelves in the field, and we then marched on, attended only by the Indians of Cempoal, and thoſe who drew the artillery. Before he entered the city he made known to theſe people the objects of his miſſion, as has been already frequently related. They replied without heſitation, that to our monarch they were perfectly ready to yield immediate obedience, which they did; but that as to abandoning their ancient religion, they could not comply with any ſuch demand. When we entered their city, we were conducted through an immenſe crowd which filled the ſtreets and terraces, to our quarters in ſome large apartments, which contained us, our allies of Cempoal, and thoſe who conveyed the artillery and baggage.

During the time we ſtayed here, a plot was concerted by the ambaſſadors of Montezuma, for the entry of twenty thouſand of his troops into this city, to fall upon us; and ſeveral houſes were filled with the poles and leathern collars, in which they were to have brought us priſoners to Mexico, but that God was pleaſed to foil their deſigns.

For the firſt two days, we were entertained as well as we could wiſh, but on the third we received no proviſions, nor did either chief or prieſt make his appearance. The few inhabitants that we ſaw, alſo, withdrew from us with a myſterious kind of ſneer in their faces, and Cortes at this time applying to the ambaſſadors ro procure for us our proviſions as uſual, all that we obtained was a little wood and water, conveyed by ſome old men, who told us that no maize was to be had.

On

On this day ambaſſadors arrived from Montezuma, who, in very diſ-reſpectful terms, forbid our approach to Mexico, and required an immediate anſwer. Cortes mildly expreſſed his ſurpriſe at this alteration; he made them a preſent, and requeſted a ſhort delay, which they acceded to. He then ſummoning his ſoldiers, warned us to be alert, for that he ſuſpected ſome great treachery. The chiefs having refuſed to attend him, he immediately ſent ſome ſoldiers to a great temple hard by our quarters, with orders to bring, as quietly as they could, two of the prieſts. In this they ſucceeded without any difficulty, and the prieſts being brought before the general, he made a preſent to each, and then enquired the reaſon of theſe extraordinary appearances. One of them was a perſon of rank, and authority over all the temples of the city, in the manner of a biſhop; this perſon aſſured him, that if he had an opportunity of ſpeaking to the chiefs, he could perſuade them to come; and being diſmiſſed for this purpoſe, he was as good as his word, for he ſoon returned accompanied by ſeveral of them. Cortes firſt aſked the cauſe of the change in their behaviour; he then demanded an immediate ſupply of proviſions, and alſo a number of their people for the enſuing day, to convey the baggage and artillery. The chiefs appeared confounded, but at length promiſed to ſend in proviſions; though they ſaid they had been forbidden by Montezuma, and that he was not ſatisfied that we ſhould go any farther. Juſt at this time three of our friends of Cempoal called out the general, and informed him, that they had diſcovered hard by our quarters, pitfalls covered with wood and earth, and that clearing away the earth, and looking into one of them, they had found it ſet with ſharp ſtakes; that the terraces of all the houſes were filled with ſtones and parapeted with ſods, and that they had ſeen a barricade of ſtrong timber in one of the ſtreets. At this inſtant arrived alſo eight Tlaſcalans, from their army which was lying in the field; they warned Cortes againſt the intended attack, for it had come to their knowledge, that the people of the place had, on the preceding night, ſacrificed to their war god ſeven victims, five of whom were children, and they had alſo obſerved, that they were withdrawing their women, children, and effects, from the place.

Hereupon

Hereupon Cortes sent orders to the Tlascalans to hold themselves in readiness, and rejoining the chiefs and priests of the town, he desired them to be under no apprehension, but warned them not to deviate from their obedience, on pain of instant punishment. He then demanded of them two thousand of their warriors to accompany him on his march, on the ensuing day; this they readily promised, thinking that it would tend to facilitate their projects; they therefore took their leave very well contented, and sent notice of our intentions to all those concerned with them. Cortes then sent Donna Marina to bring back the two priests whom he had before spoken to. In this she succeeded, and Cortes obtained from them the following intelligence.

They told him, that Montezuma, on our approach to Mexico, had become very unsettled in his mind, sometimes ordering that we should be received with honor, and at other times that we should not be permitted to pass; but that having lately consulted his gods, they had declared, that here in Cholula we were all to be put to death, or made prisoners, for which purpose he had sent twenty thousand of his troops, one half of which number was in the city, and the other concealed half a league from it. That the plan of their attack was settled, and that twenty of us were allotted to be sacrificed to the gods of Cholula. Cortes rewarded them handsomely, and enjoining strict secresy, desired them to bring to him all the chiefs, at the time he appointed. He then summoned a council of the ablest and wisest soldiers of his army, some of whom were for returning immediately, and others proposed various measures; but at length all agreed in the necessity of severely punishing this treachery, as an example to other places. It was therefore determined, that we should carry on the appearance of our intended march, preparing our baggage, and concealing our other measures, and that within the high walls of the courts where we were quartered, punishment should be inflicted on the Cholulans. With the ambassadors of Montezuma it was thought most prudent to dissemble; we therefore told them of our having discovered the treason of the people, who had aspersed Montezuma, as being the author of it; and we proposed

to

to them, to have no more intercourse with the inhabitants, but to retire to the apartment of Cortes. They folemnly declared their ignorance of the tranfaction, and contrary to their inclination we now put them under a good guard, for the night, during which our whole force remained under arms.

On this night, the wife of a cacique, an old woman, who was acquainted with the plot, came fecretly to Donna Marina whofe appearance had attracted her regard, and invited her to her own houfe, as a place of fecurity from the danger which was ready to overwhelm us, making at the fame time a propofal to her, to accept as a hufband, her fon, the brother of a boy who accompanied her. Donna Marina, with a profufion of thanks, and with her ufual acutenefs and prefence of mind, agreed to all that fhe propofed, but faid that fhe wanted fome one with whom to entruft her effects. She then obtained information of every particular of the bufinefs, all which the old woman informed her fhe had learned from her hufband, who was chief of one of the divifions of the city, and was then with his warriors, giving directions for their junction with the Mexican forces. She added, that fhe had known it three days before, in confequence of prefents which had been fent from Mexico to the different chiefs, her hufband having received at that time a golden drum.* Donna Marina, defiring this woman and her fon to remain where they were and take care of her effects, haftened to Cortes, and informed him of all that had paffed, and that the perfon from whom fhe had the information was in her apartment ; in confequence of which, Cortes immediately fent for her, and the woman on being brought into his prefence confirmed all that fhe had faid to Donna Marina, and which exactly agreed with the other information he had received.

When day broke, the hurry of the chiefs, priefts, and people, and the fatisfaction which appeared in their countenances, were as great as

R

if

---

* A golden drum was borne by a general in chief.

if they already had us in their cages. They brought many more of their warriors to attend us than we had required, infomuch that the courts, which remain at this day as a memorial of the event, large as they were, could not contain them. We were all prepared for what was to be done, the foldiers armed with fword and buckler were placed at the gate of the great court, in order to prevent any one from efcaping, and our general was on horfeback, attended by a ftrong guard. When he faw how the people crowded in he exclaimed, "How anxious are "thefe traitors to feaft upon our flefh! But God will difappoint them." He fent directions to the two priefts who had given the information, to go immediately to their houfes, and this he did in order to fave their lives; then, caufing the reft of the priefts, and all the chiefs to be brought to him, he calmly afked them what was their reafon for plotting to deftroy us, and what we had done, more than require them to abandon their abominable cuftoms, and endeavour to inftruct them in the articles of our holy faith; and that for thefe reafons only, they had made preparations to cut us all off. That their evil intentions appeared by their having withdrawn the women from the town, and that when we required the provifions which they withheld from us, they had infulted us by fending in wood and water. He faid that he knew of the ambufcade that was placed upon the road which they expected us to go, and that the recompenfe which they intended for our holy and friendly fervices was, to kill and eat us, for which purpofe the pots were already boiling, and prepared with falt, pepper, and tomatas. That if they were determined to attack us, it was better to do it in a manly way, as the Tlafcalans did; he added, that he alfo knew that twenty of us were to be facrificed to their idols, to whom they had made a propitiatory offering of feven of their brethren; but the victory the idols had promifed them, it was not in their power to give, and the effects of their treafon were now ready to fall on their own heads.

This being fucceffively explained to the natives by Donna Marina, they confeffed the whole of the charge, but faid that it was planned entirely by the orders of Montezuma. Cortes replied, that fuch crimes were

were never fuffered to pafs without punifhment, and he then commanded a mufket to be fired, as the fignal for flaughter, which was waited for by us, who were as I have related well prepared, and falling upon the multitude then inclofed within the courts, we executed their punifhment on them in a manner that they will ever remember; for a number of them were killed by us inftantly, and many afterwards burned alive, very contrary to the expectations they had formed from the promifes of their gods.† Within two hours our allies the Tlafcalans arrived, and made a defperate flaughter of them in the ftreets, and as foon as the Cholulans had ceafed to make refiftance, the former ravaged the city, plundering and making them flaves without our having it in our power to prevent them; and on the day after, when the intelligence had reached Tlafcala, frefh hordes crowded hither for the fame purpofe. It was now abfolutely neceffary to reftrain them at all rifks: Cortes therefore ordered the chiefs to withdraw their troops, which they immediately did, and foon after, fome priefts and chieftains who prefided over other parts of the town, which they alledged not to have been engaged in the confpiracy, waited on us, and requefted a remiffion of punifhment. The two priefts formerly mentioned, and the old woman who was fo anxious to be the mother-in-law of Donna Marina, came alfo, and petitioned to the fame effect. Cortes appeared greatly enraged, and calling for the Mexican ambaffadors, declared in their prefence, that if he did not deftroy the whole city as it deferved, it was out of refpect to the great Montezuma, whofe vaffals the inhabitants were; but that for his fake he pardoned them. He then commanded the Tlafcalans to deliver up thofe whom they had made prifoners: this, however unwillingly, they in a great meafure complied with, many perfons being fet at liberty, but after all they retained a good booty of gold, mantles, cotton, falt, and flaves. An amnefty for the paft being proclaimed, and Cortes having reconciled the Tlafcalans and Cholulans, the latter fuggefted that they were apprehenfive our general would appoint their new chief, the former one having been put to death. Cortes upon

R 2

this

---

† Above fix thoufand Cholulans were put to death on this occafion.

this enquired who was the regular fucceffor, and being informed that it was the brother of the late head cacique, he appointed him to the chieftainry. As foon as the inhabitants had returned, and order was reftored, he fummoned together all the priefts and chiefs, in order to exhort them upon the fubject of religion, advifing them to renounce their odious practices, and as an inftance of the inefficacy of their idols, he reminded them of the manner in which they had been lately deceived by their falfe promifes. He therefore propofed that they fhould be pulled down and broken to pieces, and an altar and crofs erected in their place. The latter was immediately done, but as to the proftration of the idols, by the advice of the reverend father it was poftponed for a time, from motives of prudence, and a juft confideration of the uncertainty of our fituation.

The city of Cholula much refembled Valladolid, being in a fertile plain, very thickly inhabited; it is furrounded by fields of maize, pepper, and maguey. They had an excellent manufacture of earthenware, of three colours, red, black, and white, painted in different patterns, with which Mexico and all the neighbouring countries were fupplied, as Caftille is by thofe of Talavera and Plafencia. The city had at that time above a hundred lofty white towers, which were the temples of their idols, one of which was held in peculiar veneration. The principal temple was higher than that of Mexico, and each of thefe buildings was placed in a fpacious court.

The Mexican troops which had been pofted in ambufcade, with ramparts and trenches to oppofe to the cavalry, hearing what had happened to their affociates, made a rapid retreat to their city, and carried the news to their monarch; but he had already heard his misfortune from two of his ambaffadors who had been with us. It is faid that he immediately ordered a facrifice to his gods, and fhut himfelf up at his devotions for two entire days, with ten of his chief priefts, in order to obtain an anfwer from them, relative to his future deftiny. The reply which they gave was to this effect; that he fhould fend an embaffy to

exculpate

exculpate himfelf in regard to what had paffed, and to invite us into Mexico, where, by cutting off the water, or raifing the bridges, he could eafily deftroy us, or retain us for breed. The news of our late fucceffes fpread rapidly, and the natives were more than ever convinced that we were beings poffeffed of a preternatural power and intelligence. My readers will be perhaps by this time as tired of the detail of the tranfaction of Cholula, as I am of writing it. I muft however mention the cages full of men and boys fattening for facrifice, which were in this city. All thefe Cortes deftroyed, and fent the poor prifoners to their homes, giving pofitive orders to the priefts to defift from the practice in future, which they promifed that they would, but what fignified their promifes!

This which I have related is the reality of the endlefs ftory of the Lord Bifhop of Chiapa, F. Bart. de las Cafas, who fays we put thefe people to death merely for paftime; but I muft obferve, that certain reverend Francifcans, after the conqueft of Mexico, being fome of the firft his Majefty fent to New Spain, went to Cholula on purpofe to make the ftricteft enquiry; the refult of which was, that they found the affair to have happened exactly as I have related it. If this punifh-ment had not taken place our lives would have been in the greateft danger, and had we been deftroyed this country of New Spain would not have been fo eafily gained, or a fecond expedition attempted; or if it had, it might have failed of fuccefs, as the natives would have defended their coafts, and have thus remained for ever in their idolatry. I have heard a reverend Francifcan named Fray Torribio de Motilinea fay, that if the punifhment could have been avoided, and that there had been no caufe given for it, it would have been better; but that fince it was done, good effects had refulted, as the natives were thereby convinced of the falfehood and deception of their idols, which they in confequence de-fpifed, as a proof of which they afterwards took down the principal one, putting another in its place.

Having now paffed fourteen days in the city of Cholula, Cortes
fummoned

summoned a council composed of certain officers and soldiers, men of equal valour and wisdom, and his particular friends, for without our advice he entered upon no measure of consequence, and it was thereby determined, to send a respectful message to the great Montezuma, and to inform him that in compliance with the orders of our king we were on our way to pay our respects to him in person. We then related the transaction of Cholula, where the treason which was meditated against us had come in sufficient time to our knowledge, from which nothing that concerned us could be concealed, adding, that if we had not punished it to the full extent, it was only out of respect to him, whose vassals the people of that city were; that the chiefs and priests had informed us, that what they did was at his instigation, which we could not believe of so great a prince, after the proffers of friendship which he had made to us, for that had he been inclined to hostility, he would have met us in the field, but that in the case of a battle, field or town, day or night, was alike to us.

The Mexican monarch was very doubtful and pensive, when he considered the events which had passed. After a variety of determinations he at length sent to us six of his first nobility, with a present of gold to the value of two thousand crowns, and several bales of fine mantles. When the ambassadors came into the presence of Cortes, saluting him with profound respect, they delivered a message from their monarch, wherein he laboured to exculpate himself in regard to what had happened in Cholula, and concluded by inviting us to his court. Cortes entertained these persons with his usual politeness, and retaining three of them to go with us as guides, sent the others back to inform their monarch that he was setting out upon his march. When the Tlascalan chiefs heard our determination, they renewed to Cortes their warnings to beware of Mexican treachery, but added, that if he was determined to proceed, they would send with him ten thousand of their warriors. Cortes thanking them observed, that such a body would not accord well with an amicable visit, but requested one thousand men for the baggage and artillery, which number was instantly provided.

Our

Our faithful allies of Cempoal being apprehenfive of the vengeance of the Mexicans, now petitioned for leave to return to their homes. Cortes difmiffed them with handfome prefents, and having written to Juan de Efcalante, informing him of his determination, we fet forward on our march.

We quitted Cholula in great regularity, fending out our cavalry patroles to reconnoitre, fupported by light infantry, our arms in order, and the cavalry by threes in front. Marching on thus, " With the " beard always upon the fhoulder," we arrived at a little place called the hamlet of Ifcalpan, in a mountainous ridge in the diftrict of Guaxocingo, four leagues diftant from Cholula, where we were met by the chiefs, accompanied by others who inhabit the fkirts of the volcano. They brought prefents of provifions and gold, of trifling value, telling Cortes he fhould receive it, not confidering how much it was worth, but the inclination of thofe who gave it. They advifed us againft going to Mexico, as being a very ftrong city and the inhabitants warlike, and they alfo told us, that on afcending the next mountain, we fhould find two roads, very broad, one whereof went to a place called Chalco, the other to Talmanalco, both, places fubject to the Mexicans. That the one road was very open and convenient, the other difficult, being obftructed by large pine trees felled acrofs it, and that the firft mentioned road, had an ambufcade of Mexicans laid hard by it, among fome rocks, in order to fall upon us as we paffed; they therefore recommended us to go by that where the trees had been felled, offering to fend a number of their people to clear it. Cortes expreffed his gratitude for their advice, faying that by God's permiffion he would purfue his route, accordingly.

Early on the morning of the next day we fet forward on our march, and reached the fummit of the ridge about twelve o'clock, where we found the roads as they had been defcribed to us, fome of the felled trees being to be feen at this day. Here we halted a little in order to confider how we fhould proceed, and Cortes calling upon the ambaffadors
dors

dors of the great Montezuma, enquired of them the meaning of thefe appearances. They replied, that we fhould take that road which led to Chalco, where we fhould be well received, and that the other road was longer and more difficult. Hereupon Cortes faid, that he would notwithftanding prefer it, and our Indian allies clearing the way before us, we proceeded up the mountain, where the weather was exceedingly cold, and prefently came a very heavy fall of fnow, fo that the whole country was covered with it. After fome time we arrived at certain houfes which are for the purpofe of lodging travellers, where we halted, and found provifions in plenty. Having placed our guards, we refted for that night, and continued our march in the morning, and at the hour of high mafs arrived at the town of Talmanalco, where we had an hofpitable reception. The people of the neighbouring diftricts, that is to fay of Chalco, Mecameca, and Acingo where the canoes are kept, waited on Cortes here with a prefent of gold worth about a hundred and fifty crowns, fome mantles, and eight women. Cortes received them kindly, promifing them his friendfhip, and a number of the natives being now collected, he defired the reverend father of the order of mercy to explain to them the doctrines of our holy faith, and require them to renounce their idolatrous worfhip; he alfo informed them of the great power of our monarch, and that we came in his name to redrefs wrongs. When the people heard this, they began to make fecret complaints of the tyranny of Montezuma, who deprived them of their wives and daughters if handfome, and took the men to work like flaves, compelling them to convey for him, ftones, timber, and corn, and feizing their lands for the fervice of his idols. Cortes condoled with them in kind words, defiring them to have patience for the prefent, and that they fhould foon be redreffed. He then defired that fome might go, and report to him the ftate of the road, but they told him there was no occafion, as it was perfectly clear.

Juft as we were fetting out attended by twenty Indians from this place, four of the principal nobility of Mexico arrived, and having paid their compliments, and delivered their prefents, thus addreffed Cortes.

Cortes. " Malintzin, this prefent our monarch fends you, faying,
" how grieved he is that you fhould take fo much trouble in coming
" from a diftant country to fee him, and that he has already told you
" he will give you gold, filver, and chalchihuis for your Teules,
" on condition that you will not approach Mexico. He now repeats
" his requeft, and promifes that he will fend after you, a great treafure
" of gold, filver, and jewels, for your king, four loads of gold for
" yourfelf, and a load for each of your brethren, on condition you
" return immediately; for as to advancing to Mexico, that, you
" cannot do, as the whole force of the Mexican warriors is in arms
" againft you: and moreover, there is no good road thither, nor are
" provifions to be had." Cortes embraced the ambaffadors with much
urbanity, and returned his thanks for the prefent, faying, that he was
furprifed to find the great Montezuma fo variable in his mind. In regard to his offers of treafure for the emperor, he thanked him, and for
what had been received, faid he hoped to pay in future fervices; but
fubmitted to him, how he could poffibly turn back, when fo near his
royal refidence, without taking that opportunity of paying his refpects,
and obeying his mafters orders; and begged him alfo to confider, what
opinion he would entertain of perfons he had fent on fimilar bufinefs,
fhould they act in the manner he required us to do. To his capital,
our monarch expected we fhould go, and therefore it was ufelefs to
fend any more fuch meffages, for he muft wait upon his Majefty, and
deliver his meffage to him in perfon: and afterwards, if our remaining
there was not agreeable, he would obey his orders, and return to the
place from whence he came.

Having thus difpatched Montezuma's ambaffadors we continued
our march. Our allies had informed us that Montezuma was to permit
us to enter the city, and there put us all to death; this we well knew,
and being like other mortals fond of our lives, it filled us with melancholy thoughts. Recommending our fouls therefore to our Lord Jefus
Chrift, who had brought us through our paft dangers, we proceeded,
and halted at a place called Iztapalatengo, one half of the houfes of
S   which

which is in the water, and the other half on firm ground, hard by a little ridge of hills, where there is now an inn.

Early in the morning, when we were on the point of marching, a centinel came to inform us, that a great number of Mexicans, richly dreffed, were upon the road. Cortes therefore ordered us to return into our quarters, and at that inftant four of the principal courtiers of Mexico arrived, and waiting on Cortes with great refpect informed him, that Cacamatzin lord of Tezcuco, the nephew of the great Montezuma, was approaching, and requefted that he would wait to receive him. Caca-, matzin followed in the greateft pomp, carried in a magnificent litter adorned with green plumes, and enriched with jewels, fet in the branched pillars of folid gold. He was borne by eight lords, who affifted him out of the litter, and fwept the way by which he was to pafs. When he came into the prefence of Cortes he faid to him, " Malintzin, here am I and thofe lords to attend you to your refidence " in our city, by order of the great Montezuma." Cortes embraced the prince, and prefented him with three jewels of that kind called margajitas, which are figured in different colours. We then fet forward on the road to Mexico, which was crowded with multitudes of the natives, and arrived at the caufeway of Iztapalapa, which leads to that capital. When we beheld the number of populous towns on the water and firm ground, and that broad caufeway, running ftraight and level to the city, we could compare it to nothing but the enchanted fcenes we had read of in Amadis of Gaul, from the great towers and temples, and other edifices of lime and ftone which feemed to rife out of the water. To many of us it appeared doubtful whether we were afleep or awake; nor is the manner in which I exprefs myfelf to be wondered at, for it muft be confidered, that never yet did man fee, hear, or dream of any thing equal to the fpectacle which appeared to our eyes on this day.

When we approached Iztapalapa, we were received by feveral great lords of that country, relations of Montezuma, who conducted us to our lodgings there, in palaces magnificently built of ftone, and

the

the timber of which was cedar, with spacious courts, and apartments furnished with canopies of the finest cotton. After having contemplated these noble edifices we walked through the gardens, which were admirable to behold from the variety of beautiful and aromatic plants, and the numerous alleys filled with fruit trees, roses, and various flowers. Here was also a lake of the clearest water, which communicated with the grand lake of Mexico by a channel cut for the purpose, and capable of admitting the largest canoes. The whole was ornamented with works of art, painted, and admirably plaistered and whitened, and it was rendered more delightful by numbers of beautiful birds. When I beheld the scenes that were around me, I thought within myself that this was the garden of the world! This place, was at the time of which I am speaking, with one half of the houses in the water, and the other half on dry land; but all is destroyed, and that which was a lake is now a tract of fields of Indian corn, and so entirely altered that the natives themselves could hardly know it.

CHAPTER VIII.

Mexico, Nov. 8th, 1519. Description of that Court and City. Transactions and Occurrences there.

ON the next day we set out, accompanied as on the former one, and proceeded by the grand causeway, which is eight yards wide, and runs in a straight line to the city of Mexico. It was crowded with people, as were all the towers, temples, and causeways, in every part of the lake, attracted by curiosity to behold men, and animals, such as never had been before seen in these countries. We were occupied by very different thoughts; our number did not amount to four hundred and fifty, we had perfectly in our recollection the accounts we had received on our march, that we were to be put to death on our arrival in the city which we now saw before us, approachable only by causeways, whereon were several bridges, the breaking of one of which effectually cut off our retreat. And now let who can, tell me, where are men in this world to be found except ourselves, who would have hazarded such an attempt?

When we arrived at a place where a small causeway turns off, which goes to the city of Cuyoacan, we were met by a great number of the lords of the court in their richest dresses, sent as they said before the great Montezuma, to bid us welcome. After waiting there some time, the nephew of Montezuma and other noblemen went back to meet their monarch, who approached, carried in a most magnificent litter, which was supported by his principal nobility. When we came near certain towers which are almost close to the city, Montezuma who

was

was then there quitted his litter, and was borne in the arms of the princes of Tezcuco, Iztapalapa, Tacuba, and Cuyoacan, under a canopy of the richeſt materials, ornamented with green feathers, gold, and precious ſtones that hung in the manner of fringe; he was moſt richly dreſſed and adorned, and wore buſkins of pure gold ornamented with jewels. The princes who ſupported him were dreſſed in rich habits, different from thoſe in which they came to meet us, and others who preceded the monarch ſpread mantles on the ground, leſt his feet ſhould touch it. All who attended him, except the four princes, kept their eyes fixed upon the earth, not daring to look him in the face.

When Cortes was told that the great Montezuma approached, he diſmounted from his horſe, and advanced towards him with much reſpect; Montezuma bid him welcome, and Cortes replied with a compliment, and it appeared to me, that he offered to yield the right hand to Montezuma, who declined it, and put Cortes on his right. Our general then produced a collar of thoſe artificial jewels called margajitas, which are of various colours, ſet in gold, and threw it upon the neck of Montezuma; after which, he advanced to embrace him, but the lords who ſurrounded the monarch, taking him by the arm, prevented him, it appearing to them not ſufficiently reſpectful. Cortes then ſaid, that he rejoiced in having ſeen ſo great a monarch, and that he was highly honored by his coming out to meet him, as well as by the many other marks of his favor. To this Montezuma made a gracious reply, and gave orders to the princes of Tezcuco and Cuyoacan to attend us to our quarters. Attended by his nobility, he then returned to the city, all the people ſtanding cloſe to the walls, without daring to lift up their eyes, and thus we paſſed, without obſtruction from the crowd. Who could count the multitude of men, women, and children, which thronged the ſtreets, the canals, and terraces on the tops of the houſes, on that day! The whole of what I ſaw on this occaſion is ſo ſtrongly imprinted in my memory, that it appears to me as if it had happened only yeſterday: glory to our Lord Jeſus Chriſt, who gave us courage to venture upon ſuch dangers, and brought us ſafely through them!

And

And praifed be he, that he has fuffered me to live, to write this my true hiftory, although not fo fully and fatisfactorily as the fubject deferves.

Our lodgings were provided in the buildings which had been inhabited by the father of Montezuma; here the monarch had the temples of his gods, and a fecret treafure of gold and valuables, which he had derived from his father Axayaca. We were lodged here, becaufe being confidered as Teules, they thought we were in our proper place amongft their idols. Be it how it may however, here they brought us to lodge in large apartments, a raifed platform being affigned for our general, and mats for each of us, with little canopies over them, fuch as are ufed in that country. The whole of this palace was very light, airy, clean, and pleafant, the entry being through a great court. Montezuma here led Cortes by the hand to the apartment deftined for him, and taking a large collar of gold, placed it round the general's neck. Cortes declared his gratitude for thefe favors, and Montezuma faid, " Malintzin, " here you and your friends are at home; now repofe yourfelves." With thefe words he departed. We were allotted to our quarters by companies, our artillery was pofted in a convenient place, and all was arranged in fuch a manner as to be prepared for any contingency; a very fumptuous entertainment was provided for us, which we fat down to with great fatisfaction, and here ends the true and full account of our adventurous and magnanimous entry into Mexico, on the eighth day of November, in the year of our Lord 1519. Glory be to Jefus Chrift for all!

When the great Montezuma had made his repaft, and underftood that we had done the fame, attended by a great body of his nobility he came to our apartments. Cortes went out to the middle of the hall to receive him, where Montezuma took him by the hand, and feats richly ornamented being brought, they both fat down, by the defire of the king, who then began a very pertinent fpeech, wherein he obferved, that he rejoiced to have in his dominions captains fo brave as Cortes and his

his affociates; that he had before heard of one who had arrived at Champoton, and alfo of another who had come with four fhips in the preceding year; that he had been anxious to fee them, but had been difappointed: now however that we were arrived, he was happy to offer us all the favor he had in his power to beftow, for we were undoubtedly thofe who had been mentioned by his anceftors, who had predicted, that there would come certain men, from that part where the fun rifes, to govern thefe countries; and it could mean no other but us, who had fought fo valiantly fince our arrival in their country; a reprefentation of each of our battles having been fent to him. Cortes replied, that he and all of us never could repay the great favors we every day received from his hands: that we certainly were thofe of whom it had been prophecied, and that we were vaffals of a potent monarch named Don Carlos, who had many and great princes fubject to him, and had fent us, hearing of the fame and grandeur of king Montezuma, to requeft in his name, that the great Montezuma and his fubjects would embrace the holy chriftian faith, which is the faith pro-feffed by our monarch, by doing which he would preferve the fouls of him, his family, and fubjects; and that he fhould in good time be in-formed of more particulars, fuch as that we worfhipped the only true God, with many other things highly edifying to the hearers. This converfation being concluded, Montezuma prefented our general with a quantity of valuable ornaments of wrought gold; to each of the captains he made a prefent of fome gold and three loads of mantles, and to each foldier of two loads of richly wrought mantles; and all this he did in the moft free and gracious manner, or to fpeak more properly, like a great monarch as he was. Montezuma then afked Cortes if his foldiers were all brothers, and vaffals of our emperor. To which Cortes replied, that we were all brothers in love and friendfhip, perfons of confequence in our own country, and fervants of our fovereign lord the king. With mutual compliments Montezuma then departed, having given orders to his officers to provide us amply according to our demands, with corn, ftone mills, and women to make bread, together with fowls, and fruit, and plenty of grafs for the horfes.

The

The next day was fixed on by Cortes, for his visit to Montezuma. Accordingly, attended by Captains Pedro de Alvarado, Juan Velasquez de Leon, Diego de Ordas, Gonzalo de Sandoval, and five soldiers, he went to his palace, which as soon as Montezuma was informed of, he came as far as the middle of the hall to meet us, attended by his relations, no other persons being allowed to enter where he was, except on most important business. With great ceremony on each side, the king took Cortes by the hand, and leading him to the elevated part of the saloon, placed him upon his right, and with much affability, desired the rest of us to be seated. Cortes then proceeded to say, that he came to him for the service of the Lord God whom the christians adored, who was named Jesus Christ, and who suffered death for our sakes. He also explained to him, that we adored the cross as the emblem of the crucifixion for our salvation, whereby the human race was redeemed, and that our Lord on the third day rose, and is in heaven, and that it is he who created heaven, and earth, and sea, and is adored by us as our Creator; but that those things which he held to be gods, were not such, but devils, which are very bad things, of evil countenances, and worse deeds; and that he might judge how wicked they were, and how little power they had, in as much as where ever we placed crosses, they dare not shew their faces. He therefore requested, that he would attend to what he had told him, which was, that we were all brothers, the children of Adam and Eve, and that as such, our emperor lamenting the loss of souls in such numbers as those which were brought by his idols into everlasting flames, had sent us to apply a remedy thereto, by putting an end to the worship of these false gods, to human sacrifices, and all other crimes; and that he now came to notify his Majesty's intentions, but our emperor would at a future period send holy men, fully capable of explaining them.

Here Cortes stopped, and Montezuma seemed to shew an inclination to reply, but Cortes observing that this was enough for the first time, proposed to us to retire, and we were preparing to do so, when we were prevented by Montezuma who spoke to him as follows.
"Malintzin,

" Malintzin, I have already heard through my ambaſſadors of thoſe
" things which you now mention, and to which hitherto we have
" made no reply, becauſe we have from the firſt worſhipped the gods
" we now do, and conſider them as juſt and good. So no doubt are
" yours. In regard to the creation of the world, our beliefs are the
" ſame, and we alſo believe you to be the people who were to come to
" us from where the ſun riſes. To your great king I am indebted.
" There have been already perſons on our coaſts, from your country ;
" I wiſh to know if you are all the ſame people." To which Cortes
having replied that they were all ſubjects of the ſame prince, Montezuma ſaid, that from the firſt time he heard of them, it had been his
wiſh to ſee them, which his gods had now granted him ; that we
ſhould therefore conſider ourſelves as at home, and if ever we were refuſed entrance into any of his cities, it was not his fault, but that of
his ſubjects, who were terrified by the reports they heard of us, ſuch
as that we carried with us thunder and lightning, that our horſes killed
men, and that we were furious Teules, with other follies of that kind ;
adding, that he ſaw we were men, that we were valiant and wiſe,
for which he eſteemed us, and would give us proofs thereof. For this
condeſcenſion we all expreſſed our gratitude. He then addreſſed himſelf
to Cortes in a laughing manner, for he was very gay in converſation
when he was in his ſtate, ſaying, " Malintzin, the Tlaſcalans your
" new friends have I know told you that I am like a god, and that
" all about me is gold, and ſilver, and precious ſtones ; but you now
" ſee that I am mere fleſh and blood, and that my houſes are built like
" other houſes, of lime and ſtone, and timber. It is true that I am a
" great king, and inherit riches from my anceſtors ; but for theſe
" ridiculous falſehoods, you treat them with the ſame contempt, that
" I do the ſtories I was told of your commanding the elements."
To which Cortes good-humouredly replied, that the accounts of enemies
were not to be relied on, paying him at the ſame time a handſome compliment, upon his power and grandeur. During this converſation
Montezuma had made a ſign to one of his principal attendants, to order
his officers to bring him certain pieces of gold, which he had laid apart

T

to give to Cortés, together with ten loads of fine stuffs, which he divided between Cortes and his captains, and to every soldier he gave two collars of gold, each worth ten crowns, and two loads of mantles. The gold amounted in value to upwards of a thousand crowns; and he gave it with an affability, and indifference, which made him appear a truly magnificent prince. It being now past midday, Cortes took his leave, observing that it was his Majesty's hour of dinner, and that he heaped obligations upon us; to which Montezuma replied, that on the contrary we had obliged him. We then retired, impressed with respect for the great Montezuma, from his princely manners and liberality.

The great Montezuma was at this time aged about forty years, of good stature, well proportioned, and thin: his complexion was much fairer than that of the Indians; he wore his hair short, just covering his ears, with very little beard, well arranged, thin, and black. His face was rather long, with a pleasant countenance, and good eyes; gravity and good humour were blended together when he spoke. He was very delicate and clean in his person, bathing himself every evening. He had a number of mistresses, of the first families, and two princesses his lawful wives: when he visited them, it was with such secrecy, that none could know it except his own servants. He was clear of all suspicion of unnatural vices. The clothes which he wore one day, he did not put on for four days after. He had two hundred of his nobility as a guard, in apartments adjoining his own. Of these, certain persons only, could speak to him, and when they went to wait upon him they took off their rich mantles, and put on others of less ornament, but clean. They entered his apartment barefooted, their eyes fixed on the ground, and making three inclinations of the body as they approached him. In addressing the king they said, " Lord, my lord, great lord." When they had finished he dismissed them with a few words, and they retired, with their faces towards him, and their eyes fixed upon the ground. I also observed, that when great men came from a distance about business, they entered his palace barefooted, and in a plain habit; and

and also, that they did not enter the gate directly, but took a circuit in going towards it.

His cooks had upwards of thirty different ways of dressing meats, and they had earthen vessels so contrived as to keep them always hot. For the table of Montezuma himself, above three hundred dishes were dressed, and for his guards, above a thousand. Before dinner, Montezuma would sometimes go out and inspect the preparations, and his officers would point out to him which were the best, and explained of what birds and flesh they were composed; and of those he would eat. But this was more for amusement than any thing else. It is said that at times the flesh of young children was dressed for him; but the ordinary meats were, domestic fowls, pheasants, geese, partridges, quails, venison, Indian hogs, pigeons, hares, and rabbits, with many other animals and birds peculiar to the country. This is certain; that after Cortes had spoken to him relative to the dressing human flesh, it was not practised in his palace. At his meals, in the cold weather, a number of torches of the bark of a wood which makes no smoke and has an aromatic smell, were lighted, and that they should not throw too much heat, screens, ornamented with gold, and painted with figures of idols, were placed before them. Montezuma was seated on a low throne, or chair, at a table proportioned to the height of his seat. The table was covered with white cloths and napkins, and four beautiful women presented him with water for his hands, in vessels which they call Xicales, with other vessels under them like plates, to catch the water; they also presented him with towels. Then, two other women brought small cakes of bread, and when the king began to eat, a large screen of wood, gilt, was placed before him, so that people should not during that time see him. The women having retired to a little distance, four ancient lords stood by the throne, to whom Montezuma from time to time spoke or addressed questions, and as a mark of particular favor, gave to each of them a plate of that which he was eating. I was told that these old lords, who were his near relations, were also counsellors and judges. The plates which Montezuma presented to them, they

received

received with high refpect, eating what was in them without taking their eyes off the ground. He was ferved on earthenware of Cholula, red and black. While the king was at table, no one of his guards, or in the vicinity of his apartment, dared for their lives make any noife. Fruit of all the kinds that the country produced was laid before him; he eat very little, but from time to time, a liquor prepared from cocoa, and of a ftimulative, or corroborative quality, as we were told, was prefented to him in golden cups. We could not at that time fee if he drank it or not, but I obferved a number of jars, above fifty, brought in, filled with foaming chocolate, of which he took fome, which the women prefented to him. At different intervals during the time of dinner, there entered certain Indians, hump-backed, very deformed, and ugly, who played tricks of buffoonery, and others who they faid were jefters. There was alfo a company of fingers and dancers, who afforded Montezuma much entertaiment. To thefe he ordered the vafes of chocolate to be diftributed. The four female attendants then took away the cloths, and again with much refpect prefented him with water to wafh his hands, during which time Montezuma converfed with the four old noblemen formerly mentioned, after which they took their leave with many ceremonies. One thing I forgot, and no wonder, to mention in its place, and that is, that during the time Montezuma was at dinner, two very beautiful women were bufily employed making fmall cakes with eggs and other things mixed therein. Thefe were delicately white, and when made they prefented them to him on plates covered with napkins. Alfo another kind of bread was brought to him in long loaves, and plates of cakes refembling wafers. After he had dined, they prefented to him three little canes highly ornamented, containing liquid amber, mixed with an herb they call tobacco; and when he had fufficiently viewed and heard the fingers, dancers, and buffoons, he took a little of the fmoke of one of thefe canes, and then laid himfelf down to fleep; and thus his principal meal concluded. After this was over, all his guards and domeftics fat down to dinner, and as near as I could judge, above a thoufand plates of thofe eatables that I have mentioned were laid before them, with veffels of foaming

chocolate

chocolate, and fruit in an immenfe quantity. For his women and various inferior fervants, his eftablifhment was of a prodigious expence; and we were aftonifhed, amidft fuch a profufion, at the vaft regularity that prevailed. His major domo was at this time a prince named Tapiea; he kept the accounts of Montezuma's rents, in books which occupied an entire houfe. Montezuma had two buildings filled with every kind of arms, richly ornamented with gold and jewels, fuch as fhields large and fmall, clubs like two-handed fwords, and lances much larger than ours, with blades fix feet in length, fo ftrong that if they fix in a fhield they do not break, and fharp enough to ufe as razors. There was alfo an immenfe quantity of bows and arrows, and darts, together with flings, and fhields which roll up into a fmall compafs, and in action are let fall and thereby cover the whole body. He had alfo much defenfive armour of quilted cotton ornamented with feathers in different devices, and cafques for the head, made of wood and bone, with plumes of feathers, and many other articles too tedious to mention.

In this palace was a moft magnificent aviary, which contained every defcription of birds that continent afforded, namely, royal eagles, and a fmaller fpecies, with many other birds, down to the fmalleft parroquets, of beautiful colours. It was here that the ornaments of green feathers were fabricated. The feathers were taken from birds which are of the fize of our pyes in Spain, and which they call here Quetzales, and other birds, whofe plumage is of five different colours, green, red, white, yellow, and blue. The name of this fpecies of bird I do not know. Here was alfo an immenfity of parrots, and certain geefe of fine plumage, and a fpecies which refembled geefe. All thefe bred here, and were ftripped of their feathers every year at the proper feafon. Here was a large pond of clear running water, where were a number of great birds, entirely red, with very long legs; there are fome like them in the Ifland of Cuba, which they call Ipiris. There was alfo a fpecies which lives entirely in the water.

We

We likewise saw another great building, which was a temple, and which contained those which were called the valiant or fighting gods, and here were many kinds of furious beasts, tygers, and lions of two species, one of which resembles a wolf, called here Adive. Also foxes, and other smaller animals, but all carnivorous. Most of these were bred in the place, being fed with game, fowls, dogs, and as I have heard the bodies of Indians who were sacrificed, the manner of which as I have been informed is this. They open the body of the victim while living, with large knives of stone; they take out his heart, and blood, which they offer to their gods, and then they cut off the limbs, and the head, upon which they feast, giving the body to be devoured by the wild beasts, and the skulls they hang up in their temples. In this accursed place were many vipers, and poisonous serpents which have in their tails somewhat that sounds like castanets; these are the most dangerous of all, and were kept in vessels filled with feathers, where they reared their young, and were fed with the flesh of human beings, and dogs; and I have been assured, that after our expulsion from Mexico, all these animals lived for many days upon the bodies of our comrades who were killed on that occasion. These beasts and horrid reptiles were retained to keep company with their infernal gods, and when these animals yelled and hissed, the palace seemed like hell itself.

The place where the artists principally resided was named Escapuzalco, and was at the distance of about a league from the city. Here were the shops and manufactories of all their gold and silver smiths, whose works in these metals, and in jewellery, when they were brought to Spain, surprised our ablest artists. Their painters we may also judge of by what we now see, for there are three Indians in Mexico, who are named, Marcos de Aquino, Juan de la Cruz, and Crespillo, who, if they had lived with Apelles in ancient times, or were compared with Michael Angelo or Berruguete in modern times, would not be held inferior to them. Their fine manufactures of cotton and feathers, were principally brought from the province of Costitlan. The women of
the

the family of the great Montezuma alſo, of all ranks, were extremely ingenious in theſe works, and conſtantly employed; as was a certain deſcription of females who lived together in the manner of nuns.

One part of the city was entirely occupied by Montezuma's dancers, of different kinds, ſome of whom bore a ſtick on their feet, others flew in the air, and ſome danced like thoſe in Italy called by us Matachines. He had alſo a number of carpenters and handicraft men conſtantly in his employ. His gardens, which were of great extent, were irrigated by canals of running water, and ſhaded with every variety of trees. In them were baths of cut ſtone, pavilions for feaſting or retirement, and theatres for ſhows, and for the dancers and ſingers; all which were kept in the moſt exact order, by a number of labourers conſtantly employed.

When we had been four days in Mexico, Cortes wiſhed to take a view of the city, and in conſequence ſent to requeſt the permiſſion of his Majeſty. Accordingly, Aguilar, Donna Marina, and a little page of our general's called Orteguilla, who already underſtood ſomething of the language, went to the palace for that purpoſe. Montezuma was pleaſed immediately to accede, but being apprehenſive that we might offer ſome inſult to his temple, he determined to go thither in perſon, which he accordingly did, in the ſame form, and with the ſame retinue, as when he firſt came out to meet us, but that he was on this occaſion preceded by two lords bearing ſceptres in their hands, which they carried on high, as a ſignal of the king's approach. Montezuma, in his litter, with a ſmall rod in his hand, one half of which was gold, and the other half wood, and which he bore elevated like a rod of juſtice, for ſuch it was, approached the temple, and there quitted his litter and mounted the ſteps, attended by a number of prieſts, and offering incenſe, with many ceremonies, to his war gods. Cortes at the head of his cavalry, and the principal part of our ſoldiers under arms, marched to the grand ſquare, attended by many noblemen of the court. When we arrived there, we were aſtoniſhed at the crowds of people, and the
regularity

regularity which prevailed, as well as at the vaſt quantities of merchandiſe, which thoſe who attended us were aſſiduous in pointing out.
Each kind had its particular place, which was diſtinguiſhed by a ſign.
The articles conſiſted of gold, ſilver, jewels, feathers, mantles, chocolate, ſkins dreſſed and undreſſed, ſandals, and other manufactures of
the roots and fibres of nequen, and great numbers of male and female
ſlaves, ſome of whom were faſtened by the neck, in collars, to long
poles. The meat market was ſtocked with fowls, game, and dogs.
Vegetables, fruits, articles of food ready dreſſed, ſalt, bread, honey,
and ſweet paſtry made in various ways, were alſo ſold here. Other
places in the ſquare were appointed to the ſale of earthenware, wooden
houſehold furniture ſuch as tables and benches, firewood, paper, ſweet
canes filled with tobacco mixed with liquid amber, copper axes and
working tools, and wooden veſſels highly painted. Numbers of women ſold fiſh, and little loaves made of a certain mud which they find
in the lake, and which reſembles cheeſe. The makers of ſtone blades
were buſily employed ſhaping them out of the rough material, and
the merchants who dealt in gold, had the metal in grains as it came
from the mines, in tranſparent tubes, ſo that they could be reckoned,
and the gold was valued at ſo many mantles, or ſo many xiquipils of
cocoa, according to the ſize of the quills. The entire ſquare was in-
cloſed in piazzas, under which great quantities of grain were ſtored,
and where were alſo ſhops for various kinds of goods. I muſt apologize for adding, that boat loads of human ordure were on the borders
of the adjoining canals, for the purpoſe of tanning leather, which they
ſaid could not be done without it. Some may laugh at this, but I
aſſert the fact is as I have ſtated it, and moreover, upon all the public
roads, places for paſſengers to reſort to, were built of canes, and
thatched with ſtraw or graſs, in order to collect this material.

The courts of juſtice, where three judges ſat, occupied a part of
the ſquare, their under officers being in the market, inſpecting the
merchandiſe.

From

From the square we proceeded to the great temple, but before we entered it we made a circuit through a number of large courts, the smallest of which appeared to me to contain more ground than the great square in Salamanca, with double inclosures built of lime and stone, and the courts paved with large white cut stone, very clean; or where not paved, they were plaistered and polished. When we approached the gate of the great temple, to which the ascent was by a hundred and fourteen steps, and before we had mounted one of them, Montezuma sent down to us six priests, and two of his noblemen, to carry Cortes up, as they had done their sovereign, which he politely declined. When we had ascended to the summit of the temple, we observed on the platform as we passed, the large stones whereon were placed the victims who were to be sacrificed. Here was a great figure which resembled a dragon, and much blood fresh spilt. Montezuma came out from an adoratory in which his accursed idols were placed, attended by two priests, and addressing himself to Cortes, expressed his apprehension that he was fatigued; to which Cortes replied, that fatigue was unknown to us.

Montezuma then took him by the hand, and pointed out to him the different parts of the city, and its vicinity, all of which were commanded from that place. Here we had a clear prospect of the three causeways by which Mexico communicated with the land, and of the aqueduct of Chapultepeque, which supplied the city with the finest water. We were struck with the numbers of canoes, passing to and from the main land, loaded with provisions and merchandise, and we could now perceive, that in this great city, and all the others of that neighbourhood which were built in the water, the houses stood separate from each other, communicating only by small drawbridges, and by boats, and that they were built with terraced tops. We observed also the temples and adoratories of the adjacent cities, built in the form of towers and fortresses, and others on the causeway, all whitewashed, and wonderfully brilliant. The noise and bustle of the market-place below us could be heard almost a league off; and those who had been

U

at

at Rome and at Conftantinople faid, that for convenience, regularity, and population, they had never feen the like. Cortes now propofed to Fra. Bartholome to apply to Montezuma for permiffion to conftruct our church here, to which the father for the prefent objected, thinking it ill-timed. Cortes then addreffing himfelf to Montezuma, requefted that he would do him the favour to fhew us his gods. Montezuma having firft confulted his priefts, led us into a tower where was a kind of faloon. Here were two altars highly adorned, with richly wrought timbers on the roof, and over the altars, gigantic figures refembling very fat men. The one on the right was Huitzilopochtli their war god, with a great face and terrible eyes; this figure was entirely covered with gold and jewels, and his body bound with golden ferpents; in his right hand he held a bow, and in his left a bundle of arrows. The little idol which ftood by him reprefented his page, and bore a lance and target richly ornamented with gold and jewels. The great idol had round his neck the figures of human heads and hearts, made of pure gold and filver, ornamented with precious ftones of a blue colour. Before the idol was a pan of incenfe, with three hearts of human victims which were then burning, mixed with copal. The whole of that apartment, both walls and floor, was ftained with human blood in fuch quantity as to give a very offenfive fmell. On the left was the other great figure, with a countenance like a bear, and great fhining eyes, of the polifhed fubftance whereof their mirrors are made. The body of this idol was alfo covered with jewels. Thefe two deities, it was faid, were brothers; the name of this laft was Tezcatepuca, and he was the god of the infernal regions. He prefided, according to their notions, over the fouls of men. His body was covered with figures reprefenting little devils with tails of ferpents, and the walls and pavement of this temple were fo befmeared with blood that they ftunk worfe than all the flaughter-houfes of Caftille. An offering lay before him of five human hearts. In the fummit of the temple, and in a recefs the timber of which was moft highly ornamented, we faw a figure half human and the other half refembling an alligator, inlaid with jewels, and partly covered with a mantle. This idol was faid to contain the
germ

germ, and origin of all created things, and was the god of harveſt, and fruits. The walls and altars were beſtained like the reſt, and ſo offenſive, that we thought we never could get out ſoon enough.

In this place they had a drum of moſt enormous ſize, the head of which was made of the ſkins of large ſerpents: this inſtrument when ſtruck reſounded with a noiſe that could be heard to the diſtance of two leagues, and ſo doleful that it deſerved to be named the muſic of the infernal regions; and with their horrible ſounding horns and trumpets, their great knives for ſacrifice, their human victims, and their blood beſprinkled altars, I devoted them, and all their wickedneſs to God's vengeance, and thought that the time would never arrive, that I ſhould eſcape from this ſcene of human butchery, horrible ſmells, and more deteſtable ſights.

Cortes, half in jeſt, addreſſing himſelf to Montezuma, expreſſed his wonder how ſo wife a prince could worſhip ſuch abſurd and wicked powers; and propoſed to him to place on the ſummit of that tower a croſs, and in theſe adoratories the image of the holy Virgin, and he aſſured him that he ſhould then be ſoon convinced of the vanity and deception of his idols. Montezuma ſhewed marks of diſpleaſure at theſe expreſſions, ſaying, that he would not have admitted us into the temple, had he thought that we would have inſulted their gods, who were kind to them, who gave them health and ſeaſonable rains, good harveſts, fine weather, victories and whatever elſe they deſired, and whom they were in duty, and in gratitude, bound to worſhip. Cortes dropped the diſcourſe, obſerving that it was time for us to go; and Montezuma aſſenting, ſaid, it was neceſſary for him to remain, to expiate by ſacrifice the ſin which he had committed, in admitting us there. Cortes then took leave, and thus we concluded our viſit to the great temple of Mexico, deſcending the ſteps with much pain to our invalids.

I will now proceed to relate other matters, in which, if I am not ſo correct as I ought to be, let it be remembered that my ſituation was

that

that of a foldier, who was obliged to be more attentive to the orders of his officer, than to the objects of curiofity around him. The ground whereon this temple ftood, was as much as fix of the largeft buildings of this country occupy. From the bafe it diminifhed to the fummit, whereon was a tower, in which the idols were placed, and from the middle of the afcent, to the top, were five concavities, like barbicans, but without parapets. However there are many paintings of temples in the poffeffion of the conquerors, one whereof I have, and thofe who have feen them will eafily form an idea of the outfide of this temple. I have heard that at the time they laid the foundations of it, the natives of all that country made offerings of their gold, filver, and jewels, of the feeds of the earth, and of prifoners, all which were buried in the foundations of the building. The inquifitive reader will naturally afk, how I came to know any thing of this, which happened upwards of a thoufand years ago. I will inform him. When we got poffeffion of this great city, and that it was to be built upon a new plan, it was determined to place the church of St. Jago on the ground where this temple ftood; and in finking the foundations, we found great quantities of gold, filver, and other valuables, and a Mexican who obtained part of the fame ground, difcovered more treafure, about which there was a law-fuit in fupport of his Majefty's right, the refult of which I am ignorant of. The account was alfo confirmed by Guatimotzin who was then alive, and who faid that the tranfaction was recorded in their ancient hiftorical paintings. The church which now ftands here is called St. Jago el Taltelulco. This temple I have before obferved, was furrounded by courts as large as the fquare of Salamanca, infide of a double inclofure of lime and ftone. At a little diftance from it ftood a tower, a true hell or habitation for demons, with a mouth refembling that of an enormous monfter, wide open, and ready as it were to devour thofe who entered. At the door ftood frightful idols; by it was a place for facrifice, and within, boilers, and pots full of water, to drefs the flefh of the victims, which was eaten by the priefts. The idols were like ferpents and devils, and before them were tables and knives for facrifice, the place being covered with the blood which was

spilt

ſpilt on thoſe occaſions. The furniture was like that of a butcher's ſtall, and I never gave this accurſed building any name except that of hell. Having paſſed this, we ſaw great piles of wood, and a reſervoir of water, ſupplied by a pipe from the great aqueduct; and croſſing a court, we came to another temple, wherein were the tombs of the Mexican nobility; it was begrimed with ſoot and blood. Next to this was another, full of ſkeletons, and piles of bones, each kept apart, but regularly arranged. In each temple were idols, and each had alſo its particular prieſts, who wore long veſtments of black, ſomewhat between the dreſs of the dominicans and our canons; their long hair was clotted together, and their ears lacerated in honor of their gods.

At a certain diſtance from the buildings of which I have laſt ſpoken were others, the idols of which were, as they ſaid, the advocates, or ſuperintendent deities of human marriages, and all round the great court were many houſes, which were not very lofty, and wherein reſided the prieſts, and others who had charge of the idols. Here was alſo a great reſervoir of water, ſupplied with pipes, excluſively for the ſervice of the two idols Huitzilopochtli and Tezcatepuca, and hard by, a large building, where were a number of the young Mexican women, who reſided there as in a nunnery, until they were married. They worſhipped two female deities, who preſided over marriages, and to them they offered ſacrifices, in order to obtain good huſbands. I have been thus diffuſe in my deſcription of this great temple, becauſe it was the moſt conſiderable in that city, amongſt the many ſumptuous buildings of that kind which it contained. The temple of Cholula however was higher than this, having a hundred and twenty ſteps; it was alſo held in great veneration, and was built on a plan different from that of Mexico. The temple at Tezcuco was very large, having a hundred and ſeventeen ſteps. All theſe were of different ſtructure, but agreed in having a number of outer courts, and a double incloſure. One ridiculous circumſtance is, that each province had its own peculiar gods, who were ſuppoſed to have no concern with any other; ſo that the idols were innumerable in this country. Having fatigued ourſelves

with

with the examination of thefe fcenes, fo new to us, we retired to our quarters.

Cortes perceiving how adverfe the king was to the converfion of his temple into a chriftian church, applied to one of the principal officers of his palace, for materials to conftruct a chapel and altar, within our quarters. His defire being made known to Montezuma, it was inftantly complied with, and timber and workmen being provided, in three days we had it completed. Here we faid mafs every day; we had however to lament the total want of wine for the holy facrament, it having been all ufed in the illnefs of Cortes, the reverend father, and others, during the wars in Tlafcala. However we were conftant in our devotions, as well on account of our duty, as in order to imprefs a proper idea of our holy religion, on the minds of Montezuma and the natives. Being employed in looking out for a proper place to fix the holy crofs, one of our carpenters obferved an appearance on the wall, as if a door had been there, and lately clofed up. When this was made known to Cortes, it was privately opened, and on entering the apartment, they found riches without end! The fecret foon tranfpired, and we went, all of us, to view them. I was then a young man, and I thought that if all the treafures of the earth had been brought into one place, they could not have amounted to fo much. It was agreed to clofe up the door again, and we determined to conceal the knowledge of it until the proper time fhould offer.

A council was now called, compofed of Cortes as prefident, with four captains, and twelve foldiers whereof I was one, and having duly confidered how evidently the Lord guided us, and what wife and valiant captains and brave foldiers we had, as alfo the fickle difpofition of the Indians, who though now kind to us, might change, there was no faying how foon, and that notwithftanding the hofpitality with which Montezuma treated us, he might at any moment fall into an oppofite line of conduct, we refolved to follow the opinion of Cortes, by adopting the moft effectual meafure, which was, to feize, and make that

monarch

monarch our prisoner; as we could not know at what moment we might be perhaps poisoned in our food, and as no gift of his, nor all his father's treasure, could make compensation to us for the alarms, and distressing thoughts, which filled the minds of those of any reflection. For these reasons it was therefore agreed to adopt the measure without delay. The captains who were present proposed, that Montezuma should be induced by a plausible pretext to come into our quarters, and when there, to seize him, and if he resisted, to make his person answer it: and they urged, that of the two great dangers, this was much the least. It was then observed by some of our soldiers, that Montezuma's officers did not provide us so plentifully as at the first, and two of our Tlascalan allies had told our interpreter, Aguilar, in confidence, that they observed a bad disposition on the part of the Mexicans towards us, for the two last days. This debate lasted a full hour; at length it was agreed to adjourn until the next day, and in the mean time we consulted our reverend father of the order of mercy, praying to God to guide us in this difficulty. On the day after this debate, arrived two Indians of Tlascala very secretly, with letters from Villa Rica, whereby we were informed, that Juan de Escalante had fallen, together with six soldiers, in a battle with the Mexicans,* and that the inhabitants of the mountains and of Cempoal were in commotion, and refused to supply provisions, or to work, so that the garrison knew not what to do. These letters added, that the opinion of the Indians were much altered since they found that the Spaniards could be killed like other men. God knows this intelligence afflicted us; it was the first defeat that we had experienced since we landed on that continent; and here let the reflecting reader ponder upon the changes which fate makes in the affairs of men. We who yesterday were honored by Montezuma, in possession of wealth, and considered invulnerable like demigods, to day found ourselves lowered in the consideration of the natives to a level with them in whose power we were. We now
therefore

---

* Cortes received the intelligence of this event in Cholula.

therefore faw in a ftronger point of view than ever, how neceffary it was for our very exiftence to feize Montezuma, and that if we failed, we might as well perifh in the attempt as meet our certain fate in any other way. But before I go farther I will give an account of the misfortune which befel Juan de Efcalante.

I have already related, that in a town named Quiabuiftlan, about thirty chiefs of the neighbouring diftricts had voluntarily come under our government. A Mexican garrifon, it appears, attempted to levy contributions upon fome of thefe people. When this was reprefented to Efcalante the commandant in Villa Rica, he fent word to the officers of Montezuma to defift, threatening them in cafe they did not, but at the fame time expreffing his wifhes to be on friendly terms with them. To this an abrupt reply was returned, that he fhould find them in the field. Efcalante was a man who had blood in his eye, and on receiving this anfwer he immediately prepared forty of his own people, and two thoufand of his allies, and put himfelf in march againft the Mexicans, whom he met out upon a pillaging expedition, and attacked. Our allies who were always afraid of the Mexicans, fled at the firft fhower of arrows, and left the poor Spaniards to get out of the bufinefs as well as they could. With great difficulty they arrived at Almeria, where Efcalante and fix foldiers foon died of their wounds. One foldier they took alive; his name was Arguello, a native of Leon; this man had a large head, and thick curled beard, and was of great bodily ftrength. Such is the truth of the affair at Almeria, which is entirely different from the account of the hiftorian Gomara, where he fays that Pedro de Ircio went to colonize Panuco with a party of foldiers, at a time when we had not a fufficiency of men to keep up our guards. In many things which that hiftorian relates concerning the feizure of Montezuma, he ought to have recollected that eye witneffes to that tranfaction were yet alive, to contradict him.

The Mexican captains reported the affair to Montezuma, and prefented him with the head of the Spanifh foldier, who died of his
wounds,

wounds, as they were bringing him prifoner.. It is faid that Montezuma trembled when he beheld it, and ordered it to be fent elfewhere. He afked his captains why, being fo numerous, they had not conquered fuch a handful of men ; they replied, that the reafon was, becaufe they beheld a fupernatural being, who encouraged the Spaniards, and ftruck terror into their people ; and this Montezuma believed could be no other than the holy Virgin Mary, with her fon in her arms, as we had explained to him that fhe was our patronefs. This I cannot teftify to, not having been there myfelf, but fome of thofe who were there affured me of the truth of it, and it was the univerfal belief amongft us. Would to God that it were fo! Certain however it is, that the divine mercy was with us throughout, for which praifed be God !

It having been decided that we fhould feize the perfon of the king; we paffed the whole of the preceding night in praying to our Lord, that he would be pleafed to guide us fo that what we were about to do fhould redound to his holy fervice, and in the morning * we proceeded to arrange the manner in which our determination was to be carried into effect. Our cavalry and infantry were as ufual in readinefs to turn out if called upon, and as it was always our cuftom to go fully armed, the appearance in that manner gave no fufpicion. Cortes having left our whole force in readinefs, proceeded to the palace, attended by the captains, P. de Alvarado, Gonzalo de Sandoval, J. V. de Leon, Fra. de Lugo, and A. de Avila, with the interpreters Donna Marina and Aguilar ; fending before him to acquaint the king, that he was on his way to pay him a vifit. This he did in order to prevent any effect arifing from an unexpected appearance. The king concluded that it was on account of the affair of Almeria, and that Cortes was enraged about that which in reality he did not care the value of a chefnut for, and fent back word to Cortes that he was welcome. Accordingly, our

X   general,

---

* Eight days after the arrival of the Spaniards in Mexico.

general, and we who attended him, having entered into the presence of Montezuma, after paying him his respects, he addressed the king through his interpreters, saying, he was astonished that a monarch who was so brave, and who had shewn himself so friendly to us, should have given orders to his troops in Tuzapan to attack the Spaniards, kill one of them, and his horse, and pillage and destroy our allies. Cortes wished to conceal the death of Escalante and the six others. He then charged the king with the treacherous attempt against us in Cholula, which he said he had hitherto been deterred from speaking of, by motives of esteem and regard; but that now, in addition to these provocations, his officers were plotting our immediate destruction, and he concluded by saying, that, in order to prevent the ruin of the city, it was necessary that his Majesty should, peaceably, and without making any opposition or remonstrance, immediately go with us to our quarters, where he should be treated with the greatest respect; but that if he said one word, or gave the least alarm, the five captains then present would instantly put him to death. On hearing this Montezuma was at first so terrified that he appeared to have lost all sensation. Having recovered himself a little, he denied his having ever given any order to his troops to attack our countrymen, and taking from his wrist the signet of Huitzilopochtli with which he was used to confirm any order of great importance, he caused the officer of whom complaint had been made, to be sent for. He then replied to the proposal of leaving his palace, and summoning up his dignity said, that he was not the person to be forced to take such a step, contrary to his inclination. The conversation was prolonged, Cortes giving him good reasons for what he proposed, and the king replying to him with better, insomuch that above half an hour had now elapsed. The captains who were standing by began at last to grow very impatient, and J. V. de Leon cried out to Cortes in his rough voice, " Why Sir do you waste so many words? " Let him yield himself our prisoner, or we will this instant plunge " our swords into his body. Tell him this, and also, that if he says a " word, he dies for it. Better for us to assure our lives now, or perish at " once." The manner in which this was spoken struck the king, and he

asked

afked Donna Marina the meaning of it. She with her ufual readinefs anfwered by requefting that he would immediately confent to what was propofed to him, and go where he fhould meet all refpect and honor, as fhe perceived that if he hefitated, they were refolved to put him to inftant death. He then addreffed Cortes and faid, " I have a legitimate " fon, and two legitimate daughters; take them as hoftages for me, " but do not expofe me as a prifoner to my own people." Cortes however replied faying nothing but what was originally propofed could do, and that remonftrances were unavailing. At length he was forced to confent, upon which our captains addreffed him with every declaration of efteem and refpect, earneftly defiring that he would not be offended at what had paffed, and that he would tell his officers and guards that he went by his own free will, and by the advice of his gods and priefts. His magnificent ftate litters were now brought, and attended by his ufual guards he proceeded to our quarters, where our pofts and centinels being duly placed, he was received and entertained with every mark of refpect. He was foon waited on by the princes of his family and the chief nobility of Mexico, who came to know the caufe of the ftep that he had taken, and alfo if it was his wifh that they fhould attack us; but he replied, that it was his intention to ftay with us for a few days, and that whatever further commands he had for them, he would fignify in due time; but charged them to do nothing to difturb the city.

Thus was the feizure of the great Montezuma effected. He was attended while with us in the fame manner as in his own palace, his wives, family, and officers, were with him, and he bathed every day: he appeared calm and refigned, and had always in his prefence twenty counfellors or chiefs. Ambaffadors came to him on affairs of importance from diftant countries, either to deliver tribute, or with bufinefs which he difpatched. I recollect that however great the prince or chief might be, before he entered the king's prefence he took of his rich drefs, and put on a plain one of the coarfe manufacture of nequen, and in this habit, and barefooted, approached the royal apartments,

which

which he entered, not directly, but making a circuit by the wall : and having come, with his eyes cast down upon the ground, into the presence of the king, he made three profound bows, and addressed him, calling him, " Lord, my lord, great lord." He then displayed before him a cloth, whereon was painted and represented the business on which he came, the particulars of which he pointed out to him with little rods, or wands, delicately wrought and polished. During this time two old lords stood by the king, and as soon as they had attentively considered all the particulars, they gave their opinions upon it to Montezuma, who dispatched the affair with a few words. The person who had brought it, then, without making any reply, withdrew from the king's presence, making three profound bows, and keeping his face towards the throne till out of sight; and as soon as he was out of the royal apartments, he put on his rich dress, and walked about the city.

The messengers, who, as it has been mentioned, were dispatched with the royal signet, to arrest and bring to Mexico the officers of whom our general had complained, soon returned with them. On their arrival and being brought into their monarch's presence, I do not know what passed, but he immediately sent them to Cortes to do with them as he thought fit. Being examined when the king was not by, they avowed all that had happened, and said they did it by the orders of Montezuma, which were, that they should if necessary recur to force, to obtain the tribute due, and attack the Spaniards if they appeared in support of his refractory subjects. Montezuma being charged by Cortes with this which now appeared, he endeavoured to exculpate himself as well as he could; but Cortes told him, that although his participation in the guilt of his officers was evident, and although the orders of our monarch were to punish with death all who inflicted death, yet such was his regard for him, that he would sooner lose his own life than do his Majesty an injury. All these assurances however could not remove the fears of Montezuma.

As to the officers, Cortes sentenced them to be burnt alive in front of of the palace of their king; this was immediately proceeded upon, and during the time of its taking place, and in order to prevent any impediment occurring, he also ordered that Montezuma should be put in irons. When this was doing, the unfortunate king could no longer suppress his emotions at the indignity, but wept aloud. In this situation he remained until the execution was over, at which time Cortes, attended by his five captains, went to his apartment, and with his own hands freed him from the irons, assuring him that he was dearer to him than even a brother, and that he trusted soon to be able to make his dominions exceed double their present extent; and also, that if he wished to go to his palace, he was at perfect liberty to do so. Montezuma's spirit was now broke, and the tears ran down his cheeks while Cortes was speaking; he declined the offer with thanks, knowing well the emptiness of his words, and added, that he considered it most prudent to remain where he was, in order to prevent disturbance and insurrection in the city. What we understood and certainly was the case, was, that Cortes had caused the interpreters to say that though he was inclined to release him, the other officers never would allow it. As soon as Montezuma had given his answer, Cortes threw his arms round his neck, and protested that he loved him as himself. The king then asked of him his page Orteguilla, a youth who had already learned the language, and Cortes immediately complied with his request, whereby Orteguilla afterwards remained about the person of the king, a circumstance very useful both to him and to us. Montezuma was very partial to the youth, from whom he was constantly used to enquire particulars relative to Europe, and Orteguilla from his knowledge of the language, was able to communicate to us whatever he observed, that was of importance for us to know. Thus Montezuma remained amongst us, treated with the greatest respect, no officer or soldier, nor even Cortes himself, coming into his presence, or passing him, without pulling off his helmet, and he always treated us most kindly and courteously.

The officers of Montezuma who were publicly executed as I have related,

related, were four in number.† Their names were Quetzalpopoca who was the principal, Coatl, Quiabuitle, and another whom I have forgotten, nor is it of much importance. As foon as this chaftifement was known through the different provinces of New Spain, it ftruck univerfal terror, and the people on the coaft returned to their fubmiffion. Now let the curious confider upon our heroic actions; firft, in deftroying our fhips and therewith all hope of retreat, fecondly, in entering the city of Mexico after the alarming warnings that we had received, thirdly, in daring to make prifoner the great Montezuma king of all that country, in his own capital, and in the centre of his own palace, furrounded by his numerous guards, and fourthly, in publicly burning his officers in front of his palace, and putting the king in irons during the execution. Now that I am old, I frequently revolve, and reflect upon the events of that day, which appear to me as frefh as if they had juft paffed, fuch is the impreffion they have made upon my mind. I fay, that it was not we who did thefe things, but that all was guided by the hand of God, for what men on earth would otherwife have ventured, their numbers not amounting to four hundred and fifty, to have feized and put in irons a mighty monarch, and publicly burned his officers for obeying his orders, in a city larger than Venice, and at a diftance of a thoufand and five hundred leagues from their native country!!! There is much matter for reflection in this, and it merits to be detailed otherwife than in the dry manner in which I relate it.

Cortes now thought it neceffary to appoint a commandant at Villa Rica. For this purpofe he chofe Alonzo de Grado, an indifferent foldier, but a perfon of good underftanding, who fpoke well, and was of a handfome appearance; he was alfo a mufician, and an excellent penman. He was always in oppofition to Cortes relative to our advance to Mexico, and was the principal orator on thofe occafions. Cortes
when

---

† They were feventeen in all: Quetzalpopoca lord of Nauhtlan, his fon, and fifteen other noblemen.

when he gave him the appointment good-humouredly said to him,
" Now Senior de Grado, go and possess your wishes; you are com-
" mandant of Villa Rica, and see that you fortify it well; and mind I
" charge you on no account to go out and fight the wicked Indians,
" nor let them kill you as they did Juan de Escalante." This Cortes
said ironically, knowing the condition of the man, and that all the
world could not have got him to put his nose out of the town. We
who were listening to this, and perceived his drift, could hardly for-
bear laughing aloud. He then gave him his instructions to behave
kindly to his Indian neighbours, and not permit them to be robbed or
oppressed: he also desired him to cause the smiths who were in that
settlement to make two large chains, out of the old iron of the ships,
and send them to him immediately, and to lose no time in proceeding
with the construction of the wooden fort. When De Grado arrived
at his government, he affected to carry on business with a lofty demeanour, and sent to the neighbouring Indians who were at peace with
us, requiring them to give him gold, and female slaves; paying no attention whatever to the fortifications, but passing his time in feasting
and play. What was worse, he combined with the adherents of Velasquez, offering to put him in possession of the post he was entrusted
with. These things being soon communicated to Cortes, he repented
of his imprudent step in appointing to such a place a man whose bad
disposition he well knew: he also foresaw that Velasquez must sooner
or later find out that he had sent agents to Old Castille, and would probably send a force against us. For these reasons it was necessary that
he should have a person of confidence in the command at Villa Rica;
he therefore sent Sandoval, who was now alguazil mayor, with whom
went Pedro de Ircio already mentioned, who gained the confidence of
Sandoval, a goodnatured man, by diverting him with anecdotes of the
families of the Count de Urena, and Don Pedro Giron, in which he
had served. De Ircio by these means gained his favor so completely,
that he never ceased promoting him, till he had got him the rank of
captain: instead of which promotion, for the licenses he gave his
tongue, and for which Sandoval at times reprehended him, he deserved

to

to have been well punifhed. Sandoval on his arrival at Villa Rica immediately arrefted De Grado and fent him prifoner to Mexico, under a guard of Indians, according to the orders of Cortes. The new governor foon made himfelf very popular amongft the natives by his affability and humanity, and he immediately began to put the fort into proper repair. Cortes would not fee De Grado on his arrival, but confined him in the ftocks, where he remained two days. I recollect that the timber whereof thefe were made has a ftrong fmell of garlic. De Grado, who was a man of great plaufibility at laft made his peace, and was employed, not in a military capacity, but in one conformable to his talents, being given the office of contador, which had been held by Avila, who was fent as procurador to the Ifland of St. Domingo. Sandoval had orders to fend the iron-work neceffary for the conftruction of two veffels, which he punctually executed, and the various articles arrived fafely in Mexico.

Cortes, regularly every day after mafs, went to wait on Montezuma, attended by all his officers, and afked him what he would be pleafed to order that they could execute; to which the king ufed to anfwer, thanking him, that he found himfelf perfectly to his fatisfaction. Thus, from one fubject to another they ufually fell into difcourfe about our holy faith, and the power of our emperor. At other times, Montezuma and Cortes ufed to play at a certain game which they call Totoloque, in which they take aim with golden balls at certain objects made alfo of gold. I remember once in particular, when Cortes and Alvarado were playing againft Montezuma and his nephew, Montezuma jocularly faid that he would not allow Tonatiu, meaning Alvarado, fo called on account of his handfome perfon, that word meaning the fun, to mark, expreffing himfelf in fuch a manner as to imply, that Alvarado did not fay that which was true; at which we all burft out laughing, becaufe Alvarado was a little addicted to exaggeration. When Cortes gained, he gave his winnings to thofe about Montezuma, and when the king gained he did the fame to our foldiers of the guard. Indeed he never let a day pafs, without making prefents of fome kind

to

to all of us, but more particularly to Velafquez de Leon who was the captain of his guard, and always paid him great attention. One night a foldier named Truxillo, was guilty of a certain piece of difrefpect within his hearing, at which Montezuma was highly offended, and enquired of the page who the perfon was. The page told him that he was a man of low birth, who knew no better. He then proceeded to tell him of our different ranks and qualities, about which he was very curious. On the next day he ordered Truxillo to be brought into his prefence, and after having reproved him, he made him a prefent worth about five crowns. The words of Montezuma made lefs impreffion on the foldier than his gold, and on the next night the fellow was guilty of the fame piece of impolitenefs, in order to get more. Of this Montezuma complained to Velafquez, who ordered the man to be relieved, and feverely reprimanded him. Another foldier one night complained that he was ill, curfing this dog of an Indian, meaning Montezuma, who gave them fo much trouble. This being overheard by the king, who difcovered what he had faid, he complained thereof to Cortes, by whofe command the man was immediately whipped, notwithftanding he was a very good foldier; his name was Pedro Lopez. After this example ftrict difcipline and filence were kept by the guard, to the great fatisfaction of the king, who was very kind to us, knew us all, and fpoke to us by our names. I was at this time a ftripling, and always behaved to him with great refpect; his page had told him that I had been twice upon his coafts before the arrival of Cortes, and I had defired the page to mention to him, that inftead of gold or mantles, he would oblige by giving me a handfome Indian girl. This requeft he gracioufly complied with, calling me to him and faying, " Bernal " Diaz del Caftillo, the young woman I prefent to you is the daughter " of one of my principal nobility; treat her well, and her friends will " give you gold and mantles, as much as you can defire." I kiffed his Majefty's hand, thanking him for his favors, and praying God to profper him; to which Montezuma replied faying, " It feems to me " that Del Caftillo is of noble condition." Wherewith he ordered me three plates of gold, and two loads of mantles.

Y

I will

I will now relate some more particulars of his course of life. In the morning, having paid his devotions, he eat a slight breakfast, not of meats but vegetables, such as agi or pepper, and then remained a full hour hearing business, in the manner I have already described. The number of judges or counsellors who attended upon him at those times amounted to twenty. His numerous mistresses he used to marry to his officers and particular friends; some of them fell to our lot; mine was called Donna Francifca; a lady of high birth, as she shewed by her manners. Thus sometimes amusing himself, and sometimes meditating on his situation, the great Montezuma passed the days of his confinement amongst us.

The materials being arrived, Cortes requested that the king would give him permission to construct two vessels, for the purpose of amusing himself upon the water, and also that he would order his carpenters to assist. The oak timber was only at the distance of about four leagues, and Montezuma having given his consent, the work went on so expeditiously, by the number of Indian carpenters, and was so ably conducted by our principal builder Martin Lopez, that in a very short space of time, they were built, launched, and rigged, with an awning over each.

Montezuma at this time requested permission from Cortes to pay his devotions, and perform sacrifices, in order that his friends and subjects might see that he lived among us by the order of his gods, and his own choice. Cortes returned for answer, that in so doing, it was his business to beware how he did any thing whereby to lose his life; for that he would send a guard of officers and soldiers with him, giving them strict orders to kill him instantly in case there appeared any thing like a commotion. With this caution he gave him his permission to visit his temple. It was also at the same time signified to him, that no human sacrifice would be permitted; to which Montezuma having agreed, he set out in his usual pomp, and accompanied by four of our captains, Velasquez de Leon, Alvarado, Avila, and De Lugo, with a
hundred

hundred and fifty foldiers. Our reverend father of the order of mercy alfo attended for the purpofe of preventing human facrifice. Montezuma on his arrival near the temple came out of his litter, and was fupported up to it as ufual, being met by a number of priefts. They had on the preceding night facrificed four Indians, nor could all our endeavours prevent that inhuman practice, which we were for the prefent obliged to connive at, fearing to do any thing which would caufe an infurrection. After Montezuma had ftaid a fhort time at his devotions he came down from the temple, and returned to our quarters in great good humour, making prefents to all of us who attended him upon the occafion.

The veffels were now afloat upon the lake, fully equipped, and manned with expert failors, and they obeyed both fail and oar, fo as to anfwer our utmoft expedition. When Montezuma was informed of it, he requefted Cortes to permit him to go hunting in a certain diftrict, which was prohibited to all others on pain of death. Cortes affented, warning him that his life paid the forfeit of any attempt at a refcue, and he offered him the ufe of his fhips to go there, which Montezuma was greatly pleafed with, and accepted.

The fwifteft failing veffel conveyed the king and his fuite, the other was occupied by his fon and a number of the nobility. They were attended alfo by a vaft number of boats, great and fmall. Cortes ordered out a party compofed of Velafquez de Leon, Alvarado, De Oli, and Avila, all men who had blood in their eyes, and two hundred foldiers, giving them orders to be very watchful over Montezuma: four brafs guns with their ammunition and artillery-men, were alfo embarked.

The wind blew very frefh, our failors took delight in exhibiting their fkill, and the fhips feemed to fly acrofs the lake, leaving the veffels of the natives far behind. Montezuma being arrived where he was to hunt, landed for that purpofe, and as the place abounded with game,

he

he had foon killed a great quantity of various kinds, fuch as deer, hares, and rabbits. After having amufed himfelf for fome time in this manner, he returned on board the veffel, and fet fail for Mexico. We dif-charged our artillery during the voyage, which afforded him amufe-ment and fatisfaction, and he delighted us all by his affable and friendly behaviour; nor is it poffible to defcribe, how noble he was in every thing he did, nor the refpect in which he was held by every one about him. One day, three of our captains were in his prefence when a hawk entered the apartments purfuing a quail, which kind of birds, as well as doves, bred in and about the palaces. As our officers and foldiers were admiring the beauty and flight of the hawk, and talking upon the fubject in general, Montezuma was curious to know what we were faying, which being explained to him, and alfo how we could tame hawks and fly them from our hands, Montezuma faid that he would order the bird to be caught for us, and giving immediate direc-tions to that purpofe, by the next morning his hunters had caught and brought to us the identical bird.

Cacamatzin the king's nephew, and prince of the city of Tezcuco, the largeft next to Mexico in the empire, having received information that the king had been now many days kept prifoner by the Spaniards, and that they had alfo opened the treafury of his anceftors, in order to fecure it by a timely effort, convoked his vaffals, and alfo the neigh-bouring princes. Amongft them was the lord of Matalcingo, a great warrior, and near relation of Montezuma, who was faid to have pre-tenfion to the throne. Thefe princes and chiefs he fummoned, in order to induce them to affemble their forces, and fall upon us in a body. When they were met in confultation upon this propofition, the prince whom I before mentioned to have had pretenfions to the throne, made the fupport of them the condition of his entering into the confederacy. Cacamatzin then brought forward a fimilar claim, declaring that he would go through the bufinefs with his own force, for which purpofe he made arrangements with his friends in the city of Mexico. This coming to the knowledge of Montezuma, he immediately forbid any
such

ſuch ſteps being taken, and communicated to Cortes the information which he had received. The tranſaction was already in a certain degree known to us, but not to the full extent. Cortes in conſequence thereof propoſed to take with him a body of Mexicans to attack and deſtroy the city of Tezcuco, but this determination not being ſatisfactory to Montezuma, Cortes ſent to Cacamatzin, deſiring him to deſiſt from his warlike preparations, as he wiſhed him for his friend. Cacamatzin replied that he was not to be duped like others by plauſible words ; that he expected ſoon to ſee us, and then we might ſay to him what we would. Cortes once again ſent to Cacamatzin warning him not to proceed to hoſtilities, the conſequence of which would be the loſs of the king's life ; to which this chief returned for anſwer, that neither the king nor Cortes were of any conſequence to him, for that he was determined to perſevere in his intentions.

He had at this time a brother in Mexico, who had been obliged to fly thither on account of a family quarrel. This being known to us, our general propoſed to Montezuma to call the reigning prince to his court, where we could ſeize on and detain him until he became more amenable, or if we thought proper elevate the brother now in Mexico to his place. Montezuma agreed to ſend for him, adding, that if he refuſed to come, he would give directions for having him brought by force. For this Cortes returned him thanks with many profeſſions of ſincere regard, aſſuring him that he ſtaid by him entirely for his protection, and that for his part he ſhould be happy to accompany him to his palace, but that he could not get his captains to conſent to it. The king thanked him, and ſaid that he would immediately ſend to inform Cacamatzin of his true ſituation, and how it was adopted of his own free will, and by the advice of his gods ; for Montezuma was perfectly well acquainted with the diſſimulation practiſed by Cortes, and that it was only done in order to found him. Montezuma according to his promiſe ſent a meſſage to the prince, who perfectly underſtood the manner in which it was obtained, and declared his determination to attack us in four days, ſaying, that his uncle the king was a pitiful

monarch,

monarch, and no better than a hen, for not having attacked us as he advifed him at the pafs of Chalco. That for his part he was determined to avenge the wrongs that had been committed by us upon Montezuma and the country, and that if in fo doing the throne of Mexico fell to his lot, he would liberally reward thofe who fupported him.

Some of the chiefs who heard thefe declarations had fcruples upon the fubject, objecting to go to war without the orders of their fovereign. This filled the prince with rage, efpecially when they propofed to fend to him for his inftructions; he caufed three of them to be taken prifoners, and the others who were prefent intimidated thereby, declared their determination to fupport him. He then fent a meffage to Montezuma, reprefenting the difgrace in which he was fallen, by connecting himfelf with wizards and magicians, and that he would come and put us all to death. Montezuma was highly offended at this, and taking off his feal, he entrufted it to the care of fix of his captains, commanding them to go and fhew it to certain perfons whom he named, as knowing they were not on terms of friendfhip with the prince, and to fignify to them his orders, that they fhould feize Cacamatzin and fend him into his prefence. Accordingly they entered where the prince was, difcourfing with fome of his chiefs, relative to his expedition, and having fecured him, together with five others, embarking them in a piragua, they brought them to Mexico, where Cacamatzin was placed in one of the royal litters, and conducted into the prefence of Montezuma. The king, after having reproached him for his difobedience and treafon, delivered him to Cortes, to do what he thought proper with him, releafing the other prifoners. Cortes thanked the great Montezuma, and made arrangements, that the brother of Cacamatzin fhould fucceed to the principality, by the name of Don Carlos, and he was accordingly invefted with this dignity in the prefence of Montezuma. The other chiefs who had joined in the meafures of Cacamatzin abfented themfelves from court through fear, but were fhortly made prifoners, and brought to Mexico in chains. Thus was concluded this important bufinefs, to our entire fatisfaction. We continued

tinued still paying our court to Montezuma, in the manner so great and generous a prince deserved, never sitting down, not even Cortes himself, in his presence, until the king commanded it. The conversation frequently turned upon our holy religion, and the truths thereof seemed to be every day making more impression upon the king's mind.

Cortes now entered again upon the subject of Montezuma's acknowledging the sovereignty of our Emperor, to which Montezuma replied, that he would summon the princes his vassals, which he accordingly did, and nearly the whole of them attended within the space of ten days. Among the few who absented themselves was that relation of Montezuma's already spoken of, as of extraordinary prowess in war, who returned for answer, that he would neither come, or pay any more tribute. The king was incensed at this, and sent officers to apprehend him, but without success. The princes being assembled and the little page present, Montezuma reminded them of the ancient prophecies, whereby they were told that from those parts where the sun rises, men were to come to rule the country, and that with their arrival should cease the empire of the Mexicans. The king added, that for his part he believed we were the people spoken of; that he had sacrificed to his gods, requesting in vain an answer from them, but they referred him to the former ones, and commanded him to ask no more, whereby he concluded their will to be that obedience should be yielded to the king of Castille, to whom these strangers were vassals. " I " now," continued he, " beseech you to give them some token of " submission; they require it of me, let no one refuse. For eighteen " years that I have reigned, I have been a kind monarch to you, you " have been faithful subjects to me; since my gods will have it so, " indulge me by this one instance of obedience." The princes, with many sighs and tears, promised Montezuma, who was still more affected than them, that they would do whatever he desired. He then sent a message to Cortes, telling him, that on the ensuing day, he and his princes would tender their allegiance to his Majesty our Emperor. This they accordingly did at the time appointed, in the presence of all

our

our officers, and many of our foldiers, not one of whom could refrain from weeping, in beholding the agitation and diftrefs of the great and generous Montezuma.

Cortes and his captains being in the prefence of Montezuma, conversing about indifferent fubjects, the general took an opportunity to afk fome queftions relative to the gold mines. Montezuma told him that the richeft were in the province of Zacatula, and he gave an account of the manner in which the gold was obtained, which was, by wafhing the earth, the fmall grains of metal finking to the bottom. He alfo informed Cortes that they obtained it in two rivers in the province of Guztepeque, where the natives did not obey him, but that if Cortes would fend fome troops thither, he would order his officers to conduct them. Cortes thanked the king, and pitched upon the pilot Umbria, and two foldiers to examine the mines of Zacatula. To thofe in the Chinantecan and Zapotecan territories he fent a captain named Pizarro, a young man, his relation; but at that time the names of Pizarro and Peru were equally unknown. The latter took with him four foldiers ufed to mining, and four noble Mexicans. Montezuma then prefented Cortes with a map, admirably painted on cloth, of the whole northern coaft as far as Tabafco, an extent of a hundred and forty leagues. Among the rivers was that of Guacacualco, which Cortes determined to have examined, and Diego de Ordas offering himfelf, was accepted by Cortes contrary to his own inclination, as he was a perfon from whofe advice and judgement he derived great advantage. Montezuma told De Ordas on his departure, that his power did not extend where he was going, but that if he wifhed for the affiftance of his frontier garrifons, he was welcome to take them.

The firft who returned was Gonzalo de Umbria. He brought with him gold to the value of three hundred crowns, and reported that the mines would be very valuable, if they were as expert at the bufinefs there, as in St. Domingo or Cuba. Two principal perfons of that country alfo attended him to Mexico, and brought a prefent of gold of

about

about a hundred crowns value, offering to become his Majesty's subjects.
The having ascertained the situation of the mines was matter of great
satisfaction to Cortes. Umbria described the country in which he had
been as very rich and populous, and indeed he and his companions
seemed to have returned no way the worse for their journey, and Cortes
intended that it should be so, in order to make up their former differences.

Diego de Ordas reported that he had passed through very populous
districts, and had been universally well received; that he had met with
bodies of the troops of Montezuma on the frontiers, of whose outrages
the inhabitants made heavy complaints, for which De Ordas severely
reprehended the military chiefs, threatening them with the punishment
of the lord of Nauhtlan. Proceeding towards the river he was hospitably received, by the caciques and inhabitants of the neighbouring
country. On sounding the mouth of the river they found three fathom
water at low-tide, in the shallowest part, and within the bar, water
sufficient for large ships, it still deepening as they went higher up. He
also found a place fit for a naval establishment, where the natives came
to him, and offered themselves as vassals to his Majesty, complaining
bitterly of Montezuma and his officers; they also pointed out to our
people the place, where, in a late action they had killed many of his
troops, and which they had in consequence named "Cuilonemequi," that
is to say the place of the slaughter of the Mexicans, giving them a most
opprobrious epithet. He further represented the soil of the country as
fit for cattle and tillage, and the port as well situated for trade with
Cuba, St. Domingo, and Jamaica, but disadvantageous in regard to its
distance from Mexico, and the Morasses in its neighbourhood. Pizarro
returned from Tustepeque with gold in grains to the value of a thousand
crowns. He related how he ascended into the mountains inhabited by
the Chinantecans, who sallied out under arms, and refused to suffer the
Mexicans to come among them, vowing that they would kill them all
if they attempted it; but our people were admitted willingly, and they
there obtained gold in its native state with a rough surface. Pizarro

Z

brought

brought with him certain of the chiefs of the country, who wished to renounce the Mexican yoke, and become subjects of his Majesty. These Cortes received most kindly, and dismissed to their homes with a promise of support and protection. He then enquired for the other soldiers; to which Pizarro replied that the country being rich, and the people well inclined to us, he had left them to make a plantation of cocoa and to collect stock and birds; as also for the purpose of exploring the rivers and mines. Cortes said nothing at the time, but severely reprimanded him in private, for going beyond his orders, and employing the soldiers in such ridiculous pursuits. He also immediately sent off a messenger, with orders to them to return to their head quarters.

Cortes now demanded of Montezuma a general contribution of gold to be made through the whole extent of his territories, to our emperor, and also that the king should deliver to us his treasure for the same purpose. Montezuma immediately sent officers to those districts where the mines were, requiring a quantity of plates of gold, of the usual size paid in tribute, two of these being sent as a standard. He at this time however remarked to Cortes, that from many of his districts gold was not to be expected in any considerable quantity, the people only possessing such toys as had been transmitted to them from their ancestors. Much gold was immediately transmitted from the rich provinces, but when the order was received by the refractory lord who was nearly related to Montezuma, the answer which he returned was, that he would pay no tribute, for that he had as good a right to the throne of Mexico as Montezuma himself. This greatly enraged the king, who immediately sending trusty officers with his token, the seal, they apprehended and brought this chief to Mexico. When he came into the presence of the king he behaved with such insolence to him as appeared to border upon madness, and Cortes learning these particulars, and also that Montezuma had ordered him to be put to death, interceded in his favor, and obtained leave to keep him in his custody. As soon as he had an interview, he addressed this chief very kindly,

and

and endeavoured to make a friend of him, offering him his liberty, which however Montezuma would not accede to, but defired he fhould be put in chains as the others had been.

In twenty days from the time of the orders being iffued, the tribute was collected. The king then fummoned Cortes, with the captains and foldiers who ufually formed his guard, and addreffed us faying, " Know, that I am indebted to your great king, and efteem him, for " having fent an embaffy to me from fuch a diftance, and alfo becaufe " I am convinced that according to what we have heard from our an- " ceftors, he is to rule us; a prophecy which is confirmed by the de- " clarations of our gods. Take this gold, which is all that could be " collected on fo fhort a notice, and alfo the treafure which I derive " from my anceftors, and which I know you have feen; fend it to " your monarch, and let it be recorded in your annals, that this was " the tribute of his vaffal Montezuma. I will give you for your " emperor fome moft valuable jewels named calchihuis, each of which " is worth two loads of gold; I will alfo fend three tubes ufed for " fhooting darts or pellets, fo richly adorned with jewels that he will " be pleafed to fee them, and this which I now give is the laft of the " treafure which has remained with me." We all took off our helmets, and returned thanks to the great Montezuma for his liberality and mu- nificence, which Cortes promifed that he would reprefent in the ftrongeft terms to his Majefty.

After fome more converfation, Montezuma commanded his officers to deliver to us the treafure which was in the concealed apartment. This was accordingly done, and we were for the fpace of three days conftantly employed in taking it to pieces, from the various manners in which it was worked up; in this we were alfo affifted by the royal goldfmiths from Efcapuzalco. When thus feparated, the articles of gold were formed in three heaps, weighing upwards of fix hundred thoufand crowns, exclufive of the various other valuables, the gold in plates and bars, and the metal in its rough ftate from the mines. The

goldfmiths

goldsmiths melted down the metal which was in the heaps, and ran it into bars of the breadth of three fingers. When this was done, another present was received from Montezuma, so rich that it was worthy of admiration, exclusive of the jewels called calchihuis, the ornamented tubes covered with jewels and pearls, the beautiful embroideries of pearls and feathers, and the penaches, and plumage, a recital whereof would be endless. The bars of gold were stamped with the imperial arms by the approbation of us all, and as to the rich ornaments, it was judged best that they should not be taken to pieces. We also caused weights to be made of iron for the purpose of ascertaining the quantity of gold in the bars. They were not perfectly exact, but perhaps an ounce more or less, being arrobas, half arrobas, and down to four ounces. The officers of his Majesty valued the gold, altogether, and exclusive of silver and ornaments, at six hundred thousand crowns; but some said that it amounted to more. Nothing farther was then thought necessary, than to deduct his Majesty's fifth, and distribute the shares to the officers and soldiers; Cortes however proposed that the division should be postponed until more treasure was brought in, and more exact weights made, but the soldiers were clamorous for an immediate division, for they perceived that since the various articles had been taken to pieces, above a third part was already gone; for Cortes, the captains, and others, were conveying it off and concealing it. At length it was determined to weigh it, and to postpone the division until the ensuing day. It was accordingly so done, and exclusive of the ornaments and plates of gold, it was found to amount to upwards of six hundred thousand crowns. I will now relate how it was divided, and how the most of it remained with Cortes and certain others.

In the partition of the treasure Cortes first laid aside his Majesty's fifth; secondly, for himself, another fifth; thirdly, a portion of the gold to reimburse the expences in the Island of Cuba, and also for the naval expenditure incurred by Velasquez, and the destruction of the ships; fourthly, for the expences of our agents in Spain; fifthly, for our soldiers in Villa Rica; sixthly, for the loss of killed horses; seventhly,

venthly, for the reverend father and the captains; eighthly, double
fhares for the cavalry, mufketeers, and crofsbow-men. Thus by the
time all thefe drafts were made, what remained for each foldier was
hardly worth ftooping for!! Many refufed to take their fhares, and the
whole, nearly, remained with Cortes. We were obliged to be filent,
for to whom could we appeal for juftice? Some at length took their
fhares at a hundred crowns, and then cried out for more; thefe men's
mouths Cortes ftopped, giving privately a little to one, and a little to
another, with promifes in abundance on condition that they kept themfelves quiet. That which was allotted to the foldiers in Villa Rica
went no better, as fhall be related in its place, and fuch was the refult
of the divifion of Montezuma's treafure.

Our captains got chains of gold made for them by the king's
workmen; Cortes had alfo fimilar works executed for him, together
with a fervice of plate. Many of our foldiers who had lined their
pockets well did the fame, and deep gaming went on, day and night,
with cards made out of the heads of drums; and thus we paffed our
time in Mexico.

Quitting for the prefent the fubject of Montezuma's gold, badly
divided, and worfe employed, I will relate what happened to a poor
fellow, one Cardenas a pilot and a native of Triana. He had a wife
and children, and like many others of us little or nothing to give them.
When he perceived that all this immenfe treafure of Montezuma's had
dwindled into a fhare of a hundred crowns, and that he, after all his
battles, had nothing to expect in future but hard blows, it made fuch
an impreffion on him, and he expreffed himfelf fo loudly, that it could
not but come to the ears of Cortes. Accordingly when he heard all
that, and much more, which had been faid, he called us together, and
in a long fet fpeech gave us a great many honied words, which he had
an extraordinary facility of doing, wondering how we could be fo folicitous about a little paltry gold, when the whole country would foon
be ours, with all its rich mines, wherewith there was enough to make
us

us great lords and princes and I know not what. To the more loud he gave some small presents, and to Cardenas, he secretly promised to send three hundred crowns for his wife and children. This Cardenas was afterwards very troublesome to him.

As all men are avaricious, as with most the desire of acquiring increases with what they possess, and as it was well known that a great quantity of valuable pieces of gold was taken out of the treasury, suspicion naturally fell on several. Juan Velasquez de Leon had then some large chains of gold, and trinkets and ornaments of that metal, in the hands of the king's workmen, and the treasurer Mexia knowing of it, 'and also how he had procured the gold, laid claim to them; but De Leon resisted, saying it had been given him by Cortes, before it was ran into bars; to which the treasurer replied, that Cortes had concealed enough, and taken enough from his soldiers already, without giving him so great a quantity. The quarrel rose so high between them, being both valiant men, that they drew their swords, and before they could be parted each had received two wounds. Cortes on hearing it ordered them to be put in arrest, and in chains; this he did to keep up appearances, having privately spoken to De Leon who was his particular friend, and desired him to submit quietly; and the other he released in consideration of his office as treasurer. Velasquez was a strong man, and used to walk much backwards and forwards in the apartment where he was confined. Montezuma hearing the rattling of his chains, enquired who it was; and being told, he interceded with Cortes for him, on the first opportunity. Cortes laughing replied that Velasquez was a mad fellow, who if he did not keep him confined, would go up and down the country robbing his majesty's subjects of their gold. The good king said, if it was only on that account he was detained, he would supply his wants, and begged that he might be released. Cortes affected to make a favor of it, but at length agreed, declaring that he would banish him from head quarters. Accordingly he went as far as Cholula, but in six days returned, richer, by the king's gold, than when he went. After this Cortes and Mexia were never great friends.

The

The king at this time made a propofal of marriage to Cortes, offering him one of the princeffes his daughters. This offer Cortes received as it merited, and fuggefted the propriety of her being previoufly
initiated into the myfteries of our holy religion, by being baptized; to
which the king who was on all occafions compliant, immediately
affented. He however continued as attached as ever to his worfhip and
facrifices, which put Cortes and his captains to a dilemma; but it was
thought moft confiftent with their duties as chriftians to incur the
danger of infurrection, and deftroy the idols of the Mexicans, in order
to plant the true crofs in their place, or if that was found impoffible,
we refolved to content ourfelves for the prefent with making a chapel
for the chriftian worfhip in the temple. Seven officers and foldiers attended Cortes, when he waited on Montezuma to fignify to him our
refolution. When it was made known to him, and he faw the violence
with which the meafure was determined to be carried into effect, he
earneftly begged permiffion to confult his priefts, and Cortes appearing
touched with his fituation, made figns to the officers and foldiers to
retire, and leave the king with him and the reverend father. He then
told him, that in order to accommodate the matter more to his fatisfaction, he would endeavour to prevail with his officers, for the prefent
to offer no violence to the idols, provided a part of the great temple was
appropriated to the purpofe of a chapel, and an altar and crucifix allowed
to be placed there; which being once done, his Majefty would in a
fhort time be convinced of the errors and falfehood of his worfhip. To
this Montezuma with much agitation, and the appearance of deep forrow, heavily confented; and in confequence, an altar and crucifix
being erected, mafs was folemnly faid, and a perfon was appointed to
take care of the chapel.

The time of our ftay in this city was one feries of alarms, fufficient in themfelves to have deftroyed the lives of thofe who were not
fupported by the divine interpofition. It appeared, that in confequence
of our late meafure, and the reprefentations of the priefts acting upon
the prejudices of the people, our dangers were now thickening on us.
Their

Their gods threatened to leave them unlefs we were put to death, for having violated their temple, and it was the determination to obey their will. This refolution was communicated to Montezuma by his priefts, and all his chief warriors, who added to their religious fubject of complaint, every other which they could collect, relative to our conduct fince we arrived in Mexico. The page Orteguilla alfo at this time came to inform Cortes of fome alarming circumftances, fuch as a number of fecret conferences which he had obferved, between Montezuma and his nobility and chiefs, the angry and melancholy countenance of the king, and other circumftances highly important and interefting to us. Cortes immediately on hearing this, taking with him five of his captains, and his interpreters, waited on Montezuma. The king feemed much diftreffed, and informed him, that he was grieved to have lately learned, that it was the determination of his gods that we fhould all be put to death, or expelled from Mexico; he, therefore, being our fincere friend, recommended to us on no account to run the rifk, but to fave our lives, whilft it could be done, by a fpeedy retreat. Cortes and the reft could not conceal their uneafinefs on hearing this, and no wonder. The general, however, immediately replied, that he was on that occafion much grieved at two things; one was, his not having veffels ready for the purpofe of returning, the other, that in cafe of his doing fo, he fhould be under the neceffity of taking his Majefty with him, in order to prefent him to his fovereign the Emperor. He therefore intreated Montezuma, that he would reftrain his priefts and warriors, until he fhould have time to build three fhips, faying if this were not acceded to, we were all refolved to die to the very laft man; and as a proof of the fincerity of his determination to depart, he declared, that he would immediately fend his fhipbuilders to fell wood and conftruct the veffels, on the coaft. The determination of Cortes to bring Montezuma with him, made that monarch more diftreffed and dejected than ever; Cortes then repeated his affurance of no unneceffary delay, and defired the affiftance of the king's carpenters in conftructing the veffels; at the fame time requefting his influence with the priefts and nobility, to prevent any infurrection in the city, and his endeavours

to

to appeafe his gods, provided it were not by human facrifices.

Cortes immediately proceeded to execute his determination of building the three ships, contrary to what is related by Gomara, who fays that the whole was a feint, in order to lull Montezuma and his fubjects. But on the contrary, Martin Lopez, the principal carpenter, who is now living, has affured me that he really, and in good earneft, did fet about the work, and that the veffels were actually on the ftocks. During this time we remained very penfive and fad, in the city of Mexico, from the precarioufnefs of our fituation, expecting every moment to be attacked. Our apprehenfions were increafed by the informations obtained by Donna Marina, and the terror and tears of the page, who, underftanding the language, obtained hints which efcaped our knowledge. We kept however good and conftant watch on Montezuma, and guard on our quarters, never fleeping out of our armour, and our horfes were conftantly bridled and faddled all night.

Without meaning to boaft I may fay of myfelf, that my armour was to me as eafy as the fofteft down, and fuch is my cuftom, that when I now go the rounds of my diftrict, I never take a bed with me unlefs I happen indeed to be attended by ftrange cavaliers, in which cafe I do it only in order to avoid the appearance of poverty, or pennrioufnefs, but by my faith, even when I have one I always throw myfelf on it in my clothes, fuch it is to be a true foldier! another peculiarity I have is, that I cannot fleep through the night, but always awaken and get up in order to contemplate the heavens and ftars, and thus I amufe myfelf, walking backwards and forwards, as I ufed to do when on guard, for a good fpace of time, without hat or cap; and glory be to God, I never yet caught cold, nor was a jot the worfe for it. And this the reader muft pardon me for mentioning, it not being from vanity, but that I wifh him to know what kind of men we, the true bred foldiers, and real conquerors of Mexico were.

CHAPTER II.

Expedition of P. de Narvaez. His army defeated by Cortes at Cempoal, May 26th. 1520.—Return of the Spaniards to Mexico. War there. Death of Montezuma. Expulsion of the Spaniards, July 1st. Battle of Obtumba. Reception of the Spaniards in Tlafcala, July 10th.

THE Bifhop of Burgos who was at this time prefident of the Indies, bore unlimited fway in that department, during the abfence of the Emperor in Flanders. He now fent out orders to Velafquez, to feize, and make us prifoners, at all events: in confequence of which the governor of Cuba fitted out a fleet of nineteen fhips, and embarked therein an army of one thoufand four hundred foldiers, and twenty pieces of cannon, with all neceffary ammunition and appointments, eighty cavalry, and one hundred and fixty mufkets and crofs-bows, the whole being under the command of Pamphilo de Narvaez. Such were his exertions, and his animofity againft Cortes and us, that he went for thefe purpofes a journey of above feventy leagues from the Havannah. While he was thus occupied, it appears, that the court of royal audience of St. Domingo, and the brethren of the order of Jeronymites, got intelligence thereof. They, knowing our good intentions, and great exertions for the fervice of God and his Majefty, and confidering alfo how injurious to the interefts thereof, the meditated expedition of Velafquez was likely to be, fent the oydor Lucas Vafquez de Aillon to Cuba, with orders to put a pofitive ftop to the failing of it. But whatever orders, oppofition, or menaces he could make ufe of for the purpofe were of no avail, Velafquez confident of the fupport of the Bifhop of Burgos, and having alfo expended all his property in the

equipment,

equipment, was more bent on it than ever, and held the oydor and his authorities in defiance. When the oydor therefore faw that his endeavours to prevent the armament from failing were in vain, he thought it moft prudent under all the circumftances to embark with it, in order to mediate, and prevent any injury to the public fervice, or, if neceffary, by virtue of his office as oydor, to take poffeffion of the country, in the name of his Majefty the Emperor.

The fleet fitted out by Velafquez and under the command of Narvaez, arrived at the port of St. Juan de Ulua without any accident, except the lofs of one fmall veffel. The whole compofed a formidable and refpectable force, confidering that it was entirely created in the Ifland of Cuba. On its arrival, the foldiers who had been fent in queft of the mines in that country, as has been before related, went on board, and it is faid that on fo doing, they returned thanks to God for their delivery from the command of Cortes, and the dangers of the city of Mexico. Narvaez finding them fo open, ordered that they fhould be plentifully fupplied with wine, to render them more communicative, in which he effectually fucceeded. Cervantes the-jefter, under colour of facetioufnefs, expofed to him all the difcontents of our people relative to the partition of the treafure, and alfo the quantity that was obtained; giving Narvaez in many points, much more intelligence than he wifhed to hear. They alfo informed him of the bad ftate of the garrifon commanded by Sandoval in Villa Rica. The news of the arrival of the fleet was foon communicated to Montezuma, who kept his knowledge of it from Cortes, and at the fame time ordered liberal gifts to be prefented to Narvaez, whereby a private correfpondence was opened between them, to the difadvantage of the former, of whom Narvaez told the king every thing that was bad, faying we were all outcafts and robbers, and that the Emperor hearing of our bad conduct, and of our having detained the great Montezuma in cuftody, had fent that force to liberate him, and punifh us, by putting us all to death. This intelligence gave the king great fatisfaction, for from the account of their force which was accurately reprefented to him in painting, he thought us loft. He fent

more

more magnificent presents to Narvaez, and could not conceal the satisfaction which he felt. It was now three days since he had received this intelligence, without communicating it to Cortes, who observed and was surprised at the alteration which he perceived in him. At the expiration of that time however, being, from the circumstance of Cortes having paid him two visits in the course of the day, apprehensive of the general having obtained the knowledge of it through some other channel, he told him the news, saying, that he had just that moment received it. Cortes demonstrated the greatest joy, and after Montezuma had shewn him the representations of it which had been transmitted to him, whereby Cortes learned all that it is was necessary for him to know, he took his leave, and communicated it to his troops, who instantly got under arms, and fired vollies. We soon however perceived that Cortes when by himself was very pensive, and shortly calling us together, he explained to us the evident destination of this armament, that it was meant against us, and he now, by gifts, as well as promises, as if what we received was his private bounty, instead of our fair right, made interest with us, to continue firm and steady to him in the contest which was to take place.

From the representation of our deserters, Narvaez was induced to send to the governor of Villa Rica, demanding of him to surrender his command. He entrusted this business to three persons, Guevara a man of talents and a clergyman, a relation of Velasquez named Amarga, and one Vergara a scrivener, who accordingly set out for Villa Rica. Sandoval had received information of the arrival of an armament, and guessing its object, prepared against an attack. He sent off all his invalids to an Indian village at some distance, and having exhorted his soldiers to stand by him, he caused a gibbet to be erected, and placed a guard on the road of Cempoal. When the deputation from Narvaez arrived at Villa Rica, they did not meet a person except Indians, for Sandoval had given orders to the Spaniards not to appear, and remained at home himself. They were perplexed how to proceed, but guessing by the appearance of the house that it must be the governors, after

going

going to mafs they proceeded thither. On entering, Guevara faluted Sandoval, and immediately began a converfation, the purport of which was, the great force Velafquez had fent, and the expence he had been at, for the purpofe of arrefting Cortes, and all with him as traitors; and he concluded by fummoning Sandoval to furrender himfelf and his poft, to General Pamphilo de Narvaez. The expreffions ufed by this churchman greatly difpleafed Sandoval, who told him, that if it was not for the protection his holy profeffion afforded him, he fhould be punifhed for his infolence, in ufing the word traitors to thofe who were more faithful fubjects to his Majefty than either Narvaez or Velafquez; and as to his demands, he referred him to Cortes, telling him to go to Mexico and fettle his bufinefs with him there. Guevara infifting on executing his miffion, called to the notary Vergara to take out his authorities, which he was preparing to do, but Sandoval ftopped him, faying, " Look you Vergara; your papers are nothing to me; I know not " if they are true or falfe, originals or copies; but I forbid you to read " them here, and by heaven if you attempt it, I will this inftant give " you a hundred lafhes." At this Guevara cried out, " Why do you " mind thefe traitors, read the commiffion." Sandoval then calling him a lying knave ordered them all to be feized; whereon, a number of Indians who were employed to work about the fortrefs, having been prepared for the purpofe, threw trammels over them like fo many damned fouls, and making them faft, inftantly fet off with them on their backs, for Mexico; they hardly knowing if they were dead or alive, or if it was not all enchantment, when they travelled in fuch a manner, poft hafte, by frefh relays of Indians, which were in waiting, and faw the large and populous towns, which they paffed through with a rapidity that ftupified them. Thus they were carried, day and night, till they were fafely depofited in Mexico. Sandoval fent to conduct them, Pedro de Solis, now firnamed De atras La Puerta, by whom he wrote a line in hafte to Cortes, informing him of the particulars. As foon as the general got intelligence of their arrival, he ordered us out under arms, and received them with the greateft honor, loofening them from their trammels, and apologizing for the rudenefs

of

of his officer, whom he highly blamed. He gave them the moſt hoſpitable entertainment, and treated them with the greateſt reſpect; and having pretty well lined their pockets with gold, he in a few days ſent back, as tractable as lambs, thoſe who had ſet out againſt him like furious lions.

As our general was one of thoſe whoſe reſources never are exhauſted, ſo alſo it is hardly neceſſary to dwell upon the merits of thoſe valiant officers and ſoldiers, who accompanied him, and by our valour in the field, and wiſdom in counſel, ſupported him through all his difficulties. On this occaſion it was determined by us, as moſt expedient, to ſend letters to Narvaez and others, which ſhould come to hand previous to the arrival of Guevara. In this we moſt earneſtly requeſted, that no ſtep might be taken which would endanger our general intereſts, or encourage the Indians to riſe upon us, and we alſo held out every inducement that friendſhip or intereſt could ſuggeſt, to bring them over to us. At the ſame time, under theſe general offers of kindneſs, we did not forget ſecretly to treat with ſuch as we thought likely to be wrought upon, for Guevara and Vergara had both informed Cortes that Narvaez was not well with his captains, and that gold would do wonders with them. Cortes adjured Narvaez in his letters, by their former intimacy, not to give cauſe by his conduct for the Mexicans to riſe and deſtroy them all, aſſuring him that they were ready to do any thing to liberate Montezuma, whoſe diſpoſition had alſo greatly altered ſince the time that Narvaez had begun to correſpond with him; adding, that he was convinced, that what was alledged to have been ſaid by him never could have come from ſo wiſe a man, but was the fabrication of ſuch wretches as Cervantes the buffoon, and the others, who had miſled and miſrepreſented him. He at the ſame time offered an unlimited ſubmiſſion to whatever Narvaez would order. Cortes alſo determined to write to the Secretary Andres de Duero, and the Oydor Lucas Vaſquez, and took care that the letters ſhould be well accompanied with preſents. When Narvaez received the firſt letter he turned it into ridicule, handing it about among his officers, calling us traitors, and ſaying
ing

ing that he would put us all to death; and as to Cortes, he would cut off his ears, and broil and eat them, with a great deal of such absurdity. Of course he sent no reply whatever. Just at this time, Guevara and his associates arrived, and they immediately launched out in the praises of Cortes, declaring the expressions of respect he had made use of relative to Narvaez, the services that he had rendered, and the advantages that would result from a junction of their forces. This put Narvaez in such a rage that he would neither see nor hear any of them again. They then began to converse with their comrades, and when the latter perceived how well furnished they had returned, they already wished themselves amongst us. At this time also, arrived the reverend father of the order of mercy, and brought with him the private letters and presents; he went first to kiss the hands of Narvaez, and to tell him how anxious Cortes was to serve under his command, but Narvaez would not see him, except to revile and abuse him. The reverend father therefore gave up that part of his commission, and applied himself to the distribution of the presents, with such effect, that in a short time all the principal officers of the army of Narvaez were in our interests.

If the oydor was originally inclined to favour Cortes, he was now much more so since he saw the magnificent presents which had been so liberally distributed. This was strongly contrasted by the miserable avarice of Narvaez, who used to say in his lofty tones to his major domo, " Take heed that not a mantle is missing, as I have duly entered down " every article." This penuriousness put his officers in an uproar of exclamation against him, all which he attributed to the intrigues of the oydor Vasquez. There was also a difference between them owing to his not keeping due accounts with the oydor, as was his duty, relative to the provisions sent in by order of Montezuma; and Narvaez being encouraged by the favour and patronage of the Bishop of Burgos, now seized the oydor, and sent him as a prisoner to the Island of Cuba, or Old Spain, and a gentleman of the name of Oblanco, a man of consideration, remonstrating with Narvaez upon this, and saying a good deal upon the merits of Cortes and his associates, was also arrested by him,

and

and thrown into prifon, which he took fo much to heart that in three days he died. The oydor Vafquez, during the voyage, prevailed on the captain of the fhip to land him in St. Domingo, where, waiting on the officers of the royal court of audience, and the Jeronymite brothers, they were highly offended at the treatment their officer had received, and made complaints upon the fubject to his Majefty's council in Caftille, without any effect however, owing to the influence of the Bifhop of Burgos.

The troops fent by Velafquez now quitting the coaft, advanced to Cempoal. The firft thing that Narvaez did upon his arrival there, was, to take forcibly from the fat cacique, all the gold and mantles, and alfo the young Indian women who had been given to Cortes and his officers by their parents, and had been left in his care on our march to Mexico. The fat cacique complained to him of this, and alfo of the robberies committed by his foldiers, faying, that it was otherwife when Cortes and his men were there; upon which Salvatierra, a very impudent boafting fellow exclaimed, "See what fear thefe Indians have of this infig-"nificant Cortes." And yet I proteft, that this man who was fo ready with his tongue on all occafions, when we came to attack Narvaez and his army, was the moft defpicable cowardly wretch I ever beheld. Narvaez at this time tranfmitted a copy of the commiffion which he held under the government of Cuba, the farther particulars relative to which I will mention in their place. Our general received conftant intelligence of whatever occurred, from his friends in the army of Narvaez, and alfo from Sandoval, who now informed him that he entertained five perfons of confideration who had quitted Narvaez, affigning as a reafon for it, that when they faw he did not refpect his Majefty's oydor, ftill lefs had they any hopes of good treatment from him, being the oydor's relations. From thefe perfons he had got information of the refolution of Narvaez, to come immediately and feek us out in Mexico.

This being made known to fuch of us as Cortes was in the habit of advifing with, he agreed with us in a general determination, to march

againft

againſt Narvaez and his forces, leaving Alvarado in the command of the city. With him remained all thoſe who were not inclined to go with us, and alſo all thoſe who we thought would be better from us, as having an inclination towards Narvaez or Velaſquez. We alſo left a ſufficiency of proviſions, which was the more neceſſary as the harveſt had been deficient, owing to a want of rain. We ſtrengthened our quarters by a good palliſade, leaving eighty three ſoldiers, with four large guns, twenty four muſquets and croſs-bows and ſeven horſes, to keep in awe, the populous city of Mexico.

Cortes having waited on Montezuma previous to our march, the king queſtioned him relative to his intention of marching againſt Narvaez, both being of the ſame country, and vaſſals of the ſame monarch. He alſo requeſted to know if he could be of any ſervice, expreſſing his apprehenſion, from what he had heard of their ſuperior numbers; and he alſo aſked of Cortes, an explanation relative to the charges brought by the new comers againſt him and us, that we were outcaſts and traitors, and that the others were ſent to bring us to puniſhment. Cortes chearfully replied, that he had not before ſpoken to him on the ſubject of his departure, becauſe he was convinced it would give his majeſty concern; that it was true we were all vaſſals of the ſame monarch, but utterly falſe that we were traitors and fugitives, for on the contrary, we had come fully authoriſed. That as for their deſtroying us by their ſuperior numbers, it did not depend upon them, but upon our Lord Jeſus Chriſt, and his bleſſed mother, who would ſupport us; and he alſo added, that as our monarch ruled many different countries, the inhabitants of ſome were more brave than thoſe of others, and that we were all natives of Old Caſtille, and called true Caſtillians, whereas our opponents were commanded by a Biſcayan; and that his majeſty ſhould ſoon ſee the difference between us, as he hoped with the bleſſing of God, to bring them back with him priſoners, and that our going ſhould not therefore give his majeſty any uneaſineſs. He alſo expreſſed his hope, that Montezuma would to his utmoſt endeavour, prevent any inſurrection in the city, as he certainly would, on his return, make thoſe who be-

B b

haved

haved ill in his abfence, dearly anfwer for it. Cortes then took his leave, embracing Montezuma twice, which the king returned, and Donna Marina acquitted herfelf fo well in her office, that fhe made the feparation a very melancholy one. Montezuma promifed to do all that Cortes defired him, and offered to affift him with five thoufand troops; an offer which Cortes, knowing indeed that he had them not to fend, declined, by faying, that he required no aid but that of our Lord Jefus Chrift; but he requefted that the king would caufe due attention to be given to that part of the temple which was confecrated to our holy religion. Having parted from Montezuma, he fummonned Alvarado and the garrifon of Mexico, and addreffing them in a body, he charged them to watch well, and not fuffer the king to efcape from them, promifing, at his return, if they did their duty properly, to make them all rich. The clergyman Juan Diaz, and certain other fufpected perfons, he left with Alvarado.

We then fet out on our march by the city of Cholula, from whence we fent to the chiefs of the Tlafcalans, requiring them to affift us with a force of four thoufand warriors. They replied, that if it was againft Indians, they were very ready to go; but if againft our countrymen, they begged to be excufed. They fent us however twenty loads of fowls. Cortes alfo wrote to Sandoval to join him, with all his force, at a place called Tampinequeta, or Mitalaquita, twelve leagues from Cempoal. We marched without baggage, in regular order, and with two confidential men, foot foldiers, a days journey before us; they did not keep the direct road, but went by thofe where cavalry could not pafs, enquiring for intelligence concerning the army of Narvaez.

When we had proceeded fome diftance upon our march, one of our advanced parties met with four Spaniards, who turned out to be thofe of Narvaez, with the proofs of his commiffion of captain general. On our coming to where they were, they faluted Cortes with great refpect, and he immediately difmounted, in order to confer with them.

Alonzo

Alonzo de Mata the principal perſon, was then proceeding to read the documents; but Cortes cut him ſhort, by aſking him if he was a royal notary, adding, that on producing his commiſſion he ſhould be obeyed, but if he had it not, he could not be permitted to read any ſuppoſed orders; that thoſe of his Majeſty he ſubmitted to, proſtrate on the ground, but deſired to ſee the original. Mata, frightened, and holding in reality no office under the crown, did not know what to ſay; but Cortes relieved him from his embarraſment, and he halted here, to give them time to refreſh themſelves. Cortes told them our deſtination, and that he was ready to receive any meſſage from their general, of whom he never uſed a diſreſpectful expreſſion; but he talked privately with theſe perſons, and uſed arguments of ſo convincing a nature, that before they ſeparated, he made them completely his friends. On their return, they were loud in their praiſes of Cortes, and his generoſity; and of the magnificence of our appearance; for many of our ſoldiers bore ornaments of gold, upon their arms, and chains and collars of the ſame about their necks. Sandoval and his party joined us on the next day, at the rendezvouz; they were in all about ſeventy. With them came the five who had quitted Narvaez, and who were moſt graciouſly received by Cortes. Sandoval told him, that he had ſome time before ſent two ſoldiers, diſguiſed like Indians, into the quarters of Narvaez; their complexions reſembled the natives, and each brought a load of fruit to ſell. They went directly to the habitation of the brave Salvatierra, who bought their fruit for a ſtring of yellow beads; he then ſent them to get graſs for his horſe, on the banks of a little river; they brought the laſt load about the hour of veſpers, and having fed the horſe, they ſat there till night, during which time they heard Salvatierra obſerve to ſome of his aſſociates, what a lucky moment they had come at, to get the ſeven hundred thouſand crowns, from that traitor Cortes. As ſoon as it was dark, our ſoldiers got out of the houſe unobſerved, taking with them the horſe, ſaddle and bridle, and on their way they met with another horſe which was lame, and which they alſo ſeized and brought off. Cortes laughed heartily when he heard it, and we afterwards learned that Salvatierra had diverted all the army of Narvaez

Bb 2

with

with his abfurdities, when he found the trick that had been played upon him. After that time they kept a better watch.

It was determined now by us, to fend the reverend father of the order of mercy, with a letter to Narváez, the contents of which were to this purpofe. That we had rejoiced on hearing of fo noble a perfon's arrival in this country, as expecting material advantage therefrom, both to our holy religion, and his Majefty's fervice; but that contrary to our expectations he had reviled us, and caufed the whole country to revolt, That our general had fent, offering to refign to him whatever territories or provinces he chofe to occupy, and to engage in new expeditions. That if he came by virtue of a commiffion from his Majefty, we demanded a fight of the original, within the fpace of three days, for which purpofe, and to obey it proftrate on the earth, we had now advanced hither; but if no fuch authority was in his poffeffion, he fhould return to the Ifland of Cuba, and not do any thing here that would throw the country into a difturbance, which if he attempted, we would as in duty bound make him prifoner, and fend him to be dealt with according to his Majefty's pleafure. That he was anfwerable for all the lamentable confequences that would enfue, and that this letter was thus fent, becaufe no royal notary dare undertake to deliver one, as according to due form ought to be done, after the violence committed againft his Majefty's officer, the oydor, a crime Læfæ Majeftatis, the perpetrator of which Cortes was in duty bound to apprehend and bring to juftice, and for which he thereby cited him to appear and anfwer, calling God to witnefs the juftnefs of his conduct. This letter concluding with expreffions of great refpect, was figned by Cortes, the captains, and feveral foldiers, and fent by the Reverend Father Olmedo, and by a foldier of the name of Ulagre, whofe brother came over with Narvaez as the commander of his artillery.

Olmedo on his arrival waited in Narvaez with great refpect, and alfo proceeded to execute the reft of his miffion, in bringing together certain officers of that army, amongft whom were Rodorigo Mira and
Ulagre

Ulagre of the artillery. To these he liberally diftributed his gold, and alfo, more privately, to Andres de Duero, with an earneft invitation to him to vifit Cortes. Narvaez foon began to fufpect what was the real object of Olmedo, and was inclined to feize and make him prifoner; which being known to Duero, who had great influence with Narvaez, not only on account of his fituation, but alfo from their being fome way related, he reprefented to him the impropriety of committing fuch an outrage againft a perfon of a holy function. He alfo furmifed to him the great probability that the foldiers of Cortes might be eafily won over to him by a little attention and policy. Having by thefe arguments and other fimilar ones appeafed Narvaez for the prefent, he took his leave, and informed Olmedo of what had paffed. Narvaez fhortly after fent for Olmedo, who waited on him, and defired permiffion to fpeak to him in private, and there in a laughing manner began to tell him how he knew that he had given orders to take him prifoner, whereas there was not a perfon exifting more devoted to his fervice, and that he knew to a certainty many perfons in the army of Cortes would be very glad to fee him delivered into the hands of his excellency; indeed he would venture to fay our whole army was of that opinion, and as a proof of it, he affured him, that he poffeffed a letter full of abfurdities, which Cortes had written by the perfuafion of thofe who wifhed to deliver him up, and which was indeed fuch ridiculous ftuff that he had been once or twice inclined to throw it away, but would with his permiffion now bring it to him. He accordingly went, as he faid, for the letter, pretending he had left it in his baggage, but in reality to call to Duero and others, to defire them to be prefent as witneffes at the delivery of it.

Duero, in order to carry on his plan of getting an interview with Cortes, then propofed, that fteps fhould be taken to open a communication between them and him, to which Auguftin Bermudez a fecret friend of Cortes added, that Duero and Salvatierra fhould be fent upon the bufinefs; this he did knowing the character of Salvatierra, who was not at all difpofed to the expedition. It was at laft fettled, that Duero fhould wait on Cortes to invite him to a meeting for the purpofe of accommodation

commodation, and the arrangement of their future meafures, at a place which lay at a convenient diftance between the quarters of the two armies, and that there Narvaez was to feize and make him prifoner, for which purpofe he prepared twenty of his foldiers in whom he placed moft confidence. Intelligence of all this was immediately conveyed to Cortes. The reverend father remained at the quarters of Narvaez, having made out a relationfhip to Salvatierra, with whom he dined every day.

Our general, on firft hearing of the arrival of Narvaez, fent a foldier who had ferved in Italy and underftood perfectly the management of the lance, to the province of the Chinantans, who had fhortly before entered into alliance with us. They ufed lances much longer than ours, with blades of fharpened ftone. This foldier, named Barrientos, was fent for the purpofe of obtaining from them three hundred of their lances, and as there was plenty of copper in that province, he gave him directions to get two heads made of this metal, for each lance. Thefe were accordingly done, being executed with fuch ingenuity that they exceeded the pattern. He alfo obtained the affiftance of two thoufand warriors of this nation, who were to rendezvouz at our quarters, armed in the fame manner. Having done this he returned, with two hundred Indians, bringing with them the lances which he had procured for us, and which we found on handling to be extraordinarily good, and we were immediately exercifed with them. A mufter was alfo taken of our army, which amounted to two hundred and fix, * including fife and drum, with five mounted cavalry, two artillery men, few crofs-bow-men, and fewer mufqueteers. And this was the force, and fuch the weapons, with which we marched againft, and were to encounter and defeat the army of Narvaez.

I muft recall the recollection of my reader to that part of my narrative, wherein I related how Andres de Duero, and the Contador de
Lares,

* Exclufive of the garrifon of Villa Rica.

Lares, negociated the appointment of Cortes to the station of captain general. Also that they were to make an equal partition of all the treasure that should be acquired by him. Duero now therefore seeing Cortes so wealthy, under colour to Narvaez of a treaty whereby to get Cortes in his power, waited on the latter, in order to obtain from him his share of the riches, for the third partner, De Lares, was sometime dead. This Cortes not only acceded to, but moreover promised him equal command with himself, and an equal share of territory when the conquest of the country should be effected; so that it was agreed between them, together with Augustin Bermudez, Alguazil major of the army of Narvaez, and many others whom I will not now name, to get rid of the command of Narvaez altogether. Cortes to confirm these, and bring over others, was more liberal than ever in his presents, with which he loaded the two Indians of Duero. On one of these days of intercourse, after they had been a considerable time together privately, and had dined, Duero having mounted his horse, asked Cortes if he had any commands for him; to which Cortes replied, that he wished to remind him not to deviate from what they had now settled, for that if he did, by his conscience, which was his usual oath, he would be in his quarters within three days, and that he should be the very first person at whom he would throw his lance; and saying this, he bid him farewell. Duero turned off laughing, and said that he would not fail. On his arrival at the quarters of Narvaez, he is said to have told him, that Cortes and all with him were ready to range themselves under his command.

Cortes now sent for Juan Velasquez de Leon, a person of much consideration, and who had always been his particular friend, though a near relation of the governor of Cuba, and on his coming to him told him, in that smooth and persuasive manner that he could put on when ever he pleased, " Senior Velasquez de Leon, Duero has informed me,
" that Narvaez is anxious to see you in his camp, and that it is report-
" ed if you go thither I am an undone man. Now my worthy friend
" mount your grey mare, put on your fanfarona, (gold chain,) take with
" you all your valuables, and more still, which I will give you, and
go

" and fix yourfelf with Narvaez immediately, and diftribute the gold
" I give you according to my directions." Velafquez replied, that
he would willingly obey his order in every thing but one, which was
that of taking his treafure with him. To which Cortes anfwered that
he believed as much, but that he did not wifh him to go on other terms
than what he had mentioned. De Leon ftill however continued firm
in what he had faid, and after a fecret conference fet out for Cempoal.
In about two hours after the departure of Velafquez, Cortes ordered the
drum to be beat to arms, whereon our little army affembled, and we fet
forward on our march. On our way we killed two wild hogs, which
our foldiers faid was a good omen. We flept all that night by the fide
of a rivulet, according to cuftom the ground our bed and ftones our
pillows, and next day arrived at the river and place where the city of
Vera Cruz is now built, but which was at that time an Indian village,
and planted with trees. As it was about midday and the weather very
fultry, we repofed here for the prefent, being much fatigued by the
weight of our arms and lances.

Captain de Leon arrived by day break at the town of Cempoal.
The Indians were overjoyed to fee him and circulated the news of his
arrival, fo that Narvaez heard of it, and immediately thereon came out
to embrace him. Velafquez having paid his compliments faid, that he
only came in the hopes of making an amicable arrangement between
him and Cortes; upon which Narvaez taking him afide, afked him
how he could talk of treating with any fuch traitor. Velafquez replied, that Cortes was a faithful and zealous officer of his majefty,
and defired that no fuch epithet fhould be applied to him in his prefence. Narvaez however perfifted, offering, if he would renounce
Cortes, to make him the fecond in command; to which Velafquez
replied that he fhould be unpardonable in quitting one who had done
fo much for the fervice of his God and king. By this time all the
principal officers had arrived to falute Velafquez, who was a favorite
amongft them, being a very polite and well bred gentleman, of a
fine figure and perfon, and he now wore a great gold chain which
made

made two returns over his shoulders, and round his body, so that he gave the idea of a truly gallant soldier, and impressed all who beheld him with respect. The Alguazil Bermudez, and Andres de Duero, wished particularly to communicate with him in private, but just at this moment arrived a Captain Gamarra, together with one Juan Yuste, Juan Buono, and Salvatierra the braggart. These persons, determined Narvaez to make him prisoner, for the freedom with which he had spoken in favour of Cortes, and Narvaez had in consequence given privately an order for the purpose, which coming to the knowledge of those already spoken of, as having embarked in the interests of Cortes, they immediately represented to him the impropriety of such a violent proceeding, and how impolitic it would be. Hereupon Narvaez again addressed him in a very friendly manner, requesting his assistance to bring Cortes and the rest of us into their power, and invited him to dine with him the next day. Velasquez promised assistance to his design, but representing Cortes as determined and head strong, he recommended a division of the country, and that each should take separate provinces. At this time Olmedo getting within hearing of Velasquez, and speaking in the manner of a person of trust, addressing himself to Narvaez said, " Let your excellency order out your troops under arms, " and shew him what your force is, that Cortes may know, and be " terrifyed at it." Narvaez agreeing to this, the troops were turned out in review order, and passed by them. Velasquez complimenting Narvaez upon their number and appearance, and wishing him an increase of his power, the latter replied, saying, he believed Velasquez was now convinced how effectually he could have crushed Cortes and all those with him: to which Velasquez only answered that he trusted they knew how to defend themselves. On the next day he dined with Narvaez, and there was in company a nephew of the governor of Cuba, a captain in the army. The conversation turning on the recent events, this gentleman used very insulting language in respect to Cortes; upon which, Velasquez rising up addressed himself to Narvaez and said, " I have already requested, general, that you would not permit in my " presence, disrespectful language of any of my friends, for we do not

deserve

" deserve it." But the other gentleman, on this, launching out into still greater liberty with Velasquez himself, the latter instantly laid his hand on his sword, desiring Narvaez to permit him to punish him as a base liar; but the officers present interfering prevented mischief, and it was recommended both to Velasquez and Olmedo to quit the place. Velasquez accordingly, on his excellent grey mare, armed in his helmet and coat of mail which he always wore, and his gold chain about his shoulders, went to take his leave of Narvaez, who returned his salute very coolly. The young man we have before spoken of was again very violent, but Velasquez gave him no other reply than swearing by his beard, that he would in a few days see what materials he was made of: then, taking hasty leave of those who were standing by, he put spurs to his good grey mare, and was soon out of sight, for he had got a hint or suspicion that Narvaez would send after him, and saw some persons on horseback, apparently for the purpose; but he was too well mounted for them, and reached our camp in safety.

We were at that time reposing by the side of the river, after the fatigues of so sultry a march, when a report came from an outpost that horsemen were in sight. On their arrival, what greeting, and embracing, and joy and congratulation! and how Cortes received them! and well he might, for they were eminently serviceable to him. We all got round to hear their narrative. Velasquez told Cortes first how he had executed his commission, and distributed his presents. Then our merry droll friar took off Narvaez when he made him order out his troops in review, to laugh at him; and told us by what finesse he got him to read the letter; and how he had persuaded the bragging fool Salvatierra that he was his cousin, the one being from Olmedo, and the other from Burgos; and of the ridiculous speeches and gestures the fellow made when he was talking how he would kill Cortes, and all of us, for the loss of his horse; mimicking him to admiration. Thus were we all together like so many brothers, rejoicing and laughing as if we had been at a wedding or a feast, knowing well that tomorrow was the day in which we were to conquer or die, opposed to five times

our

our number. Such is the fortune of war! We then proceeded on our march, and halted for the night by the river and bridge which is about a league diftant from Cempoal; at prefent there is a dairy farm at that place.

After the departure of the reverend father and Juan Velafquez from the quarters of Narvaez, it feems that certain of the officers gave advice to him of the fecret practices which had been going on, and recommended to him to be well upon his guard, as Cortes had many friends amongft his troops. The fat Cacique alfo, who was greatly in dread of being called to account by Cortes, for having delivered up the women and mantles with which he had been intrufted, was very vigilant in watching and obtaining intelligence of our motions, as he was directed by Narvaez to do.

Finding that we had now approached near to Cempoal, the fat Cacique thus addreffed Narvaez. " What are you doing, and how " carelefs are you! do you think that Malintzin and his Teules are equal- " ly fo? I tell you that when you leaft expect it he will come upon " you and put you all to death." Although Narvaez laughed at this, he did not however reject the warning. The firft thing he in confe- quence did was, to declare war againft us with fire, fword, and free rope. This we learned from a foldier named El Galleguillo, who came over to us, or was fent by Andres de Duero to Cortes. He then drew up his artillery, cavalry, and infantry, in a plain diftant a quarter of a league from Cempoal, where he determined to wait for us. It happened to rain exceedingly heavy on that day, and as the troops of Narvaez were not accuftomed to hardfhip, and moreover defpifed us, they grew reft- lefs and uneafy in their fituation, and the captains advifed their chief to march them back to their quarters, which he accordingly did, form- ing his eighteen guns in a line, in front of the building in which he lodged. His officers alfo advifed, that a grand guard of forty cavalry fhould be pofted for the night on the road of Cempoal, and that fome cavalry vedettes, and active foot foldiers, fhould be placed to watch

the

the ford which we muſt paſs.   Twenty of the cavalry were alſo to patrole during the whole night in and about the quarters of Narvaez. All this was done by the advice of his officers, who wiſhed to get back under ſhelter, and who deſpiſed Cortes, ſaying it was abſurd to ſuppoſe he would come to attack them with his pitiful handful of men, and that if he had advanced, it was only a mere oſtentation, in order to induce them to come into terms.

When Narvaez returned to his quarters, he promiſed publicly two thouſand crowns to whoever killed Cortes or Gonzalo de Sandoval. He placed as ſpies at the ford, one Gonzalo Carraſco who lives now in La Puebla, and another ſoldier of the name of Hurtado.   He alſo filled his own quarters with Soldiers armed with muſquets, croſs-bows, and partizans, and did the ſame by thoſe of the Veedor Salvatierra, Gamarra, and Juan Buono.

As ſoon as we had arrived at the river which runs through the fertile meadows at about a leagues diſtance from Cempoal, truſty perſons being ſelected and ſent to the outpoſts, our Cortes ſummoned us all, officers and ſoldiers, around him, where he was on horſeback, and earneſtly enjoining ſilence, addreſſed us as follows.   " Gentlemen, it is well " known to you that D. Velaſquez governor of Cuba ſelected me for " your captain general, not that your number did not contain many " equally worthy ; and you alſo recollect how it was believed by us, and " publicly proclaimed, that we came to colonize, when in reality our " inſtructions went no farther than to barter with the natives. You al-" ſo recollect my determination to return to Cuba, in order to give an " account of my miſſion to him by whom I was entruſted with it, but " that by your command I was required to ſtay and colonize in the " country for his Majeſty's ſervice, as, thanks to God, has been done, " and a wiſe determination it was. You alſo made me as you recollect " your captain general, and chief magiſtrate, until his Majeſty's plea-" ſure was known, and we have in conſequence rendered eſſential ſer-" vice to our God and Monarch.   I muſt now remind you how we
have

" have written to his Majesty, giving a full account of these countries,
" and requesting that the government of them may not be bestowed on any
" unworthy person, and that we, fearing the effect of the arts and influ-
" ence of the Bishop of Burgos, and of the Governor of Cuba whom he
" favors, had resolved to maintain his Majesty's government and
" right in this country, until his royal mandate duly authenticated
" should be produced to us, which we would then as in duty bound,
" obey, prostrate upon the earth. You also recollect how we have sent
" the treasure obtained by us to his Majesty. Now therefore, advert-
" ing to other matters, I must remind you how often you have all been
" at the point of death in various wars and battles, how we have suf-
" fered from fatigues, and rains, and winds, and hunger, sleeping on
" our arms, on the ground and in snow. Not to mention above fifty
" of our countrymen dead, and your own wounds as yet unhealed, our
" sufferings by sea and land, the perils of Tabasco, Tlascala, and of
" Cholula, where the vessels were prepared in which we were to have
" been boiled, and our perilous entry into Mexico. In addition there-
" to many of you have been on expeditions of adventure antecedent
" to this, and have risqued and lost your properties, and now gentle-
" men, Narvaez comes, and maligns and asperses us with the great
" Montezuma, and immediately on landing proclaims war against us,
" with fire, sword, and rope, as if we were infidel Moors." As soon
as Cortes had concluded this he proceeded to exalt our persons and valour
to the skies, and after an abundance of the most flattering promises he
concluded by observing, that Narvaez came to deprive us of our lives,
and properties; that he had imprisoned his Majesty's oydor, and that
it was uncertain if he held his command by any more than the favor of
the Bishop of Burgos. It was therefore necessary, he said, for us, as faithful subjects, to fight in defence of his Majesty's rights, our lives, and
properties, and he now demanded to hear our determination.

Our officers and soldiers all replied, that we were ready and determined to conquer or die; and we warned him not to say any more about an
accommodation, or partition of the country, for that if he did, we
would

would plunge our fwords in his body. Cortes on hearing this applauded our fpirit, faying, that he expected no lefs, and adding a profufion of promifes, and affurances that he would make us all rich and profperous. He then, adverting to our intended attack, earneftly enjoined us to obferve the ftricteft filence, faying, that to conquer in battle, prudence and filence were more neceffary than excefs of bravery; that he knew our ardour induced all to ftrive who fhould be moft forward, and that it was neceffary to diftribute us by companies, and to appoint to each his diftinct duty. Accordingly, he ordered that in the attack the firft thing to be done fhould be, to feize the artillery. For this duty he felected feventy foldiers, of which number I was one, and put us under the command of Pizarro, an active lad, whofe name however was at that time as little known as that of Peru. He gave us alfo further orders, that as foon as we were mafters of the guns, we fhould join and fupport the detachment which was to attack the quarters of Narvaez. This laft mentioned duty he affigned to Sandoval, with feventy felected men, and as this captain was alfo alguazil major, he gave him a warrant to arreft Narvaez, drawn up as follows.

Gonzalo de Sandoval, alguazil major for his Majefty in New Spain. You are hereby commanded, to feize the body of Pamphilo de Narvaez, and in cafe he makes refiftance, to put him to death; the fame being neceffary to the fervice of God, and his Majefty, whofe officer he has imprifoned. Given under my hand, at head quarters,

Counter figned,
    Pedro Hernandez, Secretary. } Hernando Cortes.

Cortes alfo promifed to the firft foldier who laid his hand on Narvaez, the fum of three thoufand crowns, to the fecond, two thoufand, and to the third, one thoufand, as he faid, to buy gloves. He appointed captain I. Velafquez de Leon to feize his relation Diego Velafquez, with whom he had the quarrel, and gave him a detachment of feventy foldiers, retaining twenty with himfelf, as a referve, to go wherever he faw moft occafion, and more particularly to fupport the attack upon the

quarters

quarters of Narvaez, and Salvatierra, in a lofty temple. Having thus arranged his troops and instructed his captains, he addressed us in a few words, saying, he well knew that the army of Narvaez was four times more numerous than ours, but that they were not accustomed to arms, and many of them were ill; he therefore trusted, that, attacking them thus unexpectedly, God would give the victory to us, who were his faithful servants, and that next to divine assistance, we were to rely on our own courage, and the strength of our arms; that now was the hour of trial, and that at worst it was preferable to die with glory.

One circumstance has struck me since, which is, that he never once said or insinuated to us that such or such persons in the army of Narvaez were our friends; and in so doing he acted like a wise captain, making us rely entirely on our own exertions, and use them to the utmost, without expecting any other assistance or support. Our three detachments were now formed, and the captains at the head of each, they and the soldiers mutually encouraging each other. Our captain, Pizarro, explained to us how we were to rush in upon the guns with our lances at the charge, and that immediately on getting them in our possession, the artillery men who were attached to his company should point and fire them against the quarters of Narvaez.

What would we not have given for defensive armour on this night! A morion, a helmet, or a breastplate, would have fetched any money. Our countersign was Spiritu santo, Spiritu santo. That of Narvaez was Santa Maria, Santa Maria.

As Captain Sandoval and I were always intimate friends, he at this time called me aside, and made me promise him that after the capture of the guns if I remained alive, I would seek out and attach myself to him for the rest of the engagement. These things being arranged, we remained with empty stomachs, reflecting on what was before us, and waiting for the orders to march. I was stationed centinel at an advanced post, and had not been there long when a patrole came to me, and
asked

afked me if I had heard any thing. I replied that I had not. A corporal foon after came to our poſt and ſaid that Galleguillo the deſerter of Narvaez's army was miſſing, and that he had come amongſt us as a ſpy; in confequence of which Cortes had given orders that we ſhould march inſtantly. Accordingly we heard our drum beat, and the captains calling over their companies.

We joined the column, and proceeding on our march, we found the ſoldier whom we had miſſed, ſleeping in the road under ſome mantles, for the poor fellow not being inured to hardſhips was fatigued. We continued our march at a quick pace, and in profound ſilence, and ſoon arrived at the river, where we ſurpriſed the two vedettes of the army of Narvaez, one of whom, by name Carraſco, we made priſoner, the other flying before us into the town, and giving the alarm. On account of the rain, we found the river deeper than uſual, and difficult to paſs, owing to the looſe ſtones under our feet, and the weight of our arms. I alſo recollect that the ſoldier whom we had made priſoner called to our general, " Senior Cortes do not advance, for I ſwear that Narvaez is " with his whole force drawn up to receive you." Cortes gave him in charge to his ſecretary, Hernandez, and we proceeded, and on coming into the town, heard the man who had eſcaped, giving the alarm; and Narvaez calling to his captains to turn out.

Our company which headed the column, charging our lances, ruſhed on, and cloſing up to the guns, made ourſelves maſters of them without giving the artillery men time to put the matches to more than four, of which one ſhot only took effect, killing three of our ſoldiers. Our whole force now advanced with drum beating, and falling upon the cavalry brought down ſix or ſeven of them, whilſt we who had got poſſeſſion of the guns could not quit them, becauſe the enemy kept up a heavy diſcharge of arrows and muſquetry from the quarters of Narvaez. Captain de Sandoval and his company coming forward, marched up the ſteps of the temple, notwithſtanding that he was ſtoutly reſiſted by the enemy with miſſile weapons, muſquetry, partizans, and lances, and then,

then, we who were in charge of the artillery, perceiving that there was no longer any danger to them, left them to our gunners, and proceeded with Captain Pizarro to fupport the attack of Sandoval, who had been forced down fix or feven of the fteps. Supported by us they again advanced, making the enemy give ground in their turn, and juft at that inftant, if I do not miftake, I heard the voice of Narvaez crying out, " Santa Maria affift me, for they have killed me, and ftruck out one " of my eyes!" On this we all fhouted out, " Victory! victory! for the " Efpiritu Santo! Narvaez is dead."

Still we could not force our way into the temple, until Martin Lopez the fhipwright, a very tall man, fet fire to the thatch of the roof, and the fire fpreading, forced thofe who were infide to rufh out and come tumbling down the fteps. P. Sanchez Farfan was the firft who laid his hand on Narvaez; we brought him prifoner to Sandoval, together with feveral of his captains, and continued fhouting, " Victory! " Live our King and Cortes! Narvaez is dead!"

During this time Cortes and the reft of our army were engaged with thofe of the troops of Narvaez who yet held out, in fome lofty temples which we now battered with the artillery. As foon as our fhouts were underftood, and the caufe of them, Cortes made proclamation that all who did not inftantly fubmit, and range themfelves under the ftandards of his Majefty, and the command of his officer Cortes, fhould be put to death. This however had no effect on thofe who occupied the lofty temples where Diego Velafquez and Salvatierra were pofted, until Sandoval with one half of our body, and the guns, proceeded againft them, and entering, made thofe officers and the people with them prifoners. As foon as this was done, Sandoval returned to keep guard upon Narvaez, who was doubly ironed. We had alfo with him under our care, Salvatierra, D. Velafquez, Gamarra, Juan Yufte, Juan Buono Vilcaino, and many other principal perfons. Shortly after, Cortes came in unobferved, fatigued, and the fweat running down his face; and addreffing Sandoval, without any congratulation or compli-

ment

ment, told him that it was impoffible to defcribe what he had gone through. Then turning about he cried, " What is become of Narvaez? " how is Narvaez? Sandoval anfwered, "Here he is very fafe. Cortes then " faid, "Son Sandoval keep good watch on him, and the other captains." After which he haftened out to caufe proclamation to be made, that all fhould immediately lay down their arms and fubmit.

All this paffed during the night, fhowers falling very frequently, and in the intervals the moon fhone; but juft at the moment of our attack it was extremely dark, and rained heavily, and a multitude of fire flies appearing at the fame time, the foldiers of Narvaez thought that they were the lighted matches of our mufquetry.

Narvaez was very badly wounded, and his eye was beaten out; he therefore requefted that his furgeon named Maeftre Juan fhould be fent for. This being done, whilft he was under the operation of having his eye dreffed, Cortes entered the room unnoticed; but being foon obferved, Narvaez addreffing him faid, " Senior Captain Cortes, " appreciate as it deferves your good fortune, in having defeated and " made me prifoner." Cortes replied that his thanks were due to God, and to his valiant officers and foldiers, but that it was the leaft of our atchievements fince our arrival in New Spain, and that for daring, he thought the arreft of his Majefty's officer much exceeded it. He then quitted the place, again warning Sandoval to keep good guard.

We foon after brought Narvaez and the reft of the prifoners to another apartment, where a guard was placed upon them compofed of our moft trufty and confidential foldiers. To this duty I was appointed, and Sandoval before he left us called me afide, and gave me a private order to permit no perfon whatever to fpeak to Narvaez. We knew that forty of the cavalry were at an outpoft on the river; it was therefore neceffary to keep a good guard until this party was difpofed of, left they fhould fall on us in order to refcue their officers. Cortes now fent to them Chriftoval de Oli, and de Ordas, mounted on two of the horfes of Narvaez which we found tied in a fmall wood clofe to Cempoal, with unlimited

offers

offers if they would come in and submit. Our officers guided by one of Narvaez's soldiers arrived at the post of the cavalry, and by their promises and arguments won them over, and they all entered the town together.

By this time it was clear day. Cortes, seated in an arm chair, a mantle of orange colour thrown over his shoulders, his arms by his side, and surrounded by his officers and soldiers, received the salutations of the cavaliers who as they dismounted came up to him to kiss his hand. It was wonderful to see the affability, and the kindness with which he spoke to and embraced them, and the compliments which he made to them; amongst the number were Augustin Bermudez, Andres de Duero, and many other friends of our general. Each, as he had paid his respects, took his leave, and went to the quarters assigned him. During all this time, and even before the arrival of the cavalry, the drums, fifes, and timbals of the army of Narvaez never ceased, having struck up at day break in honor of Cortes, without being desired or spoken to by any one of us. One of them a Negro and a comical fellow, danced and shouted for joy, crying, " Where are the Romans who with such " small numbers have ever atchieved such a glorious victory?" Nor was it possible to silence him or the rest, until Cortes was at last obliged to order one of them to be confined.

Our losses on each side on this occasion were as follow. The ensign of Narvaez, named Fuertes, an Hidalgo of Seville. A captain of the same army named Roxas, of Old Castille, and two others killed, and many wounded. One also of the three who had antecedently deserted from us to him was killed. Four of our soldiers were killed, and a number wounded. The fat Cacique on our approach had taken refuge in the quarters of Narvaez; he also received a wound. Cortes ordered him to his house, and to be there protected and taken care of. Of the two others who deserted from us, each got his deserts; Escalona being severely wounded, and Cervantes well beaten.

As

As to the fierce Salvatierra, his foldiers declared that they never faw fo pitiful a fellow, nor fo terrified a being when he heard our drum beat; but when we fhouted for victory, and cryed that Narvaez was dead, he told them that he had got a pain in his ftomach, and could fight no more. Such was the refult of his bravados. Captain Velafquez de Leon took his relation Diego Velafquez to his own quarters, where he had his wounds attended to, and treated him with the utmoft diftinction.

The reinforcement of the warriors of Chinanta, which Cortes had been promifed, marched in fhortly after the action was over, conducted by our foldier Barrientos, with great pomp and regularity, in two files, lanciers and archers alternately, and in this manner they came to the number of one thoufand five hundred, with colours, drums, and trumpets, fhouting, and making fuch a warlike appearance that it was glorious to behold. It afforded matter of aftonifhment to the army of Narvaez, for they appeared to be double their real number. Our general received them with infinite courtefy, and difmiffed them with thanks and handfome prefents.

Cortes now fent Francifco de Lugo to order all the captains and pilots of the fleet to come to him at Cempoal, or, in cafe they refufed, to make them prifoners. He alfo gave directions that the fhips fhould be difmantled, thereby cutting off all poffibility of a communication with Cuba. Narvaez had confined one Barahona, a rich man, and afterwards an inhabitant of Guatimala; him Cortes ordered to be immediately releafed, and kindly treated; I recollect when he joined us he appeared in a very weak and languid ftate. The captains and pilots of the fleet immediately came to pay their refpects to our general. He made them take an oath that they would not feparate from him, and would obey his orders; and he appointed one of them, Pedro Cavallero, his admiral of the whole fleet. Cortes warned him, that if, as he expected, more veffels arrived from Cuba, he fhould immediately difmantle them, and fend the captains and pilots to the head quarters.

Having

Having thus secured his port, he turned to other matters, and ordered Velasquez de Leon with one hundred and twenty men upon an expedition to Panuco.   One hundred of them were soldiers who had come with Narvaez; the other twenty were taken from amongst ourselves.   This force was also to have two ships with it, for the purpose of extending our discoveries.   He gave a command upon a similar plan to Diego de Ordas, to establish a colony at Guacacualco.   Ordas was also to send to Jamaica for horses and stock, to establish an independent supply in the country, the province he went to being well adapted for breeding cattle.   Cortes commanded all the prisoners to be released, except Narvaez, and Salvatierra, who still complained of the pain in his stomach.   He also ordered all the horses and arms which had been taken from the soldiers of Narvaez to be returned to them; this gave our people much discontent, but since the general would have it so, we were obliged to submit, and I for my part, was obliged to surrender a good horse which I had put in a safe place, with a saddle and bridle, two swords, three poinards, and a shield.   Hereupon Captain Alonzo de Avila, and also our Reverend Father Olmedo, took an opportunity of speaking to Cortes, and told him that they believed he had a mind to imitate Alexander of Macedon, who after his army had atchieved any glorious action, was more generous to the vanquished, than to the conquerors; for that it was observed, that, all the gold and valuable presents, as fast as he received them, he gave to the captains of the other army, quite appearing to forget us, which was not well done on his part, we having made him what he was.   To this Cortes replied by protesting, that he, and all he had was entirely at our service, and he would prove it by his future conduct; but that what he did was unavoidable for our common interest, we being so few, and the others so many. Avila in answer to this used some expressions of rather a lofty kind, upon which Cortes observed, that whoever did not wish to follow him might depart, that the women in Castille had bred good soldiers, and would continue to do so.   Avila answered again in a still more bold and imperious manner, and as Cortes could not at that time break with him, he was forced to dissimulate, knowing him to be a brave and determined

ned man. He therefore pacified him with prefents, for he always apprehended fome act of violence on his part, and for the future took care to employ him on bufinefs of importance at a diftance, as in the Ifland of St. Domingo, and afterwards in Old Spain.

Narvaez brought with him a Negro who was in the fmall pox; an unfortunate importation for that country, for the difeafe fpread with inconceivable rapidity, and the Indians died by thoufands; for not knowing the nature of it, they brought it to a fatal iffue by throwing themfelves into cold water in the heat of the diforder. Thus black was the arrival of Narvaez, and blacker ftill the death of fuch multitudes of unfortunate fouls, which were fent into the other world, without having an opportunity of being admitted into the bofom of our holy church. At this time a claim was made on Cortes by fuch of our foldiers as had been in diftant garrifons, for their fhare of the gold taken in Mexico. He, as well as I recollect, referred them to a place in Tlafcala, defiring that two perfons might be fent thither to receive it. I will at a future period relate what happened hereupon; but I muft at the prefent revert to other things.

The wheel of fortune making fudden turns, evil follows clofely upon good, as was our cafe at prefent, our late fucceffes being contrafted by melancholy news from Mexico. We now received intelligence by exprefs from that city, whereby we were informed, that an infurrection had broken out, and that Alvarado was befieged in his quarters, which they had fet on fire, having killed feven of his men, and wounded many; for which reafon he earneftly called called for fuccour and fupport. When we received this news, God knows how it afflicted us! We fet out by long marches for Mexico, leaving Narvaez and Salvatierra prifoners in Villa Rica, under the cuftody of Rodorigo Rangel, who alfo had directions to collect all the ftragglers, and to take care of the invalids, of whom there were many. At the moment we were ready to march, arrived four principal noblemen from the court of Montezuma, to lodge a formal complaint againft Alvarado, for having affaulted them

when

when dancing at a folemn feftival in honor of their gods, which he had permitted them to hold, whereby, in their own defence they had been forced to kill feven of his foldiers. Cortes replied to them in terms not the moft pleafing, faying he would foon be at Mexico, and put all in proper regulation; with which anfwer they returned, very little indeed to the fatisfaction of Montezuma who felt the infult ftrongly, many of the natives being killed.

In confequence of this intelligence, the detachments were counter-manded, and Cortes exhorted the troops of Narvaez to forget paft ani-mofities, and not to lofe this opportunity of ferving his Majefty and themfelves, expofing to their view the riches they would acquire, fo that they one and all declared their readinefs to proceed to Mexico, a re-folution they never would have taken, if they had known the force of that city. By very long marches we arrived at Tlafcala, where we learned that until the time that Montezuma and the Mexicans got in-telligence of the defeat of Narvaez, they had never ceafed making attacks upon Alvarado; but when they heard of our fuccefs they defifted, leav-ing the Spaniards greatly fatigued and diftreffed, by their continual ex-ertions and want of water and provifions. This information was con-veyed by two Indian meffengers who arrived at the moment we entered Tlafcala. Here Cortes made an infpection of our army, which now amounted to one thoufand three hundred men, nearly one hundred of whom were cavalry, and one hundred and fixty were crofsbow-men and mufqueteers. Two thoufand warriors of the Tlafcalans having joined us, we purfued our route by long marches to Tefcuco, where we were very ill received, and every thing bore the appearance of difaffection.

On St. John's day in the month of June one thoufand five hundred and twenty, we arrived in the City of Mexico, meeting with a reception very different from our former one, for none of the nobility or chiefs of our acquaintance could be recognifed, and the city feemed to be totally depopulated. When we entered our quarters, Montezuma came to em-brace Cortes, and wifh him joy of his victory, but the general would

neither

neither hear, nor fpeak to him; whereon the King retired very melancholy, to his apartment. Cortes made inquiry into the circumftances of the commotion, which evidently was not approved or inftigated by Montezuma. Indeed if he had thought fit to act againft our party, they could all have been deftroyed, as eafily as feven of them. By what Alvarado told Cortes it appeared, that a number of Indians, enraged at the detention of Montezuma, at the erection of the crucifix in their temple, and by the order of their gods as they faid, had gone thither to pull it down, but to their infinite aftonifhment, found all their ftrength utterly unable to move it. This being reprefented to Montezuma, he defired no attempt of the kind fhould be made again. Alvarado added for his own exculpation, that the attack was made upon him by the friends and fubjects of Montezuma, in order to liberate their monarch, at the time that they believed Narvaez had deftroyed Cortes and his army. Cortes now afked Alvarado for what reafon he fell upon the Mexicans, while they were dancing and holding a feftival in honour of their gods. To this Alvarado replied, that it was in order to be beforehand with them, having had intelligence of their hoftile intentions againft him from two of their own nobility and a prieft. Cortes then afked him if it was true that they had requefted permiffion of him to hold their feftival, and the other hereupon replied that it was fo, and that it was in order to take them by furprife, and to punifh and terrify them, fo as to prevent their making war upon the Spaniards, that he had determined to fall on them by anticipation. At hearing this avowal Cortes was highly enraged; he cenfured the conduct of Alvarado in the ftrongeft terms, and in this temper left him.

Alvarado farther faid, that one time when he was attacked by the Mexicans, he endeavoured to fire off one of his guns, and could not get the priming to light; but fometime after, when they were in very great danger, and expected all to have been killed, the piece went off of itfelf, and made fuch havock amongft the enemy that they were completely driven back, and the Spaniards thus miraculoufly faved. I heard feveral other foldiers alfo mention this as a fact; it was alfo faid, by Alvara-

do

do only, that when the garrifon was in great want of water, they fank a pit in the court, and immediately a fpring of the fweeteft water broke forth. I can declare, to my own knowledge, that there was a fpring in the city which very frequently threw up water tolerably frefh. Glory to God for all his mercies!

Some fay that it was avarice tempted Alvarado to make this attack, in order to pillage the Indians of the golden ornaments which they wore at their feftival. I never heard any juft reafons for the affertion, nor do I believe any fuch thing, although it is fo reprefented by Fra Bartholome de las Cafas; but for my part I am convinced, that his intention in falling on them at that time was, in order to ftrike terror into them, and prevent their infurrection, according to the faying, that, the firft attack is half the battle. A very bad plan as appeared by the refult, and it is certain, that after the affair at the temple, Montezuma did moft earneftly defire that they fhould not attack our people, but the Mexicans were fo enraged that they could not be reftrained.

Cortes during our march had expatiated to the new comers upon the power and influence he poffeffed, and the refpect with which he was treated in Mexico, and had filled their minds and heightened their expectations, with promifes and golden hopes. When on his return therefore he experienced the coldnefs and negligence of his reception in Tezcuco, and equal appearances thereof in Mexico, he grew very peevifh and irritable; and the officers of Montezuma coming to wait upon him, expreffing the wifh of their Sovereign to fee him, Cortes angrily exclaimed, "Away with him! The dog! why does he neglect to fupply " us." When the captains De Leon, De Oli, and De Lugo, heard this expreffion, they intreated him to be moderate, and reminded him of the former kindnefs and generofity of the King. But this feemed to irritate Cortes the more, confidering it a kind of cenfure, and he indignantly faid, "What compliment am I under to a dog who treated fecretly with " Narvaez, and as we fee neglects to fend provifions?" This the captains admitted ought to be done; and Cortes, confident in the great rein-

forcement

forcement of numbers he had obtained, continued a haughty demeanour. He in this manner now addreſſed the noblemen ſent to him by Montezuma, bidding them tell their maſter, immediately to cauſe markets to be held and proviſions ſupplied, and to beware of the conſequences of neglect. Theſe lords very well underſtood the purport of the injurious expreſſions which he had uſed, and on their return informed the King of what had paſſed. Whether it was from rage at the ſtory told by them, or the conſequence of a preconcerted plan to fall upon us, within a quarter of an hour after, a ſoldier entered our quarters, wounded dangerouſly, and in great hurry, and told us that the whole people were in arms. This man had been ſent by Cortes to bring to our quarters ſome Indian ladies, and amongſt them the daughter of Montezuma, whom Cortes, when he marched againſt Narvaez, had left in the care of their relation the Prince of Tacuba. He was on his return with them when he was attacked by the people who were aſſembled in great numbers, had broken a bridge upon the cauſeway of Tacuba, and had once had him in their hands and were hurrying him into a canoe to carry him off for ſacrifice, but that he extricated himſelf from them, with two dangerous wounds.

Cortes immediately on receiving the intelligence ordered out a party of four hundred men, under the command of Captain de Ordaz, to go and ſee what foundation there was for the account given by the ſoldier, and to endeavor if poſſible to pacify the minds of the people. De Ordaz had hardly proceeded the length of half a ſtreet, when he was attacked by immenſe numbers of Mexicans in the ſtreets, and on the terraces of the houſes, who by their firſt diſcharge killed eight ſoldiers on the ſpot, wounded moſt of the reſt, and De Ordaz himſelf in three places. Finding it therefore impoſſible to proceed, he retreated ſlowly to our quarters, in doing which he loſt another good ſoldier named Lezcano, who with a two handed ſword had performed many feats of great force and valour. Our quarters had been attacked by multitudes at the ſame moment; they poured in ſuch diſcharges of miſſile weapons upon us there that they immediately wounded upwards of forty ſix, twelve of

whom

whom afterwards died. The ſtreets were ſo crowded, that De Ordas when he endeavored to reach us could not proceed, and was inceſſantly attacked in front, in rear, and from the roofs of the houſes. Neither our fire arms, nor our good fighting could prevent the enemy from cloſing in upon us for a length of time; however De Ordaz at laſt forced his way back, with the loſs of twenty three men. The enemy ſtill continued their attacks, but all we had hitherto ſuffered was nothing to that which ſucceeded. They ſet fire to various parts of the buildings which we occupied, thinking to burn us alive, or ſtifle us with the ſmoke; and we were obliged to ſtop it by tearing down the building, or by throwing earth upon it. All the courts and open ſpaces of our quarters were covered with their arrows and miſſile weapons, and in repelling their attacks, repairing the breaches which they had made in the walls, dreſſing our wounds, and preparing for enſuing engagements, we paſſed that day and night.

As ſoon as the next morning dawned we ſallied out with our whole force upon the enemy, being determined if we could not conquer, to make them fear us. The Mexicans came to meet us with their whole force, and both parties fought deſperately; but as the numbers of our opponents were ſo immenſe, and as they conſtantly brought up freſh troops, even if we had been ten thouſand Hectors of Troy, and as many Roldans, we could not have beaten them off; nor can I give any idea of the deſperation of this battle; for though in every charge we made upon them we brought down thirty and even forty, it was of no avail; they came on even with more ſpirit than at firſt, nor could we, by our cannon or fire arms, make any impreſſion on them. If at any time they appeared to give ground it was only to draw us from our quarters, in order to enſure our deſtruction. Then the ſtones and darts thrown on us from the terraces of the houſes were intolerable. But I deſcribe it faintly; for ſome of our ſoldiers who had been in Italy ſwore, that neither amongſt Chriſtians nor Turks, nor the artillery of the King of France, had they ever ſeen ſuch deſperation as was manifeſted in the attacks of thoſe Indians. We were at length forced to retreat to our quarters, which we reached with great difficulty.

On

On this day we loft ten or twelve foldiers, and all of us who came back were feverely wounded. From the period of our return we were occupied in making preparation for a general fally on the next day but one, with four military machines conftructed of very ftrong timber, in the form of towers, and each capable of containing twenty five men under cover, with port holes for the artillery and alfo for the mufquetiers and crofsbow-men. This work occupied us for the fpace of one day, except that we were obliged likewife to repair the breaches made in our walls, and refift thofe who attempted to fcale them in twenty different places at the fame time. They continued their reviling language faying, that the voracious animals of their temples had now been kept two days fafting, in order to devour us at the period which was fpeedily approaching, when they were to facrifice us to their gods; that our allies were to be put up in cages to fatten, and that they would foon repoffefs our ill acquired treafure. At other times they plaintively called to us to give them their king, and during the night we were conftantly annoyed by fhowers of arrows, which they accompanied with fhouts and whiftlings.

At day break on the enfuing morning, after recommending ourfelves to God, we fallied out with our turrets, which as well as I recollect were called burros or mantas, in other places where I have feen them, with fome of our mufquetry and crofs-bows in front, and our cavalry occafionally charging. The enemy this day fhewed themfelves more determined than ever, and we were equally refolved to force our way to the great temple, although it fhould coft the life of every man of us; we therefore advanced with our turrets in that direction. I will not detail the defperate battle which we had with the enemy in a very ftrong houfe, nor how their arrows wounded our horfes, notwithftanding their armour, and if at any time the horfemen attempted to purfue the Mexicans, the latter threw themfelves into the canals, and others fallied out upon our people and maffacred them with large lances.

As to fetting fire to the buildings, or tearing them down, it was
utterly

utterly in vain to attempt; they all ſtood in the water, and only communicating by draw bridges, it was too dangerous to attempt to reach them by ſwimming, for they ſhowered ſtones from their ſlings, and maſſes of cut ſtone taken from the buildings, upon our heads, from the terraces of the houſes. Whenever we attempted to ſet fire to a houſe, it was an entire day before it took effect, and when it did, the flames could not ſpread to others, as they were ſeparated from it by the water, and alſo becauſe the roofs of them were terraced.

We at length arrived at the great temple, and immediately and inſtantly, above four thouſand Mexicans ruſhed up into it, without including in that number other bodies who occupied it before, and defended it againſt us with lances, ſtones, and darts. They thus prevented our aſcending for ſome time, neither turrets, nor muſquetry, nor cavalry availing, for although the latter body ſeveral times attempted to charge, the ſtone pavement of the courts of the temple was ſo ſmooth, that the horſes could not keep their feet, and fell. From the ſteps of the great temple they oppoſed us in front, and we were attacked by ſuch numbers on both ſides, that although our guns ſwept off ten or fifteen of them at each diſcharge, and that in each attack of our infantry we killed many with our ſwords, their numbers were ſuch that we could not make any effectual impreſſion, or aſcend the ſteps. We were then forced to abandon our turrets, which the enemy had deſtroyed, and with great concert, making an effort without them, we forced our way up. Here Cortes ſhewed himſelf the man that he really was. What a deſperate engagement we then had! every man of us was covered with blood, and above forty dead upon the ſpot. It was Gods will that we ſhould at length reach the place where we had put up the image of our Lady, but when we came there it was not to be found, and it ſeems that Montezuma, actuated either by fear or by devotion, had cauſed it to be removed. We ſet fire to the building, and burned a part of the temple of the gods Huitzilopochtli and Tezcatepuco. Here our Tlaſcalan allies ſerved us eſſentially. While thus engaged, ſome ſetting the temple on fire, others fighting, above three thouſand noble Mexicans with their

prieſts

priefts were about us, and attacking us, drove us down fix and even ten of the fteps, while others who were in the corridores, or within fide the railings and concavities of the great temple, fhot fuch clouds of arrows at us that we could not maintain our ground, when thus attacked from every part. We therefore began our retreat, every man of us being wounded, and forty fix left dead upon the fpot. We were purfued with a violence and defperation which is not in my power to defcribe, nor in that of any one to form an idea of who did not fee it. During all this time alfo other bodies of the Mexicans had been continually attacking our quarters, and endeavoring to fet fire to them. In this battle, we made prifoners two of the principal priefts. I have often feen this engagement reprefented in the paintings of the natives, both of Mexico and Tlafcala, and our afcent into the great temple. In thefe our party is reprefented with many dead, and all wounded. The fetting fire to the temple when fo many warriors were defending it in the corridores, railings, and concavities, and other bodies of them on the plain ground, and filling the courts, and on the fides, and our turrets demolifhed, is confidered by them as a moft heroic action.

With great difficulty we reached our quarters, which we found the enemy almoft in poffeffion of, as they had beaten down a part of the walls; but they defifted in a great meafure from their attacks on our arrival, ftill throwing in upon us however fhowers of arrows, darts, and ftones. The night was employed by us in repairing the breaches, in dreffing our wounds, burying our dead, and confulting upon our future meafures. No gleam of hope could be now rationally formed by us, and we were utterly funk in defpair. Thofe who had come with Narvaez fhowered maledictions upon Cortes, nor did they forget Velafquez by whom they had been induced to quit their comfortable and peaceable habitations in the ifland of Cuba. It was determined to try if we could not procure from the enemy a ceffation of hoftilities, on condition of our quitting the city; but at day break they affembled round our quarters and attacked them with greater fury than ever, nor could our fire arms repel them, although they did confiderable execution.

Cortes

Cortes perceiving how defperate our fituation was, determined that Montezuma fhould addrefs his fubjects from a terrace, and defire them to defift from their attacks, with an offer from us to evacuate Mexico. He accordingly fent to the King to defire him to do fo. When this was made known to Montezuma, he burft out into violent expreffions of grief faying, "What does he want of me now? I neither " defire to hear him, nor to live any longer, fince my unhappy fate " has reduced me to this fituation on his account." He therefore dif-miffed thofe fent to him with a refufal, adding as it is faid, that he wifhed not to be troubled any more with the falfe words and promifes of Cortes. Upon this the Reverend Father Fray Bartholome and Chrif-toval de Oli went to him, and addreffed him with the moft affectionate and perfuafive language, to induce him to appear, to which he repli-ed, that he did not believe that his doing fo would be of any avail, that the people had already elected another fovereign, and were determined never to permit one of us to quit the city alive. The enemy continued their attacks, and Montezuma was at length perfuaded. He accord-ingly came, and ftood at the railing of a terraced roof, attended by many of our foldiers, and addreffed the people below him, requefting, in very affectionate language, a ceffation of hoftilities, in order that we might quit the city. The chiefs and nobility, as foon as they perceived him coming forward, called to their troops to defift and be filent, and four of them approached, fo as to be heard and fpoken to by Montezuma. They then addreffed him, lamenting the misfortunes of him, his chil-dren, and family, and alfo told him that they had raifed Coadlavaca Prince of Iztapalapa to the throne, adding, that the war was drawing to a conclufion, and that they had promifed to their gods never to defift but with the total deftruction of the Spaniards; that they every day offered up prayers for his perfonal fafety, and as foon as they had refcu-ed him out of our hands, they would venerate him as before, and truft-ed that he would pardon them.

As they concluded their addrefs, a fhower of arrows and ftones fell about the fpot where Montezuma ftood, from which the Spaniards, in-terpofing

terpofing their bucklers, protected the King; but expecting that while fpeaking to his people they would not make another attack, they unguarded him for an inftant, and juft then three ftones and an arrow ftruck him in the head, arm, and leg.

The King when thus wounded refufed all affiftance, and we were unexpectedly informed of his death. Cortes and our captains wept for him, and he was lamented by them and all the foldiers who had known him, as if he had been their father; nor is it to be wondered at, confidering how good he was. It was faid that he had reigned feventeen years, and that he was the beft King Mexico had ever been governed by. It was alfo faid that he had fought and conquered in three occafions that he had been defied to the field, in the progrefs of fubjugating different ftates to his dominion.

All the endeavors of our Reverend Father Fray Bartholome, could not prevail on the King to embrace our faith, when he was told that his wounds were mortal, nor could he be induced to have them attended to. After the death of Montezuma, Cortes fent two prifoners, a nobleman and a prieft, to inform the new fovereign, Coadlavaca, and his chiefs, of the event, and how it had happened by the hands of his own fubjects. He directed them to exprefs our grief on the occafion, and our wifh that he fhould be interred with the refpect due to fo great a monarch. Cortes farther fignified to them, that he did not admit or acknowledge the right of the fovereign that they had chofen, but that the throne fhould be filled either by a fon of the great Montezuma, or his coufin who was with us in our quarters. Alfo, that we defired unmolefted egrefs from the city, on condition of our committing no more acts of hoftility by fire or fword. Cortes then caufed the body of the King to be borne out by fix noblemen, attended by moft of the priefts whom we had taken prifoners, and expofed it to public view. He alfo defired them to obey the laft injunctions of Montezuma, and to deliver his body to the Mexican chiefs. Thefe noblemen accordingly related the circumftances of the King's death to Coadlavaca, and we could hear

the

the exclamations of forrow which the people expreffed at the fight of his body. They now attacked us in our quarters with the greateft violence, and threatened us that within the fpace of two days we fhould pay with our lives the death of their king, and the difhonor of their gods, faying that they had chofen a fovereign whom we could not deceive, as we had done the good Montezuma.

In confequence of the fituation to which we were reduced, Cortes determined to make on the enfuing day another fally, and to march towards that part of the city which contained many houfes built on the firm ground, there to do all the injury we could, and that our cavalry taking advantage of the caufeway, fhould ride the enemy down; which he hoped would make them tired of hoftility, and induce them to come into terms. We accordingly made our fally, and proceeded to that part of the city, where, notwithftanding the refiftance and inceffant attacks of the enemy, we burned about twenty houfes, approaching very near the firm ground; but whatever injury we did them was dearly paid for by the lofs of twenty foldiers killed, nor could we get poffeffion of a fingle bridge, all of them being partly broken, and the enemy had alfo made barricades and parapets to obftruct the cavalry, in every part where they expected to be able to act. Thus our difficulties and troubles increafed upon us. This fally I recollect took place on a thurfday; Sandoval and many other good cavalry men were prefent at it; but thofe of Narvaez not being ufed to fervice, were timorous in comparifon to our veterans.

As our numbers diminifhed every day, whilft thofe of the enemy increafed, as alfo did the fury of their attacks, at the fame time that we from our wounds were lefs able to make refiftance; our powder being almoft exhaufted, our provifions and water intercepted, our friend the good Montezuma dead, and our propofals for peace rejected, the bridges by which we were to retreat broken down, and in fine, death before our eyes in every direction, it was determined by Cortes and all of the officers and foldiers, to quit the city during the night, as we hoped at

F f

that

that time to find the enemy lefs alert. In order to put them the more off their guard, we fent a meffage by a chief prieft, informing them, that if we were permitted to quit the city unmolefted within the fpace of eight days, we would furrender all the gold which was in our pof-feffion.

There was with us a foldier named Botello, of refpectable demean-our, who fpoke latin, had been at Rome, and was faid to be a necro-mancer; fome faid he had a familiar, and others called him an aftrolo-ger. This Botello had difcovered by his figures and aftrologies, and had predicted four days before, that if we did not quit Mexico on this night, not one of us fhould ever go out of it alive. He had alfo foretold that Cortes fhould undergo great revolutions of fortune, be deprived of his property, and honours, and afterwards rife to a greater ftate than ever; with many other things of this kind.

Orders were now given to make a portable bridge of very ftrong timber, to be thrown over the canals where the enemy had broken down the bridges, and for conveying, guarding, and placing this, were af-figned, one hundred and fifty of our foldiers and four hundred of the allies. The advanced guard was compofed of Sandoval, Azevido el Pu-lido, F. de Lugo, D. de Ordas, A. de Tapia, and eight more captains of thofe who came with Narvaez, having under them one hundred picked foldiers, of the youngeft and moft active. The rear guard was compofed of one hundred foldiers, moftly thofe of Narvaez, and many cavalry, under the command of Alvarado and Velafquez de Leon. The prifoners, with Donna Marina and Donna Luifa, were put under the care of thirty foldiers and three hundred Tlafcalans; and Cortes, with A. de Avila, C. de Oli, Bernardino Vafquez de Tapia and other offi-cers, with fifty foldiers, compofed a referve, to act wherever occafion fhould require.

By the time that all this was arranged night drew on. Cortes then ordered all the gold which was in his apartment to be brought to the

great

great faloon, which being done, he defired the officers of his Majefty, A. de Avila and Gonzalo Mexia, to take his Majefty's due, in their charge, affigning to them for the conveyance of it eight lame or wounded horfes, and upwards of eighty Tlafcalans. Upon thefe were loaded as much as they could carry of the gold which had been run into large bars, and much more remained heaped up in the faloon. Cortes then called to his fecretary Hernandez and other royal notaries and faid, " Bear witnefs that I can be no longer refponfible for this gold; here is " to the value of above fix hundred thoufand crowns, I can fecure no " more than what is already packed; let every foldier take what he will, " better fo than that it fhould remain for thofe dogs of Mexicans." As foon as he had faid this, many foldiers of thofe of Narvaez, and alfo fome of ours fell to work, and loaded themfelves with treafure. I never was avaricious, and now thought more of faving my life which was in much danger; however when the opportunity thus offered, I did not omit feizing out of a cafket, four calchihuis, thofe precious ftones fo highly efteemed amongft the Indians; and although Cortes ordered the cafket and its contents to be taken care of by his major domo, I luckily fecured thefe jewels in time, and afterwards found them of infinite advantage as a refource againft famine.

A little before midnight the detachment which took charge of the portable bridge fet out upon its march, and arriving at the firft canal or aperture of water, it was thrown acrofs. The night was dark and mifty, and it began to rain. The bridge being fixed, the baggage, artillery, and fome of the cavalry paffed over it, as alfo the Tlafcalans with the gold. Sandoval and thofe with him paffed, alfo Cortes and his party after the firft, and many other foldiers. At this moment the trumpets and fhouts of the enemy were heard, and the alarm was given by them, crying out, " Taltelulco, Taltelulco, out with your canoes! the Teules " are going, attack them at the bridges." In an inftant the enemy were upon us by land, and the lake and canals were covered with canoes. They immediately flew to the bridges, and fell on us there, fo that they intirely intercepted our line of march. As misfortunes do not come

fingle,

single, it also rained so heavily that some of the horses were terrifyed, and growing restive fell into the water, and the bridge was broken in at the same time. The enemy attacked us here now with redoubled fury, and our soldiers making a stout resistance, the aperture of water was soon filled with the dead and dying men, and horses, and those who were struggling to escape, all heaped together, with artillery, packs, and bales of baggage, and those who carried them. Many were drowned here, and many put into the canoes and carried off for sacrifice. It was dreadful to hear the cries of the unfortunate sufferers, calling for assistance and invoking the Holy Virgin or St. Jago, while others who escaped by swimming, or by clambering upon the chests, bales of baggage, and dead bodies, earnestly begged for help to get up to the causeway. Many who on their reaching the ground thought themselves safe, were there seized or knocked in the head with clubs.

Away went whatever regularity had been in the march at first; for Cortes and the captains and soldiers who were mounted clapt spurs to their horses and gallopped off, along the causeway; nor can I blame them, for the cavalry could do nothing against the enemy, of any effect; for when they attacked them, the latter threw themselves into the water on each side the causeway, and others from the houses with arrows, or on the ground with large lances, killed the horses. It is evident we could make no battle with them in the water, and without powder, and in the night, what else could we do than what we did; which was, to join in bodies of thirty or forty soldiers, and when the Indians closed upon us, to drive them off with a few cuts and thrusts of our swords, and then hurry on, to get over the causeway as soon as we could. As to waiting for one another, that would have lost us all; and had it happened in the day time, things would have been even worse with us. The escape of such as were fortunate enough to effect it, was owing to Gods mercy, who gave us force to do so; for the very sight of the number of the enemy who surrounded us, and carried off our companions in their canoes to sacrifice, was terrible. About fifty of us, soldiers of Cortes, and some of those of Narvaez, went together in a body, by the causeway;

way; every now and then parties of Indians came up, calling us Lui-
lones, a term of reproach, and attempting to feize us, and we, when
they came within our reach, facing about, repelling them with a few
thrufts of our fwords, and then hurrying on. Thus we proceeded, until we reached the firm ground near Tacuba, where Cortes, Sandoval,
De Oli, Salcedo, Dominguez, Lares, and others of the cavalry, with
fuch of the infantry foldiers as had croffed the bridge before it was deftroyed, were already arrived. When we came near them, we heard the
voices of Sandoval, De Oli, and De Morla, calling to Cortes who was
riding at their head, that he fhould turn about, and affift thofe who
were coming along the caufeway, and who complained that he had
abandoned them. Cortes replied that thofe who had efcaped owed it to
a miracle, and if they returned to the bridges all would lofe their lives.
Notwithftanding, he, with ten or twelve of the cavalry and fome of the
infantry who had efcaped unhurt countermarched, and proceeded along
the caufeway; they had gone however but a very fhort diftance when
they met P. de Alvarado with his lance in his hand, badly wounded,
and on foot, for his chefnut mare had been killed; he had with him
three of our foldiers, and four of thofe of Narvaez, all badly wounded,
and eight Tlafcalans covered with blood. While Cortes proceeded along
the caufeway, we repofed in the enclofed courts hard by Tacuba. Meffengers had already been fent out from the city of Mexico, to call the
people of Tacuba, Ezcapuzalco, and Teneyuca together, in order to intercept us. In confequence they now began to furround and harrafs us
with arrows, and ftones, and to attack us with lances headed with
the fwords which had fallen into their hands on the preceding night.
We made fome attacks upon them, and defended ourfelves as well as
we could.

To revert to Cortes and his companions, when they learned from Alvarado that they were not to expect to fee any more of our foldiers, the
tears ran from their eyes, for Alvarado had with him in the rear guard,
Velafquez de Leon, with above twenty more of the cavalry, and upwards of one hundred infantry. On enquiry Cortes was told that they
were

were all dead, to the number of one hundred and fifty and more. Alvarado alſo told them that after the horſes had been killed, about eighty
aſſembled in a body and paſſed the firſt aperture, upon the dead bodies
and heaps of luggage; I do not perfectly recollect if he ſaid that he paſſed upon the dead bodies, for we were more attentive to what he related
to Cortes of the deaths of J. Velaſquez and above two hundred more
companions, thoſe of Narvaez included, who were with him, and who
were killed at that canal. He alſo ſaid that at the other bridge God's
mercy ſaved them, and that the whole of the cauſeway was full of the
enemy.

As to that fatal bridge which is called the leap of Alvarado, I ſay
that no ſoldier thought of looking whether he leaped, much or little,
for we had enough to do to ſave our own lives. It muſt however have
been as he ſtated when he met Cortes, that he paſſed it upon the dead
bodies and baggage, for if he had attempted to ſuſtain himſelf upon his
lance, the water would have been too deep for him to have reached the
bottom of it; and the aperture was too wide, and the ſides too high for
him to have leaped, let him have been ever ſo active. For my part
I aver that he could not have leaped it in any manner, for in about a year
after, when we inveſted Mexico, I was engaged with the enemy on
that which is now called the bridge of the leap of Alvarado, for they
had there made breaſtworks and barricades; and we many times conver-
ſed upon the ſubject at the ſpot, and all of us agreed that it could not
have happened. But as ſome will inſiſt upon the reality of it I repeat it
again, it could not have been done, and let thoſe who wiſh to aſcertain
it view the place; the bridge is there, and the depth of the water will
prove no lance could reach to the bottom. There was in Mexico afterwards one Ocampo, a ſoldier who came with Garay, a prating fellow
and very ſcurrilous, amuſing himſelf with making defamatory libels.
Many of thoſe he made upon our captains, too bad to be repeated. He
ſaid of Alvarado, that he left his companion Velaſquez and two hundred
more, and that fear made him give that great ſpring, for that as the ſaying goes, he leaped for his life.

As

As our captains found from the information of Alvarado that they were not to expect any more of our companions, for that the caufeway was full of warriors of the enemy, and if any had hitherto efcaped they muft now be intercepted, as we alfo found that all the people of thofe countries were preparing to attack us in Tacuba, it was determined under the guidance of fix or feven of our allies well acquainted with the country, to endeavor to reach Tlafcala. Accordingly we fet out, and proceeding by an indirect road came to fome houfes hard by a temple on a hill. During our march we were harraffed by the enemy, who threw ftones and fhot their arrows at us. I fear to tire the reader with the prolixity of thofe repeated details, but I am compelled to relate what was of fuch defperate confequence to us, for many of us were in this manner killed. Here we defended ourfelves, and took what care we could of our wounds. As to provifions, we had none.

After the conqueft of Mexico, a church was founded on the fcite of this temple, and dedicated to Nueftra Senora de los Remedios, and thither many ladies and inhabitants of Mexico go in proceffion, and to pay the nine days devotions.

Our wounds, having taken cold and being only bound with rags, were now in a miferable fituation, and very painful; we had alfo to deplore the lofs of many valiant companions. As for thofe of Narvaez, moft of them perifhed in the water, loaded with gold. Numbers of Tlafcalans alfo loft their lives in the fame manner. Poor Botello too! the aftrologer! his ftars bore an evil afpect for he was killed with the reft. The fons of Montezuma, Cacamatzin, and all the other prifoners, amongft whom were fome princes, loft their lives on this fatal night. All our artillery was loft, we had very few crofs-bows, only twenty three horfes, and our future profpect was very melancholy, from our uncertainty as to the reception we might meet in Tlafcala, which was our only refource.

Having dreffed our wounds and made arrows for our crofs-bows,
and

and being inceffantly harraffed in our prefent poft, we proceeded at midnight upon our journey, under the guidance of our faithful Tlafcalans.
Thofe who were very badly wounded we carried between us; the lame
were fupported upon crutches, and fome who were utterly unable to help
themfelves on, were placed upon the croups of lame horfes. Thus,
with what cavalry we had able to act, in front and on the flanks, and
as many of the infantry as were fit to bear arms making head to the
enemy, we proceeded on our march, our wounded Spaniards and allies
in the centre, the reft oppofing the enemy, who continued to follow,
harrafs, and revile us, faying we were now going to meet our deftruction. Words which we did not at that time underftand.

I have hitherto forgotten to mention the fatisfaction we had, in
feeing Donna Marina and Donna Luifa rejoin us. Having croffed the
bridge amongft the firft, they had been faved by the exertions of two
of the brothers of Donna Luifa, all the reft of the female Indians having been loft there. On this day we arrived at a great town named Gu-
altitlan, from whence we continued our march, harraffed by the enemy,
whofe numbers and boldnefs increafed, infomuch that they killed two
of our lame foldiers and one horfe in a bad pafs, wounding many more.
Having repulfed them, we proceeded until we arrived at fome villages,
and halting there for the night, we made our fupper on the horfe which
had been killed. On the next morning we fet out very early, and having proceeded little more than a league, juft as we began to think ourfelves in fafety, three of our vedettes came in with a report that the
whole plains were covered with the armies of the enemy. This intelligence was truly frightful and we felt it as fuch, but not fo as to prevent
our determination to conquer or die, or our arranging all matters to the
beft effect for action.

A halt being made, orders were given to the cavalry, that they
fhould charge at half fpeed, not ftopping to make thrufts, but pointing
the lances at the faces of the enemy, until they were put to flight; the
infantry were warned to thruft with their fwords, and to pafs them
clear

clear through the bodies of their opponents, fo that at worft we fhould fell our lives dearly, and this being done, as we faw that the enemy began to furround us, after recommending ourfelves to God and the Holy Virgin, and invoking the aid of St. Jago, the cavalry formed in bodies of fives, and the infantry in concert with them, proceeded to the attack.

Oh what it was to fee this tremendous battle! how we clofed foot to foot, and with what fury the dogs fought us! fuch wounding as there was amongft us with their lances and clubs and two handed fwords, while our cavalry, favoured by the plain ground, rode through them at will, galloping at half fpeed, and bearing down their opponents with couched lances, ftill fighting manfully, though they and their horfes were all wounded; and we of the infantry, negligent of our former hurts, and of thofe which we now received, clofed with the enemy, redoubling our efforts to bear them down with our fwords.

Cortes, De Oli, Alvarado mounted on a horfe of one of the foldiers of Narvaez, and Sandoval, though all wounded, continued to ride through them. Cortes now called out to us to ftrike at the chiefs; for they were diftinguifhed by great plumes of feathers, golden ornaments, richly wrought arms, and devices.

Then to hear the valiant Sandoval, how he encouraged us crying out, "Now gentlemen is the day of victory; put your truft in God, " we fhall furvive for he preferves us for fome good purpofe." All the foldiers felt determined to conquer, and thus animated as we were by our Lord Jefus Chrift, and our lady the Virgin Mary, as alfo by St. Jago who undoubtedly affifted us, as certified by a chief of Guatimotzin who was prefent in the battle, we continued, notwithftanding many had received wounds and fome of our companions were killed, to maintain our ground.

It was the will of God, that Cortes, accompanied by the captains

G g

De

De Oli, Sandoval, Alvarado, and several others, should reach that part of the army of the enemy which was the post of their general in chief, who was distinguished by a standard, arms covered with gold, and a great penache ornamented in the same manner. As soon as Cortes perceived the chief who bore the standard, and who was surrounded by many others bearing also great penaches of gold, he cried out to Alvarado, Sandoval, De Oli, Avila, and the rest, "Now gentlemen, let " us charge them." Then, recommending themselves to God, they rode into the thickest of them, and Cortes with his horse struck the Mexican chief, and threw down the standard; the cavaliers who supported him at the same moment effectually breaking this numerous body. The chief who bore the standard, not having fallen, in the charge made upon him by Cortes, Juan de Salamanca, mounted on his good pyed mare, pursued him, and having killed him, seized the rich penache which he bore, and presented it to Cortes, saying, that as he had given the Mexican general the first blow, and struck down his standard, the trophy of the conquest was due to him.

It was God's will, that, on the death of their general, and of many other chiefs who surrounded him being known, the enemy should relax in their efforts, and begin to retreat. As soon as this was perceived by us, we forgot our hunger, thirst, fatigue, and wounds, and thought of nothing but victory, and pursuit. Our cavalry followed them up close, and our allies, now become lions, mowed down all before them with the arms which the enemy threw away in their flight.

As soon as our cavalry returned from the pursuit, we all gave thanks to God, for never had there appeared so great a force together in that country, being the whole of the warriors of Mexico, Tezcuco, and Saltocan, all determined not to leave a trace of us upon the earth. The whole nobility of these nations were assembled, magnificently armed, and adorned with gold, penaches, and devices. This battle was fought near a place named Obtumba. I have frequently seen it represented in paintings amongst the Mexicans, in the same manner as

I have

I have the other battles fought by us antecedently to the final conqueſt. I muſt now recall to the readers recollection, that our entry into Mexico to relieve Alvarado was on the day of St. John in the month of June one thouſand five hundred and twenty. We entered that city with upwards of one thouſand three hundred ſoldiers, cavalry included, which latter body was ninety ſeven in number, and of our infantry eighty were croſsbow-men, and as many muſqueteers. We had alſo with us a great train of artillery and two hundred Tlaſcalan allies. Our flight from Mexico was on the tenth of July following, and the battle of Obtumba was fought on the fourteenth day of that month.

I will now give an account of all our countrymen who loſt their lives in Mexico, at the cauſeway, in battle, and on the road. In five days were killed and ſacrificed upwards of eight hundred and ſeventy ſoldiers, including ſeventy two of thoſe of Narvaez put to death together with five Caſtillian women, in a place named Tuſtepeque. One thouſand two hundred and upwards of our allies of Tlaſcala were alſo killed. Juan de Alcantara and two more, who came for the ſhare of the gold aſſigned to them, were robbed and murdered, and if we examine throughout we ſhall find, that all who were concerned with the treaſure came to ill fortune. Thus it was with the ſoldiers of Narvaez, who periſhed in a much greater proportion than ours did, on account of their having followed the dictates of their avarice.

After the battle we continued our march to Tlaſcala, chearfully, and eating certain gourds named ayotes, which we found by the way, the enemy only ſhewing themſelves at a diſtance, until we arrived at a village where we took up our quarters in a ſtrong temple, and halted for the night, occaſionally alarmed by the Mexicans, who kept about us as it were to ſee us out of their country. From this place we to our great joy perceived the mountains of Tlaſcala, for we were anxious to be convinced of the fidelity of our friends, and to know ſomething of our companions in Villa Rica. Cortes warned us, as we were ſo few in number and had eſcaped by God's mercy, to be cautious not to give

offence;

offence; this he particularly enforced to the foldiers of Narvaez who were not fo much habituated to difcipline. He added that he hoped to find our allies fteady to us, but that if it turned out otherwife, though but four hundred and forty ftrong, ill armed, and wounded, we had vigorous bodies and ftout hearts to carry us through.

We now arrived at a fountain on the fide of fome hills, where is a circular rampart built in old·times, at the boundary of the ftates of Mexico and Tlafcala. Here we repofed, and then proceeded to a town named Gualiopar, where we procured a little food which we were obliged to pay for, and halted one day. As foon as our arrival was known in the head town of Tlafcala, our friends Maxicatzin, Xicotenga, Chichimecatecle, the chief of Guaxocingo, and others, came to fee and embrace Cortes and the reft of our captains and foldiers. They wept for our loffes, and kindly blamed Cortes for having neglected the warning they had given him of Mexican treachery. They then invited us to their town, rejoicing at our efcape, and congratulating us on our valiant actions. They alfo affured us that they were affembling thirty thoufand warriors to join us at Obtumba. Cortes thanked, and diftributed prefents to all. They were rejoiced at feeing Donna Marina and Donna Luifa, and lamented the lofs of others; Maxicatzin in particular bewailed his daughter, and V. de Leon to whom he had given her. Thus we were received by our friends in Tlafcala, where we repofed after our dangers. Cortes lodged in the houfe of Maxicatzin, Alvarado in that of Xicotenga; and here we recovered from our wounds, lofing but four of our number.

THE TRUE HISTORY

OF

THE CONQUEST OF MEXICO.

PART THE SECOND.

CHAPTER I.

Tlaſcala, July, 1520. Tranſactions and occurrences there. Foundation of the colony of Segura de la Frontera. Subjugation of the neighbouring diſtricts by the Spaniards.

WE were thus, as I have mentioned, by the friendſhip of the Tlaſcalans, hoſpitably received and entertained in their city, after our fatigues, dangers, and loſſes, in the retreat from Mexico.

One of the firſt things done by Cortes on our arrival was, to enquire after the gold which had been brought there, to the value of forty thouſand crowns, and which was the ſhare of the garriſon of Villa Rica.

Rica, He was informed by the Tlascalan chiefs, and also by one of our invalids who remained there when we marched to Mexico, that the persons who had been sent from Villa Rica to receive it, had, on their return, been robbed and murdered on the road, at the time we were engaged in hostilities with the Mexicans. Another cause of uneasiness to us was, our uncertainty as to the situation of our countrymen at Villa Rica. Letters were sent, to inform them of the events which had lately taken place, and desiring them to send us what arms and ammunition they could spare, and a strong reinforcement. We were informed by the return of the messengers, that all continued well in the neighbourhood of that garrison. The reinforcement also, which had been required, was immediately sent. It consisted of seven men in the whole, three of whom were sailors, and every one of them invalids. They were commanded by a soldier named Lencero, the same who kept the inn at present called by his name. For a long time afterwards, a reinforcement of Lencero, was a proverbial expression with us.

We had now some trouble given us by the younger Xicotenga, This chief on hearing of our misfortunes in Mexico, and of our being in march for his country, conceived the project of taking us by surprise, and putting us all to death; for which purpose he was very active in forming his party, and having assembled many of his friends, relations, and adherents, he exposed to them the facility with which it could be done. These intrigues however could not go on long, without coming to the knowledge of his father, who reproached him severely for his treacherous conduct, assuring him that if it came to be known, it would cost the lives of him and all those concerned with him. The young man however persevered, paying no regard to what his father said, and the affair at length coming to the ears of his mortal enemy Chichimecatecle, he immediately gave information of it; whereupon, a council was summoned of all the chiefs to take the affair into consideration, and Xicotenga was brought prisoner before them. Maxicatzin was the orator upon the occasion and spoke at considerable length in favour of the Spaniards; he said that prosperity had attended their nation ever since

our

our arrival amongſt them. That we had enabled them to eat ſalt with their proviſions, and that we were certainly thoſe of whom their anceſtors had ſpoken. He then reprobated and expoſed the conduct of the younger Xicotenga. In reply to this, and to the diſcourſe of his father to the ſame purpoſe, the young man made uſe of ſuch outrageous and diſreſpectful language, as induced them to ſeize him by the collar, and throw him down the ſteps of the building into the ſtreet, and he very narrowly eſcaped with his life; but Cortes did not think it prudent in his preſent ſituation to carry matters any farther. Such was the fidelity of our Tlaſcalan allies, with whom we at this time ſtaid two and twenty days.

Cortes meditated an attack upon the adjoining provinces of Tepeaca and Zacatula, on account of the murders committed by theſe people upon the Spaniards, and determined to ſet out upon it, at the expiration of the above mentioned period; but when he came to propoſe this to his troops, he found the univerſal ſentiment of the ſoldiers of Narvaez decidedly againſt it. They thought that they never could get back ſoon enough to their houſes and mines in the Iſland of Cuba, and the ſlaughter of Mexico, and battle of Obtumba, made them deſire to renounce all connexion with Cortes, his riches, and his conqueſts. But beyond all others Andres de Duero, his friend and companion, moſt heartily curſed the day he had embarked with him in the buſineſs, and the gold which he had been forced to leave in the ditches of Mexico. They all totally declined any connexion with his new ſchemes, and finding that words did not avail them they made a requiſition in form to that effect, ſtating the inſufficiency of our force, and demanding licences to return to Cuba. Cortes having received and read the memorial, replied to it, giving at leaſt ten reaſons for his plan, to every one they alledged againſt it; his own ſoldiers alſo addreſſed him on the occaſion, requeſting him on no account to give permiſſion to any one to depart, but that we ſhould all remain together, as being moſt conducive to the ſervice of God, and his Majeſty. At length they were obliged to acquieſce, with a very ill grace, and much murmuring againſt Cortes, and his expeditions, and againſt us who ſupported him in them, and who as they ſaid had no-

H h

thing

thing to lofe but our lives. Cortes on his part made them a general promife, that by the next convenient opportunity he would fend them to their Ifland of Cuba.

The hiftorian Gomara in his account of this tranfaction makes no diftinction between us and the foldiers of Narvaez, as if we were equally concerned in prefenting the memorial; and this he does in order to enhance the merits of his hero, Cortes, and to depreciate us the true conquerors of Mexico, becaufe we did not think it became us to bribe him with gifts to fpeak favourably of us, when we were thofe, and thofe only, who fupported Cortes. And now this hiftorian would annihilate our reputations, in faying, forfooth, that we memorialled!!

It would have better become this hiftorian to attend more to matters of fact, and lefs to his figures of rhetoric in what he writes. I have been aftonifhed at that part of his relation, where he affigns the victory at Obtumba folely to the valor of Cortes. I have faid before, that it was in the firft inftance owing to God's mercy; I fay alfo that Cortes did every thing that ought to be expected from a wife and valiant general, and that he owed his fuccefs, under God, to the ftout and valiant captains, and to us brave foldiers, who broke the force of the enemy, and fupported him by fighting in the manner we fought, and as I have related. What that hiftorian fays relative to his charging the general and bearer of the royal ftandard of Mexico is true, and it was Juan de Salamanca, afterwards alcalde major of Guacacualco, who killed him with his lance, and prefented the ornamented plume to Cortes; which plume his Majefty was afterwards pleafed to give Salamanca in his coat of arms. Not that I am unwilling to afcribe all due honour to our Cortes; for I know that he deferves it; and if it was the cuftom, as formerly, to give triumphs to generals, he is more worthy of one than any Roman. Gomara alfo greatly exaggerates the numbers of our Indian allies, and the population of the country beyond all reafon; for it was not the fifth part of what he reprefents it. According to his account there would have been more thoufands here, than inhabit all Caftille; but where

he

he has written eighty thoufand we fhould read one thoufand. All this he has done in order to make his narrative the more agreable. In my hiftory I tell the truth, word for word as it happened, without looking to ornaments of rhetoric; for I confider myfelf obliged to adhere to matter of fact, and do not deal in flatteries.

We now fet out on our march, to punifh the diftricts of Cachula, Tepeaca, and Tecamachalco, without artillery or fire arms of any kind, for all had been left in the ditches of Mexico. Our force confifted of fixteen cavalry and four hundred and twenty infantry, moftly armed with fword and target, with about four thoufand Tlafcalans. We halted at night, at the diftance of three leagues from Tepeaca; but the people of the place had deferted their houfes on our approach. We made fome prifoners on our way, by whom Cortes fent to the chiefs, to inform them, that we came for the purpofe of obtaining juftice for the murder of eighteen Spaniards, who had been without any caufe put to death in croffing their territories; and alfo to know the reafon of their entertaining Mexican troops, and to warn them, that if they did not immediately treat with us for peace, we would make war againft them with fire and fword. However terrible our language was, that of their anfwer conveyed by our meffengers and two Mexicans, was much more fo; for the Mexicans were elevated by their fucceffes againft us at the bridges. Cortes treated them very kindly, and declared every wifh to forget and forgive the paft, but all could not do; they fent back for anfwer, that if we did not return immediately, they would put us all to death and make a feaft upon our bodies.

Upon this Cortes called a council of the officers, and it was then determined, that a full ftatement of all which had paffed fhould be officially drawn up by a royal notary, whereby all the Mexicans and allies of the Mexicans who had killed Spanifh fubjects, after having given obedience to his Majefty, fhould be declared in a ftate of flavery. This being duly drawn up and attefted, we once more fent to require them to come in, giving them notice of the confequences of their contumacy,

but

but they returned an anſwer ſimilar to their former one. Both ſides then prepared for battle, and on the next day we came to an action with them. This battle taking place in open fields of maiz, our cavalry ſpeedily put the enemy to flight, with confiderable loſs, though they made a ſtout reſiſtance; but our allies fought gallantly, and purſued them hotly, and we took many boys, for ſlaves.

The Mexicans being thus defeated, the natives came in, to ſue for peace; we accordingly proceeded to the town of Tepeaca, to receive their ſubmiſſion, and on that ſpot was founded our ſettlement of Segura de la Frontera, the ſituation being eligible, as on the road to Villa Rica, and in a fertile diſtrict. The municipal officers were immediately appointed, and the iron brand was made here, for the purpoſe of marking thoſe natives who were taken for ſlaves; they were marked with the letter G, for "Guerra," or war. We made excurſions through the diſtrict, and to the towns of Cachula, (where they had put fifteen Spaniards to death in the houſes,) Tecamechalco, Las Guayavas, and many others whoſe names I do not recollect; taking a number of priſoners, who were immediately branded for ſlaves. By theſe means, in about the ſpace of ſix weeks, we reduced the people to order and obedience.

At this period another prince of the blood royal was elected to the throne of Mexico, for the former one who had expelled us from that city, was dead of the ſmall pox. The new king was named Guatimotzin; he was a young man about the age of twenty five years, of elegant appearance, very brave, and ſo terrible to his own ſubjects that they all trembled at the ſight of him. When the intelligence reached this prince of what had happened in Tepeaca, he began to be apprehenſive for his other provinces, neglecting, however, nothing that it was in his power to do, to induce the chiefs to continue ſteady to him; and he alſo ſent confiderable bodies of troops to watch our movements.

Cortes now received letters from Villa Rica informing him, that a veſſel had arrived at the port, commanded by a gentleman named Pedro
Barba,

Barba, who was his intimate friend. He had been lieutenant under Velafquez at the Havannah, and had now brought with him thirteen foldiers and two horfes; he alfo brought letters from Velafquez the governor of Cuba to Narvaez, who was thought to be by this time all powerful in New Spain, ordering him, if Cortes was not already dead, to fend him to Cuba, that he might be thence tranfmitted to Caftille, fuch being the directions of the bifhop of Burgos. As foon as Pedro Barba arrived in the harbour, the officer whom Cortes had appointed admiral went to vifit him, taking with him in his boat a ftrong crew, with their arms concealed. When he came on board, he faluted Barba and the reft courteoufly, and enquired after the health of the governor of Cuba. The others in their turn enquired after Narvaez, and what had become of Cortes. They were told that Cortes was a fugitive with about twenty of his companions, and that Narvaez had eftablifhed himfelf, and was in poffeffion of great riches. They then invited Barba and the reft on fhore to refrefh themfelves, to which they affenting defcended into the boats, where they were bid to furrender themfelves inftantly prifoners to Cortes. They had no alternative, and were obliged to fubmit. The fhip was difmantled, and the captain and crew fent to us in Tepeaca, to our great fatisfaction, for though we did not fuffer much in the field, yet continual fatigue had made us very unhealthy, five of our foldiers having died of pleurifies within a fortnight. With this party came Francifco Lopez, afterwards regidor of Guatimala. Barba was exceedingly well received by Cortes, who was informed by him that he might expect the arrival of another fmall veffel with provifions, within the fpace of a week, which accordingly happened. On board the laft mentioned fhip came a gentleman, native of Medina del Campo, by name Rodorigo de Lobera, eight foldiers, and one horfe. Our friends purfued the fame method with this veffel that they had done with the former, and with the fame fuccefs. The party joined us in a few days, it being no fmall fatisfaction to us, thus to find our army recruiting its numbers.

The new king of Mexico having fent large bodies of troops to thefe provinces

provinces that were neareſt to the Spaniſh army, they became very diſorderly, robbing and outraging the people. Theſe provocations induced the natives to ſend four chiefs ſecretly to negotiate with Cortes, offering to ſurrender themſelves to him, provided he would give them his aſſiſtance to expell the Mexicans. Cortes immediately acceded to the propoſal, and ordered for this ſervice the whole of the cavalry and croſsbow-men, under the command of Chriſtoval de Oli. A conſiderable number alſo of Tlaſcalans were joined in the expedition. Several of the captains who had come with Narvaez were appointed to command in this detachment, which amounted in the whole to above three hundred ſoldiers. As our people were on their march, converſing with the Indians, they received ſuch accounts from them of the force of the enemy, as entirely deprived the ſoldiers of Narvaez of what little inclination they ever had for military expeditions, and made them doubly anxious to return to their Iſland of Cuba, being utterly averſe from a repetition of the days of Mexico, and Obtumba. They began to grow very mutinous, and told their chief in plain terms, that if he was determined to perſiſt in his attempt, he might do it by himſelf, for that they were all reſolved to quit him. De Oli remonſtrated with them upon the impropriety of ſuch conduct, in which he was ſupported by all the ſoldiers of Cortes, but in vain; he was compelled to yield to their perverſeneſs, and halt at Cholula, from whence he wrote to Cortes, informing him of his ſituation. When Cortes received his letter, he immediately returned an angry meſſage, ordering him poſitively to advance with his whole force, at all events. When De Oli received this, he fell in a violent rage with thoſe who had brought that reprimand on him, and ordering the whole to march immediately, declared he would ſend back any one who heſitated to Cortes, to be treated by him as a coward deſerved.

When he arrived within a league of Guacacualco, he was met by ſome chiefs, who informed him in what manner he might beſt come upon the enemy. Having in conſequence ſettled his plan of attack, he marched againſt, and after a ſharp action defeated the Mexican troops,
and

and put them completely to flight, with the lofs on his part, of two horfes, and eight wounded. Our allies this day made a great flaugh-ter of the Mexicans, who fell back, and rallied at a large town called Ozucar, where were other great bodies of their troops. Here they made a poft, fortifying themfelves and breaking down the bridges; but De Oli, turned into a tiger by the reproof of Cortes, purfued them without halting, with as many of his troops as he could bring up. By the af-fiftance of his Indian friends of Guacachula, he contrived to pafs the river, and falling on the Mexicans, difperfed them again, with the lofs of two more horfes killed; his own horfe was alfo wounded in feveral places, and De Oli himfelf received two wounds. Here he halted for two days after the action, and all the principal people waited on him, to fubmit as vaffals to his Majefty. Their allegiance being accepted, and the country reftored to peace, he returned with his force to the town of Segura de la Frontera.

Not having been on this expedition, the account I have given is fuch as was related to me, by thofe who were. De Oli was received by Cortes and all of us with great fatisfaction; we laughed heartily at him for his counter march, in which he joined with us, and fwore that for the next expedition he was fent on, he would take the poor fol-diers of Cortes, and not the rich planters of Narvaez, whofe minds were more intent upon their houfes and eftates, than upon feats of arms; and who were much more ready to command, than to obey. Gomara fays that it was the people of Guaxocingo who gave the information to the officers of Narvaez; but this is abfurd, for the laft mentioned town was entirely out of their route, and it is exactly the fame thing as fay-ing, that if we were to fet out now from Medina del Campo to travel to Salamanca, we fhould go round by Valladolid.

While we were here, Cortes received letters from Villa Rica, whereby he was informed, that a veffel had arrived there commanded by a perfon of the name of Camargo, having on board upwards of fe-venty foldiers, all very fickly. She was one of thefe which had been

fent

fent to eftablifh a colony at Panuco, * and brought intelligence that the other captain who had been fent thither, named Pineda, with all his foldiers, had been put to death by the Indians; and that their fhipping had been burned. Camargo therefore finding the ill fuccefs of that attempt, had come to Villa Rica for affiftance, his men being afflicted with liver complaints, which their yellow and dropfical appearance demonftrated. This officer was very well acquainted with the fituation of affairs, and had been it is faid, a Dominican friar. Having difembarked his foldiers, he fet out with them, and arrived by flow marches at La Frontera, where they were kindly received by Cortes, and attended with as much care as we could beftow upon them, but the captain and many of the foldiers very foon died. On account of their morbid colour and fwollen bodies, we ufed to call them "the green paunches." In order to avoid the interference of foreign matters with the thread of my narrative, I will now inform my reader, that one after another, at different and irregular periods, all the remains of this armament arrived at the port of Villa Rica. Amongft others was an Arragonian named Miguel diaz de Auz. He brought upwards of fifty foldiers, with feven horfes; with which he immediately joined us, being the moft effectual reinforcement we had for a long time received. This Captain de Auz ferved very well during the war in New Spain; it was he who afterwards had a law fuit with a brother in law of Cortes, named Andres de Barrios, whom we ufed to call "the dancer." The law fuit was about the divifion of Meftitan, which was awarded afterwards as follows; he had the furplus of the rents, beyond two thoufand five hundred crowns, on condition of not entering upon the diftrict for the fpace of two years, becaufe he was accufed of having killed Indians there, and in other places where he had been. Another of Garay's veffels arrived fhortly after at our port. In this came an officer named Ramirez, called by us, "the old." He brought with him forty foldiers, ten horfes, crofs-bows and other arms. Thus Garay continually fent us reinforcements, thinking that his colony was going on well in Panuco. All thefe foldiers joined us at Tepeaca. Thofe who came with Miguel diaz de Auz, as they were plump and in good condition, we named "the Sir loins;" and as the

foldiers

---

* By F. de Garay governor of Jamaica.

foldiers of old Ramirez wore cotton armour which was very thick and clumfy, fo that no arrow could penetrate through it, we called them "the pack-horfes."

Cortes having been thus reinforced to the amount of an hundred and fifty foldiers and twenty horfes, determined to punifh the Cacatame and Xalacingo Indians, with feveral others who had been concerned in the murders of Spaniards. Twenty cavalry and twelve crofsbow-men, made part of the force fent againft them, the whole of which confifted of two hundred of the veterans of the army of Cortes, and a body of Tlafcalans, commanded by Gonzalo de Sandoval. Our detachment received intelligence that the enemy were in arms, fortified, and rein-forced by Mexican troops. Sandoval therefore arranged his plan of at-tack, firft fending to inform them, that he would pardon the deaths of the Spaniards, provided they fubmitted, and returned the treafure. The anfwer they fent back was, that they would eat him, and all thofe with him, in the fame manner that they had done the others. Sandoval then proceeded to attack them, which he did in two places at the fame inftant, and notwithftanding that both the natives and the Mexicans fought with great fpirit, they had no better fuccefs than on former oc-cafions, being defeated and purfued with a confiderable lofs. Our peo-ple after the action going into fome of their temples, found cloaths, arms, bridles and faddles, prefented as offerings to their gods. Sando-val declared his intention of halting three days there, and he alfo now again demanded from them the treafure which had been taken. They readily fubmitted themfelves to his Majefty, but in regard to the trea-fure, they faid, that it was no longer in their power, having been tranf-mitted to Mexico. Sandoval referred them to the general for their par-dons, and returned with his troops, having made a confiderable number of women and boys prifoners, all of whom were immediately marked with the iron. I was not on the expedition, being ill of a fever, and throwing up blood at the mouth; but I was bled plentifully, and thanks to God recovered. In confequence of the directions given by Sandoval, the chiefs of thefe nations, and alfo of many others in their neighbourhood,

I i

came

came in and made their submissions to Cortes. This expedition was productive of the very best effects. The fame of Cortes extended through all their countries, for valor and for justice, and he was much more dreaded and respected than Guatimotzin, the new sovereign of Mexico; insomuch that his decision was requested in the most important litigations. The small pox was now so prevalent in New Spain, that many of the great lords of the natives died of it. In such cases the claimants to the succession called on Cortes for, and abided by his decision, as sovereign lord of the country. There were at this period great disputes relative to the lordships of Ozucar and Guacachula, which being referred to Cortes he decided the cause in favor of a nephew of Montezuma, whose sister had married the cacique of that district.

At this time Cortes sent Sandoval to punish the people of the district called Cocotlan, where they had put to death nine Spaniards. Sandoval took with him thirty cavalry and one hundred infantry, with a strong body of Tlascalans. On his entry into the district he summoned these people, holding out as usual threats on the one hand, and invitations on the other, to which the Indians replied, that they acknowledged no other government than that of Mexico, and that they were very well able to defend themselves. They had here a considerable force of Mexican auxiliaries, who encouraged them to resistance. As soon as Sandoval received this message he put his troops in order, and cautioned his allies not to advance to the attack at first, on account of their disordering the cavalry, but to wait until the enemy were broken by our troops, and then to fall on the Mexicans. Two large bodies of the enemy were met by our army, in a strong situation; they made a firm resistance, and before Sandoval could extricate his cavalry from the difficult and rocky ground, they had killed one and wounded nine of his horses and four soldiers. At length having driven them from this post, he advanced to their town, and there assaulting them and the reinforcements which had joined them, at their post in the temples, and large walled inclosures, with the good assistance of his Indian allies, whose keenness was increased by the abundance of plunder, he totally defeated
ed

ed, and put them to flight. Sandoval halted here for two days, during which the chiefs came in and made their submissions. He demanded of them the property and effects of the Spaniards whom they had put to death, but they replied that it was out of their power to return them, they having already burned the whole. They also said that most of the Spaniards they had killed were eaten, five of them having been sent to their monarch Guatimotzin. They promised a plentiful supply of provisions, apologized for what was passed, and Sandoval being able to do no more was fain to accept their submissions.

As all this country was now brought under subjection, Cortes determined, with the approbation of his Majesty's officers to mark the prisoners and slaves, previous to the taking out the royal fifth, and his own. An order was in consequence given out, that the soldiers should bring all their prisoners to an appointed place, which was a large house in the town, for this purpose. It was accordingly done; they consisted of women, boys, and girls of the Indians, for as to the men they were too troublesome to keep, and our Tlascalan friends did us all the service we could desire from them. The prisoners remained in confinement during the night, and in the morning the repartition took place. First the royal fifth was selected, and then that of Cortes; and thus far all went on very well, but when the soldiers shares came to be allotted, behold! we found that some one had been there in the night, and taken every handsome and good Indian that was there, leaving us nothing but a herd of old, ugly, and miserable jades. This of course made a great murmur amongst the soldiers, who loudly charged Cortes with having conveyed away and concealed all the valuable slaves, and the soldiers of Narvaez swore they never heard of such a thing as two kings, and two fifths, in his Majesty's dominions! among the rest one Juan de Quexo said he would make it known in Castille how they were treated, and another plainly told Cortes how he had abused them in regard to the gold in Mexico, for that when the division was made there appeared only three hundred thousand crowns in value, and when our flight took place he produced above seven hundred thousand; all which had been

regularly

regularly attefted. And now the poor foldier, who had worn himfelf to nothing with fatigue, and was full of wounds, when he had gotten a good female Indian prifoner, and given her cloathing and ornaments, found that fhe was taken from him! "When the order was given," faid the foldier, " Every one thought that the flaves were only put in " to be marked and valued, and that each would get his own back, pay- " ing the fifth of the value which fhe was rated at to his Majefty, and " that Cortes was to have no farther claim on them whatever." He added a great deal more to the fame purpofe, but worfe than what I have mentioned. When Cortes heard thefe exclamations againft him, he made anfwer, fwearing by his confcience! his ufual oath, that it never fhould happen fo again, and he protefted that in future better regulations fhould be adopted. Thus with fmooth words, and fair promifes on his part, the affair paffed over.

But I have now fomething to mention worfe than this; it has been already related how in the fatal night of the retreat from Mexico, the treafure was produced and all the foldiers given liberty to take as much as they chofe of it; many of thofe of Narvaez loaded themfelves with gold, fome alfo of ours did the fame; to a great many this coft their lives, and none who efcaped with life and what they had carried off, but were feverely wounded. After all this however Cortes came to know that in our garrifon here at La Frontera, a quantity of gold in bars was in circulation, and that deep gaming was going on amongft our foldiers; wherein our companions had forgot the old proverb which fays, that " wealth and amours fhould be kept concealed." He iffued an order for all the gold to be brought in within a given time, under the fevereft penalty in cafe of difobedience, promifing, on a fair delivery, to return the third part, but threatening in cafe of failure or evafion, that the whole fhould be forfeited. Many of the foldiers refufed, and from fome Cortes took it by way of loan; but indeed rather by main force than free will. As many of the captains and alfo of thofe who had offices under his Majefty were poffeffed of gold, a compromife took

place

place whereby no more was faid about the order; but it was a very bad tranfaction on the part of Cortes.

The officers of Narvaez thought this a good juncture to renew their folicitations to Cortes for permiffion to return to Cuba. After much trouble and many efforts on their part, Cortes affented, promifing that on the conqueft of Mexico, he would give his friend Andres de Duero much more wealth than he had ever poffeffed. He made fimilar offers alfo to the other captains, efpecially to Auguftin Bermudez. Thofe who were determined to return he ordered to be provided with whatever was neceffary for their voyage, fuch as maiz, dogs falted, fowls, &c, and giving them one of the beft fhips in the harbour, he wrote letters by them to his wife Donna Catalina Xuarez Marcayda, and to his brother in law Juan Xuarez, informing them of all that had happened; and he alfo tranfmitted to them by the fame opportunity fome bars and ornaments of gold. The following perfons were among thofe who returned to Cuba at this time, with their pockets well lined after all their difafters. Andres de Duero, Auguftin Bermudez, Juan Buono de Quexo, Bernardino de Quefada, Francifco Velafquez the hump backed, a relation of the governor of Cuba, Gonzalo Carrafco who returned afterwards to this country and lives in La Puebla, Melchor Velafco, and one Ximenes who lives in Guaxaca: he went for his fons; alfo the commendador Leon de Cervantes who went to bring over his daughters; after the conqueft of Mexico he married them to very honourable connexions; one Maldonado alfo of Medellin, an invalid; not he who married Donna Maria del Rincon, nor the big Maldonado, nor the other of that name whom we called Alvaro Maldonado "the fierce," who was married to a lady named Maria Arias; there was alfo one Vargas whom we nicknamed "the gallant;" I do not mean the Vargas who was father in law to Chriftoval Lobo; Cardenas the pilot alfo went; it was he who talked of the two kings; Cortes gave him three hundred crowns for his wife and children; with many others whom it would be too prolix to enumerate. When Cortes was remonftrated with on letting fo many quit us in our weak ftate he replied, that he did it partly

to

to get rid of their importunities, and partly becauſe they were not fit for war, and that it was better to be alone than badly accompanied. He ſent Alvarado with them in order to ſee them ſhipped, and at this time he alſo diſpatched De Ordas and Alonzo de Mendoza to Caſtille, with certain inſtructions, the tenor of which we were ignorant of; as we alſo were of what was going on in that country relative to us, except that the Biſhop of Burgos declared us all traitors, and that Diego de Ordas anſwered very well for us, and got for himſelf the order of St. Jago, and for his coat of arms the volcano which is between Guaxocingo and Cholula. But theſe affairs ſhall be related in their proper time. Cortes alſo ſent Captain Alonzo de Avila contador of New Spain, and Franciſco Alvarez, a man of buſineſs, to make a report to the royal court of audience and the brothers of the order of Jeronymites in St. Domingo, of all that had happened, more particularly relative to Narvaez; and alſo to inform them, how he had puniſhed by ſlavery, thoſe guilty of revolt and murders, and meant to purſue the ſame meaſures with all thoſe people who adhered to the alliance of the Mexicans. He alſo ſupplicated their intereſts in repreſenting our faithful ſervices to the Emperor, and their ſupport againſt the miſrepreſentations and enmity of the Biſhop of Burgos.

Cortes likewiſe at this time ſent a veſſel to Jamaica for horſes, commanded by one De Solis, whom we afterwards called De Solis de la Huerta. Some will aſk how he was able to ſend agents to Caſtille, to St. Domingo, and Jamaica, without money. To this I reply, that on the night of our retreat from Mexico, though many of our ſoldiers were killed, yet a conſiderable quantity of gold was ſaved, as the firſt who paſſed the bridge were, the eighty loaded Tlaſcalans; ſo that though much was loſt in the ditches of Mexico, yet all was not left there, and the gold which was brought off by the Tlaſcalans, was by them delivered to Cortes. But as to us poor ſoldiers who had no command, but were commanded, it was enough for us to eſcape with our lives, and all badly wounded too, without troubling ourſelves what was done with the gold, nor how much of it was brought off; and it was alſo ſhrewd-

ly

ly fufpected, that the treafure which fell to the fhare of the garrifon of Villa Rica, and of which thofe who were entrufted with the conveyance were robbed, went after all to Old Caftille, Jamaica and elfewhere. But the ingots of gold in the captains pockets ftopped all inquiry upon that head.

The fiege of Mexico being now determined on, Cortes left a garrifon of twenty men moftly fick and wounded, under the command of Francifco de Orozco in the town of Frontera, and proceeded with the reft of his force to the country of Tlafcala, where he ordered timber to be cut for the conftruction of the veffels to command the lake of Mexico. The fhips were to be conftructed under the directions of Martin Lopez, an excellent fhipwright, and one who was moft highly ferviceable to his Majefty's interefts here in other refpects, befides being a valiant foldier. When we arrived at Tlafcala, we found that our good friend and the faithful ally of our Monarch, Maxicatzin, had fallen a victim to the fmall pox. Cortes lamented him as if he had been his father, and put on mourning in refpect to him, as did many of our captains and foldiers. As there was fome difpute in regard to the fucceffion, Cortes fettled that it fhould be with the legitimate fon of our friend, as he had defired at his death; a fhort time previous to which, having fummoned his family into his prefence, he had ftrictly enjoined them never to quit our alliance, as we were undoubtedly thofe who were deftined to rule that country. The other chiefs of that nation offered their affiftance in providing timber, and alfo to aid us in the war againft the Mexicans. Cortes received their propofals with every mark of attention and gratitude, and at that time propofed to one of them, the elder Xicotenga, to turn chriftian; to which he readily affented, and was baptized in great ceremony by the name of Don Lorenzo de Vargas.

Our fhipwright Lopez managed his bufinefs fo well, that in a few days he had all his timber cut, fhaped, and marked for each particular part of the veffels. He was affifted by a good foldier named Andres Nunez,

Nunez, and by old Ramirez the carpenter, who was lame with a wound. Cortes obtained from the port of Villa Rica the iron work, fails, and other neceffaries to equip the veffels; and he alfo ordered to be fent to him what fmiths were there, amongft others, Aguilar, of which name there were three amongft us, but this was the man we called "the iron-mauler." As pitch was wanting, and was unknown to the natives of thofe countries, he fent four failors to the pine woods of Guaxacingo, which are very confiderable, to obtain a fupply of that article. Some curious perfons have afked me, why Cortes fent Alonzo de Avila who was fo valiant a captain on an affair of negociation, when he had men of bufinefs fuch as Alonzo de Grado, and Juan de Caceres the rich, and others whom they have named to me. To this I reply, that Cortes fent Avila becaufe he was a brave man, and would not be afraid to fpeak out on any neceffary occafion in order to obtain juftice; and therefore, to avoid being oppofed and thwarted by him, and to give his company to Andres de Tapia, and his office of contador to Alonzo de Grado, Cortes chofe to fend him upon bufinefs to St. Domingo.

Now that the timber of the veffels was all ready for the dock yard, and that thofe who came with Narvaez no longer molefted us with their fears and furmifes, there was great difference of opinion amongft us on the fubject of eftablifhing our poft, in order to prepare for the inveft-ment of Mexico. Some ftrongly recommended Ayotcingo as moft convenient on account of the canals, others, amongft whom was Cortes, as ftrongly infifted on the elegibility of Tezcuco as moft advantageous for making incurfions upon the Mexican territory. The decifion being at length for Tezcuco, juft as we were ready to march we were interrupted in our movements for an inftant, by intelligence that a veffel had arrived at Villa Rica from Europe and the Canary Iflands, loaded with military ftores, merchandife, and horfes. It was commanded by one Francifco Medel, but the owner of the property, who came with it, was one Juan de Burgos. There were alfo on board thirteen foldiers. We were in high fpirits on receiving this intelligence, and Cortes having fent orders to purchafe the whole cargo, we loft not a moment in

fetting

fetting forward on our route for Tezcuco, after we were joined by the people who came on board the veffel. Amongft thefe were one Juan del Efpinar, afterwards a very rich man, one Sagredo uncle to the woman called La Sagreda, in the Ifland of Cuba, and a Bifcayan named Monjaraz, uncle to two of that name who were foldiers with us, and father to the handfome woman who afterwards came to Mexico called La Monjaraza. This man never was in any expedition or engagement with us, always pretending to be fick, though he miffed no opportunity of boafting of his valour. When we befieged Mexico, he faid he would fee how the natives fought, for he had no opinion of their bravery. He accordingly went to the top of a very high temple like a turret, and no one ever could tell how it was, but certain Indians killed him on that very day. Thofe who had known him in the Ifland of St. Domingo faid, that it was God's judgment on him for having had his wife, a good, honourable, and beautiful woman, put to death, by the perjury of falfe witneffes.

Kk

CHAPTER II.

————◆————

March of the Spaniards to besiege Mexico, December 28th.
1520. Investment of Mexico, May 30th. 1521. Siege of
that city, and final conquest August 16th. 1521.

ON the day after the feast of the nativity, we set forward towards
Tezcuco with our full force, and accompanied by ten thousand of our
Tlascalan allies. On the same night we halted in a part of the territory
of Tezcuco, the inhabitants of the place supplying us with provisions.
The next night we halted at the foot of the ridge of mountains, having
made a march of about three leagues; we found here a very severe cold.
Early the next day we ascended the mountains, the bad roads through
which were made more difficult by cuts, or dikes, abbatis of trees, and
the like, which required the utmost exertions of our allies to remove.
Proceeding thus however with much regularity and precaution, we
reached the summit, a company of musqueteers and crossbow-men being
in our front, and our allies clearing the way for the cavalry. Descend-
ing a little, we came to that part from whence we discover the whole
extent of the city, lake, and plain of Mexico, with all its towns rising
as it were out of the water, and here we returned thanks to God for permitting us again to behold this city.

We now observed signals made by smoke in the different places
towards Mexico, and a little farther on we fell in with a body of the
enemy who were posted at a bad pass, where a broken wooden bridge
crossed a deep water cut. We soon drove them from thence, and passed over without difficulty, the enemy contenting themselves with shouting at us from a distance. Our allies pillaged as they went along, contrary

trary to the inclination of Cortes, who was not able to reftrain them. We halted for this night at a town in the territory of Tezcuco, which the inhabitants had abandoned. We had got intelligence by fome Mexicans we made prifoners in the laft fkirmifh, that large bodies of the enemy waited for us in front; but it afterwards appeared that they had feparated, in confequence of feuds, and indeed a civil war which exifted between the Mexicans and thofe of Tezcuco. The fmall pox alfo, which was at the fame time very deftructive in the country, contributed in a confiderable degree to prevent their armies from affembling.

On the next morning we again fet forward on our march for Tezcuco, which was diftant about two leagues; but we had proceeded a very fhort diftance, before one of our patroles came to us with intelligence that ten Indians were on the road, with figns of peace. The whole of the country alfo through which we marched exhibited every fign of moft perfect tranquillity. When thefe Indians arrived, we found that they compofed an embaffy, confifting of feven chieftains of Tezcuco. A golden banner borne upon a long lance was carried before them, and when they came near us the banner was lowered, and they bowed their bodies. Addreffing Cortes in the name of their lord Cocoivacin, the prince of Tezcuco, they then requefted to be received under our protection, inviting us to their city, and prefenting to us, as a token of peace, their golden banner. They utterly denied having any part in the attacks with which we had been threatened, and requefted that no injury might be done to their city by us or our allies. Three of thefe embaffadors were perfonally known to moft of us, for they were relations of the good Montezuma, and captains of his guards. Cortes earneftly requefted the Tlafcalan chiefs to prevent their people from pillaging, and his wifhes were ftrictly attended to, excepting only in the article of provifions.

It clearly appeared that this embaffy was a mere pretence; neverthelefs the embaffadors were affured that every protection fhould be afforded to the country, but were at the fame time told, that it could not

be

be unknown to them, how, above forty of the Spaniards and two hundred of our allies were put to death within their territories, when we retreated from Mexico. For the loss of lives Cortes said no restitution could be made, but the gold and other property they might return. They in reply threw the blame upon the prince who had succeeded Montezuma, and who they said received the spoil, and sacrificed the prisoners. Cortes therefore found that little was to be got from them, and we proceeded to a village in the outskirts of Tezcuco, named Guatinchan, or Huaxutlan, where we halted for the night. On the ensuing morning we arrived at Tezcuco, and immediately remarked that neither women or children were to be seen, and the men appeared as if they were meditating some mischief against us. We took up our quarters in some buildings which consisted of large halls and enclosed courts, and received orders not to quit them, and to be very alert. Alvarado, De Oli, and some soldiers whereof I was one, then ascended to the top of the great temple, which was very lofty, in order to notice what was going on in the neighbourhood. We observed that all the people were in movement, carrying off their children and effects to the woods, the reedy borders of the lake, and to a number of canoes collected for the purpose. Cortes now wished to seize the chief who had sent him the embassy, but found that he had fled to Mexico, with many other persons of rank. We posted strong guards for the night, and as in so large a city there are many different parties and factions, and those persons who were adverse to the present chief having remained, Cortes on the next morning sent for them, and enquired into the state of their government. They assured him that their present chief, Cocoivatzin, was an usurper, having murdered his elder brother Cuscuxca, and was supported only by the prince then on the throne of Mexico, and whose name was Guatimotzin. They pointed out the youth who was the right heir, and who was immediately conducted into the presence of Cortes, by whose order he was baptized with much solemnity, being called after his godfather, Don Hernando Cortes; after which he was appointed lord of Tezcuco. Cortes in order to retain him in our holy faith and in the interests of Spain, and also to instruct him in our language, ordered three persons to

attend

attend upon him; Anthonio de Villaroel married to the handsome Isabel de Ojeda, a batchellor named Escobar captain of Tezcuco, and Pedro Sanches Farfan, a good soldier, married to the worthy and honorable lady Maria de Estrada. Cortes then required of him a number of Indian labourers to open the canals, in order to bring his vessels to the lake. He also explained to him his plan of attacking Mexico, to which the young prince offered assistance to the utmost of his power.

Our captains were at this time assigned their different posts, in case of a sudden attack upon our quarters, the reigning prince in Mexico frequently sending out his troops upon the lake, in expectation of taking us unprepared. Some neighbouring people, whose district is called Guatinchan, and who had been guilty of offences in the murders of our countrymen, now petitioned for, and obtained pardon. The work upon the canals went on most rapidly, as we never had less than from seven to eight thousand Indians employed.

Cyoadluanaca

Guatimotzin now upon the throne of Mexico, was lord of Iztapalapa, the people whereof were bitter enemies to us, and our declared allies of Chalco, Talmalanco, Mecameca, and Chimaloacan. As we had been twelve days in Tezcuco, so large a force caused some scarcity of provisions; idleness had also made our allies grow impatient, and for those reasons it became necessary to take the field. Cortes therefore proceeded towards Iztapalapa at the head of thirteen cavalry, two hundred and twenty infantry, and the whole body of our Indian confederates. The inhabitants had received a reinforcement of eight thousand Mexicans, and as we approached, they fell back into the town. But this was all a concerted plan; they then fled into their canoes, the reeds by the side of the lake, and also to those houses which were in the water, where they remained quietly, leaving us in possession of that part of the town which was on the firm land. As it was now night we posted our guards, and were reposing contentedly in our quarters, when all on a sudden there came on us such a body of water by the streets, and into the houses, that if our friends from Tezcuco had not called to us at that moment,

moment, we fhould have been all drowned; for the enemy had cut the banks of the canals, and alfo a caufeway, whereby the place was laid under water as it were inftantaneoufly. As it happened two of our allies only, loft their lives, but all our powder was deftroyed, and we were glad to efcape with a good wetting. We paffed the night badly enough, being fupperlefs, and very cold; but what provoked us moft was the laughter and mockings of the Indians upon the lake. Worfe than this however happened to us, for large bodies from the garrifon of Mexico, who knew of the plan, croffed the water and fell on us at day break with fuch violence that it was with difficulty we could fuftain their attacks. They killed two foldiers and one of our horfes, and wounded a great many. Our allies alfo fuffered a confiderable lofs on this occafion. The enemy being at length beaten off we returned to Tezcuco, in very bad humour, having acquired little fame or advantage by our expedition.

Two days after our return from our laft expedition, the people of three neighbouring diftriĉts, viz Tepetezcuco, Obtumba, and another which I do not recolleĉt, fent to follicit pardon for the offences they had committed, excufing themfelves, by alledging the commands of Coadlavaca. Cortes making a merit of neceffity gave them a free pardon, knowing very well that he was not in a fituation to do otherwife. The people alfo of that place called Venezuela, or Little Venice, who had always been at enmity with the Mexicans, now follicited our alliance; a circumftance highly ufeful, from the fituation of that town within the lake; and they promifed alfo to bring over their neighbours to us.

Intelligence was foon received, that large bodies of Mexican troops had fallen upon the diftriĉts in alliance with us, the inhabitants of which being afraid to remain at home, were flying to the woods or to our quarters for proteĉtion. Cortes ordered out twenty cavalry and two hundred infantry, twenty three mufqueteers and crofsbow-men included, and taking Alvarado and De Oli with him, proceeded to the towns of Guatinchan, and Huaxutlan. The reports appeared to have foundation,

but

but the real caufe of contention was, the crop of Indian corn on the borders of the lake, which was now fit to reap, and from which the people of Tezcuco and the others fupplied our provifions; but the Mexicans alfo laid claim to it, and it appeared that the produce of thefe fields went to the priefts of Mexico. Cortes told them to inform him when they thought it neceffary to cut the corn, and accordingly, at that time, a body of one hundred or upwards of our foldiers, attended by the allies went out to cover the reapers. I was twice on that duty, and had one fmart fkirmifh. The Mexicans croffed over in upwards of a thoufand canoes, and attacked us in the maize fields, but we and our allies, drove them back to their boats, with the lofs of one foldier of our's killed, and many wounded. They fought like men, and left behind them twenty dead, and we alfo took five prifoners. At this time other neighbouring diftricts folicited our alliance.

There were two places, named Chalco and Talmalanco, of fome confequence, as being between our army and Tlafcala. They were now poffeffed by the Mexican troops, and though Cortes had feveral petitions for protection, he thought it neceffary above all things, immediately to diflodge thefe Mexicans, that fuch of his allies as wifhed it might return home, and alfo in order to obtain his fhip timber from Tlafcala. He therefore fent a force for this purpofe under Sandoval and De Lugo, confifting of fifteen cavalry and two hundred infantry, and he gave thefe officers orders to break completely the Mexican force, whereby we fhould obtain a clear communication with Villa Rica. Our allies of Chalco were fecretly informed of our intention, in order that they fhould be ready to fupport us. Sandoval had put ten of his party in the rear as a guard, and to protect the allies who were returning home with his detachment, and who were loaded with plunder. The Mexicans fell upon them on their march with confiderable impreffion, owing to the weaknefs of the rear guard, of which they killed two, and wounded the reft; and although Sandoval inftantly flew to their relief, the Mexicans contrived to reach the lake. Sandoval cenfured the people in the rear for this, throwing the whole blame on them; he then put the
Tlafcalans

Tlafcalans in fecurity, and having fent the letters with which he was intrufted to the commandant of Villa Rica, in which Cortes ordered him to fend what reinforcements he could to Tlafcala, there to wait until it fhould be afcertained that the route from thence to Tezcuco was clear, he difmiffed the allies to their province, and returned to Chalco, which diftrict he had reafon to apprehend was filled with the troops of he Mexicans.

On his road he was attacked in a plain covered with maize and maguey, by a body of the enemy who wounded feveral of his party; the cavalry drove them to a diftance, after which he purfued his route to Chalco. Having informed the principal people of this place of his intention to march to Tezcuco on the enfuing day, they informed him of their determination to go with him, and for the following reafon. Their lord was lately dead of the fmall pox. He had on his death-bed recommended his fons to the protection of Cortes, being convinced that we were thofe of whom their anceftors had prophefied, when they faid that men with beards fhould come to govern them; and he there-fore enjoined his fons to receive their dominions from the hands of our chief. Sandoval accordingly marched for our head quarters, bringing with him the young lords of Chalco, who experienced a moft gracious reception from Cortes, and they prefented him with ornaments of gold amounting in value to about two hundred thoufand crowns. Cortes divided the diftrict between them, giving Chalco and the larger part to the elder brother, and Talmalanco, Ayocingo, and Chimalcan, with other places, to the younger. By fome Mexican prifoners Cortes fent a meffage to the reigning prince in that city, couched in the moft in-viting and amicable terms, in order to induce him to come to an accom-modation; but Guatimotzin would not hear them, and perfifted in the moft active hoftility againft us. Frequent complaints came to us at this time of the incurfions made by the enemy upon our allies of Gua-tinchan and Huaxutlan, in the neighbourhood of the lake, upon the old caufe of the fields fown for the fervice of the Mexican temples; in confequence of which, Cortes being determined to put a ftop to thefe

inroads

inroads, and marching with a ſtrong party for that purpoſe, came up with the enemy at the diſtance of about two leagues from Tezcuco, and ſo completely broke and defeated them, though with no very conſiderable loſs on their ſide, that they did not ſhow themſelves there again.

As it was reſolved to loſe no time in the grand objeƈt of our enterpriſe, Sandoval attended by twenty of the principal people of Tezcuco, marched with a detachment of two hundred ſoldiers of the infantry, twenty muſqueteers and croſsbow-men included, and fifteen cavalry, from Tezcuco, in order to bring the timber to conſtruƈt our ſhips on the lake of Mexico. Before they ſet out, Cortes effeƈted a reconciliation between the Tlaſcalans and the Indians of Chalco, who had long been hoſtile. He gave direƈtions to Sandoval, after he had left the chieftains of Chalco in their own town, to proceed by a place named by us Puebla Moreſca, the inhabitants of which had robbed and put to death upwards of forty of our ſoldiers, who were on their march from Vera Cruz to Mexico, when we went to the relief of Alvarado. Sandoval had orders to infliƈt an exemplary puniſhment on them, not that their guilt was more than that of the people of Tezcuco, who were the leaders of the buſineſs, but becauſe they could be puniſhed with leſs inconvenience. The place was put under military execution. Some few of the inhabitants were made priſoners, and when Sandoval enquired of them in what manner they had deſtroyed the Spaniards, they informed him that they were fallen on by the troops of Mexico and Tezcuco, by ſurprize, in a narrow paſs where they could only go in ſingle file, and that it was done in revenge for the death of Cacamatzin. Not more than three or four of theſe people loſt their lives, as Sandoval had pity on them. In the temples were found many traces of the blood of our countrymen upon the walls, their idols were beſmeared with it, and we found the ſkins of two of their faces with their beards, dreſſed like leather, and hung upon the altars, as were alſo the ſhoes of four horſes, together with their ſkins very well dreſſed. The following words were found written upon a piece of marble fixed in the wall of one of the houſes. "Here was taken the unfortunate Juan Juſte, with many

L l   others

" others of his companions." This Jufte was a gentleman who came with Narvaez, and ferved in the cavalry. Thefe fad remains filled the minds of Sandoval and his party with rage and grief, but there was no poffibility of obeying the dictates of their feelings, for the men were all fled, and the women and children bewailed their fate in the moft affecting terms. Sandoval therefore fent them to their hufbands and fathers, whom they induced to come in and fubmit. In anfwer to the queftions put to them relative to the gold, they declared that it had all been claimed by the Mexicans. Sandoval now continued his march to Tlafcala, and when he came near the capital of that country, he fell in with a vaft body of Indians employed in tranfporting the timber, and conducted by Chichimecatecle, and our fhipwright Martin Lopez. The order thefe people came in was as follows. Eight thoufand men carried the timber ready fhaped for every part of the thirteen veffels, eight thoufand more followed as a guard with their enfigns and arms, and a third body of two thoufand, as a relief, and with provifions for the whole. Several Spaniards joined us with this efcort, and alfo two great Tlafcalan chiefs named Teuleticle, and Teatical. The enemy appeared only in fmall bodies at a diftance, but it was thought neceffary to ufe much precaution, confidering the extent of the line of march, and the danger of a furprife. Sandoval fent fome of his troops in front, and pofted others on the flanks, while he remained at the rear guard with the Tlafcalans, to whom he affigned that poft. This arrangement gave their chief, Chichimecatecle, great offence, but when he was informed that it was there the Mexicans were moft likely to attack, his pride became pacified. In two days more the whole body arrived at Tezcuco, in great triumph and pomp, the allies wearing their fineft habits and great plumes of feathers, with drums, horns, and trumpets, founding. Thus they continued marching into our quarters, without breaking a file, for the fpace of full half the day, fhouting out, "Caftilla! Caftilla! Tlafca-" la! Tlafcala! live his Majefty the Emperor."

Our timber being all now laid ready at the docks, in a very fhort time, by the great exertions of Lopez, the hulls were completely finifhed;

ed; but we were obliged to keep the ſtricteſt guard, as the Mexicans ſent three parties to endeavour to ſet them on fire.

The Tlaſcalans were anxious to be ſent on ſome enterpriſe, and Cortes indulged them by declaring his intention to march on the enſuing day to Saltocan, a town which had neglected our ſummons to a ſubmiſſion. For this purpoſe he ordered two hundred and fifty infantry and thirty cavalry, the whole of the Tlaſcalans, and a body of the warriors of Tezcuco. He appointed the captains Alvarado and De Oli to act under him, and having left the poſt of Tezcuco, where it was always neceſſary "to have the beard upon the ſhoulders," under the care of Sandoval, and ordered Lopez to have the veſſels ready to launch within the ſpace of fifteen days, he ſet out with the above force upon his expedition. When he approached Saltocan, he was met by large bodies of the Mexican troops, whom the cavalry drove to the woods. The troops halted for the night in ſome villages, in a country thickly inhabited. They were kept very alert, for it was known that the enemy had a conſiderable force in Saltocan; and a body of Mexicans had been ſent thither in large boats, and was at this time concealed in the deep canals of the neighbourhood.

On the enſuing day, at the commencement of the march, our troops were aſſailed by the enemy, and ſeveral were wounded, without our cavalry having it in their power to retaliate, on account of the number of canals. The only cauſeway which led to the town on the land ſide, they had completely inundated, and our muſquetry was of no effect againſt the enemy in their canoes, being ſo well guarded by ſtrong ſcreens of timber. All this contributed to give our people a diſguſt to the expedition. Some Indians of Tezcuco who had joined our army, at this time pointed out a paſs to one of our ſoldiers; upon which, our people put themſelves into march, and under the direction of their guide croſſed the canals and waters, and at length reached the road which led to the town, Cortes with the cavalry remaining on the other ſide. Our troops advanced againſt the town, and made a conſiderable ſlaughter of

the

the Mexicans, driving the remainder, and the natives of the place, to their boats. They then returned to Cortes, with a confiderable booty of flaves, mantles, falt, and gold. We loft one foldier by this expedition.

On the enfuing day Cortes marched againft a large town called Culvatitlan, through a very populous country. We found the place to which we marched totally deferted, and here we halted for the night. On the enfuing day we proceeded to another large town called Tenayuco, but which we named the town of the ferpents, on account of the enormous figures of thefe animals which we found in their temples, and which they worfhipped as gods. This place we alfo found deferted, and we proceeded a league farther to that which we called the town of the gold-fmiths. This place was alfo deferted, and our troops marched half a league farther, to Tacuba, our foldiers being obliged to cut their way through confiderable numbers of the natives. In this town our troops halted for the night, and on the next day they were affailed by bodies of the enemy, who had fettled a plan to retreat by their caufeways, in order to draw us into an ambufcade. This in part fucceeded; Cortes and our troops purfued them acrofs a bridge, and were immediately furrounded by vaft numbers on land and in the water. The enfign was thrown over the bridge, and the Mexicans were dragging him to their canoes, yet he efcaped from them with his colours in his hand. In this attack they killed five of our foldiers, and wounded many. Cortes perceived his imprudence, and ordered a retreat, which was effected with regularity, our people fronting the enemy, and only giving ground inch by inch. Juan Volante, the enfign who fell into the lake, had a jealoufy with one of our foldiers, Pedro de Ircio, about a certain woman. The latter in order to affront him ufed fome abufive language, which Volante did not deferve, being a very valiant gentleman, as he had fhown on that and many other occafions. Cortes halted here for five days, and then returned to Tezcuco, the Mexicans harraffing his march; but having been once defeated in an ambufcade which Cortes laid for them, they defifted. When our troops arrived at head quarters, the

Tlafcalans,

Tlafcalans, who had enriched themfelves by plunder, were anxious to go home, which Cortes readily gave them permiffion to do.

During four days after this expedition, the Indians of feveral neighbouring diftricts came in with prefents and declarations of fubmiffion. Cortes received all in good part, although he knew very well that they had been concerned in murders, difmiffing them with promifes of protection. Other applications of a more embarraffing nature were alfo made at this time, for the nations in our alliance came with painted reprefentations of the outrages committed on them by the Mexicans, and requefting fuccour. Cortes was hardly able to grant them affiftance, from the ftate of our army, which, exclufive of our lofs by killed and wounded was grown very unhealthy. He however promifed them his fupport, bnt told them to rely more on their own exertions, and that they fhould be affifted by the neighbouring people of our alliance. For this purpofe he gave them letters of fummons to the refpective diftricts, to affemble againft the common enemy. The different diftricts having affembled their forces, met the Mexicans in the field, and had an action with them, in which they exerted themfelves with fuccefs. The province of Chalco however was an object of more importance; the poffeffion of that country was requifite for our communication with Villa Rica and Tlafcala, and for the fubfiftence of our troops, as it was a corn country. It was much harraffed, and therefore Cortes fent Sandoval with about two hundred and fifty of our troops, cavalry and infantry, accompanied by what few of our Tlafcalan allies remained with us, and a company of thofe of Tezcuco, to clear it of the enemy.

On the twelfth day of March, one thoufand five hundred and twenty one, after hearing mafs, Sandoval fet out, and arrived in the diftrict of Chalco. On the enfuing morning he reached Talmanalco, where he received information that the Mexican force was pofted at a large town called Guaztepeque. The warriors of Chalco accompanied our troops, who halted for the night at the town of Chimalcan. On the next morning Sandoval ordered the crofsbow-men and mufqueteers to attack the

enemy

enemy in the broken ground, and forming the cavalry into small divisions of three in front, directed them to charge as soon as the firing had made any impression; those who were armed with sword and buckler he formed in a compact body as a reserve. Advancing in this order, he shortly perceived the Mexicans in three large battalions or columns, and sounding their warlike music. As soon as Sandoval perceived their disposition he thought proper to give up his original plan, and to break the enemy by a charge of cavalry. Putting himself therefore at the head of this body of troops, he attacked them, crying out "St. Jago for us! comrades fall on!" The main body of the Mexicans was partly broken by the charge, but they immediately closed and fronted again. The ground was much in their favor, so that Sandoval saw it was absolutely necessary to drive them from this post, into the open ground in their rear. For this purpose he ordered the musqueteers and crossbow-men to engage them in the front, and the troops armed with sword and target to turn their flanks, and he gave directions, that at the proper time, the cavalry should fall on the enemy by a signal. He also now ordered our allies to come forward to the attack. Our troops at last forced them to retreat; they fell back however no farther than to a second strong position, nor could Sandoval with his cavalry do any considerable execution among them. Here we lost Gonzalo Dominguez, whose horse fell with him, whereby he died in a few days. He was much regretted, for we esteemed him to be as brave a soldier as De Oli or Sandoval. Our army having broken the enemy again, pursued them to the town, where they were suddenly attacked by at least fifteen thousand fresh warriors, who attempted to surround them; but our troops falling on both their flanks, the whole faced about and fled, endeavoring to rally behind some works which they had constructed. They were however so closely followed that they had not time to do so, and were driven compleatly withinside the town. Sandoval then thought it necessary to give his soldiers some repose, and as a considerable spoil of provisions had fallen in the way of the troops, they began to prepare their dinners, during which time the patroles came galloping in, crying "To arms! the enemy are coming!" There was hardly a moments interval until they

were

were prepared, and advancing againſt the enemy, they met them in an open ſpace, and had a ſevere ſkirmiſh, after which the enemy fell back behind their works; but Sandoval attacked them with ſuch impetuoſity that he drove them completely away, forcing them to evacuate the town.

In this place was a very magnificent and extenſive garden, in which Sandoval took his quarters for the night, and certainly it was a beautiful one to behold; it contained a number of large and handſome buildings, and ſuch varieties that it was truly admirable, and fit for the reſidence of a great prince; nor had our ſoldiers time to ſee the whole of it, for it was above a quarter of a league in length. I was not in this action, being very ill by the wound of a lance, which I received in my throat at the affair of Iztapalapa, the marks of which I carry to this day; but I ſaw the garden about twenty days afterwards, when I accompanied Cortes. Not having been on this expedition for the reaſon I have before aſſigned, as I was then almoſt at death's door, I do not in my narrative ſay we, and us, but they, and them; but notwithſtanding that, all is true to the letter as I have related it, for the tranſactions of an expedition are immediately known in quarters, nor is there any opportunity of adding to, or diminiſhing the truth, as is ſometimes the caſe elſewhere.

Sandoval thought it a good time to ſummon all the neighbouring diſtricts to ſubmiſſion, which he accordingly did, but with very little effect, thoſe of Acapiſtlan, eſpecially, anſwering by a defiance. This made our allies of Chalco uneaſy, as well knowing that they and the Mexicans were only waiting until the return of the Spaniards, in order to fall upon them. For ſeveral reaſons it was neceſſary therefore to humble theſe people, but a great difference of opinion exiſted on the ſubject. Sandoval was adverſe to any new expedition on account of the number of his wounded, and the ſoldiers of Narvaez were adverſe, becauſe they diſliked riſques of any kind; but our allies were for it, and Captain Luis Marin, a wiſe and valiant officer, ſtrongly ſupported them. As the

the diftance was but two leagues Sandoval acquiefced. When he advanced, the enemy attacked him with their miffile weapons, and after wounding fome of his men, returned to their ftrong poft in the town. Our allies did not exhibit much alacrity in going to the attack, in which the Spaniards were obliged to fhew them the way, and difmounting fome of the cavalry, and leaving the reft in the plain to guard the rear, they advanced againft the place, which they entered, having a number wounded in the afcent, and amongft others Sandoval himfelf. But if the Indians were tardy before, they made up for it now; the Spaniards not having the trouble of putting the enemy to death, it being entirely faved them by their allies. Indeed our countrymen thought their time employed to much better purpofe in fearching for gold, or making good female prifoners, than in cutting to pieces a parcel of poor wretches who did not any longer defend themfelves. They frequently blamed the cruelty of their allies, and faved many Indians from them. Gomara fays that the Spaniards fuffered thirft here becaufe the water was not to be drank, on account of the quantity of blood with which it was difcoloured; the fact is, that many of the wounded Mexicans did come from the rocks and ridges down to the water in making their efcape, and it was difcoloured the length of time that it would take to fay an Ave Maria, but as to our people fuffering thirft on that account, that muft be untrue, for there were feveral fountains of the fineft water, in the town.

After this fuccefs Sandoval returned to Tezcuco, with a number of flaves and confiderable fpoils. Guatimotzin the reigning prince of Mexico was enraged when he heard of the hoftilities committed againft him by his own people of Chalco, and determined to inflict immediate punifhment. He now fent acrofs the lake twenty thoufand of his warriors in two thoufand canoes, to wafte the province with fire and fword, fo that at the very moment when the brave Sandoval had arrived at head quarters, and before he could make the report of his expedition to the general, there arrived expreffes from Chalco ftating their being in a more defperate fituation than ever. This put Cortes in a violent paffion with

Sandoval,

Sandoval, thinking that he had been the caufe of this misfortune; and thus, without hearing him out, when he came to wait upon him, he commanded his inftant return. This gave Sandoval pain, thinking that he was unworthily treated by Cortes. However he was obliged to return to Chalco. On his arrival he found the bufinefs entirely over, for the people of that province had fummoned their allies, and repulfed the Mexicans, fo that our countrymen returned with the prifoners to head quarters. Cortes was delighted when he heard the event, but Sandoval would not fpeak to him. The general made every apology, and protefted that the whole was owing to a miftake, however, it is unneceffary to fay any more upon the fubject, as they fhortly after became as good friends as ever.

At this time, according to a general proclamation, the Indian flaves were brought together in order to be marked. The reader is already acquainted with the tranfactions at Tepeaca. It was if poffible worfe now at Tezcuco. Firft there was a fifth for his Majefty, then another fifth for Cortes, and then the fhares of the captains. What was worft, moft of the good female flaves had difappeared during the night! it had been promifed that they fhould be rated, and the proprietor charged according to the value; but the royal officers or commiffaries valued them as they thought proper, fo that the poor foldier fell from bad to worfe. The confequence of this was, that in future, to avoid lofing them thus, the foldiers concealed their flaves or paffed them as fervants and not prifoners of war, and thofe who were in favor with Cortes brought them to be marked privately and paid the value to him. Thofe flaves who fell to the lot of fuch mafters as treated them ill, or had the name of doing fo, immediately deferted and were no more to be found; but the owners always remained debtors for fo much upon their value in his Majefty's books, fo that many were in debt more than their fhare of prifage of gold could pay off.

At this time arrived a fhip, with arms and gunpowder, from Old Caftille, in which came Julian de Alderete treafurer for the crown; he

M m   was

was from Tordefillas, as was also Orduna the elder, who, after the conquest, brought over five daughters whom he married very honorably. A brother of the order of St. Francis also came; he was named Fra Pedro Malgarejo de Urrea. He brought with him a number of bulls of our lord St. Peter, in order to compose our consciences if we had any thing to lay to our charge on account of the wars. The reverend father made a fortune in a few months, and returned to Castille. Anthonio Carajaval who now lives in Mexico, though very old, Geronymo Ruiz de la Mora, one Briones, who was about four years afterwards hanged in Guatimala for sedition, Alonzo Diaz de la Reguera now living in Valladolid, and many others came by this vessel. We now learned that the Bishop of Burgos had no longer any power, his Majesty having been displeased with his conduct ever since he knew of our eminent services. Another message arrived at this moment from Chalco for assistance against the Mexicans, upon which Cortes gave his promise that he would immediately march thither, although the brigantines were now ready to launch, and the soldiers were anxious to begin the siege of Mexico.

Cortes, leaving the town of Tezcuco to the care of Sandoval, set out after mafs, upon his expedition, to clear the district of Chalco, and reconnoitre the country adjacent to the lake, on friday the fifth of April, one thousand five hundred and twenty one, at the head of three hundred infantry, twenty crofsbow-men and fifteen musqueteers included, and thirty cavalry, with a large body of the auxiliaries of Tezcuco and Tlafcala. The general was accompanied by the treasurer Alderete, Fray Pedro Melgarejo, the captains Alvarado, De Oli, and Tapia, and in this expedition I also went. The first night we halted at Talmanalco, and on the next day reached Chalco, whither Cortes summoned all the chiefs, and informed them of his intention immediately to attack Mexico, requiring their assistance, which they most readily promised. On the next day, Cortes continuing his march, arrived at the town of Chimalacoan, in the same province, where above twenty thousand warriors had affembled to meet us. From the time of my first arrival in this

country,

country, I never had feen fo many of our allies in one body. They were thofe of Chalco, Guaxocingo, Tlafcala, Tezcuco, and other places, and they certainly were attracted by the hope of fpoil, and a voracious appetite for human flefh, juft as the fcald crows and other birds of prey follow our armies in Italy, in order to feed on the dead bodies after a battle.

We here received intelligence, that the Mexican forces and their allies of that neighbourhood, were ready and in the field. Cortes therefore warned us to be alert, and early the next morning after mafs, as we proceeded on our march, our route being between two ridges of rocks the fummits of which were fortified and garrifoned, the enemy endeavored by outcries and reproaches to draw us to an attack; but we purfued our march, by a large town named Guaztepeque, which we found abandoned, and paffing through, we arrived at a plain where were fome very fcanty fountains of water, and hard by was a great rock with a fortrefs on the fummit. We obferved it to be filled with troops, who faluted us on our approach with fhouts, fhowers of ftones, and arrows, by the firft difcharge of which they wounded three of our foldiers. Cortes then ordered us to halt, and obferving that the Mexicans feemed to defpife us for not attacking them, he fent a party of cavalry to examine the rock. On their return they told the general, that no part feemed to them fo acceffible as that where we then were. Cortes then ordered us to afcend, Enfign Chriftoval del Corral with the colours leading us, and Cortes with the cavalry remaining in the plain to protect the rear.

When we began to afcend the mountain, the Indians threw down large maffes of rock, and it was dreadful to fee them roll among us, and a wonder how any of us efcaped, as they bounded over us. The order was a very inconfiderate one, and very unlike a wife captain. One foldier though he wore a helmet was killed at my foot; he never uttered a word; his name was Martin Valenciano. As we continued to afcend, the ftones ftill came rolling down upon us, and two more foldiers, one named Gafpar Sanches, nephew to the treafurer of Cuba, and the other

named

named Bravo, were the next who loft their lives, and immediately after, Alonzo Rodriguez was killed, and two more knocked down. Moft of the reft received wounds, but ftill we afcended. I was at that time an active young man, and followed clofe to our enfign, taking advantage of the concavities that we found from time to time in the rock. Corral was wounded in the head, his face covered with blood, and the colours tattered to pieces. "Oh fignor Bernal Diaz del Caftillo" faid he to me, " here is no advancing; remain under cover, for it is as much as I can " do to keep my hold, and preferve myfelf from falling." Looking downward I at this time perceived Pedro Barba captain of the crofsbow-men, with two foldiers, climbing up as we had done under the cover of the projections in the face of the rock. I called to him not to ad-vance, for that it was impoffible to climb much farther. He replied in lofty terms, that I fhould defift from talking, and proceed on. I was a little piqued at this, and exerting my utmoft activity, mounted to a confiderable diftance higher, telling him I fhould fee how he would do. At this moment a fhower of large rocks came down, and crufhed one of the foldiers who were with Barba to death; after having feen which he did not ftir a ftep. Corral called out to thofe below defiring them to report to the general the impoffibility of proceeding, and that even the defcent was full of danger. When Cortes was informed of this, for he could not fee us on account of the inequalities of the rocks, and underftood that moft of us were wounded and many killed, a circum-ftance which he could the readier believe from having had three of the cavalry killed on the plain by the rolling down of the maffes of rocks, feven alfo being wounded in the fame manner, he gave fignals for us to defcend, which we accordingly did, in a very bloody and bruifed con-dition, leaving eight of our party dead.

Bodies of the Mexicans were watching us during this time, con-cealed in different places, in order to fall upon us when we were enga-ged in the attack, for it was a concerted plan. They now fhewed themfelves, and advanced againft us; we attacked them in the plain and drove them to fome other ridges of rocks, and advancing through nar-

row

row paffes like roads between them, we found another very ftrong fortrefs fimilar to that we had juft been repulfed from. We now defifted
for the prefent, and returned to our former pofition, in order to procure
water, the men and horfes not having drank during the whole day.
We found fome fprings at the foot of the rock, but the numbers of the
enemy had drained them, and left nothing but mud. We then proceeded to the other fortrefs which we had obferved; there was a diftance of about a league and a half between the two. Here, in a grove
of mulberry trees we found a fountain, but very fcanty of water, and
under thefe trees we halted for fome time. At the foot of the rock
whereon the fort was, ftood a fmall village. The people above began
at our approach to fhoot at us, and appeared in much more confiderable
numbers than in the former place, and their fituation was fuch that no
fhot from us could take effect upon them. For fome diftance from the
level ground, there was an appearance of paths up the rock, but it altogether prefented extreme difficulties.

On the enfuing day we attacked, our principal body climbing the
rock very flowly and with great fatigue, nor could we have ever afcended to the works, for they were wounding and deftroying us by rolling
down maffes of rock on our heads, but that fortunately for us there was
within fhot of the poft another rock which commanded it, and to this
all our fire arms and crofsbow-men were detached; and although they
were rather too far off to have much effect, yet having killed feveral of
the enemy over their ramparts, it threw them off their defence, and they
offered to fubmit. Cortes called for five of their chiefs to defcend, and
reprehending them for having been the aggreffors, he told them that he
would pardon them on condition that they induced thofe who were in
the other fortrefs to give themfelves up, which they undertook to do.
Cortes then ordered the two captains Juan Xaramillo and Pedro de Ircio,
and the enfign, Corral, to afcend to the fort which had been furrendered,
bidding me accompany them, and he at the fame time warned us not to
touch a fingle grain of maiz. This expreffion I confidered as implying
that we fhould do ourfelves what good we had in our power. We

found

found it to confift of an extenfive plain on the fummit of a perpendicular rock; the entrance was by an aperture not much larger than twice
the fize of the mouth of an oven.   It was completely filled with men,
women, and children, but they had not a fingle drop of water, and about
twenty of their warriors were killed, and many wounded.   Their property was all packed up in bales, and here was alfo a confiderable tribute, collected in order to be fent to Mexico.   I had brought four of
my Indian fervants with me, and began to load them, and alfo four of
the natives; upon which Captain De Ircio came and told me to lay down
the packs immediately, or he would report me to the general, afking if
I had not heard his orders not to touch a grain of maize.   I replied that
I had heard the orders that the maize fhould not be taken, and that was
the reafon why I took the packages; but he would not fuffer any of it
to go, and on our return reported me to Cortes, expecting that I fhould
receive blame; but Cortes was not fo difpofed, faying on the contrary,
that he was forry I had not got the fpoil, and that the dogs fhould keep
their property, and laugh at us, after all the mifchief which they had
done.   De Ircio on this wifhed to return thither; but Cortes told him
that the time did not then admit of it.   By this, the chiefs had arrived
from the firft fortrefs, the garrifon of which agreed to fubmit, and we
returned, being compelled by want of water, to the town of Guaztepeque, where was the noble garden I have before mentioned.   In this
garden our whole force lodged for the night; I certainly never had feen
one of fuch magnificence, and Cortes and the treafurer Alderete, after
they had walked through and examined it, declared that it was admirable, and equal to any that they had ever feen in Caftille.

On the enfuing day we marched for Cuernabaca.   The Mexicans
who were in that town came out and attacked us, but we defeated and
drove them to a town named Tepuztlan, which we took by furprife,
making a great booty of Indian women, and other fpoils. Cortes fummoned the chiefs three or four times, to fubmit, and on their refufal to
come in, and in order to ftrike terror into others, fet fire to about one
half of the houfes.   At this time the chiefs of a diftrict named Yauh-
                                                                    tepeque

tepeque came to wait on Cortes and make their fubmiffion. On the next day we arrived at the large town of Cuernabaca, or Coadlavaca, in a very ftrong fituation, on account of a deep ravine caufed by a rivulet which runs at the depth of at leaft forty feet, although there is not much water, and which precluded all accefs to the town except by two bridges, which the inhabitants had broken upon our approach. Cortes however being informed that about half a league higher up was a paffage practicable for the cavalry, went thither with them, and we all fearched for paffes, and at length difcovered a very dangerous one, over fome trees which hung acrofs from the two oppofite fides of the ravine. About thirty of us, and many Tlafcalans, made our way over, by the help of thofe trees, with great difficulty, three fell into the water, and one broke his leg. It was indeed a truly frightful attempt; I for a time entirely loft my fight, from the depth and danger. We who got over, falling on the flank and rear of the enemy unexpectedly, and being juft then joined by part of our cavalry who had croffed a bridge which was not entirely deftroyed, now drove the enemy from this poft, to the neighbouring woods and rocks. In the town we found confiderable property, and here we were again lodged in a large garden, belonging to the lord of the diftrict. A deputation of twenty of the principal Indians waited on Cortes, apologizing for the hoftilities committed, the blame of which they threw on the Mexicans, offering to fubmit themfelves and obferving, as I recollect, that their gods had been permitted by ours to punifh them.

Suchimileco, the object of our march, is a large city on the frefh water lake, in which moft of the houfes are built. As it was late when we fet out from Coadlavaca, and the weather exceffively fultry, our troops fuffered dreadfully from the want of water, not a drop whereof was to be met with on our route. Our allies fainted on the road in numbers; one of them died, and alfo one of our foldiers. Cortes feeing the diftreffes of the army, halted under fome pine trees, and fent a party forward to feek for relief. When I faw them about to fet off, my friend Chriftoval de Oli being one of them, I brought three of my Indian fervants
vants

vants with me, and followed the party, which they obferving, halted in order to make me return, but I was refolved, and De Oli at laft affented, telling me I muft expect to fight my way. About half a league in front were fome villages on the fide of a ridge. The cavalry went thither and found water in the houfes, and one of my fervants brought me from thence a large jar, which they ufe in that country, full of water. I then determined to return, for the inhabitants of the village had begun to take the alarm. I found Cortes juft fetting forward on his march, and gave him and the captains a hearty draught each out of the jar, which my fervants carried very well concealed, for thirft confiders itfelf before any one. We arrived at the villages and found water, though not much; the fun was then near fetting, and our cavalry came in and reported that the whole country was in movement againft us; we therefore halted here. I was on the night guard, and recollect that it was very windy and rainy. Several of our foldiers were taken ill with inflamations in the mouth and throat, from eating a fpecies of thiftle or artichoke, to quench their thirft.

Early the next morning we purfued our route, and about eight o'clock arrived at Suchimileco. I can give no idea of the number of the enemies troops which were gathered here, they were in fuch vaft bodies. They had broken down the bridge which was in front, and fortified themfelves with parapets and pallifades; their leaders were armed with fwords which they had taken from us in the fatal night of Mexico, and which they had polifhed and made very bright. The attack lafted for half an hour at the bridge. Some of our people paffed the water by fwimming, and fome loft their lives in it. What was worft, feveral bodies fell on our flanks and rear. When our cavalry had got on firm ground, with the lofs of two more of our foldiers killed, we drove them before us, but a reinforcement of at leaft ten thoufand Mexicans juft then arrived, and received the charge of our cavalry, four of whom they wounded. Here the good chefnut horfe which our Cortes rode tired under him amongft a croud of the enemy, who pulled or knocked the general down, with the intention of taking him alive; more crouds now

gathered

gathered about him, and were hurrying him off, but a body of our Tlafcalan allies headed by the brave Chriftoval de Olea came to his ref_ cue, and remounted him, though he was feverely wounded in the head. Olea alfo received three defperate wounds from the fwords of the enemy.

As all the ftreets of the town were full of Mexican troops, we were obliged to divide into bodies and fight feparately; but thofe who were neareft, knowing by the outcry and noife that it was very ferious in that part where Cortes commanded, hurried thither, and found him with about fifteen of the cavalry in a very embarraffed fituation, among the canals and parapets. We then forced the enemy to give ground, and brought off our Cortes and Olea. On firft paffing the bridge, Cortes had ordered the cavalry in two divifions, to clear our flanks. At this time they returned to us, every one of them wounded, and re_ ported that the numbers were fuch that their efforts were unavailing.

We were in an enclofed court, dreffing our wounds with burnt oil, and tearing cloth to bind them, when the cavalry came in; and in a fhort time after, fuch a volley of arrows came among us that very few efcaped unhurt. We now, together with the cavalry, fallied out among the enemy, and ufed our fwords to fuch effect that they left a confide_ rable number behind them on the ground; our lofs being, one man and two horfes killed. Having now a little breathing time, for the enemy defifted from their attempt to ftorm our poft, Cortes brought his troops to the large enclofures where were the temples of the Indians, and fome of our party going to the top, which commanded Mexico and the whole lake, perceived above two thoufand canoes coming from the city againft us full of troops. A body of ten thoufand men alfo marched on the land fide, to attack us on that night, and another body of ten thoufand was in readinefs as a relief. All this we learned from five of the chiefs whom we made prifoners. We pofted ftrong guards at thofe places where the enemy were to difembark, the cavalry were in readinefs to act upon the roads and firm ground, and conftant patroles were kept

N n

going

going during the night. I and ten more soldiers were posted as a guard upon a wall of lime and stone, which commanded one of the landing places. While we were on the watch, we heard a noise which we knew to be occasioned by the approach of a party of the enemy. We were prepared, and beat them off, sending one of our soldiers to make a report to Cortes. The enemy returned in a very short time, and attacking us again, knocked down two of our party, and then drew off to attempt a landing at another place, which was a small gate upon a deep canal. The night was very dark, and as these people are not accustomed to fight during that season, it appeared that their two armies fell into confusion, and contrary to the orders they received, formed in one body, making at least fifteen thousand men.

I must now speak of myself, not meaning it however in the way of boast. When our report reached Cortes, he came to us with ten of the cavalry, and as he approached without speaking, I challenged, " who goes there?" and getting no answer, I and my comrade, one Gonzalo Sanchez a Portuguese of Algarve, sent three or four shots at them. Cortes knowing our voices observed to those with him, that this post required no visiting, for we were two of his veterans. He then remarked to us that our station was a dangerous one, and turning about without saying any more, he continued his rounds. I afterwards heard that one of Narvaez's soldiers was whipped for negligence on this night.

Our powder being all exhausted, Cortes ordered us to prepare a good store of arrows, which we were employed during the night in heading and feathering, under the directions of Pedro Barba the captain of the crossbow-men. At day break the enemy attacked us, but without much success; for we killed several of their leaders, and took many of them prisoners, with the loss of but one Spaniard killed. Our cavalry who had advanced, fell in with the Mexicans, and not being strong enough to attack them, sent back for assistance; on which the whole of our force sallied out. We charged and defeated the enemy,

and

and made several prisoners, who informed us of the plan of the Mexicans to wear us out by inceffant attacks. We therefore determined to quit that place on the enfuing day. In the interim, our troops and allies having intelligence of the wealth which was in the town, got fome of the prifoners to point out to them the houfes that contained it, the approach to which was by a caufeway with fmall bridges over the canals, for they ftood on the frefh water lake. From thefe they returned loaded with cotton cloths and other valuables, and this example induced others to follow it. Unfortunately, while thus employed, a body of Mexicans in canoes came upon them, and wounding many, feized four foldiers of the company of Captain De Monjaraz, alive, and hurrying them into their veffels, carried them to Mexico in triumph. From thefe men Guatimotzin the King of Mexico was informed of the fmallnefs of our numbers, and our great lofs in killed and wounded. After having queftioned them as much as he thought proper, he commanded their hands and feet to be cut off, and in this lamentable condition fent them through many diftricts of the neighbourhood, as a fample of what he expected to do by us all, and after having thus exhibited them through the country they were put to death. The enfuing morning afforded opportunity for frefh attacks upon us, as had been regularly the cafe for the four days during which we ftaid in Suchimelco.

Previous to our march, Cortes drew his troops to an open place a little out of the town, where the market was held. Here he formed us, and then made a fpeech, wherein he dwelt upon the dangers we had to go through in our retreat, and the great bodies of the enemy that waited us on the road; for which reafon, he ftrongly infifted on the neceffity of leaving all the luggage behind; but we replied that we were men able to defend our properties, our perfons, and his alfo; and that it would be very paltry in us to abandon what we had acquired. When he faw our determination, he put us in order for the march, the baggage in the center, and the cavalry forming the advanced and rear guard; and it was protected alfo by our crofsbow-men, for as to our mufquetry it was ufelefs from want of powder. The enemy attacked us upon our

retreat,

retreat, purfuing us as far as Cuyocan. There were in this neighbour-hood clufters of towns, each of confiderable magnitude, built in the water, at the diftance of two leagues from Mexico, and about a league and an half from each other. They amounted to above ten in number. It was the inhabitants of all thofe who had joined together at this time to attack us; their names were Suchimelco, Cuyoacan, Chohuilobufco, Iztapalapa, Coadlavaca, Mefquique, and others. We halted for two days at Cuyoacan, which we found abandoned, attending the wounded, and making arrows for our crofsbows. On the third morning we fet out upon our march for Tacuba, and were attacked as ufual, but our cavalry drove the enemy to their ditches and canals.

Cortes at this time determined to lay an ambufcade, and accordingly fet out with ten of the cavalry and four fervants. He foon fell in with a party of Mexicans who fled before him, and imprudently prefling them too far, a large body of their warriors ftarted out upon him, and in their firft attack wounded all the horfes, and getting two of the at-tendants of Cortes in their hands, carried them to Mexico to be facrifi-ced, the reft having a moft narrow efcape. Our main body reached the head quarters at Tacuba with the baggage in fafety, and not hearing any thing of Cortes or his party of cavalry, we fufpected fome misfor-tune. Alvarado, De Oli, Tapia, I, and fome more therefore went in fearch of him, towards that part whither we faw them go, and we foon met two of his fervants, who informed us of what had happen-ed. In a fhort time Cortes came up to us; he was very fad, and weeping.

When we arrived at our quarters at Tacuba it rained heavily, and we remained under it for two hours in fome large enclofed courts. The general, with his captains, the treafurer, our reverend father, and ma-ny others of us, mounted to the top of the temple which commanded all the lake, and afforded a moft furprifing and pleafing fpectacle, from the multitude of cities rifing as it were out of the water, and the innu-merable quantity of boats employed in fifhing, or rapidly pafling to and fro.

fro. All of us agreed in giving glory to God, for making us the inftruments of rendering fuch fervices: the reverend father alfo confoled
Cortes, who was very fad on account of his late lofs. When we contemplated the fcenes of what had happened to us in Mexico, and which
we could well trace from where we ftood, it made Cortes much more
fad than before. It was on this that the romance was written which
begins,

" In Tacuba was Cortes, with many a gallant chief,
" He thought upon his loffes, and bowed his head with grief.

One of our foldiers, the bachelor Alonzo Perez, who was afterwards
fifcal near Mexico, in order to confole him, obferved, that thofe things
were the common fortune of war, and that they could not at prefent
compare him to Nero viewing Rome on fire. Cortes anfwered that he
was only fad from the reflection of the dangers and fatigues that we
fhould have to go through, but that he would fhortly put his hand to
the bufinefs. Our captains and foldiers now confulted, whether it would
not be eligible to take a view of the caufeway, but it was thought not
prudent, and we continued our march by Efcapuzalco, which was
abandoned, to Tenayuca, where, in the great temple, they worfhipped
three ferpents. From this place, which was alfo abandoned, we proceeded to Guatitlan, and during the whole days march it never ceafed
raining; whereby, together with the weight of our arms, we came in
dreadfully fatigued.

The enemy gave us fome alarms in the night, during which it
rained heavily, no watch being kept by us on account of the feverity of
the weather, as I can teftify, my poft not having been vifited either by
rounds or corporal. Marching through four or five towns which were
abandoned, by a road deep in mud, we arrived in two days more at
Aculman in the diftrict of Tezcuco, where we found that a reinforcement to our army had newly arrived from Caftille. On the next day
we

we proceeded to Tezcuco, and arrived fatigued, worn out, and diminifhed in numbers.

A confpiracy againft the life of Cortes was at this time formed, by
an adherent of the governor of Cuba, one Anthonio de Villafana, native of Zamora or of Toro, and fome of the other foldiers of Narvaez,
whofe names I will not mention. The affaffination was to have been
executed in the following manner. A veffel having lately arrived from
Caftille, a letter was to be brought to the general, as from his father,
and as if it had come by that opportunity; which letter was to be delivered as he fat at table with his officers and foldiers, and when he had
opened, and was in the act of reading it, the confpirators were to fall
on and affaffinate him with their poinards, together with all of us who
were in his company. When every thing was arranged, the confpirators communicated their intentions to two principal perfons whom I will
not name, but who had been on the expedition with us, one of whom
on the death of Cortes they meant to have appointed captain general.
The offices of alguazil major, enfign, alcaldes, regidor, contador,
treafurer, veedor, and others of this kind were to have been filled up
from among the foldiers of Narvaez, and they had divided amongft
them our properties and horfes. The bufinefs was difcovered two days
after our arrival at Tezcuco, by God's mercy, who did not chufe that
New Spain fhould have been fo loft; for if we had been put to death,
all would have fallen into confufion and faction.

It feems a faithful foldier made the difcovery to Cortes, who immediately took proper fteps to prevent the mifchief from fpreading, for
he underftood it to be conducted by perfons of quality. As foon as it
was made clear to him, he gave large rewards for the information.
He then communicated it to all our captains, namely, alvarado, De
Lugo, De Oli, Sandoval, and Tapia, alfo to me, and to the two Alcaldes of that year, Luis Marin, and Pedro de Ircio; in fhort to all of
his party. As foon as we knew of it we prepared ourfelves, and attended Cortes to the quarters of Villafana, where we found him and many
others

others of the conspirators. The four alguazils seized Villafana; the others attempted to escape by flight, but Cortes ordered them to be detained, and some of them he committed to prison. Cortes then took from the bosom of Villafana a paper, with the signatures of those who were concerned with him, in consideration for whom however, he caused the report to be circulated, that it had been swallowed by Villafana, without his having seen it. He was immediately put upon his trial, but voluntarily made a confession, according to which, and to the testimony of many witnesses, he was condemned by his judges, the two alcaldes, conjointly with Cortes, and De Oli who sat by virtue of his office. Shortly after his condemnation, having confessed himself to the reverend Father Juan Diaz, he was hanged from a window of the apartment.

Of the several others who were arrested, no more were proceeded against; enough having been done for example and intimidation. Cortes however to prevent such attempts in future thought it prudent to appoint a guard for his person, composed of valiant and faithful soldiers. They were selected from those who had been with him from the first, and were commanded by a gentleman named Anthonio de Quinones. Henceforward, although he showed great attention to those who had been in the conspiracy, and treated them in the best manner, he took care to be on his guard with them.

At this time came out an order for all the prisoners to be brought to an appointed place, in order to be marked. Not to take up time with repetitions of the story I will sum up all in one observation which is, that if what was ill done the first time, was worse done the second, this third was worst of all; for after the royal fifth had been drawn out, Cortes took his own, and then came no less than thirty successive drafts for the captains. Besides, those handsome and good female prisoners which we put in to be marked were stolen out of the crowd, and were kept concealed until it was no longer inconvenient to produce them.

The

The brigantines were now finifhed, and the canal brought to a fufficient width and depth to float them to the lake. Cortes therefore iffued a circular notice to all the diftricts of our alliance in the neighbourhood of Tezcuco, to fend him each within the fpace of the next eight days, eight thoufand arrow heads made of copper; alfo an equal number of fhafts, of a particular wood. By the expiration of the given time the whole number was brought, executed to a degree of perfection which exceeded the pattern. Captain P. Barba who commanded the crofsbow-men ordered each of his foldiers to provide themfelves with two cords and nuts, and to prove the range of their bows, for one of the laft fhips which came from Caftille had brought out a fupply of the materials to make cords, and alfo of powder. Cortes ordered the cavalry to have their lances well pointed, and to ufe their horfes to daily exercife; and he at this time fent an exprefs to Xicotenga the elder, otherwife Don Lorenzo de Vargas, for twenty thoufand of the warriors of his nation, and thofe of Guaxocingo and Cholula; and he fent fimilar notices to Chalco and Talmalanco, fummoning them to a general rendezvous, on the day after the feaft of the Holy Ghoft, at which time Don Hernando our ally of Tezcuco was alfo to join us with all his forces.

On the day after the feftival of the Holy Ghoft, Cortes infpected his army in the large quadrangles of Tezcuco. They amounted to eighty four cavalry, fix hundred and fifty infantry with fword and buckler or lances, and one hundred and ninety four mufqueteers and crofsbow-men. Out of this number he took for the fervice of his fleet twelve of the mufqueteers or crofsbow-men, and twelve of the other infantry for rowers, under the command of a captain, to each veffel; he alfo diftributed twenty cannoniers through the whole fleet, which he armed with what guns fit for this fervice we had in our ftores.

Having thus diftributed his force, Cortes gave the following orders. Firft, no perfon to utter any blafphemy againft our Lord Jefus Chrift, the Holy Virgin his mother, the Holy Apoftles, nor any other

of

of the faints, under heavy penalties. Second, no foldier to ill treat our allies in their perfons or properties. Third, no foldier to abfent himfelf from his quarters on any pretence. Fourth, every foldier to be fully provided with arms offenfive and defenfive. Fifth, no foldier to ftake his horfe or arms at gaming. Sixth, no foldier to fleep out of armour, or without his weapons befide him, except in cafe of wounds or ficknefs. Laftly, penalty of death for fleeping on, or abfence from a centinels poft, abfence from quarters without leave, quitting the ranks in the field, or flight in battle.

Although a number of our people had ferved as failors before, there was a great averfenefs on the prefent occafion among them to act as rowers. The general was therefore obliged to make enquiry, and confidering all thofe who belonged to, or were natives of Palos, Moguer, Triano, El Puerto, or any other feaport, or who had been known to have been employed in fifhing, as being of the profeffion, he ordered them to the oars, and although many of thefe brought their gentility as an objection, he would not hear of it, but enforced his orders; by which he obtained one hundred and fifty, who were, as it will appear in the fequel, better fituated than any of us who had to bear the weight and dangers of the field. The crews being embarked, each brigantine hoifted a royal ftandard, and alfo its peculiar one. The general then appointed the captains as follows: Garci Holguin, Pedro Barba, Juan de Limpias Carvajal the deaf, Juan Xaremillo, Geronymo Ruiz de la Mora, Carvajal his companion who is now very old and lives in the ftreet of St. Francis, one Portillo, a good foldier with an handfome wife, Zamora, mafter of a fhip, now living in Guaxaca, Colmenero a mariner and brave foldier, Lerma, Gines Nortes, Briones native of Salamanca, another whofe name I have forgotten, and Miguel diaz de Auz. To thefe he gave inftructions how they were to act, and with what officers of the land forces they were to cooperate.

At this time arrived the army of our allies of Tlafcala under the command of the younger Xicotenga. He brought with him his two

O o

brothers. In this army alfo came fome of the warriors of Cholula, and Guaxocinga, but not in any confiderable number. The alacrity of the whole body appeared in their arrival a day previous to that appointed; they advanced in great parade, each chief having a ftandard with their national device, a white fpread eagle, embroidered upon it. They entered the town in high fpirits, fhouting " Caftilla! Caftilla! Tlafcala! " Tlafcala! live the Emperor!" and it was about three hours from the time of the arrival of their advanced party, until the rear had come in. Cortes, with many compliments, difmiffed them to their quarters, and promifing to make them all rich on their return to their native country. We now heard that the Mexicans had put to death three of our foldiers who had been left by Pizarro to fearch for mines, one only, named Barrientos, efcaping to Chinanta, where he was protected.

Our general made his difpofition for the attack upon the city of Mexico as follows.

Pedro de Alvarado, with one hundred and fifty infantry, thirty cavalry, eighteen mufqueteers and crofsbow-men, and eight thoufand Tlafcalans was to take poft at Tacuba, having to affift him Jorge de Alvarado his brother, Gutierre de Badajos, and Andres de Monjaras, each of whom was captain of a company, confifting of fifty infantry, and a third of the crofsbow-men and mufqueteers, the cavalry being commanded by Alvarado in perfon. To this detachment I was appointed.

Chriftoval de Oli, having under him the captains Andres de Tapia, Francifco Verdugo, Francifco de Lugo, thirty cavalry, one hundred and feventy five infantry, twenty mufqueteers and crofsbow-men, and eight thoufand Indians was to take poft at Cuyoacan, and Gonzalo de Sandoval, with captains Luis Marin and P. de Ircio, at the head of twenty four cavalry, one hundred and fifty infantry, fourteen mufqueteers and crofsbow-men, and upwards of eight thoufand Indians was to take his poft at Iztapalapa. The two firft named divifions were to march by the right, the third in the oppofite direction. Sandovals

party

party had alſo orders not to march, until Cortes who commanded the flotilla in perſon ſhould launch out upon the lake.

I muſt now advert to another affair which happened at this time. The diviſions of the two captains in chief Alvarado and De Oli being prepared to ſet out, in order not to be incumbered with our Indian allies on the march, we ſent them off one day before us, with orders to halt and wait for our arrival when they came upon the Mexican territory. The Tlaſcalans purſuing their march, Chichimacatecle remarked the abſence of the younger Xicotenga, the commander in chief. On enquiring it was found that he had ſecretly gone away on the preceding night to Tlaſcala, there to ſeize and poſſeſs himſelf of the property and territory of Chichimacatecle, thinking this a good opportunity, in the abſence of that chief and of the other warriors of his nation, and fearing no oppoſition ſince the death of Maxicatzin. His diſinclination to the expedition had alſo been apparent from the firſt. Chichimacatecle, on diſcovering the deſign againſt him, immediately returned to Tezcuco to inform Cortes, who on hearing it diſpatched five of the chiefs of Tezcuco and two of Tlaſcala after Xicotenga, with a meſſage from him to requeſt his return. His anſwer was, that if Maxicatzin and his old father had believed him, they would not be now ridden by Cortes in the manner they were, and he abſolutely refuſed to return. This anſwer being ſent back to Cortes, he commanded an alguazil attended by four of the cavalry and five chiefs of Tezcuco, to ſet out immediately, giving them orders, wherever they found Xicotenga, to ſeize and hang him without ceremony. Alvarado interceded ſtrongly for him, but ultimately to no purpoſe, for although Cortes appeared to liſten to him, the party which arreſted Xicotenga in a town ſubject to Tezcuco, there hung him under private orders of Cortes not to let him go from them alive, and as ſome ſay with the approbation of his father.

This affair detained us one day, and on the next, the two detachments of Alvarado and De Oli marched by the ſame route, and halted

for

for the night, in a place subject to Tezcuco named Aculma. Here a disagreeable affair had like to have taken place. It appeared that De Oli had sent forward to take quarters, and had appropriated every house in the town to his own company, marking them by putting green branches on the terraces, so that when Alvarado's detachment arrived, we had not a place to lodge in. Our soldiers immediately stood to their arms to fight those of De Oli, and the two captains had already challenged each other, but several of the more moderate officers interfering, they were pacified for the present. An express was immediately sent to Cortes, who wrote to every one of any influence amongst our detachments, condemning the steps which had been taken, and earnestly recommending a reconciliation. After this Alvarado and De Oli never were friends.

We continued our march for two days more, by Mexican cities which were abandoned, the last of which was Guatitlan; and on the third, passing the towns of Tenayuca and Escapuzalco where we found our allies * waiting for us, we proceeded to Tacuba.

The enemy gave notice by their noises that they were about us in great numbers, and our two detachments, it was settled, should on the ensuing day go to cut the aqueduct of Chapultepeque. At the time appointed, we set out with our allies, and though the enemy attacked us in our march, we succeeded, destroying the pipes, so that from that day, no more fresh water came to Mexico. It was now determined to try our fortune against the city, and see if we could not at least get possession of a bridge upon the causeway of Tacuba. When we arrived there, the immense number of boats, and of their troops on the land, was a subject of astonishment. By the first volley of their arrows they killed three and wounded thirty of our soldiers; nevertheless we advanced to the bridge, the enemy, as it were by stratagem, receding, and now we were upon a causeway twenty feet wide, exposed as a butt to the arrows of those on the water on both our flanks. Our musquetry and crossbows had no effect whatever on their canoes they were so well protected; as

to

---

* The whole number of whom amounted to seventy thousand.

to the cavalry their horfes were all wounded, and if they purfued the enemy a little diftance on the caufeway, they were ftopped by the parapets which they had built acrofs it, and which they defended with long lances; and when our infantry advanced againft them in front, the enemy threw themfelves into the water. Thus we were fighting them for upwards of an hour, their numbers increafing from every part of the lake, and our allies only encumbering the caufeway. Being utterly unable to refift the enemy who were on the water we determined to retire, which we did, leaving eight dead and having above fifty wounded, the enemy purfuing us clofely.

On the enfuing day, Captain De Oli proceeded with his detachment for Cuyoacan; he talked in terms of difapprobation of the preceding expedition, laying the blame on the rafhnefs of Alvarado. We all were folicitous that the two captains fhould remain together, and certainly their feparation was very imprudent, for had the enemy known the fmallnefs of our number, they would have fallen on and deftroyed either detachment, during the four or five days that we were feparated, and before the arrival of Cortes with the flotilla. In thefe two pofitions our detachments remained for the above period, without venturing to pay another vifit to the Mexican caufeways. During this time the enemy frequently fent bodies of their troops to the main land, and annoyed us with attacks in our quarters.

Sandoval with his detachment left Tezcuco on the fourth day after the feaft of Corpus Chrifti, and marching through a friendly country, arrived in front of the town of Iztapalapa. On his arrival he immediately attacked the enemy in that place, and burned many of the houfes which were built on the firm ground; but frefh bodies of Mexicans came both by land and water to their relief, and while thus occupied, our troops obferved a fmoke to rife from the top of a hill above the town, which was anfwered in the fame manner at other points round the lake, and this we found to be a fignal for the information of the enemy, that our flotilla was launched; a circumftance which occafioned them to

relax

relax in their hostilities against Sandoval. He now remained unmolested in his insulated situation, in a part of the town of Iztapalapa, between which and Cuyoacan there were no means of communication but by a causeway which crosses the lake, and the passage of which was impracticable in the face of the enemy.

Cortes when he brought his flotilla upon the lake, first went to attack a rock which forms a small island just by Mexico, and on which many of the natives as well of that neighbourhood as of other parts had taken refuge. As soon as the enemy discovered his intention, their whole force from every part of the lake proceeded against him. When our general perceived the immense number of large boats full of fighting men, for it exceeded four thousand, he drew his flotilla into an open part of the lake, and ordered his captains to wait patiently for a breeze of wind which was just then begining to spring up. The enemy thinking this was owing to fear, began to close round him with great triumph, and just at this moment the wind rising in his favor, the whole fleet set sail, plying their oars at the same time; bearing down upon the Mexican canoes in this manner, they sunk a number of them, and compelled the rest to take shelter in the recesses on the sides of the lake.

After this Cortes sailed for Cuyoacan. Here he had another attack by the Mexicans, who assailed his vessels from the temples on the land, as well as with their canoes; but he brought four guns to bear upon them, and did considerable execution; although, by some mismanagement of the gunners, his powder magazine blew up, wounding many of his people. This misfortune obliged him to detach his lightest vessel to Sandoval for a supply. At Cuyoacan he remained with the flotilla for two days, and here I will leave him to relate what passed in the detachment of Alvarado. When we perceived that the flotilla was upon the lake, we marched out upon the causeway as far as the bridge, where we passed our time in a repetition of engagements with the enemy, but to little effect, farther than repairing the passes in our rear as

we

we advanced, nor did we now suffer the cavalry to come to the causeway.

Sandoval had found that in his present position he could not sufficiently annoy the enemy, who were established in the houses built in the water; he therefore advanced by a causeway to a place which commanded them better. This being perceived from Mexico, a large detachment was sent in canoes, with directions to cut the causeway behind our troops. Cortes observing this set sail with his vessels for their relief, ordering De Oli to go thither with a body of troops by the causeway. Having relieved Sandoval, the general ordered this detachment to a place named Tepeaquilla, where is now built the church of Nueftra Senora de Guadelupe, in which many wonderful miracles have been, and are, performed.

As it was impossible for our troops to advance upon the causeways without their flanks being secured on the water, the flotilla was formed into three divisions, and one of them attached to each of the three corps of our army; that is to say, four ships to Alvarado, six to De Oli, and two to Sandoval, making in all twelve, for the thirteenth, named " Busca Ruido, or follow the noise," being found to be too small, was ordered to be laid up, and her crew divided among the rest, as we had twenty very badly wounded already on board the ships. Alvarado now ordered us out upon the causeway, and placing two of the ships on each side, he thereby protected the flanks. We drove the enemy from several bridges and barricades, but after fighting during the whole day, we were obliged at night to retreat to our quarters, almost every man of us wounded by the showers of arrows and stones, which exceeded imagination; for we were attacked constantly by fresh troops bearing different devices, by land, while from the terraces of the houses, the enemy commanded our ships. As we could not leave a party to secure what we got in the day, at night the enemy repossessed themselves of the bridges, and put better defences on them. They deepened the water in some places, and in the shallow part they dug pits, and placed canoes in in ambufcade, which they fecured from the attacks of our veffels by pallifades under the water. This was the manner in which they oppofed us every day. The cavalry as I before obferved could do nothing; the enemy had built parapets acrofs the caufeways which they defended with long lances, and even had an attack been practicable, the foldiers would not rifk their horfes, which at this time coft eight hundred crowns, and fome more than one thoufand; nor indeed were they to be had at any price.

When we arrived at night, we were employed in curing our wounds, and a foldier named Juan Catalan alfo healed them by charms and prayers, which, with the mercy of our Lord Jefus, recovered us very faft. But wounded or not, we were obliged to go againft the enemy every day, as otherwife our companies would not have been twenty men ftrong. When our allies faw that the before mentioned foldier cured us by charms and prayers, all their wounded came to him, fo that he had more bufinefs on his hands than he knew what to do with. Every day our enfign was difabled, not having it in his power to carry the colours, and defend himfelf. Corn we had fufficiency of, but we wanted refrefhments for the wounded. What preferved us was the plant called "quilites," cherries while in feafon, and "tunas" or Indian figs. The fituation of our other parties round the lake was fimilar to what I have here defcribed.

The enemy in the city rufhed out on the fignal being made from the top of the great temple of Taltelulco; and thefe attacks were made every day, and repeated by frefh troops, who were formed and marched out in fucceffion. Finding that we gained fo little and loft fo much, we refolved to change our plan of operations. There was on our caufeway a fmall open place, where were fome buildings for religious worfhip; here we eftablifhed a poft, and lodged ourfelves, though very badly, as every fhower of rain came in upon us, leaving our cavalry and Indian allies to fecure our rear in Tacuba, from which place we were fupplied with bread. From this time, as we advanced, we filled the water cuts

which

which interfected the caufeway, and proftrated the houfes which were on each fide of it; for it was exceeding difficult to fet them on fire, nor could the flames communicate from one to another, on account of the water which was between them, and if we threw ourfelves into the water to fwim to a houfe, the enemy deftroyed us from their terraffes. We guarded every pafs day and night as we gained it, and our method of keeping guard was as follows.

The company which was firft for duty took it from fun fet to midnight with forty men; the fecond company with the fame number came on at midnight, and remained u▮▮ two hours before day break, the firft guard not quitting the poft, but fleeping on the ground; this fecond guard watched the hours of lethargy, and after them came on the third company for the two hours until day, at which time, as thofe who were relieved did not quit the poft, there were an hundred and twenty men at the guard. Sometimes our whole detachment remained under arms during the night, for our prifoners had informed us that it was the intention of the Mexicans, by a great effort, to force our poft, as they knew that by fo doing they would entirely difconcert the plans of the other two; and it was intended that the nine towns in and about the lake, including ours of Tacuba, together with Ezcapuzalco and Tenayuca, fhould make a joint effort, and attack us in the rear while the Mexicans attacked us in front. It was at the fame time intended to carry off our luggage and bakery in Tacuba. This intelligence we immediately communicated to our cavalry, warning them and our allies to be well on their guard.

As we had been informed, fo it happened; we were attacked for feveral nights in fucceffion, from midnight to the break of day. The enemy fometimes came on with great noife, at others ftole upon us in filence, but during the night their attacks were never made with fo much refolution as in the day. We were however harraffed to death with wounds, fatigues, wind, rain, and cold. The place where we were pofted was now mud and water, and our miferable food of maize, and

P p

herbs

herbs withall! but, as our officers faid, fuch is the fortune of war! with all our fufferings nothing effectual was gained: the parapets we threw down, or the ditches we filled up during the day, the enemy replaced in the enfuing night. What ufe was our cutting off their water, or clofing their caufeways againft them, when they were fupplied by canoes with whatever they wanted from the neighbouring towns on the lake? In order to prevent this, it was determined that two of our veffels fhould cruife during the night, to intercept them. This was found to anfwer in a confiderable degree, but ftill fome efcaped into the city.

The Mexicans had the b●●●hefs at this time to form a plan for the furprife of thefe veffels. For this purpofe they prepared thirty of their largeft piraguas, and concealed them among reeds, fending two or three canoes along the lake, as if conveying provifions, by way of a bait for our veffels. The Mexicans had alfo fixed piles of large timber below the water, in the direction which our fhips were to be drawn in. The canoes being perceived by our people, two veffels fallied out upon them; the others appeared to take fright, and rowed towards the ambufcade, followed by our veffels, which as foon as they arrived near enough, were furrounded by the thirty piraguas. By the firft difcharge they wounded every officer, foldier, and rower, on board; and the veffels could not ftir on account of the piles of timber. The enemy continuing their attacks, killed a captain named Portilla; he was a gentleman who had ferved in Italy. Captain Pedro Barba alfo of the crofsbowmen died of his wounds, and the veffels fell into their hands. Thefe belonged to the principal divifion, which Cortes commanded; he was much exafperated, but in the courfe of a fhort time repayed them well in their own way.

Cortes as alfo our other chiefs, by his order, purfued their plan of advancing againft the city. As they gained ground, they threw down the houfes, and with the materials filled up the ditches or canals which croffed the caufeways; and our brave Tlafcalan allies rendered us the greateft fervices, during the whole war. The Mexicans oppofed our

progrefs

progrefs by breaking a bridge in the rear of their parapets and barricades, where the water was very deep, leaving one obvious pafs as a decoy, and in other parts, pit falls under the water; they alfo made parapets on both fides of the breach, they placed palifades in the deep water where our veffels could approach, and they had canoes manned ready to fally out upon the fignal given. When they had made thefe preparations they advanced againft us in three bodies, one by the fide of Tacuba, the other by the ruins of the houfes which had been deftroyed, and the third by the caufeway, where they had made the works. Alvarado had brought part of his cavalry to our poft, fince the houfes were deftroyed. We repulfed the enemy on all fides, and one party of us having forced them from the work I have mentioned, croffed the water, up to our necks, at the pafs they had left open, and followed them, until we came to a place where were large temples and towers of idols. Here we were affailed by frefh troops from the houfes and roofs, and thofe whom we purfued faced about and came againft us. We were obliged to retreat, which we did with regularity, but when we came to the water, we found that the enemy in their canoes had got poffeffion of the pafs where we had croffed. We were therefore obliged to look for other places, but as they came preffing on us, we were at length compelled to throw ourfelves into the lake and get over as we could. Thofe who were not able to fwim fell into the pits; the enemy clofed in upon them, wounded moft, and took five of our foldiers alive. The veffels which came to our relief could not approach, being embarraffed among the palifades, and here they loft two foldiers. It was a wonder that we were not all deftroyed in the pit falls; a number of the enemy laid hands on me, but our Lord Jefus Chrift gave me force to difengage my arm, and by dint of a good fword, I got free from them, though wounded, and arrived on the dry ground, where I fainted away, and remained fenfelefs for a time. This was owing to my great exertions, and lofs of blood. When this mob had their claws on me, I recommended myfelf to our Lord and his bleffed mother, and they heard my prayer, glorified be they for all their mercies! one of our cavalry croffed the water with us this day; he and his horfe were killed. Fortunately,

nately,

nately, the reft were with Alvarado in Tacuba; had they been with us they muft have been all deftroyed from the tops of the buildings, for the action took place as it were within the very city. After this fuccefs the enemy kept us conftantly employed during the day and night, by attacks upon our pofts. Cortes was much diffatisfied at hearing of our defeat, which he confidered as owing to our neglect of his directions that the cuts acrofs the caufeways fhould be filled with timber and fods as we advanced.

In the fpace of four days, and with the lofs of fix foldiers, we completely filled up this great aperture, and here we eftablifhed our advanced poft, the enemy having one oppofite to us. Their method of keeping guard was this; they made a great fire in their front, which concealed them from our view, except when they came to renew the fire, as it was fometimes extinguifhed by the rains, which were at that feafon frequent and heavy. They kept profound filence on guard, nor was it ever interrupted except by their fignals, which were given by a whiftle. Our fhot did no execution among them, for they fortified their poft by a parapet and a new ditch. Having defcribed the manner in which guard was kept on each fide, I will now give an account of our daily employment. In the morning we marched againft the enemy; after engaging them during the whole day we retreated, towards evening, covered with wounds, firft clearing the caufeway of our allies whofe numbers embarraffed us, a circumftance the enemy were watchful to take advantage of; after which we fell back ftep by ftep, firing at the enemy as they advanced, and being flanked by the armed veffels, until we reached our poft. When we arrived in our quarters we fat down to our mifery of maize cakes, herbs, and tunas, curing our wounds with oil, and remaining all night fubject to conftant alarms.

Cortes and his party were employed in the fame manner, and his lofs in killed and wounded was by this time become very confiderable. He conftantly fent out veffels at night to fcour the lake, and one night they brought in to him fome prifoners of confequence; from them he
learned

learned that the enemy had formed an ambufcade fimilar to their former one, of forty piraguas and the fame number of canoes. Cortes then prepared fix veffels, and fent them during the night, and with muffled oars, to a place of concealment within a quarter of a leagues diftance of that of the enemy. It muft be obferved that the bufhes and tall reeds, and the water cuts at the edges of the lake, favored thofe deceptions. Early in the morning one of our veffels was fent as if in fearch of the Mexican canoes which went with provifions to the city, the prifoners being put on board it in order to point out the place where their flotilla was concealed. The enemy alfo played off the deception of loaded canoes to draw us thither, and thefe canoes pretending to endeavor to efcape, rowed towards the ambufcade laid by their party; our veffel purfued them very near it, and then brought to, as if from apprehenfion. The enemy's flotilla perceiving that fhe did not advance, fallied out on her, thofe on board of her rowing towards that part where our fhips were concealed. When they found that the enemy were brought to that point where we wifhed them to be, the crew fired two fhots as a fignal to our ambufcade, immediately on which the veffels pufhed out, and falling on the enemy ran down feveral, and difperfed the reft, making a number of prifoners. This gave them enough of ambufcades, nor did they from that time run acrofs to Mexico fo openly as before.

The people of the cities in the lake growing tired of this warfare, waited on Cortes at this time in order to make fubmiffion, declaring that they had been forced into hoftility by the Mexicans. Cortes received them with affability, gave them affurances of protection according to their behaviour, and at the fame time told them that he expected their affiftance in the fupply of boats and provifions, and in erecting barracks for the troops. This they promifed readily, but performed very badly. Cortes had huts built for his detachment, but the reft remained expofed to the weather, a very fevere duty in itfelf in that climate, where during the months of June, July, and Auguft, it rains continually.

O

Our detachment perfevered in filling up every ditch and canal as we proceeded with the materials of the houfes which we deftroyed; and conftantly gained temples, bridges, or houfes which ftood feparate from each other, and were acceffible by draw-bridges only. To prevent jealoufy, the companies took the working and covering parties alternately, and towards evening, when we drew off, the whole ftood to their arms, and retreated, fending our Indian allies before us. The latter rendered us moft important affiftance in the working duty, both in pulling down the houfes, and filling the apertures. Sandoval during this time was obliged to fuftain conftant attacks, and Cortes on his fide attacked one of the out pofts of the city, where the canal which croffed the caufeway was too deep to be forded. The enemy had fortified it ftrongly, and defended it both by land and water. Cortes commanded the attack in perfon, and with fuccefs; but at night he was obliged to retire without filling the ditch, and with the lofs of four Spaniards killed and above thirty wounded, for the pafs was commanded from the terraces, and the pallifades made in the water prevented the approach of the veffels.

Guatimotzin now determined to wear us out by continual efforts. Accordingly, on the twenty firft of June, the anniverfary of the day of our entry into Mexico, the enemy attacked us at every point with their whole force by land and water, at the hour of the fecond fleep, or of lethargy, that is two hours before day. The number fit for duty at our poft was one hundred and twenty; our allies we had fent entirely off the caufeway, and it was with our utmoft efforts that we could refift the enemy; we at length however repulfed them from all our pofts, but with the lofs of many killed and wounded. Alvarado's detachment loft two foldiers on this occafion. The enemies attacks were continued for two nights fucceffively upon the different pofts, and they afterwards concentrated their whole force in an affault upon ours, which took place at day break. This was the moft defperate of all; if our allies had been with us we fhould have been loft. Our cavalry on this occafion faved our flanks, and we had confiderable fupport from our fhips. Eight of
our

our soldiers were killed in this attack, and Alvarado was wounded; but we ultimately beat the enemy off, and also made four of their chiefs prisoners. I fear to tire my readers with this repetition of battles. For ninety three days together were we employed in the siege of this great and strong city, and every day and every night we were engaged with the enemy. Of course they must pardon what my duty as an historian compels me to relate; still were I to extend my narrative to include every action which took place, it would be almost endless, and my history would resemble that of Amadis, and the other books of chivalry.

Cortes growing weary of delay, called a council of war, relative to a general assault upon the city. His plan was, to march by the three causeways, and to endeavour to gain the great square, where, uniting our whole force, we should command all the streets leading to it. Upon this proposal there was a great difference of opinion, for many thought our present method of proceeding by filling the canals as we advanced, destroying the houses, and making a road with the materials, was preferable to that recommended by Cortes, whereby, in going into the heart of the city, we should become the besieged instead of being the besiegers, and fall exactly into the situation in which we were when obliged to fly from Mexico. We should also they said be involved in greater difficulties than formerly, for the enemy would now bring their whole power by land and water upon us, so that we should have to contend with them in the city, on the lake, and all round it, without the possibility of retreat, which they could preclude by cutting the causeways. When Cortes had heard the opinions of all, and the good reasons upon which they were founded, the result was, that he gave orders for our whole force, together with our allies, to attack the city on the ensuing day, and to get possession of the great square.

On the next morning therefore, having heard mass, and recommending ourselves to God, our three detachments marched against the enemy's posts in their front. Those commanded by Cortes and Sandoval

val met with lefs violent oppofition than that which fell to the lot of the division of Alvarado, to which I belonged. In our attack upon the firft dike, moft of the Spaniards received wounds, one was killed, and above one thoufand of our allies killed or wounded. Cortes at firft bore down all before him, and having driven the enemy from a poft where the water was very deep and the caufeway very narrow, he was induced to purfue them in their retreat to the city, his Indian allies crouding clofe after the Spaniards. The enemy induced him by frequent halts and feigned attacks to continue the purfuit, and the caufeway had been narrowed, to anfwer their defign. It was the will of our Lord that Cortes and his captains fhould be fo negligent as to omit filling the ditch, which they had paffed. The caufeway was alfo in fome parts covered with water, and deep in mud. When the enemy faw our Cortes thus run into the trap which they had laid, multitudes in canoes fallied out againft him and took him on his flanks and rear, his own veffels not being able to approach on account of the pallifadoes. It became now neceffary for the troops to retreat, which they did at firft with great regularity, but when they came to the narrow pafs I have before mentioned, the difficulty of the ground, with the fury of the attack, from a retreat turned it into a race, our people flying before the enemy without attempting to defend themfelves. Our Cortes ufed every exertion to rally them but in vain; he received a wound in the leg from the enemy on board the canoes at the pafs, where they killed fix of our horfes, and carried off feventy two Spaniards alive. Six chiefs feized upon Cortes, but it was the will of God that he fhould efcape, for that valiant foldier Chriftoval de Olea, feeing his general's danger, flew to his affiftance, as did another brave man named Lerma. Olea with his own hand killed four of the fix Mexican chiefs, gallantly lofing his own life in defence of his general, and Lerma efcaped with the greateft difficulty. Other foldiers now arrived to the affiftance of our Cortes; amongft the number was Quinones captain of his guards. They took him out of the water in their arms, and placing him on a horfe, hurried him off from the crowd of enemies, and fhortly after, his major domo named Chriftoval de Guzman brought one of his own horfes for him. The

enemy

enemy followed up their attack with ardour, and the unfortunate Guz-man being feized by them was carried alive to Mexico. Cortes and the fhattered remains of his troops, purfued to the laft, arrived with great difficulty at their quarters, where I will leave them for the prefent, to relate what happened in the divifion commanded by Alvarado.

After our firft attack, wherein we defeated the enemy, as we were advancing, we were met by frefh troops in great parade, bearing plumes of feathers, and devices on their ftandards. When we came near them they threw down before us five bleeding heads, crying out to us that they were thofe of Cortes and his officers, and that we fhould meet the fame fate with our companions; they then marched up, and fighting us foot to foot, compelled us to retreat. We as ufual called to our allies to clear the way for us, but in the prefent cafe there was no occafion; the fight of the bloody heads had done it effectually, nor did one of them remain on the caufeway to impede our retreat. Before we arrived at our quarters, and while the enemy were purfuing us, we heard their fhrill timbals, and the difmal found of the great drum, from the top of the principal temple of the god of war, which overlooked the whole city. Its mournful noife was fuch as may be imagined the mufic of the infernal gods, and it might be heard at the diftance of almoft three leagues. They were then facrificing the hearts of ten of our compani-ons to their idols. Shortly after this the king of Mexico's horn was blown, giving notice to his captains that they were then to take their enemies prifoners, or die in the attempt. It is impoffible to defcribe the fury with which they clofed upon us when they heard this fignal. Though all is as perfect to my recollection as if paffing before my eyes, it is utterly beyond my power to defcribe; all I can fay is, it was God's will that we fhould efcape from their hands, and get back in fafety to our poft. Praifed be he for his mercies, now, and at all other times!

Our cavalry made feveral charges this day, but our great fupport was in two guns which raked the caufeway, and were commanded by a gentleman named Pedro Moreno de Medrano, who always bore a

Q q

high

high reputation as an officer, but whose services on this day were most important, for the whole causeway was crouded with the enemy. We were as yet ignorant of the fate of our other detachments. Sandoval was above half a league distant, and Cortes still farther. The melancholy sight of the remains of our countrymen, and the loss of one of our vessels, three of the soldiers of which the enemy had killed, impressed our minds with despair, and we thought this the last hour of our lives. The vessel was afterwards recovered by that commanded by Captain Juan Xaramillo. Captain Juan de Limpias Caravajal, who now lives in La Puebla, a most gallant officer, had the honor of being the first who with his vessel broke through the enemies pallisades, totally losing his hearing, from this day, by excess of courage.

Cortes, most of whose soldiers had been killed, and what remained alive, wounded, was attacked in his quarters by a great body of the enemy, who threw over to him the heads of four of our companions, alledging them to be those of Alvarado, Sandoval, and others, in order to impress the soldiers of Cortes and our allies with the idea, that they had been equally successful against the other detachments. When Cortes beheld the horrid spectacle his heart sunk within him, but he kept up appearances, and ordering all to stand to their arms, made a front to the enemy. He then sent Andres de Tapia with three more mounted men to our quarters, in order to ascertain what the state of affairs was. In their way thither they were attacked by many bodies of the enemy, whom the king of Mexico had placed upon a plan of intercepting our communications. On their arrival they found us engaged with the Mexican forces. They at that time concealed the loss of Cortes, stating it at no more than five and twenty.

It is now necessary to advert to Sandoval, who had gone on victorious until the defeat of Cortes; after which the enemy turned on him, and in their first attack killed two soldiers and wounded all the rest, giving Sandoval himself three wounds, one of which was in the head. As they had done elsewhere, they threw before his troops six heads of

their

their companions, recently taken off, threatening them with the like fate. Sandoval was not to be terrified; he warned his soldiers to preserve a good countenance, and seeing no hopes of success brought his division back to their quarters, with many wounds it is true, but with the loss of only two of their number. Sandoval then, wounded as he was, leaving the command of his post to Captain Luis Marin, set out on horseback to have an interview with Cortes. As he went he was assailed by the enemy, but he arrived at the general's quarters, and addressing him in terms of surprise and condolance, asked him how this ill success had happened. "Son Sandoval" said Cortes, with tears in his eyes, "it is for my sins that this misfortune has befallen me; but " the fault is with the treasurer Alderete, who was ordered by me to " fill up the bad pass where the enemy threw us into confusion." The treasurer then exclaimed, that it was with Cortes himself the fault lay, he having never given any such orders, but hurrying on his men after the enemy in their feigned retreat, crying, "forward! gentlemen for- " ward!" Cortes was also very much blamed for not having sent his allies out of the way early enough; however I will omit to detail any more of the conversation which passed at this time between Cortes and the treasurer, as it happened in the heat of anger and disappointment. Cortes was agreeably surprised by the arrival of two of his vessels which he had given up for lost, although he did not express himself so. Cortes desired Sandoval to go to our quarters at Tacuba, as he apprehended that the weight of the enemy's attack would fall upon this post, and recommended that he should pay attention to our affairs, as he himself was at present unable to do so. Sandoval setting out, arrived at Tacuba about the hour of vespers. He also found us as Tapia had done, occupied in repelling the enemy, some of whom were attacking us by the causeway, others by that of the ruined houses. I was at this time together with others of our soldiers up to my waist in the water defending a vessel which was aground, and engaged with the enemy who were endeavouring to get possession of her. Just as Sandoval arrived however, by a great effort we got the vessel afloat, but with the loss of two of the crew killed, and every man on board wounded. The enemy

now

now attacked us with more violence. Sandoval received a blow on the
face with a ftone, and called to us loudly to retreat; we not falling back
as faft as he wifhed, he called again to us, afking if we wanted to have
all the cavalry deftroyed. We then retreated until we reached our poft,
during the time of which, our two guns, under the direction of Medrano, though they frequently fwept the caufeway, could not prevent
the enemy from following us clofely.

Here we were for a time at reft, and engaged in relating the events
which had happened at each poft, when on a fudden our ears were
ftruck by the horrific found of the great drum, the timbals, horns, and
trumpets, in the temple of the war god. We all directed our eyes thither, and fhocking to relate! faw our unfortunate countrymen driven by
force, cuffs, and baftinades, to the place where they were to be facrificed, which bloody ceremony was accompanied by the mournful found
of all the inftruments of the temple. We perceived that when they had
brought the unfortunate victims to the flat fummit of the body of the
temple, where were the adoratories, they put plumes upon their heads,
and with a kind of fan in the hand of each, made them dance before
their accurfed idols. When they had done this, they laid them upon
their backs, on the ftone ufed for the purpofe, where they cut out their
hearts, alive, and having prefented them, yet palpitating, to their gods,
they drew the bodies down the fteps by the feet, where they were taken
by others of their priefts. Let the reader think what were our fenfa-
tions on this occafion. Oh heavenly God! faid we to ourfelves, do
not fuffer us to be facrificed by thefe wretches! do not fuffer us to die
fo cruel a death! and then how fhocking a reflection, that we were unable to relieve our poor friends who were thus murdered before our eyes!
at this moment the enemy affailed our poft in great force, reviling us
and faying their gods had promifed us all to them. Our Indian allies
funk under the dreadful ideas they expreffed, when they threw among
them alfo fome of the mangled remains of their horrid feafts, other parts
being fent round all the neighbouring diftricts, as a triumphant memorial.

morial. We still however maintained possession of our post, one half of our cavalry being on the causeway and the other half in the town.

Our new allies on the lake had suffered considerably by the enemy, having lost half their canoes, but they continued firm to us, from animosity to them, or contented themselves with being mere lookers on, and did not molest us. Cortes in consequence of our losses ordered a cessation of attacks, which lasted for the space of four days, during which we did not quit our posts, having lost near eighty men, and seven horses, in the last engagement. The enemy also gained ground on us, and made new ditches and water cuts, but we had a very deep and defensible one in front of our quarters. Sandoval and Tapia on their return to the general, reported to him the valiant manner in which our soldiers were behaving when they arrived at our post; Sandoval also mentioned me particularly, and said those things in my commendation, which, exclusive of the facts being known to our whole army, would not be proper to repeat of myself.

During this cessation, our whole force of infantry kept guard on the causeway at night, flanked by the brigantines, one half of the cavalry patroling in Tacuba, the other half on the causeway. In the morning we prepared to receive the enemy, who every day continued sacrificing our poor companions, and when they attacked, reviled us saying, that our flesh was too bitter to be eaten, and truly it seems that such a miracle was wrought. For five days together the enemy continued their assaults, being promised, as they said, our destruction, by their gods, within the space of eight days; but their gods as it appears to me, were perverse and treacherous to them, not permitting them to think of peace, and thus leading them to ruin. This language however, and the last menace in particular, had such an effect upon our allies, together with the bad appearance of our affairs, that they almost entirely deserted us in the course of a night. The only one who remained with Cortes, was, Suchel, otherwise Don Carlos, brother of Fernando lord of Tezcuco. He was a man of great bravery. His friends who staid

by

by him amounted to about forty. With Sandoval remained the chief
of Guaxocingo, with about fifty, and in ours the brave Chichimecatecle, the two fons of our friend D. Lorenzo de Vargas, and about eighty
Tlafcalans. Being queftioned as to the flight of their countrymen they
faid, that the gods of the Mexicans had predicted our deftruction ; that
they faw us all wounded, and many killed, that their own lofs was
above one thoufand two hundred killed, and that the younger Xicotenga had from the firft foretold that we fhould be all put to death; and
therefore, confidering us as loft, their countrymen had quitted us. Cortes though he thought what they faid much too true, put on a chearful appearance, ridiculed the predictions of the enemy, and affured them
that all would do well. He thereby was fortunate enough to induce
the few who yet remained to ftay with us to the laft. The Indian Don
Carlos, a brave and wife man now reprefented to Cortes the erroneous
fyftem on which he had acted, and alfo that which the fituation of the
enemy pointed out, advifing him not to fuffer his troops to fight. "Cut
" off" faid he "their provifions and water; there are in Mexico fo ma-
" ny Xiquipils of warriors, how can they fubfift ? their provifions muft
" at fome time be expended, the water which they get from the wells
" is falt, and they have no refource but from the frequent rains; fight
" them by hunger and thirft, and do not throw away your own force."
Cortes embraced D. Carlos for his advice; not that the fame had not
occurred to many of us before, but we were too impatient.

Cortes began upon his new fyftem, by fending orders to all the
detachments to remain in their quarters for the next three days. As
the enemy were fo ftrong upon the lake, we always fent out two veffels
in company; they had now acquired the method of breaking through
the pallifadoes by the force of oars and fails, when there was a good
wind. Thus we were mafters of the lake, and alfo of all the houfes
which were at any little diftance from the city. This flackened the
triumphs of the Mexicans. As our veffels broke through the enemy's
pallifadoes, they could flank us while we carried on our work, filling
the

the ditches in our front. This we effected at all our posts in the space of four days, Cortes himself carrying the beams and earth.

During each night of this period the enemy continued beating their accursed drum in the great temple; nothing can equal the dismal impression its sound conveyed. They were then in the execution of their infernal ceremonies; the whole place was illuminated, and their shrieks at certain intervals pierced the air. For ten nights together were they thus employed in putting to death our unfortunate companions; Christoval de Guzman was the last sacrificed; he was in their hands eighteen days; this we were informed by some of our prisoners, and for every sacrifice, we were told that their war god renewed to them the promise of victory. The enemy at times during the foregoing period brought our own crosbows against us, and made the unfortunate prisoners shoot them; but our post derived its safety from the excellent management of the two guns under P. M. Medrano, and we still advanced, gaining every day a bridge or a parapet. Our vessels also continually intercepted their canoes loaded with provision and water, also those which were employed in procuring that nutritive substance which when dry resembles cheese, and is found at the bottom of the lake. In this manner of proceeding twelve or thirteen days had now passed, our lives therefore exceeded the date allowed them by the prediction of the Mexican priests. This gave our allies courage, and in compliance with the requisition of our steady friend Suchel, two thousand warriors from Tezcuco returned to us. There came with them Captain Pedro Sanchez Farfan, and Anthonio de Villaroel, afterwards married to La Ojeda, who had been left behind in Tezcuco. Many bodies also of our Tlascalan and other allies arrived about the same time. Cortes having summoned their chiefs, made them a speech, partly of reprimand and partly of hopes and promises, concluding it with an admonition to them not to put to death any of the Mexicans, as it was his wish to negociate for peace.

The heavy rains at this season of the year were much in our favor, the enemy always relaxing in their exertions when they came on. We

had

had now advanced confiderably into the city at each of the three attacks; we had alſo reached the fountains of brackiſh water, which we totally deſtroyed, and the cavalry could act through the whole ſpace which we had gained, as it was our care to make it level for them.

Our general thought the preſent a good juncture to offer peace to the Mexicans; he therefore propoſed to three of his principal priſoners to go with his meſſage to their king, Guatimotzin, but they declined it, alledging that he would certainly put them to death. At length however he prevailed with them to carry his propoſal, which was to this purport. That from the affection he bore to all the family of the great Montezuma, in order alſo to prevent the deſtruction of that great city, and the loſs of lives, he was willing to treat of peace, calling to the recollection of Guatimotzin, that his troops and people were cut off from proviſions and water, and that all thoſe nations which had former-ly been the vaſſals of Mexico were now the allies of the Spaniards; with many more ſtrong arguments to the ſame purpoſe, which the embaſſa-dors very well underſtood. Previous to their going they deſired that the general would provide them with a letter, under which authority they waited on the monarch, ſobbing and wailing bitterly, as knowing the danger which attended their buſineſs. At firſt Guatimotzin and his chiefs appeared enraged, but the moderation of his diſpoſition prevailed, and he reſolved to call a council compoſed of the princes, chiefs, and prieſts of the city. Guatimotzin opened the buſineſs by expreſſing his own inclination to come into terms, expoſing the inefficacy of their re-ſiſtance, the deſertion of their allies, and the diſtreſſes of the people. The prieſts took the oppoſite opinion. They repreſented the conduct of the Spaniards from the firſt, their treatment of his uncle the great Mon-tezuma, of Cacamatzin, and of various other princes as ſoon as they had got them in their power; alſo the death of the two ſons of Mon-tezuma, which they laid to their charge, the deſtruction and waſte of the wealth of Mexico, and the marks of ſlavery with which they had branded other nations. They reminded him of his own martial fame and conduct, of the inſidiouſneſs of Cortes and his offers, and the

promiſes

promises of victory they had obtained from their gods. Guatimotzin then expressed his determination to fight to the last man and gave orders to spare the provisions as much as possible, to sink wells in various places, and to endeavour to obtain supplies by night.

Our army remained at their posts for two days quietly, expecting the answer from Mexico. We were then attacked at all points by great bodies of the enemy, who fell on us like lions, closing upon and endeavouring to seize us in their hands, whenever the horn of Guatimotzin was sounded. For seven days were we thus engaged, watching in a body during the night, at day break going into action, fighting during the day, and in the evening retiring to console ourselves with our misery of maize cakes, agi or pepper, tunas, and herbs. Our offer of peace only served for new matter for the enemy to revile us on, reproaching us as cowards, and saying, that peace was for women and arms for men.

It has been mentioned that the wretched remains of our countrymen were sent round to different provinces, to summon and encourage them to come to the aid of the Mexicans. In consequence, a force assembled from Matalzingo, Malinalco, and other places at the distance of eight leagues from Mexico, to fall on our rear, while the enemy from the city attacked us in front. When they had assembled as above mentioned, they began to commit outrages upon the country between them and us, seizing the children in order to sacrifice. Complaints of this coming to Cortes, he detached Andres de Tapia with twenty cavalry and one hundred infantry against the enemy. This officer executed his mission completely, driving them back to their own country with loss.

Cortes then sent Sandoval to assist the people of the district called by us Cuernabaca, who were attacked in the same manner. There is much to say in respect to this expedition; too much indeed to be able to do justice to it without going into the details; suffice it that it was

R r

more

more peaceable than warlike, and of the happiest effect for us, Sandoval returning accompanied by two chiefs of the nation he had marched against. His return was very sudden, in order to protect our posts, which were in a most perilous way; for this draft had dismantled them, as he had with him every man really fit for duty, being twenty cavalry and eighty infantry. However he by his expedition saved both our allies and us.

Cortes now again sent an embassy to Guatimotzin, saying he had his Monarch's orders to save if possible that fine city; he reminded Guatimotzin of the distress of the wretched people, and to convince him that he had no hope from his allies, he sent the message by the two chiefs who accompanied Sandoval. The Mexican monarch returned no answer, except ordering the ambassadors immediately to quit the city. The enemy now increased every day the fury of their attacks; their expressions were, "Tenitoz re de Castilla! Tenitoz Axaca?" which means, " what says the king of Castille? what does he now?" We still continued advancing towards the heart of the city, and observed that notwithstanding the rage with which they assailed us, for it seemed as if they wished to meet their deaths, there was not so much movement among them as formerly, nor did they so busily employ themselves in opening the ditches. We also had cause for reflection of a less pleasant nature which was, that our powder was almost reduced to nothing. At this moment most fortunately, arrived at the port of Villa Rica, a vessel with soldiers and ordnance stores, one of an armament fitted out by the Licentiate Lucas Vasquez de Aillon, which had been destroyed or dispersed near the Islands of Florida. The relief and reinforcement were immediately forwarded to Cortes, by his lieutenant, Rangel. It was now determined by Cortes and all the army to push for the great place or Taltelulco of the city, on account of the principal temples and strong buildings being there. Each of our detachments therefore advanced for the purpose. Cortes got possession of a small square at which were some temples; in those temples were beams whereon were placed the heads of many of our soldiers; their hair and beards had much

grown;

grown; I could not have believed it had I not feen it with my own eyes in three days after, when our party had advanced near enough to get a view of them, after having filled two canals. I recognifed the features of three of our friends, and the tears came into my eyes at the fight. In twelve days they were all buried by us in that which is now named the church of the martyrs.

The detachment of Alvarado continued to advance, and after an engagement of two hours forced the enemy from their barricades in the great fquare. The cavalry now rendered good fervice in the open fpace, and the enemy were driven before us into the temple of the war god Alvarado divided his forces into three bodies, and while he occupied the attention of the enemy with two, he ordered the third, commanded by Gutierre de Badajoz, to drive them from, and take poffeffion of the great temple. The enemy, headed by their priefts, occupied the adoratories or fanctuaries of their idols, and repulfed our troops, driving them down the fteps; which being obferved by Alvarado, he then fent us to fupport them, and on our arrival, having afcended to the top, we completely drove the enemy from that poft; having done which, we fet fire to the images of their falfe gods, and planted our ftandard on the fummit of the temple. The view of this fignal of victory rejoiced Cortes, who would fain have joined us, but he had it not in his power. He was then diftant a quarter of a league, and had many ditches to fill as he advanced. In four days from this time, both he and Sandoval had worked their way to us, and the communications to the three pofts were opened through the centre of the city of Mexico. This attack upon the temple was truly perilous; the edifice was very lofty, and the enemy numerous; and they continued to engage us on the flat ground at the fummit, from the time that we had fet fire to the idols and their adoratories, until night. The royal palaces were now levelled to the ground, Guatimotzin and his troops having retired to a quarter of the city more diftant from the centre, and towards the lake.

Still they attacked us in the day, and at night purfued us to our

quarters,

quarters, and thus time paſſed over, and no propoſition was made concerning peace. Our chiefs then propoſed a plan of laying ambuſcades.
Thirty cavalry and one hundred infantry of the prime of our army, together with one thouſand Tlaſcalans were poſted in concealment, in
ſome large houſes which had belonged to a nobleman of the city. This
was done during the night. Cortes with the reſt of his troops, in the
morning went to attack a poſt at a bridge, which Guatimotzin had ordered to be ſupported by a large force. Cortes after his firſt attack retreated, drawing the enemy after him, by the buildings where the troops
were placed in concealment. At the proper moment he fired two ſhots
cloſe together as a ſignal to us; we. ſallied out, and the enemy being
encloſed between us, our allies, and the party of Cortes which. faced
about, a dreadful havoc was made of them, and from that time they
no more annoyed us in our retreat. Another trap was alſo laid for them
by Alvarado, but not with the ſame ſucceſs; I was not preſent at it,
being ordered by Cortes to do duty for that time with his party.

From our quarters we had to march above half a league to meet
the enemy; we now therefore quitted that poſt altogether, and lodged
ourſelves in the great ſquare or Taltelulco. Here we were for three days
without doing any thing worth mentioning: we alſo abſtained from deſtroying any more of the city, in the hopes of peace.

Cortes at this time ſent to Guatimotzin requeſting him to ſurrender,
under the ſtrongeſt aſſurances of enjoying the plentitude of power and
honors. He accompanied this embaſſy with as handſome a preſent as
his ſituation permitted, of proviſions, bread, fowls, fruit, and game.
Guatimotzin as he was adviſed to do by thoſe whom he conſulted, dif-
ſimulated, and ſeemed inclined to a pacification. He ſent four of his
principal nobility, with a promiſe to come to an interview with Cortes
in three days. But this was all feigned; he employed the time in fortifying his quarter of the town, and making preparations to attack us.
He alſo endeavoured to amuſe us by a ſecond embaſſy, but we were
now adviſed of his ſchemes. In fact, from what he was told by thoſe

about

about him, and from the example of his uncle Montezuma, he was afraid to truft himfelf in our hands. But the mafk was foon thrown off; we were attacked by great bodies of the enemy, with fuch violence that it appeared as if all was beginning anew. Having been rather taken by furprife, they did us at firft fome mifchief, killed one foldier, and two horfes; but in the end we fent them back with very little to boaft of. Cortes ordered his troops now to proceed againft that part of the city where the quarters of Guatimotzin were; accordingly we began upon our former fyftem, and gained ground as we had before done elfewhere. When the king perceived this, he defired an interview with Cortes, on the fide of a large canal which was to feparate them. To this Cortes readily affented, and it was to take place on the enfuing morning. Cortes attended, but Guatimotzin never appeared; inftead of which he fent feveral of his principal nobility, who faid that the king did not think proper to come, from an apprehenfion that we might fhoot him during the parley. Cortes then engaged by the moft folemn oaths not to do him any injury whatever, but it was of no effect. A ridiculous farce was played here: two of the nobility who attended on the part of Guatimotzin, took out of a fack, bread, a fowl, and cherries, which they began to eat, in order to imprefs the Spaniards with an idea that they were not in want. Cortes feeing the manner in which he was treated, fent back an hoftile meffage and retired; after this we were left unmolefted for the fpace of four or five days. During this time numbers of wretched Indians, reduced by famine, furrounded our quarters every night. Cortes pitied their miferable fituation, and hoping that it might induce the enemy to come into terms of accommodation, ordered the ceffation of hoftilities to be ftrictly adhered to; but no overture of the kind was made.

There was in the army of Cortes a foldier who boafted of having ferved in Italy, and of the great battles which he had feen there. His name was Sotelo, and he was a native of Seville. This man was eternally talking of the wonderful military machines which he knew the art of conftructing, and how he could make a ftone engine which

fhould

should in two days destroy that whole quarter of the city where Guatimotzin had retreated. He told Cortes so many fine things of this kind, that he persuaded him into a trial of his experiments, lime, stone, and timber being brought, according to his desire; the carpenters were also set to work, two strong cables were made, and stones the size of a bushel were prepared. The machinery was now all ready, the stone which was to be ejected was put in its place, and the whole apparatus was played off* against the quarters of Guatimotzin. But behold! instead of taking that direction, the stone flew up vertically into the air, and returned exactly into the place from whence it had been launched. Cortes was enraged and ashamed: he reproached the soldier, and ordered the machinery to be taken down; but still it continued the joke of the army.

Cortes now gave orders to Sandoval, to go with the flotilla against that part or nook of the city whither Guatimotzin had retired, cautioning him at the same time not to kill or injure any Mexican, unless he was attacked, nor even then to do more than was absolutely necessary for his own defence; but to level all the houses, and the many advanced works which the enemy had made in the lake. Cortes ascended then into the great temple, with several of his officers and soldiers, to observe the movements of his fleet. When Sandoval approached the quarters of Guatimotzin, that prince, who had great apprehensions of being made prisoner, availed himself of the preparations which he had made for his escape, and embarking himself, his family, his courtiers, and officers, with their most valuable effects, on board fifty large piraguas, the whole body set off for the main land, as did all his nobility and chiefs in various directions. Sandoval who was at this time occupied in making his way by tearing down the houses, received immediate notice of the flight of Guatimotzin. He instantly set out in the pursuit, giving strict orders that no injury or insult should be offered, but that each should keep a steady eye upon the royal vessel, and do his utmost to get possession of it. He particularly directed however Garci Holguin, his intimate friend, and captain of the quickest sailer of the fleet, to

make

---

* From the platform of a theatre.

make for that part of the fhore whither Guatimotzin was moft likely to go. Accordingly this officer followed his inftructions, and falling in with the veffels, from certain particulars in its appearance, ftructure, and awning, he afcertained that which the king was on board of. He made figns to the people in it to bring to, but without effect; he then ordered his crofsbow-men and mufqueteers to prefent, upon which Guatimotzin called out to them not to fhoot, and approaching the veffel, acknowledged himfelf for what he was, declaring his readinefs to fubmit, and go with them to their general, but requefting that his queen, his children, and attendants fhould be fuffered to remain unmolefted. Holguin received him with the greateft refpect, together with his queen, and twenty of his nobility. He feated them on the poop of his fhip, and provided refrefhments for them, commanding, that the piraguas which carried the kings effects, fhould follow untouched.

Sandoval at this moment made a fignal for the flotilla to clofe up to him, and perceived that Guatimotzin was prifoner to Holguin, who was taking him to Cortes, Upon this he ordered his rowers to exert their utmoft to bring him up to Holguin's veffel, and having arrived by the fide of it, he demanded Guatimotzin to be delivered to him as general of the whole force; but Holguin refufed, alledging that he had no claim whatever. A veffel which went to carry the intelligence of the great event, brought alfo to Cortes who was then on the fummit of the great temple in the Taltelulco, very near the part of the lake where Guatimotzin was captured, an account of the difpute between his officers. Cortes inftantly difpatched Captain Luis Marin and Francifco de Lugo, to bring the whole party together to his quarters, and thus to ftop all litigation; but he enjoined them not to omit treating Guatimotzin and his queen with the greateft refpect. During the interval, he employed himfelf in arranging a ftate, as well as he could, with cloths and mantles. He alfo prepared a table with refrefhments, to receive his prifoners. As foon as they appeared, he went forward to meet them, and embracing Guatimotzin, treated him and all his attendants with every mark of refpect. The unfortunate monarch, with tears in his eyes, and

and finking under affliction, then addreffed him in the following words. "Malintzin! I have done that which was my duty in the de-" fence of my kingdom and people; my efforts have failed, and being " now brought by force a prifoner in your hands, draw that poinard " from your fide, and ftab me to the heart." Cortes embraced, and ufed every expreffion to comfort him, by affurances that he held him in high eftimation for the valour and firmnefs he had fhewn, and that he had required a fubmiffion from him and the people at the time that they could no longer reafonably hope for fuccefs, in order to prevent further deftruction; but that was all paft, and no more to be thought of; he fhould continue to reign over the people, as he had done before. Cortes then enquired after his queen, to which Guatimotzin replied, that in confequence of the compliance of Sandoval with his requeft, fhe and her women remained in the piraguas, until Cortes fhould decide as to their fate. The general then caufed them to be fent for, and treated them in the beft manner his fituation afforded. The evening was draw-ing on, and it appeared likely to rain; he therefore fent the whole roy-al family to Cuyoacan, under the care of Sandoval. The reft of the troops then returned to their former quarters; we to ours of Tacuba, and Cortes, proceeding to Cuyoacan, took the command there, fending Sandoval to refume his ftation at Tepeaquilla. Thus was the fiege of Mexico brought to a conclufion by the capture of Guatimotzin and his chiefs, on the thirteenth of Auguft, at the hour of vefpers, being the day of St. Hyppolitus, in the year of our Lord one thoufand five hun-dred and twenty one. Glorified be our Lord Jefus Chrift, and our la-dy the Holy Virgin Mary his bleffed mother, amen!

In the night after Guatimotzin was made prifoner, there was the greateft tempeft of rain, thunder, and lightening, efpecially about mid-night, that ever was known; but all the foldiers were as deaf as if they had been for an hour in a fteeple, with the bells ringing about their ears. This was owing to the continual noife of the enemy for ninety three days; fome preparing their troops and bringing them on, fhout-ing, calling, and whiftling, as fignals to attack us on the caufeway;

others

others in the canoes coming to attack our veffels; fome again at work upon their pallifadoes, or opening the ditches and water cuts, and making ftone parapets, or preparing their magazines of darts and arms, and the women fupplying the flingers with their ammunition. Then from the temples and adoratories of their accurfed idols, the timbals and horns, and the mournful found of their great drum, and other difmal noifes, were inceffantly affailing our ears, fo that day or night we could hardly hear each other fpeak. But thefe dins immediately ceafed on the capture of Guatimotzin, for which reafon as I have obferved, we felt like fo many men juft efcaped from a fteeple where all the bells were ringing about our ears.

Guatimotzin was of a noble appearance both in perfon and countenance; his features were rather large, and chearful, with lively eyes. His age was about twenty three or four years, and his complexion very fair for an Indian. His queen the niece of Montezuma, was young, and very handfome.

In regard to the difpute between Sandoval and Holguin, Cortes related to them the circumftance from the Roman hiftory, of the capture of Jugurtha, and the difpute of Marius and Sylla, about which of them fhould have the honor of it, and that this difpute was productive of moft fatal civil wars; but faid that he would lay the whole affair before his Majefty, by whofe arbitration it fhould be decided, which of the two fhould have the action emblazoned in his arms. In two years from this time the Emperor's orders upon the fubject arrived; they were to this purpofe; that Cortes fhould bear in his arms the feven kings, reprefenting Montezuma, Guatimotzin, and the princes of Tezcuco, Iztapalapa, Cuyoacan, Tacuba, and Matalzingo.

What I am going to mention is truth, and I fwear and fay amen to it. I have read of the deftruction of Jerufalem, but I cannot conceive that the mortality there exceeded this of Mexico; for all the people from the diftant provinces which belonged to this empire had concentrated

S s
themfelves

themfelves here, where they moftly died. The ftreets, the fquares, the houfes, and the courts of the Taltelulco were covered with dead bodies; we could not ftep without treading on them; the lake and canals were filled with them, and the ftench was intolerable. For this reafon, our troops immediately after the capture of the royal family retired to their former quarters. Cortes himfelf was for fome time ill from the effect of it.

The veffels were now the beft fituation, thofe on board carrying away all the plunder, for they had accefs to houfes in the water which were not in our reach. They alfo found what the Mexicans had concealed in the reeds, and on the borders of the lake, and intercepted that which was carried out of our reach by water. We on land gained nothing but honor and wounds. The wealth our navy got was much more than we could guefs at; Guatimotzin and all his chiefs declaring, when enquiry was made as to the public treafure, that it had moftly fallen into their hands.

To return to the ftate of Mexico. Guatimotzin now requefted of Cortes, that permiffion fhould be given to clear the city entirely of the inhabitants, in order to purify it, and reftore its falubrity. Accordingly they were ordered to remove to the neighbouring towns, and for three days, and three nights, all the caufeways were full, from one end to the other, of men, women, and children, fo weak and fickly, fqualid and dirty, and peftilential, that it was mifery to behold them. When all thofe who were able had quitted the city, we went to examine the ftate of it, which was as I have defcribed. The ftreets, courts, and houfes were covered with dead bodies, and fome miferable wretches were creeping about, in the different ftages of the moft offenfive difor_ders, the confequences of famine and improper food. The ground was all broken up to get at the roots of fuch vegetation as it afforded, and the very trees were ftripped of their bark! There was no frefh water in the town. During all their diftrefs however, though their conftant practice was to feaft on fuch as they took prifoners, no inftance occurred

of

of their having preyed on each other; and certainly never exifted fince the creation a people which fuffered fo much from hunger, thirft, and warfare.

After having returned thanks to God, Cortes determined to cele-brate his fuccefs by a feftival in Cuyoacan; a veffel had arrived at Villa Rica with a cargo of wine, and hogs had been provided from the Ifland of Cuba. To this entertainment he invited all the officers of his army, and alfo the foldiers of eftimation, and all things being prepared, on the day appointed, we waited on our general. When we came to fit down to dinner there were not tables for one half of us; this brought on great confufion among the company, and indeed for many reafons it would have been much better let alone. The plant of Noah was the caufe of many fooleries and worfe things; it made fome leap over the tables who afterwards could not go out at the doors, and many rolled down the fteps. The private foldiers fwore they would buy horfes with golden harnefs; the crofsbow-men would ufe none but golden arrows; all were to have their fortunes made. When the tables were taken away the foldiers danced in their armour, with the ladies, as many of them as there were, but the difproportion in numbers was very great. This fcene was truly ridiculous. I will not mention the names, fuffice it to fay a fair field was opened for fatire. Fray De Olmedo thought what he obferved at the feaft, and in the dances too fcandalous, and com-plained to Sandoval; and the latter directly told Cortes how the reverend father was fcolding and grumbling. Cortes, difcreet in all his actions, then came to him and affecting to difapprove the whole, requefted that he would order a folemn mafs and thankfgiving, and preach a fermon to the foldiers on the moral and religious duties. Fra Bartholome was highly pleafed at this, thinking it had originated fpontaneoufly from Cortes, and not knowing that the hint had been given him by Sandoval. Accordingly, the crucifixes and the image of our Lady were borne in fo-lemn proceffion, with drums and ftandards; the litany was fung during the ceremony, Fra Bartholome preached and adminiftered the facrament, and we returned thanks to God for our victory.

Cortes

Cortes now took leave of his allies, the Tlafcalan chiefs, and alfo of Suchel otherwife Don Carlos, a very brave man, as was another, a captain of fome city near the lake the name of which I forget; but he did wonders. Many others who had rendered us moft important fervices departed at the fame time. Cortes difmiffed them all to their homes with many embraces, thanks, and compliments, promifing that he would foon make them rich, and great lords, and give them lands and vaffals, fo that they took their departure in high fpirits. They had however fecured fomething more fubftantial than promifes, for they were well loaden with the plunder of Mexico, nor were they behind the enemy in their cannibal feafts, carrying with them portions preferved, to fupply their friends on their return home.

Now that I am paft thefe furious combats, through which, praifed be God he was pleafed to conduct me fafe, I have to mention a certain particularity relative to myfelf, and it is this. When I faw the facrifice of our feventy two countrymen, and their hearts taken out and offered to the war god of the Mexicans, I had a fenfation of fear. Some may confider this as want of firmnefs; but if they weigh it duly, they will find that it was in truth the refult of too much courage, which caufed me to run into extreme and uncommon dangers; for in that day I confidered myfelf a moft valiant foldier, and was fo efteemed by all; and was ufed to do that which was attempted by the boldeft, and I was always under the eye of my captain. As I have before obferved, when I faw my companions facrificed, their hearts taken out palpitating, and their legs and arms cut off and eaten, I feared it might one day or other be my own lot, for they had me in their hands twice, but it was God's will that I fhould efcape; but I remembered, and thought on what I had feen, and from this time I feared that cruel death; and this I mention, becaufe before I went into battle, I felt a great depreffion and uneafinefs about my heart, and then recommending myfelf to God and his bleffed mother our Lady, the inftant I was engaged with the enemy it left me. Still I am furprifed that it came upon me when I fhould have felt more valiant than ever, on account of the many battles in which I

had

had been engaged. But I declare I never knew what fear was, until I saw the maffacre of the feventy two foldiers. Let thofe cavaliers who have been in defperate battles and mortal dangers now decide what was the caufe of my fears; I fay that it was excefs of courage; and for this reafon; that I knew the greatnefs of the danger into which I was determined to go, and knowingly, and voluntarily, encountered it. Many engagements are related in my hiftory befides thofe I was at; but if my body were of iron, I could not have been at all; and I was much oftener wounded than whole.

I muft obferve, that the Mexicans did not kill our foldiers, but wounded, and carried them off, to facrifice alive, to their gods.

THE TRUE HISTORY

OF

THE CONQUEST OF MEXICO.

PART THE THIRD.

CHAPTER I.

*Tranſactions and occurrences in New Spain ſubſequent
to the conqueſt.*

AFTER the conqueſt, as ſoon as Cortes had leiſure to turn his
mind to objects of police and internal regulation, he directed that the
aqueducts ſhould be reſtored, and the city cleared of the dead, ſo that
within two months it might be inhabited as before. The palaces and
houſes he ordered to be repaired, and pointed out that part which was
to be inhabited by the natives, and that which was to be reſerved for
the Spaniards.

Guatimotzin now applied in the name of many of his principal
nobility to Cortes, requeſting that he would order ſuch of their women

of

of rank as had been taken by our foldiers, to be delivered to their hufbands, and fathers. The general found fome difficulty in this, but
agreed to permit them to make fearch, and fuch as wifhed to return, he
affured them that he would caufe to be given up. They fearched
through every houfe, and though the women hid themfelves they found
many, but very few were inclined to return; they declared that they
detefted the idolatry of their countrymen, and in addition they were
many of them pregnant, fo that of the whole number three only went
back to their families.

One of the firft public works undertaken was an arfenal in the
city, fo fituated as to include our flotilla. Alvarado was to the beft of
my knowledge appointed alcalde, until the arrival of Salazar de la Pedrada. All the gold, filver, and jewels, which were now collected in
Mexico, amounted to the paltry fum of three hundred and eighty thoufand crowns. It was reported that Guatimotzin had thrown great
quantities into the lake four days before the furrender of the town, and
it was well known that a confiderable fhare had fallen to our allies, and
to thofe who ferved on board the fleet. Cortes was not forry to think
Guatimotzin had it concealed, in hopes of obtaining it all for himfelf.
It was then propofed to put both Guatimotzin and his confidential friend
the prince of Tacuba to the torture, to extort confeffion from them; this
was certainly very contrary to the inclination and difpofition of Cortes,
who could not approve of fuch an act of cruelty being committed on a
perfon fo diftinguifhed as Guatimotzin; one who was abfolute monarch
of a country three times larger than Caftille. In anfwer to all enquiries
the king's officers protefted that there was no more than what had been
produced, which when melted and run into bars did not exceed three
hundred and eighty thoufand crowns. From this the fifth for the Emperor and another for Cortes were deducted; what remained did not at
all fatisfy thofe of the conquerors of Mexico who were not before friends
to Cortes. They fuggefted to the treafurer Alderete that the general
objected to Guatimotzin being tortured, in order to get the gold himfelf. Cortes was therefore obliged to leave the unfortunate king at their
difpofal,

difpofal, as well as the lord of Tacuba. What this inhuman procefs extorted from them was, a confeffion that they had, four days previous to the furrender, thrown treafure into the lake, and alfo the mufquets, bows, and other arms taken from us in our flight, and in the laft defeat of Cortes. The place which Guatimotzin pointed out was fearched by the beft fwimmers, to no effect whatever. In a deep pond at his palace was found a fun of folid gold, fimilar to that which Montezuma had given us, with many ornaments of fmall value, the private property of Guatimotzin. On the torture the Prince of Tacuba declared that he had gold at fome large houfes he poffeffed four leagues from the town of Tacuba, and that, if there, he would point out to us where it was buried. Alvarado and fix foldiers whereof I was one accompanied him thither; when we arrived he declared he had faid fo in hopes of dying on the road, for that he had no treafure whatever; fo we remained without any more gold to melt. The fact is that the treafury was diminifhed to a mere trifle before it came into Guatimotzin's hands; and I and many others who faw it at firft knew it appeared to be then worth twice what it was when brought out to have his Majefty's fhare deducted: I obferved many articles of remarkable and curious workmanfhip miffing at that time; they were taken for the public fervice.

I and feveral good divers fearched that part of the lake which had been pointed out by Guatimotzin, and we found fome pieces of gold of little value, which were immediately claimed by Cortes and Alderete. They alfo fent down perfons and were themfelves prefent, but all they obtained amounted to lefs than the value of ninety crowns. This made us very penfive and grave, when we found what mere trifles our fhares as they were called came to. For this reafon Fra Bartholome, and other cavaliers and captains, reprefented to Cortes that it would be beft to divide that which fell to the lot of the whole army, among the wounded, the halt, the blind, the deaf, the fcorched, and the fick; and that thofe who had efcaped found would renounce their claims. This they faid upon an expectation that it might draw out fome of the treafure which they fufpected was concealed. Cortes replied that he

T t

would

would enquire, and rectify all. Our captains and foldiers were then curious to know what the fhares came to for each man. On cafting it up it appeared, that to each horfeman there came one hundred crowns, and to each infantry foldier I forget how much, but no one would accept it. This did not quiet the foldiers; they murmured loudly and accufed the treafurer. He to exculpate himfelf faid, that they fhould blame Cortes, who had taken out a fecond fifth for himfelf, and alfo a deduction for lofs of horfes, and had retained from the common ftock many pieces of wrought gold to fend to his Majefty. The foldiers of Narvaez who never liked Cortes thoroughly, would not take their paltry fhares, and as Cortes now lodged at Cuyoacan, in large buildings with white walls, very well adapted for fcribbling on, there appeared every morning libels againft him in profe or verfe. The idea of one of them was, that as the planets fometimes went a little out of their courfe, but by the order of nature fpeedily reverted to it again, fo it was with Cortes and his ambition. Another faid we were more conquered by Cortes than Mexico by us, and that we were not the victors of New Spain, but the vanquifhed of Cortes. Some faid that he had taken his fifth as general, and a fecond as king; and others again that Velafquez had incurred all the expence, and Cortes reaped all the profit. I recollect the words of one only: they were

" Que trifte efta el alma mea,
" Hafta que la parte vea.*

Many were written in fuch a ftile as is not fit for me to relate, and fome had a turn and witty point in them which I am not able to give. Cortes was a poet, and prided himfelf on giving anfwers in that way to fuch complimentary addreffes as he received; he alfo ufed to reply in pointed epigrams to thefe pafquinades which grew every day more indecent. One day obferving the walls covered with them he wrote, "a white wall is paper for fools." Next morning was found added, "and for truths." At length Fra Bartholome told Cortes the thing was going too
far

---

* How anxious I am for a partition of plunder!!

far, and advifed him to ftop it, which he did by threats of fevere punifhment.

Among the foldiers of our army very heavy debts were contracted;
a crofs-bow was fold for fifty crowns, a mufquet coft one hundred, a
horfe eight hundred, one thoufand, and even more; and every thing
elfe was in proportion. Then our furgeon Maeftre Juan charged high,
as did a Doctor Murcia who was an apothecary and barber. There were
befides various other money traps, all which were to be fatisfied out of
our dividends. This required fome regulation: Cortes accordingly appointed Sancta Clara, a very honorable perfon, and one Lerena, to appreciate each claim, which was to be paid according to their award,
within two years. The value of the gold was alfo altered by increafing
the alloy; this was intended to ferve us in our dealing with the merchants from Europe or Cuba, but it had a contrary effect, as they were
prepared, and added twice as much to the price of their goods. The
alloy was copper, called here Tepuzque; for which reafon we call any
one of an inferior degree to another of the fame name, Don Juan, or
Don Alonzo Tepuzque, or the copper Don Juan &c. The abufes refulting from this being made known to his Majefty, he was pleafed to
forbid the currency of this bafe metal, ordering it to be taken in duties
until it was all drawn over to Caftille, and that no more of it fhould be
made. At this time two gold-fmiths were hanged here for running bafe
metal with the legal mark.

I have digreffed for fome time paft, and will now return to the
thread of my narrative. Cortes, as the beft way to get rid of troublefome companions and demands, determined now to fend out colonies,
and make fettlements at convenient fituations. For this purpofe Sandoval was ordered to Tuftepeque, and Guacacualco. Juan Velafquez was
to go to Colima, one Villa Fuerte to Zacatula, Chriftoval de Oli to
Mechoacan, (he was at this time married to a Portugueze lady named
Donna Phillipa de Aranja,) and Francifco de Orozca to Guaxaca.

At

At this time the chiefs of the diſtant provinces could not bring themſelves to believe that Mexico was deſtroyed: they therefore ſent deputations to aſcertain the truth, and alſo to offer themſelves as vaſſals to his Majeſty the Emperor. All made great preſents of gold to Cortes, and many came in perſon, and brought their children to ſee the ſtate of that power once ſo feared by them, and uſed to expreſs themſelves as we ſay, "here Troy town ſtood."

Curious readers will be deſirous to know how it happened, that the conquerors of Mexico who had gone through ſuch dangers to obtain poſſeſſion of that city, ſhould now quit it to ſearch for new ſettlements. To this I reply, that the books which contained the accounts of Montezuma's revenues were examined to find from whence the gold, and other valuable articles of tribute, ſuch as cacao, and cotton manufactures, were ſent; and it was to theſe productive diſtricts that we wiſhed to go. Eſpecially, we were led by the example of Sandoval, who being known to be the particular friend of Cortes, it was not to be ſuppoſed would go upon an unprofitable enterpriſe. We alſo ſaw that the vicinity of the city of Mexico had neither mines, plantations, nor manufactures, but was intirely occupied by the cultivation of maize, and of maguey. This we thought did not afford us proſpects ſufficiently advantageous, and we went to other places where we were ſadly diſappointed. I waited upon Cortes to requeſt permiſſion to attend Sandoval; "brother B. Diaz del Caſtillo" ſaid the general to me, "by my con-" ſcience you will find yourſelf miſtaken; you had better ſtay with me, " but if you are determined on going with your friend Sandoval, go in " God's name; I will always do my utmoſt to take care of you, but I " tell you that you will repent of it." All the gold remained with the Emperor's officers, the ſlaves having been purchaſed by the ſoldiers according to their valuation at a public ſale. The detachments were ſent out to colonize the provinces at different periods, for two months after the capture of Mexico; however I will not any farther particularize them, not to treſpaſs unneceſſarily on my reader's time.

At

At this time arrived at the port of Villa Rica, Chriftoval de Tapia, veedor of the Ifland of St. Domingo, with a commiffion to take upon him the government of New Spain, by order of his Majefty, and under the direction of the Bifhop of Burgos. He brought with him letters from the faid Bifhop of Burgos to Cortes and many others of his army, recommending him, to be honoured by us as governor of New Spain, and befides thofe which were clofed and fealed, he had alfo with him letters filled up and which he was authorifed to addrefs as he faw occafion for his own intereft. Great promifes were held out to fuch as would come over to the new governor, and violent threats of punifhment to thofe who made any oppofition to him. Tapia firft prefented his commiffion to Alvarado, then commandant in Villa Rica. Alvarado received it with the higheft refpect, and faid that as he was not able of himfelf to decide any thing, it would be neceffary to affemble the alcaldes and regidors of the town, to have the commiffion verified before them, and alfo to prove the manner in which it had been tranfmitted, that they might know for a certainty that it came in a proper form from his Majefty's hand. This did not exactly agree with the views of Tapia. Being advifed to proceed to Mexico and produce his commiffion to Cortes himfelf, he forwarded the letter of the bifhop, and alfo wrote to Cortes upon the fubject of his miffion. The ftile of the letters was fmooth and perfuafive, but the anfwer of Cortes was ten times more fo. Cortes immediately fent expreffes to fome of the different officers he had detached, ordering them to go and meet Tapia who had already fet out for Mexico, but was, in confequence of the direction of Cortes, met on the road by Alvarado, Sandoval, De Soto, Valdenegro, Captain Andres de Tapia, and the reverend father Fra Malgarejo. Thefe gentlemen with much compliments and ceremony, induced Chriftoval de Tapia to go to Cempoal; they there requefted to fee his commiffion, which being verified, and acknowledged, they placed it on their heads in token of refpect and fubmiffion; but in regard to the admitting him as governor by the virtue of it, that was quite another affair; it was firft neceffary to know what his Majefty's pleafure was touching the affairs of New Spain, the true ftate of which had been

concealed

concealed from him by the Bishop of Burgos, who did it to serve his own private views, and to favor Velasquez and Tapia, one of whom he intended should marry his niece. By all this it was pretty evident to Tapia, that he would not very speedily enter upon his office, and the disappointment affected him to that degree that he fell sick. Our captains wrote to Cortes letting him know all that had passed, and recommending him to send a good quantity of golden ingots, and try their effect in mollifying the fury of the would-be governor. These arrived by the return of the express, and with them they bought from him some negroes, three horses, and one of his ships; in the other Tapia embarked himself, and set sail for the Island of St. Domingo, where he was very ill received by the court of royal audience and the brothers of the order of Jeronymites, he having undertaken the business contrary to their express command; but they would not exert their power farther against one patronised by the Bishop of Burgos, his Majesty being at that time in Flanders.

I have formerly made mention of some particulars relative to an expedition set on foot by one Garay. It was to colonize and settle upon the river of Panuco. Cortes had received intelligence of it, and resolved to anticipate him by sending thither a party for the same purpose. He also now again sent Rangel to Villa Rica as commandant, and ordered Narvaez to be sent to him at Cuyoacan, where he resided until the palace which he was to inhabit in Mexico was compleated. The reason he sent for Narvaez was this; he was told that the latter had held a conversation with Tapia, in which he advised him to quit the country on as good terms as he could get, and go to his patron the Bishop of Burgos in Castille, to lay the whole state of affairs before him; telling him also to profit by the example which his misfortunes set him, as, if he staid, he certainly would be put to death, and that success attended all the measures of Cortes. When Narvaez was brought before Cortes, he fell on his knees and attempted to kiss his hand, but our general would not permit it; he raised, and embracing Narvaez, treated him with all respect and regard, and made him sit by his side.

Cortes

Cortes now proceeded to take his refidence in the city of Mexico. He divided the ground into lots for the churches in the firft place, then for the monafteries, the public buildings, and fquares. He divided the reft of the ground among the inhabitants that were to be, and not to wafte more time upon the fubject, all thofe who have feen the prefent city of Mexico agree, that there is not in Chriftendom one more populous, larger, or better built.

While Cortes was thus employed, intelligence arrived that the province of Panuco was in arms. They are a warlike people, very numerous, and having rebelled, had killed many foldiers of the party which Cortes had fent to form a colony there. He refolved therefore to go thither in perfon: indeed all his captains were now abfent on different duties. Our numbers had by this time received a confiderable reinforcement as well of thofe who had come with the veedor Tapia, as of fuch as had been on the expedition to Florida with Vafquez de Aillon, and of many others lately arrived from the iflands. He left a good garrifon in Mexico under Diego de Soto, and fet out on his march with one hundred and thirty cavalry, two hundred and fifty infantry, and ten thoufand Mexicans. Juft at this time De Oli returned from Mechoacan which he had reduced to a ftate of fubmiffion and peace, bringing with him the principal chief and feveral others, and a quantity of gold. This expedition to Panuco was very expenfive; Cortes applied for a reimburfement from the crown, which could not be acceded to; his Majefty's officers objected that it was undertaken on a private account, to prevent the eftablifhment of a colony by Garay, and not for the public fervice. When he arrived at Panuco he found the people very rebellious. In the courfe of a few days he had two battles, in which he loft three foldiers, four horfes, and above one hundred Mexicans. The number of the enemy amounted to above feventy thoufand warriors, but it was God's will that we fhould obtain the victory, with fuch a flaughter of the rebels as deprived them of all thoughts of making any head for the prefent. Thefe people are called the Guaftecas, and Naguatecas. After the laft battle Cortes again fent to fummon them to fubmiffion.

fubmiffion. He employed for this purpofe fome of the prifoners, and fent with them Fra Bartholome, by whofe exhortations they were induced to fubmit.

Cortes then went with one half of his troops to the river Chila, to reduce the Indians on the oppofite fide. He fummoned them, but they murdered his meffengers. He then paffed over one hundred and fifty infantry, and fifty cavalry, during the night. The enemy on their landing fell on them in great numbers, but they were foon driven from the field, and our troops advancing took their quarters in a town where they found plenty of provifions. In the morning fome of them entering the temple found remains of the bodies and clothes of our countrymen; fome of our foldiers thought they recognifed the features of their friends, and it was a melancholy fight to all; their remains we carefully collected and buried.

From this place our detachment marched to another, where an out party reported, that great bodies of the enemy were pofted in concealment in the houfes to fall upon our people when the cavalry had difmounted; their plan being difcovered failed of fuccefs, but they fought valiantly for half an hour, and three of our foldiers died afterwards of their wounds. Thefe people contrary to the general practice of Indians, rallied no lefs than three times. On the enfuing day our foldiers fcoured the neighbourhood, and entering fome towns which had been abandoned, found a quantity of earthen veffels, full of the wine of the country, in cellars under ground. After a ftay of five days they returned to the river of Chila. Cortes now again fummoned them, to which they returned for anfwer that they would come within four days; which Cortes waited out, but to no effect. He therefore determined to punifh them, and during a dark and rainy night, embarking a large body of Mexicans, he fent them acrofs a lake to one of the enemy's largeft towns, which they totally deftroyed. This brought in moft of that country to fubmit. Cortes founded a town of one hundred and thirty houfes, fixty three of the inhabitants whereof were foldiers. He

named

named it Villa de St. Eftevan del Puerto. It is fituated about a league from Chila. He allotted to it all the neighbouring diftricts which had fubmitted, and gave the command to Pedro Valego. Cortes was informed that three diftricts which had been concerned in the murder of many Spaniards, but which had been now received under allegiance, intended to fall on this poft as foon as he quitted the country. He in confequence marched againft them and deftroyed their towns, but they foon eftablifhed them again.

A veffel which Cortes had ordered to come to him with provifions and neceffaries was at this time loft in fome ftrong gales from the north, whereby the new fettlement was much diftreffed.

Cortes on his return to Mexico was informed of depredations committed on the peaceable diftricts, by fome of the inhabitants of the neighbouring mountains, whom he determined to chaftife in his way, but they anticipated him, by falling upon his rear and robbing the baggage in a bad pafs; our allies the Mexicans made them pay well for this infult, and two of their chiefs were hanged. Cortes then ordered hoftilities to ceafe, and the people, on being fummoned, came in and fubmitted. In the place of the chief, who was executed, Cortes appointed his brother, after which he proceeded to Mexico. In all the provinces of New Spain none was fo bad for favage and evil manners, as that of Panuco. They made human facrifices, and were cruel to an excefs, drunkards, filthy, and wicked, with thirty other turpitudes. They were punifhed with fire and fword two or three times, and greater misfortunes befell them when Nuno de Guzman came to be their governor, for he made them all flaves, and fold them in the iflands.

Alonzo de Avila whom I have formerly mentioned, was now returned with powers from the court of royal audience and the brothers of the order of St. Jeronymo, whereby we were authorifed to purfue our conquefts, to mark flaves, and to make fettlements according to the practice in the Iflands of Hifpaniola and Cuba. They alfo fent a report

U u

of

of what steps they had taken, to Castille. His Majesty was then in Flanders, where it was laid before him. Had De Avila been here at the time of Tapia's arrival he might have been very troublesome, for he was an adherent of the Bishop of Burgos, and had been bred up in his house. For these reasons, and by the advice of Almedo, Cortes to put him in good humour gave him the district of Guatitlan, one of the richest in that country. He also presented him with a considerable quantity of gold, and a much greater of kind words and promises, by which he won him so completely over to his interest that he afterwards sent him as his agent to Castille; at which time several gigantic human bones were transmitted, together with a quantity of gold, pearls, and valuable jewels. The bones were found in a temple at Cuyoacan; they were prodigiously large, and similar to those which we had procured in Tlascala and sent to Castille. The agents also brought over with them three tigers, and many other things of a curious nature, which I do not recollect. One part of their business was to transmit memorials to his Majesty from the council of Mexico, and from us the conquerors of New Spain, requesting that he would send us over holy men of good life and example, as bishops and clergymen. Also praying, that in consideration of our meritorious services, all offices of honour and emolument should be given amongst us, and the government to Cortes, as the only fit and proper person. Also that his Majesty would be pleased not to suffer any scholars, or men of letters to come into this country, to throw us into confusion with their learning, quibbles, and books. We further represented the insufficiency of Christoval de Tapia, who was only sent by the Bishop of Burgos to effect a marriage between the said Tapia, and the bishop's niece, Donna Petronila de Fonseca. We also deprecated the interference of the bishop in the affairs of this country as being obstructive of our plans of conquests for his Majesty's service, adding that we were ready to receive his Majesty's commands, prostrate on the ground, but had thought it our duty to inform him of these particulars, which had been artfully kept from his knowledge. All this, and more, was represented in the fullest light, for his Majesty's information, and to do away the misrepresentations of the said

Bishop

Bifhop of Burgos, whofe enmity was manifeft in his having prohibited the Cafa de Contraction of Seville from fending us any fupplies.
Cortes alfo left nothing in his inkftand which could be of fervice to our
interefts, for he wrote a memorial of twenty one pages, which I read,
and certify to be to the full tenor and effect of what I have related. He
alfo farther petitioned, that his Majefty would permit him to go to the
ifland of Cuba, to apprehend Velafquez the governor thereof, and fend
him as a prifoner to Caftille, for the injuries done by him to the general fervice, more efpecially in fending an order to put Cortes to
death.

Our agents failed from the port of Vera Cruz, on the twentieth of
December one thoufand five hundred and twenty two, without any particular occurrence on the voyage to the Terceras, except the breaking
loofe of two tigers, who wounded fome failors, and their being obliged
to kill the other on account of his ferocity. At the Ifland of Tercera
Captain Anthonio de Quinones loft his life. He was very amorous,
and in a quarrel concerning a lady there, as he piqued himfelf upon his
valor a duel enfued, in which he received a fword wound on the head,
and died in three days. Thus the bufinefs remained in the hands of
Alonzo de Avila only. As he purfued his voyage to Europe, he fell in
with a French privateer commanded by Juan Florin, who made prize
of him, his fhip, and all the treafure. This captain took another fhip
from St. Domingo with a valuable cargo of fugar, and hides, as alfo
twenty thoufand crowns of gold, and a quantity of pearls, fo that he
returned to France very rich, and made great prefents to the King, and
alfo to the admiral of France, the people whereof were aftonifhed at the
magnificence of what we fent to our great Emperor. The King of
France faid that the wealth we fupplied was fufficient alone to enable
our Monarch to wage war againft him, and yet Peru was not at this
time known. It is alfo reported that the King fent to our Emperor, to
fay, that he and the King of Portugal had divided the world between
them, without giving him a fhare, and that he defired to fee the will
of our father Adam, to know if he had made them exclufively his heirs.

Florin

Florin in his next expedition fell in with a ftrong Bifcayan fquadron, by which he was defeated and made prifoner, and being tranfmitted to Spain, he was hanged at the Ifland of Teneriffe. Thus was an end of him, his fhips, and our treafure.

Avila was confined a clofe prifoner in France, but he fucceeded in gaining the friendfhip of the officer in whofe cuftody he was, and obtained means of communicating with his friends in Spain, to whom he tranfmitted all the papers and documents with which he had been entrufted, and which were laid before his Majefty by the means of the licentiate Nunez, coufin to Cortes and relator of the royal council, Martin Cortes his father, and Diego de Ordaz. The Emperor was pleafed on due confideration to order, that all favor fhould be fhewn to Cortes, and that farther proceedings fhould be fufpended until his Majefty's return to Spain.

The intelligence of the lofs of the treafure was received by us as a moft ferious difappointment. The diftrict of Guatitlan was honorably referved by Cortes for Avila, notwithftanding his captivity, and his brother fucceeded to it three years after, Alonzo de Avila being then appointed contador of Yucatan.

The two captains, Sandoval and Alvarado, after the fettlement with Tapia, returned to their detachments, and proceeded on their expeditions, of which I will now give an account.

CHAPTER II.

Expeditions of G. de Sandoval and P. de Alvarado.

WHEN our party (for I went with Sandoval) arrived at Tuſtepeque, I took up my lodgings in the ſummit of a tower in a very high temple, partly for the freſh air and to avoid the muſquitos which were very troubleſome below, and partly to be near Sandoval's quarters. It was here that ſeventy two ſoldiers of thoſe who came with Narvaez, and ſix Caſtillian women had been put to death. The whole province on our arrival came in and ſubmitted, except the Mexican chief, who had been the cauſe of the deaths of our ſoldiers. Him Sandoval got arreſted, and he was ſhortly after executed, being burned alive. There were many more as guilty but this example was judged ſufficient. After this was done a meſſage was ſent to the Zapotecan mountaineers to come in and ſubmit. Their country is about ten leagues diſtant from Tuſtepeque. On their refuſal an expedition was ordered againſt them, under the command of a Captain Briones, who according to his own account had been a great officer in Italy. He marched with one hundred infantry and about the ſame number of Indian allies; the enemy were prepared for him, and laid a plan for a ſurpriſe, which they effected ſo completely that they drove our party over the rocks, rolling down to the bottom, and above a third of them were wounded, one of whom afterwards died. The diſtrict is ſo very difficult of acceſs, that troops can only paſs in ſingle file, and the climate is very miſty and humid. The natives are armed with large lances with an ell of blade, with two edges of ſtone as ſharp as a razor, and pliable ſhields which cover the whole body. They are very nimble, and give their ſignals by whiſtlings which echo among the rocks with inconceivable ſhrillneſs. This diſtrict

is

is called Tiltepeque. After it had been brought to fubmiffion the government of it was affigned to a foldier named Ojeda, who now lives in St. Ildefonfo. Sandoval who was a good humoured man began to joke with Briones at his return, upon the bad fuccefs of his expedition, afking him if ever he had feen the like in Italy; for Briones was always giving accounts how he had fevered men in two, and cut their heads off, &c. He was not pleafed with Sandoval's jocularity, and fwore he had rather fight the Turks and Moors, than the Zapotecans. This expedition was of little ufe, but on the contrary injurious. There was another diftrict of the Zapotecans which was called Xaltepeque, the people of which were at war with their neighbours, and immediately on being fummoned waited on Sandoval with handfome prefents, and a confiderable quantity of gold partly formed into toys, and the reft in ten little tubes; their chiefs wore very long robes of cotton reaching to the feet, richly embroidered, and refembling the upper robes of the Moors. They applied to him for fome of his foldiers to affift them againft their enemies named the Minxes. This the ftate of his force did not permit him to comply with, but he promifed to tranfmit an application to Mexico for a reinforcement for them, and in the interval would fend fome of his men to fee the country and the nature of the paffes; but his real object was to examine their mines. Thus he difmiffed them all except three, fending eight of us upon the bufinefs I have mentioned.

There were two of the fame name in this party, for we had three Caftillos in our army. I who at that time prided myfelf upon my drefs, was named Caftillo "the gallant." My namefake who went on his expedition was a man of very flow fpeech, not replying to a queftion for a length of time, and then he came out with fome abfurdity; he was named Caftillo "the thoughtfull." The other who was very fmart and ready in all he faid was called Caftillo "the prompt." But to have done with our witticifms and proceed with my narrative. On our arrival, the Indians turned over the earth in three different rivers, and in each they found gold, filling four tubes of the fize of the middle finger with it, and with thefe we returned. Sandoval thought that all our fortunes

were

were now made; he took a diftrict to himfelf from which he immediately procured fifteen thoufand crowns. To Captain Luis Marin he gave Xaltepeque from whence we had obtained the gold. This turned out however very indifferently. He gave me a very profitable diftrict there; would to God I had kept it! it confifted of three places named Matallan, Ozotequipa, and Oriaca, where is now the ingenio of the viceroy: but I thought it more confiftent with my character to go with Sandoval upon his expeditions. Sandoval called his town Medellin, after the birth place of Cortes. The river De las Vanderas from which the fifteen thoufand crowns were procured is the port, and it was here that the merchandife from Caftille was difcharged until Vera Cruz became the emporium.

We now proceeded on our route for Guacacualco. The province of Citla through which we paffed has the moft pleafant climate, and the greateft plenty of provifions, of any we had feen in this continent; its extent is about twelve leagues, in length and breadth, and it is very populous. The chiefs immediately fubmitted. On our arrival at the river of Guacacualco, thofe of that diftrict, which is the head one of all the neighbouring people, on being fummoned did not appear, which we confidered as a declaration of hoftility, and fuch in fact was their firft determination; but after five days had paffed, they waited on Sandoval with a prefent of fome trinkets of fine gold. By his directions they collected one hundred canoes, in which our troops croffed the river, after we had firft fent four foldiers to obferve and report the ftate of the people. The town which we founded here we called Del Efpiritu Santo, which fublime name was given to it becaufe it was on that day we defeated Narvaez; it was alfo our word in the battle, and it was on the fame day that we croffed this river. Here the flower of our army was eftablifhed, and it is certain that when we went out to the fquare upon a feftival or review, we muftered eighty cavalry; a greater number in proportion than five hundred now, horfes were then fo fcarce and dear. Sandoval having examined and confidered the fituation of the neighbouring diftricts, made repartitions of them as moft convenient to the
different

different settlements. The districts he allotted to his of Guacacualco were Guazpaltepeque, Tepeca, Chinanta, the Zapotecas, Copilco, Cimatan, Tabasco, Cachula, the Zoques, Techeapa, Cinacatan, the Quilenes and Papanahausta. We had much trouble afterwards on account of litigation with Vera Cruz concerning three of them, Guazpaltepeque, Chinanta, and Tepeca; with the town of Tabasco concerning two others, Cimatan, and Copilco, also with Chiapa concerning two, the Quilenes and Zoques, and with St. Ildefonso about the Zapotecas. I was very sorry I fixed myself here; the lands were very poor, and it turned out altogether to my disadvantage. Still we should have done very well had we been left as we were at first; but when the new settlements were formed our possessions were clipped, to accommodate them; whereby our colony fell to decay, from being the best, and containing the greatest number of the generous conquerors of Mexico; but it is at present a place of very few inhabitants.

Sandoval now received intelligence of the arrival of Donna Catalina lady of our general Hernando Cortes, and her brother, at the river of Aguayalco. La Zambrana also and her family arrived with them, and Elvira Lopez " the tall," married to Juan de Palma who was afterwards hanged. We all set out to pay our respects to these ladies, and I recollect the roads were almost impassable from the constant and heavy rains. Donna Catalina and the rest were escorted by us to our town of Guacacualco, and we sent word to Cortes of their arrival. After a short stay with us they set out for Mexico. Cortes was very sorry for their coming, but he put the best face upon it, and received them with great pomp and rejoicings. In about three months after the arrival of Donna Catalina, we heard of her having died of an asthma.

Villafuerte who had been sent to Zacatula, and Alvarez Chico who had also gone to Colima, were unsuccessful in their endeavours to bring those provinces into submission. Cortes then sent a party thither commanded by Christoval de Oli; the natives attacked him on his march, killing two of his soldiers; but he reached the station of Villafuerte who

was

was afraid to ftir out of it, and the enemy had even killed four of his men in the town. De Oli however before he departed reduced both thefe diftricts to fubmiffion. I do not know what became of Captain Juan Alvarez, but I believe he was killed in fome of the actions with the natives at this time. De Oli returned to Mexico, but had hardly got there when intelligence arrived of three provinces being again in rebellion. Sandoval had at this time arrived at Mexico with the ladies. Cortes fent him with a fmall party of our veterans to take thefe diftricts into his hands, which he did, and punifhed, and regulated them in fuch a manner, that we heard no more of their being refractory.

Several of the diftricts fubject to Guacacualco rebelled on the departure of Sandoval, killing the Spaniards employed in the management of the tribute; amongft others were the Xaltepeque Zapotecas, Cimatan, and Copilco; the firft of which is difficult of accefs on account of its mountains, the two others on account of lakes and marfhes, and they were not brought to fubjection but with the greateft difficulty.

At this time, and while Captain Luis Marin was employed in fubjugating thefe diftricts, arrived at our fettlement in a fmall veffel which came up to the town, Juan Buono the Bifcayan. He immediately fummoned us all to a meeting, where, after fome compliments on both fides, he opened his bufinefs to us, which was, to induce us to accept as governor Chriftoval de Tapia, of whofe return to St. Domingo Buono was ignorant. Large offers were made by the Bifhop of Burgos in unaddreffed letters, which Buono had a difcretionary power of directing to fuch as would fupport his views. Thefe he accordingly fent to fuch as he found to hold offices; I was offered a regidor's place. When Buono heard that Tapia was no longer in the country he was very much difappointed. We referred him to Cortes at Mexico, whither he went; I do not know what paffed between them, but I believe Cortes fent him back to Caftille with fome money in his pocket.

Amongft

Amongst others who courted the alliance of the Spaniards after the conquest of Mexico, were the people called the Tutepeque Zapotecans. They applied very earnestly for our assistance against a nation which was in hostility to them, named likewise the Tutepeques, whom they represented as possessing a very rich country. Accordingly in the year one thousand five hundred and twenty two, Alvarado, by the order of Cortes, marched from Mexico with one hundred and eighty soldiers, infantry and cavalry, with an order to take twenty more in his march to the province of Guaxaca, and also to visit certain rocky districts said to be in rebellion. He was forty days upon his route from Mexico to Tutepeque; on his arrival he was hospitably received, and lodged in the most populous part of the city, where the houses joined, and were roofed with straw, it not being the custom of that country to have terraces on their house-tops, as the climate is very sultry. By the advice of Olmedo it was determined that our troops should remove to a more open part of the town, left, in case of any treachery on the part of the people, their quarters should be set fire to. When they were fixed the chief of the town brought them provisions, and every day some rich present of gold. Alvarado desired a pair of stirrups of this metal, which was done according to the pattern. In a few days after, the chief was made prisoner, on an information from the Indians of Teguantepeque, who were in hostility to these, of his intention to burn the Spaniards in the quarters which they had first assigned to them in the temples. Some of the Spaniards say, it was to extort gold from him; however it was, he died in prison, after Alvarado had got from him to the value of thirty thousand crowns. Apparently his death was owing to vexation, though Fra Bartholome did what he could to console and encourage him. His son was permitted to succeed him in the chieftainry. Alvarado obtained from him more than he had got from the father, and then proceeded to establish a colony which he named Segura, as the colonists were mostly from Tepeaca, named by us Segura de la Frontera.

Alvarado then set out on his return, with all his wealth; for Cortes
had

had written to him to collect what he could, to send to Caftille. The foldiers being thus excluded from any fhare, fome of them formed a confpiracy to affaffinate Alvarado and his brothers. They were principally mufqueteers and crofsbow-men. A foldier of the name of Tribejo gave information to Fra Bartholome, a few hours before it was to be attempted. The reverend father having called Alvarado afide, and informed him of what he had heard, at the hour of vefpers, when the latter was riding out in company with feveral of the confpirators, and paffing by fome houfes, he faid to them, "gentlemen I am fuddenly " taken ill with a pain in my fide, let us return, and call a barber to bleed me." On his arrival he immediately fent for his brothers George and Gonzalo, together with the alcaldes and alguazils. He then ordered them to arreft the affaffins, two of whom were hanged; one was named Salamanca; he had been a pilot. The other was called Barnardino Levantifco. They both died like good chriftians, the reverend father taking great pains to bring them to a due fenfe of their fituation.

Alvarado now returned to Mexico, leaving a colony in this place; but when the colonifts found that the gold had been drawn away, that the climate was hot and unhealthy, and infefted with mufquitos, bugs, and other vermin, and that they and their flaves were dying faft, they determined to abandon it, fome going to Mexico, and fome to other places. Cortes on hearing of the fettlement being thus renounced, caufed an enquiry to be fet on foot, and found that it had been determined by the alcaldes and regidors in council, for which he condemned them to fuffer death, which was afterwards mitigated at the interceffion of Olmedo to banifhment. Thus fell to the ground the colony of Segura or Tutepeque, a very fertile country, but unhealthy. The cruelty and extortion of Alvarado alienated the minds of the people, and they threw of their allegiance; but that officer returning thither brought them again to fubmiffion, and they afterwards continued peaceable.

CHAPTER III.

Armament of Francisco de Garay.

I HAVE already made mention of F. de Garay, who was governor of the Island of Jamaica. When he heard of the riches that had been acquired here by Diego Velasquez, and of the fertile countries which had been discovered, stimulated by his avarice, and encouraged by the reflection on his wealth and means, Garray was induced to try his fortune.

Having therefore sent for, and discoursed with Alaminos our principal pilot upon the subject, his account was so favorable that he determined on sending a confidential person one Juan de Torralva, to obtain from the Bishop of Burgos the government of the country about the river Panuco. His application having been successful he sent an armament of three ships, with two hundred and forty soldiers, under the command of Alonzo Alvarez Pinedo or Pineda, which was defeated by the Indians of Panuco, one ship only escaping, and joining us at Villa Rica.

Garay receiving no intelligence of his first armament, sent a second, which also arrived at our port; and having now expended much treasure, and learning the good fortune of Cortes, he was more than ever stimulated to make exertions. He therefore fitted out a fleet of thirteen ships, and embarked one hundred and thirty six cavalry, and eight hundred and forty foot soldiers, mostly musqueteers and crossbow-men. The fleet under his command sailed from Jamaica in the year one thousand five hundred and twenty three, on the day of St. John, and arrived

ved

ved without any particular occurrence at a port called Xagua in the Island of Cuba. On his arrival here, he learned the news of Cortes having brought the province of Panuco under fubjection, and that he had fent a petition to his Majefty to be appointed to the government of it. He was alfo told of the heroic actions of Cortes and his companions in arms, and of our having defeated Narvaez with only two hundred and feventy foldiers. He was therefore ftruck with awe at the power of our chief, and the more fo when he was vifited by the Licentiate Zuazo. One day difcourfing with this gentleman on the fortunes of Cortes, he expreffed his apprehenfions of a difference between them relative to the government of Panuco, and requefted that Zuazo would mediate with Cortes in his favor, to which the other affented.

Shortly after this, Garay with his armament fet out, and being forced by a ftorm into the river Palmas, he there difembarked and marched for Panuco. Knowing alfo that Cortes had made an eftablifhment there, he thought it neceffary to take an oath of fidelity from thofe under his command, and he nominated the officers requifite for the eftablifhment of his colony, which he meant to name the city of Garayana.

Having advanced for two days march along the fea fhore through an uninhabited and marfhy country, he with his troops arrived at fome villages, whofe inhabitants received and entertained them hofpitably, but, many of the foldiers ftaying behind, robbed and injured the people. Garay continued his march and at length arrived at Panuco, which the troops had painted to themfelves as the end of their labours, but were fadly undeceived by finding it almoft a defert, for the war of Cortes had wafted it, or what remained was concealed on the approach of the Spaniards, who found nothing but bare walls, where they were to fuftain the attack of flies, and vermin of every defcription. One misfortune following another, he could get no intelligence from his fleet, but learned by a Spaniard who having committed fome crime was a fugitive among the Indians, that it had not arrived at the port. The

fame

same person gave a very unfavorable account of the country of Panuco, enhancing that of Mexico, and this making a strong impression on the minds of Garay's soldiers, they began to disband, and went towards Mexico, robbing the natives in their way.

All these things combined reduced Garay to a bad situation, and he sent one of his officers named Diego de Ocampo, to sound the disposition of the governor under Cortes in the colony of Santistevan, to whom he notified the appointment he had obtained from his Majesty. This officer answered Garay's message politely, and returned a favorable answer as to their reception, requesting that the soldiers might not outrage the inhabitants; Pedro de Vallejo, for that was his name, at the same time sent an express to Cortes with Garay's letter, and sollicited a strong reinforcement, or the presence of Cortes himself.

On the receipt of the intelligence from Vallejo, Cortes dispatched Fra Bartholome, Alvarado, Sandoval, and Gonzalo de Ocampo, brother to the person of that name who was with Garay, and entrusted to them the instructions he had received, whereby his Majesty's pleasure was signified, that all his conquests should be left under his command, until the matters in dispute between him and Velasquez should be brought judicially to an issue.

I will now return to my relation of the steps taken by Garay, who advanced with his force into the neighbourhood of St. Estevan del Puerto. On receiving intelligence thereof, Vallejo concerted a plan with the inhabitants of the neighbourhood, and being guided by five deserters who told him that Garay's troops were scattered negligently in a large town called Nacoplan, he came upon them by surprise, and made forty of them prisoners, assigning as a reason, their coming without producing any commission, and the outrages which they committed on the inhabitants. This being reported to Garay, he demanded the prisoners, threatening Vallejo with the vengeance of government. Vallejo replied, that when he saw his Majesty's orders he would obey them with all humility,

humility, and requefting that they fhould be fent to him. At this moment the perfons deputed by Cortes arrived, and Diego de Ocampo being at that time firft alcalde under Cortes in Mexico, began to remonftrate againft the entrance of Garay's force into that country, and feveral days were paffed in remonftrances and replies. During this time numbers of Garay's foldiers deferted from him; thus he faw every day his force diminifhing, and that of Cortes encreafing. From his fleet he had intelligence, that two of his fhips had been loft in a tempeft, and that the remainder, which were at the mouth of the river, had received and rejected a friendly invitation from Vallejo to remove higher up to a place of fecurity, threatening at the fame time, that in cafe of refufal he would confider them as pirates.

Vallejo continued fecretly to negociate with the officers of the fleet, and having fucceeded with two of them, they went to the fhip of the commodore Juan de Grijalva, and informed him that he fhould either bring his veffel into the river, or quit the place entirely. To this Grijalva only anfwered by difcharging his artillery, but on the receipt of certain letters from Alvarado and Fra Bartholome, accompanied with promifes conveyed by a royal notary he was at laft induced to accede to the firft propofition. No fooner had he brought his fhip into port than Vallejo declared all on board prifoners to his general Cortes; he was perfuaded however by Fra Bartholome to give them their liberty, from motives of humanity, which as he faid was the method of acting moft agreeable to God and to Cæfar.

The unfortunate Garay entreated the officers of Cortes to reftore his fhips, and to compel his troops to return to him, promifing to give up his intended eftablifhment, and make the beft of his way to the river Palmas. This propofal was acceded to, and every meafure taken to deliver up to him his deferters, though with little effect; for the foldiers defpifed Garay, and as to the oath of fervice, they faid that they had complied with it in coming to Panuco. Garay was then in the utmoft defpair, and finally agreed to adopt the meafure advifed by the officers of

Cortes,

Cortes, in writing to that general, stating his situation, and praying his protection in consideration of their former intimacy. This request was acceded to by Cortes, who sent an invitation to him to come to Mexico. Garay set out upon his journey, and when he approached the city of Mexico, he was met by Cortes at the head of a number of Spanish gentlemen on horseback, who conducted him to his newly built palace, and having heard the detail of his distresses, he promised him redress, and referred the affair to Fra Bartholome, Alvarado, and Sandoval. Fra Bartholome, to bind Cortes and Garay in stronger ties of friendship proposed an alliance between the daughter of Cortes, named Donna Catalina Cortes or Pizarro, and the eldest son of Garay, who then held a command in his fleet. Cortes accepting the proposal gave his daughter a liberal fortune, adding an assent to Garay's colonizing on the river of Palmas, and a promise to support the undertaking.

Garay was now induced to intercede with the general, and obtained permission for Narvaez to visit the Island of Cuba; for which favor Narvaez was very thankful, and took his leave of Cortes with many professions of gratitude and service. As to Garay and his expedition, both one and the other approached their end, for he, attending Cortes to early mattins, and having walked about the church, and eaten his breakfast, was suddenly seized with a pleurify, which after a course of bleeding and purging was declared mortal. This was anounced to him by Fra Bartholome, who accompanied the fatal news with earnest exhortations to him, to advert to the state of his soul, and not lose that in the next world, as he had already thrown away his fortune in this. Garay was impressed by the arguments of the good father, and having confessed, and had the rites of the church administered, he made his will, leaving Cortes and Fra Bartholome his executors, and in four days from the time he was first seized he gave up the ghost. This we observe peculiarly to belong to the climate of these countries; that in four days pleurifies are fatal, of which we had many instances amongst our soldiers, both in Tezcuco and in Cuyoacan. However Garay being now dead, God pardon him his fins! amen. He received an honourable

able funeral, and Cortes and the other officers put themselves into mourning. Thus died Garay in a distant country, a strange house, and far from his wife and children. As to his armament, being now left without any head a competition arose for the command, between Juan de Grigalva, Gonzalo de Figueroa, Alonzo de Mendoza, Lorenzo de Alloa, Juan de Medina, Juan de Villa, Anthonio de la Cerda, and a certain Tobarda the most seditious fellow in the whole army. The young Garay however was ultimately made general, contrary to the inclination of every soldier; the consequence of which was, that they separated in small bodies of fifteen or twenty, and went through the country pillaging as if they had been amongst Moors. This enraging the Indians they laid a plot to cut all the Spaniards off, which they so effectually executed, that in a few days they had sacrificed and eaten more than five hundred of Garay's soldiers. In some towns upwards of a hundred Spaniards were sacrificed together. In other places they fell on and massacred these wanderers without resistance, and encouraged thereby, they rose against the settlement of St. Estevan in such numbers, that it was with great difficulty they could be kept out of it, nor would they have been, but for seven or eight of the veterans of Cortes, who supported Vallejo, a brave man, and experienced officer. These gallant veterans induced many of Garay's Spaniards to abide by them in the open field, being obliged to fight three battles, in one of which Vallejo was killed, and many were wounded. So desperate did the Indians grow, that one night they killed and burned forty Spaniards and fifteen horses, and among the soldiers who were killed were several of those of Cortes.

When the general heard of these outrages he was exceedingly displeased, and determined to go in person to suppress them; but being at that moment prevented, having broken his arm by accident, he dispatched Gonzalo de Sandoval, with one hundred infantry, fifty cavalry, two pieces of artillery, and fifteen arcabusiers, to whom he joined eight thousand Mexicans and Tlascalans, with orders not to quit those dis-

tricts

tricts until he had so completely subjugated them, as that it should not
be in their power again to make disturbance. Sandoval was a man who
did not sleep at night when on any business of importance; of course
he made no delay upon his route, towards the enemy, who expected
him in two narrow defiles, where they had concentrated the whole force
of the refractory provinces. Sandoval on learning this divided his force
into two bodies, and attacked each of these posts. The Indians resisted
with their darts and arrows, whereby many of our soldiers were wounded, insomuch that he was obliged to halt the body which he commanded in that bad position, and send orders to his other detachment to do
the same for that night. The Indians retaining their first position, Sandoval recalled his detachment, and began his retreat towards Mexico.
When the enemy perceived this, they thought themselves conquerors,
and began to follow and surround the Spaniards from all parts, shouting at, and reviling them. This Sandoval seemed not to regard, but
continued his retreat, by which having completely deceived them, he
made a sudden countermarch at midnight, to gain the passes. This he
effected, but not without the loss of three of his horses, and considerable danger to his whole army, many of whom were wounded. No
sooner were his two columns clear of the defiles, than he perceived in
front vast bodies of Indians, who had arrived there that very night, on
hearing that he had countermarched. He therefore again brought his
whole force into one body, and perceiving the desperation with which the
Indians fought, and that they had actually wrested the lances out of the
hands of six of his soldiers, while his cavalry was composed of men
unused to such service, he gave them full instructions how to act, telling them not to halt to give thrusts, because the first thing
that the Indian does when wounded is, to seize the lance. He farther
directed, that if such a thing happened, the soldier should put spurs
to his horse, and with the lance firmly grasped in his hand, and under
his arm, wrest it from the enemy by the force of the horse. Having
then placed watches, guards, and patroles, he gave orders that the cavalry should remain saddled all night, and the troops went to their repose

pofe on the bank of a riyer. The Mexicans and Tlafcalans were pofted at a little diftance, for Sandoval knew by experience, that if the enemy attacked him in the night, he would be little benefited by them.

As foon as daylight appeared, Sandoval put his army into march, but had hardly advanced half a mile when he heard the found of the drums of the Indians, and he was fhortly after fronted by three large bodies of their warriors, who attempted to furround him. As foon as Sandoval perceived this, he made an attack upon them with his cavalry in two fquadrons with fuch fpirit that he entirely broke and difperfed them. This was not however effected without the lofs of two foldiers and three horfes. Our allies then made confiderable deftruction, burning all before them, until the army arrived at St. Efteyan del Puerto. The remains of this colony Sandoval found in a wretched ftate, and he was received as one who faved them from deftruction, and the foldiers of Garay who were there affured him, that the prefervation of what remained was folely owing to our veterans. Sandoval then divided his cavalry, mufqueteers, and crofsbow-men, into different bodies, and placed them under the command of the veterans, with orders to carry on the war with vigour againft the neighbouring Indians, and to fend in what provifions they could collect, for he was unable to go out, in confequence of a bad wound. During three days his parties fent in a number of prifoners of the lower clafs, together with five chiefs, the former of whom Sandoval releafed. He then gave out an order to his troops not to fend in any but fuch as had been prefent at, or concerned, where the lives of Spaniards had been loft.

Sandoval now prepared for an expedition againft the enemy, and on the day after, marched out with thofe troops which he had brought from Mexico, and by fkilful meafures fucceeded in taking twenty caciques, who had commanded where no lefs than fix hundred Spaniards had been put to death. Purfuing mild and fevere meafures at the fame time, according to the circumftances, he fummoned the neighbouring

towns

towns to a treaty of peace. Some acceded to his proposals, but others neglected to attend. With the latter he dissimulated, thinking it best not to notice their contumacy, and wrote to Cortes giving a full account of what he had done, and desiring to know how the prisoners should be disposed of. Cortes on receiving these satisfactory accounts appointed Sandoval to succeed Vallejo, as commandant at St. Estevan, and informed him, that for the sake of justice, and to prevent future mischief, it was necessary to punish with death those who had been any way concerned in, or who had abetted the murders of Spaniards, and he gave directions to the alcalde Diego de Ocampo, to take the necessary steps against them, with orders to execute such as should be legally condemned. He gave orders that every necessary measure also should be taken to conciliate the natives of that province, and that proper steps should be adopted to prevent any future outrages on the part of Garay's troops. These letters, the contents of which were highly satisfactory to Sandoval having reached him, he proceeded conjointly with Ocampo to put the orders of Cortes into execution. In two days after their receipt they proceeded to the trial of those caciques who were accused, and many being found guilty by evidence, or their own confession, were put to death. Some were burnt and others hanged; many also were pardoned, and the districts were given to the children and heirs of such as suffered. These acts of justice being done, Ocampo in compliance with the farther instructions he had received from Cortes, proceeded against all those Spaniards who had committed outrages, robberies, or murders; or who, going through the country in bands, had invited other soldiers to desert to them; and having seized and collected together these public disturbers, he caused them to embark for the Island of Cuba. To Juan de Grijalva Cortes offered the alternative of accepting a present of two thousand crowns, and a passage to Cuba, or if he preferred staying in the country, an honorable reception at Mexico; Grijalva and all the others were anxious however to return and accordingly they set sail for that island.

Sandoval

Sandoval and Ocampo having thus cleared the colony of thefe troublefome inmates, returned to Mexico, leaving an officer of the name of
Vallecillo governor of the fettlement. On their arrival they were received
by Cortes and every one there as their fervices merited, for a general
apprehenfion prevailed of fome misfortune occurring on that expedition.
Such was the fuccefs of the meafures purfued as I have above related,
that there never was another infurrection in that province.

The reader has been told how the Licentiate Zuazo met with Garay
in the Ifland of Cuba, and that the latter made preffing invitations to
him to take a part in his expedition. Zuazo agreed to this propofal,
and promifed to follow, as foon as he could give up his office. Having effected this he embarked, taking with him two brothers of the order of mercy, Fra Gonzalo de Pontevedra, and Fra Juan de Varillas.
Thefe three perfons purfuing their voyage, fell among fome fmall iflands
named Las Viboras, very fatal to veffels. Here, they were obliged to
throw overboard their provifions, and the pieces of pork attracted a
number of fharks, one of which feized a failor, and tore him to pieces,
fo that the whole water round them was difcoloured with his blood.
They were then obliged to run the veffel on fhore, and in this fituation
they were left. Two Indians of Cuba who were with them had the art
of obtaining fire by rubbing two dry fticks together; in the fand they
found fome brackifh water, and a quantity of turtles came afhore to lay
their eggs. Thus they obtained provifions fufficient to fuftain thirteen
perfons. The failors alfo contrived to kill the fea wolves which in the
night were frequently found on the fhore. Amongft the crew were
two fhip carpenters, who had preferved their working tools. Out of
the wreck of the veffel they conftructed a fmall failing boat in which
three mariners and one Indian embarked for New Spain, and made the
port of Calchocuca in the river Vanderas. From thence they went to
Medellin, and informing the governor of the fituation in which they
had left the Licentiate, he fent a veffel in fearch of them. The veffel
arrived

arrived at the island but Fra Gonzalo died a few days before. The rest, shortly arrived at Medellin; from whence they went to Mexico, where they had all reason to be satisfied with the reception they met with from Cortes, who made Zuazo his alcalde major.

CHAPTER IV.

Expeditions under various officers.

AS the views of Cortes were always lofty and tending towards domination, and as he was well supported by the talents and bravery of
his captains and soldiers, after having established his power in the great
city of Mexico, and in Guaxaca, Zacatula, Colima, Vera Cruz, Panuco, and Guacacualco, he learned that in the province of Guatimala,
there were populous nations, and rich mines. He therefore determined
to send a force under Pedro de Alvarado, to conquer and colonize that
country, and having first sent an embassy thither, ineffectually, Alvarado at the head of three hundred infantry, and one hundred and thirty
five cavalry, two hundred Tlascalans and Cholulans, and one hundred
Mexican allies, with four pieces of cannon, was ordered to march to
that province.

Cortes gave instructions to Alvarado, that he should if possible
bring those nations over to him by peaceable methods, and that Frá
Bartholome should preach to them upon the articles of our holy religion;
that all prisons and cages should be broken in pieces, and the prisoners
set at liberty.

The expedition set out from Mexico, on the thirteenth day of December, one thousand five hundred and twenty three. On his march
Alvarado received the submission of the district named the rocks of Gu-
elamo, and there obtained many rich presents of Gold. When the army, passing the provinces of the Zapotecas of Teguantepeque, and by
Soconusco,

Soconusco, which last place contained upwards of fifteen thousand houses, came into the neighbourhood of a place called Zapotitlan, at a river over which there was a bridge, they perceived a number of bodies of warriors drawn up to dispute the passage with them. An action ensued in which many soldiers were wounded, and a horse killed. So numerous were the Indians, that the Spaniards could not break or disperse them without three very hard fought battles.

From this place Alvarado continued his march, under constant alarms from the neighbouring Indians of Quetzaltenango, and after some time he arrived at a defile which ascends a mountain, for the length of about a league and a half. When he arrived at the summit, he found there an Indian woman, very fat, and having with her a dog of that species which they breed in order to eat, and which do not bark. This Indian was a witch; she was in the act of sacrificing the dog, which is a signal of hostility. Shortly after, our army perceived multitudes of armed Indians advancing upon them on all sides, in a difficult broken tract of ground, where the cavalry could not charge. The infantry advanced, but our troops soon perceived that these Indians acted upon a regular plan; for they retreated into the most rough and difficult ground, where above six thousand of the warriors of Utatlan, which is adjacent to Quetzaltenango, fell upon our people. They were howeve rfor the present put to flight, but soon rallied, being reinforced by fresh troops in great numbers, who waited our advance, and fought our troops foot to foot parties of three or four of them seizing a horse before and behind, and endeavouring to pull him to the ground. During this time the exertions of Alvarado, and the exhortations of Fra Bartholome, who represented to our soldiers the service which they owed to God, and that they must conquer or die, for the extension of our holy faith, never ceased; thus animated, our troops completely succeeded in dispersing the Indians. They then halted in the field and were unmolested by the enemy for three days; after which they advanced to the town of Quetzaltenango.

Meaning

Meaning to give fome repofe to his troops, Alvarado was difappointed to find that the Indians were now affembled in greater force, and determined to attack him in his poft. On their approach, to the number of about fixteen thoufand, for their army was compofed of two Xiquipils, Alvarado drew out his troops in a plain, and advancing upon the enemy, completely defeated them, with fuch lofs, that for a long time after, they remained completely under awe of the Spaniards.

The chiefs now propofed to treat for a peace, and fent ambaffadors to Alvarado who received them kindly, but they had at the fame time arranged a plan for the deftruction of the Spanifh force, and it was this. Not far diftant was a place called Utatlan, in a difficult country, and furrounded with defiles, whither they perfuaded him to march, and it was determined, that when the Spaniards were arrived, they fhould be fallen on by furprife with the forces of both the diftricts. Alvarado marched for Utatlan, but on his arrival remarked the bad fituation of the place. This town was of confiderable ftrength, having only two gates, to one of which was an afcent of about five and twenty fteps, and the other opened to a very bad and broken caufeway. The ftreets were very narrow, and the houfes joined; and in cafe of being attacked, the ground about the town was unfit for cavalry. The Spaniards obferved alfo that the women and common people had difappeared; and fome Indians of the place which they had left told them, that warriors were pofted in ambufcade round the town, which it was intended that night to fet fire to, and that was to be a fignal for a general attack.

Alvarado therefore ordered his troops under arms, and marched out into the open country, telling the caciques that it was to give his horfes grafs. They did not feem pleafed with this change, and as foon as Alvarado had his troops clear of the town he feized the cacique who governed it, and reproaching him for his treafon, ordered that he fhould be burnt alive, but Olmedo obtained a refpite and permiffion to ufe his

Z z   endeavours

endeavours to convert him to our holy faith; he accordingly preached an entire day, and at laſt ſucceeded, and as an indulgence, inſtead of being burned he was hanged, and his territory given to his ſon. Alvarado now fell upon, and diſperſed ſuch of the natives as remained about the town, and his ſucceſs having become known in Guatimala, previous to his arrival on the frontiers of that nation which was in hoſtility with the people of Utatlan, they determined to treat; for that purpoſe they ſent an embaſſy charged with a quantity of gold, and to declare their ſubmiſſion as vaſſals to his Majeſty; they offered at the ſame time to ſerve in his wars. Alvarado accepted their ſubmiſſion and their offer of ſervice, deſiring them to ſend to him two thouſand of their warriors, which requiſition was immediately complied with. As the people had rebelled again, Alvarado continued in the country of Utatlan about eight days, collecting a conſiderable ſpoil and many ſlaves, and then ſetting forward on his march, he ſoon arrived at the city of Guatimala, where he was hoſpitably received.

During this time the greateſt harmony prevailed between Alvarado and his troops, and the natives, the chiefs of whom informed him that in their neighbourhood was a nation called the Altitans, who poſſeſſed ſeveral ſtrong fortreſſes on the ſide of a lake, and who refuſed to come in and make ſubmiſſion. They alſo repreſented them as a bad and malicious people. To theſe Alvarado ſent an invitation, but they maltreated the perſons who brought it, in conſequence of which, he found it neceſſary to go with an armed force, and taking with him one hundred and forty Spaniſh ſoldiers, and two thouſand Guatimalans, he marched againſt them, renewing his offer, which was returned by a diſcharge of arrows from their warriors, who marched out armed in coats of mail, and ſounding warlike inſtruments. Alvarado put them to flight, and purſued them, with conſiderable loſs, to their fortreſſes which were over the lake. He then drove them from thence, and making ſeveral priſoners, compelled them to take to the water, and croſs over to an iſland. The principal perſons whom he had taken, he ſet at liberty, and bid them go and uſe their endeavours to perſuade their countrymen to a peace.

Between

Between threats and promifes Alvarado at length fucceeded, after which he returned to Guatimala. Fra Bartholome exerted himfelf with effect in his holy office, for, erecting an altar and an image of our Lady, he explained the mysteries of our faith to the natives, who imitated our example in adoring the Holy Virgin.

A people who came from a diftance towards the fouth, to make fubmiffion, and who were named the Pipiles, told our chief, that in their way was a nation called the Izcuintepeques, of a very malignant and obftinate difpofition, who maltreated all fuch as went through their country. To them he fent an invitation to come in and make fubmiffion, which they neglecting, he marched againft them with his whole force and a body of his allies of Guatimala, and coming on them by furprife he made great deftruction among them. This was an unfortunate event, productive of mifchief, and directly contrary to his Majefty's orders. I have now given the reader a fummary account of the conqueft and pacification of Guatimala and its dependencies, but it may be found at full length as written by Gonzalo de Alvarado. I was not prefent at it, nor did I go into that province until my return from Higueras. The Indians of this province are not good foldiers; only waiting the attack in broken ground.

Cortes had been informed that the provinces of Higueras and Honduras contained rich mines, and certain failors alfo told him, they had met with the natives fifhing, and that they ufed nets which had weights of gold mixed with copper; as alfo, that a ftraight, or paffage, was probably fomewhere about that coaft. In compliance with his Majefty's orders, he therefore determined to fend a body of troops thither under Chriftoval de Oli to fearch for this paffage to the Spice Iflands, and to make enquiry concerning the mines. As the way thither by land was very tedious and difficult, it was determined he fhould go by fea, and accordingly fix fhips were provided, and three hundred and feventy foldiers embarked, of whom one hundred were mufquetéers and crofsbowmen, and twenty two, cavalry. Five alfo of the old conquerors of

Mexico,

Mexico, the companions of Cortes and his Majesty's veteran servants, who had retired to their houses and repose, were commanded to take up arms again on this occasion; and it was of no use to tell Cortes that any one had served long enough, or suffered hardships, for when Cortes ordered no remonstrances availed. There was also one Briones, a seafaring man, of a seditious disposition, and a bitter enemy to Cortes, and many of the soldiers who embarked thought they had been ill used in the distribution of lands and property.

The instructions given to De Oli were, to sail to the Havannah, to receive provisions and necessaries, and pursue his voyage to Higueras, where he was to make enquiry whether any harbour, straight, or passage lay to the southward; also to search for mines of gold, and silver, and in some commodious situation to build a town, not neglecting the interests of the church, for the extension whereof, two reverend friars, one of whom spoke the Mexican language, were to attend the expedition.

De Oli embarked from Villa Rica, and arrived at the Havannah, where he took on board his provisions and horses and also five persons of those who had come out with Garay, and who had been expelled from the settlement of Panuco for seditious conduct. These persons attached themselves to De Oli, and began to instil their poisonous counsels in his mind, advising him to renounce his obedience to Cortes. Briones also laboured in this, and having concerted matters with Velasquez the mortal enemy of Cortes, it was settled amongst them, that De Oli should put himself under Velasquez, who would support him in his expedition, and also make such representations at court, that the new settlement should be taken out of the hands of Cortes, and the government thereof given to De Oli. This man was of great personal valour, a very good soldier, but unfit to be a commander; he was at this time about thirty six years of age, and was a native of Baeza or Linares; he had a good person and countenance, a cleft in his under lip, and his voice was rough and fierce; he was endued with many

good

good qualities, being fincere, and for a long time much attached to Cortes; until the ambition of governing, and diflike of being governed, perverted his mind, by the influence of bad advifers. He had been brought up in the houfe of Velafquez, but was under much greater obligations to Cortes.

De Oli fet fail from the Havannah, and on the third of May arrived at his ftation, which he on that account named El Triumpho de la Cruz. Here he appointed his civil adminiftration, making his alcaldes and regidors of thofe whom Cortes had recommended to him. He alfo took poffeffion of the country for his Majefty in the name of Cortes. His motive for doing this was, becaufe he wifhed to conceal from thefe perfons his feceffion from his general, and wifhed to keep them his friends until he could afcertain how the bufinefs was likely to turn out; for, if the country was as rich as he had reafon to fuppofe, he intended to throw Cortes off and fet up an independent government; if on the other hand, it fhould appear not to be valuable, he could return to his poffeffions at Mexico, and glofs over to Cortes his negociations with Velafquez, by pretending it was done in order to put him in good humour, and induce him to give him the neceffary fupplies. Thus was the new colony of El Triumpho de la Cruz eftablifhed, from whence no intelligence reached Cortes for upwards of eight months.

In the town of Guacacualco were a confiderable number of veterans, and Spaniards of quality, who were entrufted with the government of the province of that name, together with thofe of Citla, Tabafco, Cimatan, Chontalpa, Cachula, Zoque, the Quilenes, Cinacatan, and Chamuela, Chiapa of the Indians, Papanaufta, Pinula, Xaltepeque, Guazpaltepeque, Chinanta, and Tepeque. In the whole of New Spain, the demand of tribute was the fignal for an infurrection, and thofe who attempted the collection of it were killed, as indeed were all Spaniards who fell into the hands of the natives. In thofe provinces the refiftance was univerfal, and we were under the neceffity of going round from one city or town to another with a company of foldiers, to preferve the peace.

The

The diſtrict of Cimatan being particularly refractory, and Captain Luis Marin being unwilling at that time to ſend a body of troops thither, it was determined that four neighbours, whereof I was one, ſhould be ſent to try if we could bring the people to reaſon. Accordingly, ſetting out upon our journey, when we approached the principal town, we diſpatched meſſengers to acquaint the people with our buſineſs. When we came nearer to it we were met by a large body of Indians, armed with lances, and bows and arrows, who killed two of my comrades, and wounded me deſperately in the throat. My ſurviving companion after a few blows provided for himſelf by making off to ſome canoes by the bank of the river Macapa, ſo that I was left alone; I however retained ſufficiently my ſenſes, to creep into ſome buſhes where recovering a little, I addreſſed myſelf to heaven, and implored the aid of our Holy Virgin, beſeeching her not to let me die in the hands of thoſe dogs of Indians. Then, feeling my powers return to me, I ſallied out, and forcing my paſſage through the natives, giving many good cuts by the way, I made my eſcape to where my comrade was in the canoes, with four Indians whom we had brought with us to carry our baggage, which they had thrown away, and which the natives quitted us, to pillage. As it was the will of God that we ſhould not loſe our lives on this occaſion, we then got acroſs the river, which is very broad and deep, and full of alligators. To avoid the Indians we were obliged to remain eight days concealed in the woods, and from our not appearing, we were all concluded to be loſt. As was the cuſtom at that time, our property was forthwith divided amongſt the other Spaniards, however at the end of twenty three days we returned to our town, to the great joy of our friends, and diſappointment of thoſe who had gotten poſſeſſion of our lands and Indians.

Captain Marin now thought proper to go to Cortes to repreſent the ſtate of affairs, and demand more ſoldiers. He accordingly ſet out and waited on Cortes, who gave him thirty ſoldiers, commanded by Alonzo de Grado, with orders for the whole body of Spaniards to march for the province of Chiapa which was in a ſtate of war. Accordingly we ſet out

for

for the purpofe of reducing it, and of building a town there, to keep the inhabitants in check.

The firft thing neceffary was to make a road through the woods, in a very marfhy country where we were obliged to make caufeways for the horfes to pafs. Proceeding thus, we arrived at a place called Tezpuztlan, and continued our route to another town named Cachula, from whence we proceeded, there being no paffage previous to our expedition, from the fear the other natives have of thofe of Chiapa, who undoubtedly were at that time the braveft warriors in America; they alfo robbed paffengers and travelling merchants, and brought off the inhabitants of thefe diftricts to colonize and till their ground, nor could the Mexicans ever fubdue them. This our expedition took place in Lent, the year I cannot bring to my recollection, but think it was one thoufand five hundred and twenty four. When we came near the city of Chiapa, we made a review of our force, which confifted of twenty feven horfemen, twenty three mufqueteers, and a field piece under the direction of a gunner who told us that he had ferved in Italy; however that was, he was of no ufe, being a very cowardly fellow. We had feventy foot foldiers armed with fword and target, and about eighty Mexicans. The cacique of Cachula with fome of his principal people attended us, trembling with fear; four foldiers of the moft active of our little army, of whom I was one, were always fent forward to reconnoitre; the ground not being fit for a horfe I left mine behind, and we were ufually in front of the army about half a league. The people of Chiapa being much accuftomed to hunting, fome of them who were thus employed perceiving us at a diftance gave the alarm, and made fignals by fmoke.

As we approached their firft fettlement, which is called Eftapa, and is diftant four leagues from the principal town, we found the roads, which ran through cultivated grounds, wide and convenient; and on each fide were plentiful crops of corn, and vegetables. We entered this town, but the inhabitants had quitted it, and having pofted our guards and fent out patroles, the remainder went to reft; but we were foon roufed

by

by the arrival of two of our out party, who came in at full fpeed to tell us, that the natives were collecting from all parts to attack us. We ftood to our arms, and advanced to meet them out of the town, where a very fevere action enfued, for they were provided with darts hardened in fire, war clubs, and lances larger than ours, and alfo a good defenfive armour made of cotton. As the field of battle was very ftoney, their flingers did us infinite mifchief. They approached us fo clofe that in the firft attack they killed two of our foldiers, and four horfes, wounded our reverend father, Fra Juan, and thirteen foldiers, and deftroyed many of our allies. Our captain, Marin, alfo was wounded in two places. This action lafted till dark night, when, having made an unfatiffactory experiment of the fharpnefs of our fwords and the effect of our mufquetry, the enemy retired, leaving behind them fifteen killed, and many wounded, from two of whom, apparently principal people, we learned, that on the next day a general attack was intended upon us.

The manner in which the enemy had fought convinced us that they were no defpicable warriors: for when a cavalry man halted to make a thruft the Indians feized the horfe, and wrefted the lance out of the horfeman's hand, or pulled him to the ground.

On the next day we purfued our route to the city of Chiapa, and a city it might truly be called, from the regularity of its ftreets and houfes. It contained not lefs than four thoufand families, not reckoning the population of the many dependent towns in its neighbourhood. At the diftance of about a quarter of a league from the place which we had left, we found the whole force of Chiapa drawn up to receive us. Their troops were adorned with plumage, and well armed, offenfively and defenfively, and the hills refounded with their fhouts on our appearance. It was dreadful to behold the fury with which they threw themfelves upon us like enraged lions; as for our black artillery man, and black he was indeed to us, he was fo ftupified with fear, that he ftood trembling and unable to put the match to the gun, and when at

laft

laft we fucceeded in roufing him, he fired the piece with no other effect than that of wounding three of our own men. Our captain gave orders to the cavalry to form in fmall bodies, and the mufqueteers, crofsbowmen, and fword and buckler men, to clofe into one compact battalion, whereby the cavalry and infantry fupported each other. The enemy were fo numerous that had we not been the men we were, it would have gone very hard with us, and we ourfelves were aftonifhed at the bravery of our adverfaries; but good father Bartholome ftood firmly by us, and adminiftered comfort to us by his exhortations, promifing that we fhould be rewarded for our exertions, both by God and by Cæfar. Our Captain Marin likewife frequently encouraged us, calling out to charge them in the name of St. Jago. We at length forced them to fly before us; but as there were hard by, tracts of very rocky ground where the cavalry could not follow them, frefh bodies of Indians fell upon us by furprife, while we, thinking the day our own, were returning thanks to God and our Lady. Of thefe troops a number were prepared with long thongs to twift round the horfes, and throw them down, and they had aifo ftretched out the nets which they ufed in hunting, for the fame purpofe. The enemy attacked us here fo defperately that hardly one of our foldiers efcaped without a wound; they wrefted the lances from fome of our cavalry, and killed two foldiers and five horfes. In the centre of their army was a woman, aged, and immoderately fat, who was efteemed by them a goddefs, and had promifed them the victory. They had alfo incenfe in a pan, and certain idols made of ftone. This woman, who had her body painted, and cotton mixed with the paint, advanced without any fear among our allies, who were formed by companies, and by whom this infernal deity was in a very fhort time torn to pieces.

During this time the battle raged, and we and our captain recommending ourfelves to our Lady, and befeeching the reverend father to pray for us, threw ourfelves into the thickeft of it, and forced the enemy to fly, fome to the rocks, others to the river, whereby they effected their efcape, being excellent fwimmers. We then halted to take breath,

and

and our good friar, joined by the foldiers, fang the hymn which begins " Salvé &c," and we returned thanks to God for the victory. Our army then advanced towards a town by the fide of a river, where we remained the entire day and night, paying particular attention to the concealment of our dead.

About midnight, ten chieftains of the neighbouring diftricts came down the river which is very broad and deep in five canoes; they difembarked at one of our pofts, and were made prifoners. Being brought before our captain, they told him they belonged to a nation called the Xaltepeques, againft whom the people of Chiapa had made war; their object was, to offer their fupport, and to obtain from us a promife, that in cafe of fuccefs againft the Chiapans, we fhould fet free from them the nations to which thefe Indians belonged; in the hopes of which, they promifed us affiftance to pafs the river, which could not otherwife be done. This was very fatisfactory to us, and therefore leaving two of their party behind, the reft went immediately to provide twenty canoes. The remainder of the night was paffed under a ftrict watch, for the drums and horns of the enemy were heard, from the banks of the river, where they were collecting to attack us. As foon as it was light we faw our friends arrive with the canoes; they alfo fhewed us a ford, though a very dangerous one, and were urgent to us to lofe no time in paffing, to fave the lives of fome of their countrymen who had been made prifoners. Accordingly we paffed the river, formed into a folid column, at the ford, which took us up to our armpits, and where we loft one of our cavalry. On the oppofite bank we were affailed by the enemy with fuch a difcharge of darts and arrows, that not one of our party efcaped without two or three wounds before we could get out of the water, but vaft bodies of other Indians appearing in our rear, and declaring for us, by attacking the Chiapans, they were foon forced to turn their backs and fly towards their city, whither we advanced in good order, with colours flying, and accompanied by our allies. On our arrival there, we found it too clofe built to be fafely occupied by us, and we therefore pitched our camp in the open field.

Our

Our captain now fent meffengers inviting them to peace, and fhortly after, they fent a deputation of their chiefs, praying forgive-nefs, and requefting to be admitted fubjects to his Majefty. They alfo defired that the neighbouring nations might not be permitted to de-ftroy their houfes and plantations, which requeft was readily granted. When we went into this town we found many prifoners confined in wooden cages, who had been feized by them when travelling. All thefe were releafed and fent to their homes. In their temples we found idols of horrid figure, which Fra Juan broke to pieces, and alfo many remains of men and boys juft facrificed, and other traces of their moft abominable cuftoms.

Our captain then fent orders to all the neighbouring nations to come in; amongft the firft who obeyed were thefe of Chinacatan, Gopa-nauftla, Pinola, Gueguiztlan, Chamula, the Quilenes, and others of the Zoque language, with many more which I do not recollect. Thefe people were much furprifed when they perceived with how fmall a body we had ventured to attack the warlike nation of the Chiapans, whom the Mexicans never could conquer. Fra Juan preached to them with great fuccefs, and many came to him to be baptifed.

While this was paffing, a certain Spanifh foldier, attended by eight Mexicans, went to a town called Chamula, and there demanded with-out any authority a contribution of gold in the name of his captain. A portion was collected for him, but not fatisfied therewith he attempted to feize the cacique, which caufed an infurrection in that and a neigh-bouring town named Guehuiftlan. As foon as our captain got intelli-gence of it, he caufed him to be feized, and immediately fent him off by exprefs, prifoner, to Mexico. This man was one who confidered himfelf of confequence amongft us, very evil difpofed, and cruel to the Indians.

We then proceeded to Chamula, which in confequence of the above related outrage continued in rebellion. We were affifted on our march

by

by the people of Cinacatan, a polifhed and mercantile nation, and arriving at Chamula, we found this place ftrongly fortified by nature, and the inhabitants well armed, having a large kind of fhield with which they could cover the whole body, and which when not wanted was rolled up. When we approached we were attacked with fhowers of arrows, upon which our captain ordered the cavalry to go into the plain, there to watch the infurgents of the neighbouring diftricts of Quiabuitlan. Our mufqueteers then fired upon the enemy, but with very little effect, whereas their miffile weapons injured us who were uncovered, materially. We were during this whole day fighting thus, to very little purpofe, and when we attempted to force the ramparts, we found them guarded by above two thoufand men armed with lances. Finding our endeavours ineffectual, it was determined to procure timber from another town which was depopulated, and to conftruct of it the machines named burros or mantas, under cover of which twenty men or more could approach, and remain under the walls, fo as to work an entrance. We therefore drew off for that time, and having procured the timber and conftructed thefe machines, we again proceeded to the attack. Under cover of them our men endeavoured to undermine the wall, the enemy throwing down upon us fcalding water mixed with blood, fire, and heavy ftones, infomuch that we were quite in defpair, and forced to retreat to repair the machines, which having done, we again brought them to the walls, and working under them we made different breaches. As foon as the enemy perceived this, they fent up to the top of their ramparts four of their principal perfons, priefts, and others, who addreffed us covered with their thick fhields, and told us, that fince we wanted gold we might have it; and therewith threw over feven crowns of fine gold, together with a quantity of gold trinkets, and other things made of that metal, caft in the forms of fhells and birds; and they alfo at the fame time fent among us frefh fhowers of arrows, darts, and ftones. We had fucceeded in making two confiderable breaches in the walls, but it was now dark, and a heavy rain began to fall; we were therefore obliged to defift for that night, keeping good watch all round our poft, and the cavalry remaining on the plain

ground,

ground, faddled and bridled. The enemy during the whole night were founding their warlike inftruments, fuch as timbals, and fmall trumpets, yelling, and threatening us with destruction on the next day, which they faid had been promifed to them by their gods.

At day break we again brought forward our machines, to work at their walls, which the enemy defended with the greateft obftinacy, wounding five of our people, and amongft them myfelf by a thruft, and were it not for the ftrength of my cotton quilted armour, the lance would have gone through me. Thus we were employed during the whole day, and the evening was drawing on, with a heavy fall of rain and a very thick mift, as is frequently the cafe in that mountainous country. In confequence of this our captain called us off from the engagement, and about the fame time the enemy ceafing to fhout and make the noifes they had hitherto done, I, who was accuftomed to bufinefs of the kind, and alfo perceived that their lances were refted againft the walls, barbicans, and battlements, except about two hundred that ftill appeared to be in hand, began to fufpect they were going to abandon the place; in confequence whereof, I and one of my comrades getting in at a fmall breach in the wall, to fee what they were doing, fell fuddenly in upon upwards of two hundred of them in arms, who attacked us with their lances, and would fpeedily have put an end to us, but that fome of our Indian allies who perceived our fituation, called out to the reft of our foldiers, who crouded in to where we were furrounded by thefe Indians, who only compofed the rear guard of the garrifon, for all the reft, men, women, and children, had evacuated the place by the other gate.

Thefe who remained we quickly put to flight, and purfuing them, we came up with many of the others, and made prifoners feveral men, women, and children. We now quitted the town, and purfued our route towards Chinacatan, halting for that night at a place where at prefent the city of Chiapa de los Efpanoles is built. Being arrived here, our captain difcharged fix of his prifoners, with orders to inform their
countrymen

countrymen that if they fubmitted, he would deliver up to them the whole of thofe he had taken, which meffage was delivered, and chearfully complied with.

In confequence of the orders which Cortes had given to our captain, who was alfo my particular friend, to give me fome good fituation, I was appointed to the command of this encomienda which I held for eight years. The firft thing I did was, to get a reverend father to preach to the Indians, and convert them to the chriftian faith; we accordingly erected an altar and crucifix, and he preached to them to good effect. The firft day we baptifed fifteen, to my great fatisfaction, for I loved and wifhed well to them, they being now my own. There was in this neighbourhood a people who inhabited three fortified towns, and were in rebellion againft us, named the Guegueftitlans, and it became neceffary to march againft and reduce them. Leaving therefore our wounded and baggage behind, the moft ftout and active among us proceeded againft them; they had barricaded all their approaches with fallen trees, which we cleared by the affiftance of our Indian allies, and arrived under their fortreffes, which appeared likely to give us enough to do, for the firft we came to was full of warriors who were well appointed, offenfively and defenfively. When we mounted to the affault they all fled and left the place to us, but our allies made two of them prifoners, who were immediately releafed, and fent with offers of peace and good treatment to their friends, on fubmiffion. Thefe conditions they accepted and came in, bringing with them fome trifling prefents of gold, and feathers of the quetzal.

Having thus effected our bufinefs here, we proceeded according to the directions of Cortes, to eftablifh a colony. Hereupon there was a difference of opinion amongft us, for fome were for it, but others who had plantations and Indians in Guacacualco were adverfe, objecting to it as an unfit fituation for cavalry, and faying alfo that our force in its prefent reduced ftate was infufficient, the diftrict being populous, and the towns built in the faftneffes of the mountains. Thus our party fell

into

into difputes upon this and other fubjects, for our captain, Marin, and Diego de Godoy who was a royal notary and a very bufy perfon, were adverfe to the plan. That troublefome fellow Alonzo de Grado, alfo it appeared, was poffeffed of a patent from Cortes, giving him an enco-mienda in the province of Chiapa, when it was reduced to obedience. By virtue of this he demanded from Marin the gold which had been obtained from the Indians of Chiapa, and alfo that which had been found in the temples, amounting to one thoufand five hundred crowns. This Marin refufed, alledging that it was neceffary to employ it in re-placing the horfes which had been killed in the expedition. All thefe differences together brought matters to fuch an extremity, that our cap-tain put both of them in irons, determining to fend De Grado to Mex-ico; as to Godoy, by dint of interceffion and promifes he obtained his releafe. Godoy made but a very bad return to Marin for his lenity, for he immediately entered into a cabal with De Grado, and it was agreed between them to make a formal complaint to Cortes against him. I was applied to alfo to write to him in exculpation of De Grado, becaufe they faid that Cortes would believe my reprefentations. I did write in-deed, but it was to let Cortes know the true ftate of the cafe, and by no means charging Marin with any impropriety. De Grado was fent to Mexico under an oath to prefent himfelf to Cortes within eighty days; that time being allowed on account of the diftance, which is upwards of one hundred and ninety leagues.

It was now determined by us, to chaftife thofe people who killed the two foldiers of that party wherewith I was fent, as formerly men-tioned. In our way we marched through a diftrict fo very rugged, that the paffage was impoffible to our horfes without affiftance, which, on an application to the caciques was readily afforded us. Thefe people are named Tapelola. Continuing our route by the Silo, Suchiapa, and Coyumelapa diftricts we came to thofe of the Tecomayatacal and Atea-pan Indians. The houfes in the chief town, which belonged to my dif-trict, joined each other, and formed a very populous and extenfive place.

Near

Near this was a large and deep river, which it was neceſſary to paſs, and here we were oppoſed by the people of the town and vicinity, but after a ſharp action, wherein we had ſix ſoldiers wounded and three horſes killed, we put them to flight, they all taking to the mountains and woods, having firſt ſet fire to their town. We ſtayed here five days taking care of the wounded, and having made many of the women of this place priſoners, our captain ſent to invite the people to peace, which was accepted, and they returned to their homes. Godoy was averſe from this lenity, and told our captain that theſe people who had revolted without any reaſon ſhould be puniſhed, or at any rate made to pay for the horſes which were killed in the action. I was of a different opinion, and thought that ſince they came peaceably they ſhould not be made to ſuffer; and giving my opinion freely, Godoy became enraged and broke out into angry words, from which we came to blows, and drew our ſwords. A good many cuts paſſed between us before we could be parted, and if we had not been ſo, one or other of us would have loſt his life. Marin, who was a good and mild man, ſaw the impropriety of uſing harſh meaſures with theſe people, and reſtoring all their property to them, left them in peace.

We continued our march, and paſſing by other diſtricts of Cimatlan, and Talatiopan, we were aſſailed by a number of their archers, who gave us a volley whereby above twenty of our ſoldiers were wounded, and two horſes killed; and but that we immediately attacked and drove them from their poſt, they would have done us much miſchief. I muſt obſerve, that theſe are the ſtrongeſt archers that ever I met with, for they drive their arrows through two ſuits of cotton mail well quilted; which is a wonderful force. Their country is in great part marſh, which ſhakes when a foot-man walks upon it. It was therefore in vain to purſue the natives, and as for our offers of peace they treated them with neglect. We therefore thought it beſt to make our ſhorteſt way to our town of Guacacualco. We took our route for it by the diſtrict of Guimango, Nacaxa, Xuica, Teotitlan, Copilco, and others which

I do

I do not recollect, to Ulapa, and acrofs the rivers Agaqualulco, and Tonala, to Guacacualco, where the killed horfes were paid for at a penny a pound.

As to De Grado, when he arrived at Mexico and waited on Cortes, the general was highly difpleafed with him, telling him to take three thoufand crowns and go to the Ifland of Cuba, and give him and others no farther trouble. De Grado however made fuch apologies that they were afterwards good friends.

Bbb

CHAPTER V.

Tranſactions in Old Spain.

IN the year one thouſand five hundred and twenty one, our moſt Holy Father Pope Adrian of Lobayana ſucceeded to the ſovereign pontifi-
cate. He was then governor of Caſtille, and reſided in the city of
Vittoria, where our agents waited upon him to kiſs the foot of his holineſs. At the ſame time arrived a great nobleman from Germany,
called Moſiur de Laſoa, chamberlain to his Majeſty, by whom he was
ſent to congratulate his holineſs on his election. This M. de Laſoa,
having heard the heroical actions of the conquerors of Mexico, and the
great works they had done for the extenſion of our holy faith, by the
converſion and baptiſm of ſo many thouſands of Indians, was intereſted
in our behalf, and applied to the Holy Pontiff, requeſting him to accelerate the buſineſs wherein our agents were employed. This requeſt
was readily granted, for independent of what was laid before him by
our agents, our holy father had received many complaints againſt the
Biſhop of Burgos from perſons of high honour and quality, whereby
our agents were encouraged to proceed in a formal accuſation againſt
him. Thoſe who were moſt active in the buſineſs were Franciſco de
Montejo, Diego de Ordas, the licentiate Franciſco Nunèz couſin to
Cortes, and Martin Cortes our general's father, who were aſſiſted by
many great and powerful noblemen, but principally by the Duke de
Bejar; and thus countenanced, they brought forward their charges with
great effect.

The firſt was, that Velaſquez had bribed him with a diſtrict, with
the people of which he worked gold mines. Secondly, that in the
year

year one thoufand five hundred and feventeen, when one hundred and
ten of us procured veffels at our own expence and fet out for the difcovery of New Spain, the Bifhop of Burgos informed his Majefty that it
was Diego de Velafquez who had done fo, contrary to the truth.

Thirdly that Velafquez had fent twenty thoufand crowns in gold,
which his nephew Juan de Grijalva had obtained, to the bifhop, and
fio part to his Majefty; and that when Cortes fent a prefent of gold the
bifhop feized it, fuppreffing our letters, and fubftituting others, afcribing the faid prefent to Velafquez. Alfo that the bifhop retained one
half of the treafure, and when Puertocarrero applied to him for permiffion to wait upon his Majefty, he caufed him to be feized and thrown
into prifon, where he died. Alfo, that he fent orders to the officers of
the Cafa de Contractacion of Seville, that they fhould not give any affiftance to Cortes. Farther, that he appointed as officers to the military
fervice in New Spain, fuch as were not fit for it, as was the cafe in regard to one Tapia, to whom, in order to bring about a marriage between
his niece and the faid Tapia, he promifed the government of New Spain.
Alfo, that he approved for good, the falfe relations tranfmitted by the
agents of Velafquez, which he forwarded to his Majefty, fuppreffing
thofe of Cortes which were the true ones. There were befides many
other charges, all very well fubftantiated, and which he could not
deny.

Thefe things being all brought to light, his holinefs was pleafed
to order, that the Bifhop of Burgos fhould have no farther authority in
New Spain, that Cortes fhould be declared governor thereof, and that
Velafquez fhould receive compenfation for the expences he had been
at, and could duly prove. His holinefs fent alfo to New Spain a number of indulgences for the hofpitals and churches, and was pleafed to
direct Cortes and us the conquerors to pay unremitting attention to the
converfion of the Indians, adding how much it was the duty of himfelf
and all Chriftendom to pray for thofe who had done fo much for the
advancement of our holy faith. He alfo was pleafed to fend to us his

holy

holy bulls of abfolution. All this his Majefty gracioufly thought proper to confirm, fo far as relates to the civil and military eftablifhment, adding thereto his order to Velafquez to give up his government of Cuba, on account of his having fent out the armament under Narvaez in defiance of the peremptory orders of the royal chamber of audience, and of the brethren of the order of St. Jerome. The Bifhop of Burgos was fo affected by the cenfure which his holinefs the Pope paffed upon his conduct, and by his Majefty's orders in confequence thereof, that when he retired to his country feat at Toro he fell dangeroufly ill.

At this period arrived in Old Caftille, Pamphilo de Narvaez, and Chriftoval de Tapia, whom the Bifhop of Burgos had created governor of New Spain, together with the pilots Umbria and Cardenas. Thefe perfons waited on the bifhop to demand his permiffion to lay their accufations againft Cortes before his Majefty, and as the bifhop defired nothing better than to hear complaints of Cortes and of us, he fhewed them every favour in his power. When the agents of Velafquez perceived this, they gladly joined the party, and all together went to prefer their charges before the Emperor.

They made ftrong accufations againft Cortes; firft, that Velafquez fitted out armaments three times to his own great coft, and entrufted the command of the laft to Cortes, who broke his engagement. Farther, that when Velafquez fent Narvaez with his Majefty's commiffion as governor general of New Spain, Cortes made war upon, and defeated him. Alfo, that when the Bifhop of Burgos fent Tapia to take the government of thofe countries in his Majefty's name, he refufed to obey, and by main force compelled him to reimbark. They alfo accufed Cortes of having obtained a quantity of gold in the name of his Majefty, and converting it to his own ufe; of having taken to himfelf a fifth of all prizage; of having burnt the feet of Guatimotzin; of retaining the foldiers fhares; and building palaces and fortified houfes that were as large as whole villages, making the inhabitants round Mexico work at them, and forcing them to draw large cyprefs trees, and ftones, from a great distance;

diſtance; and that he had given poiſon to Franciſco de Garay, to get from him his troops and ſhipping. There were many other accuſations brought forward, ſo that his Majeſty was at laſt tired of hearing them, believing them to be true.

Narvaez, when admitted into the Emperor's preſence addreſſed him in his pompous tone of voice, as follows. "Your Majeſty muſt fur-
" ther know, that on the night I was taken priſoner, having your
" royal commiſſion in my pocket, my eye put out, and in apprehenſion
" of being burnt alive, for the apartment was in flames, one of Cor-
" tes's captains, Alonzo de Avila at preſent priſoner in France, violent-
" ly tore your commiſſion out of my pocket, and when I claimed it,
" declaring what it was, he denied the fact, and ſaid that they were
" bonds for money owing me by Spaniards in Mexico, and which I
" was coming to enforce." At this the Emperor could not refrain from laughing. In regard to the charges, his Majeſty ſaid, he would give orders that ſtrict juſtice ſhould be done; and he forthwith commanded, that certain perſons of his royal privy council ſhould be formed into a court of enquiry to hear and decide upon theſe allegations. The perſons who compoſed this court were Mercurio Catarinario grand chan-
cellor of Italy, De la Soa, and Doctor De la Roche, Flemings, Hernando de Vega lord of Grajales, the Doctor De Garavajal, and the Licentiate Vargas.

This court gave notice to the parties to come forward; and accord-
ingly they produced their charges in the ſame form that they had been laid before his Majeſty. To the charges brought by Velaſquez it was replied, that De Cordova was the diſcoverer of New Spain, who did it with his companions at their own coſt, and that Velaſquez was here alſo criminal, in that he ordered him to go to the Iſland of Los Guanajes, to take Indians by force, and make ſlaves of them. Farther, that admitting he ſent Juan de Grijalva thither, it was not for the purpoſe of colonization but only for trade. That for the expences incurred, the principal part was born by the different captains, and not by Velaſquez,

and

and thefe captains had there collected twenty thoufand crowns, the principal part of which went to Velafquez. Farther, that Velafquez gave the Bifhop of Burgos Indians in the Ifland of Cuba to procure gold, neglecting his duty to his Majefty. Alfo, that admitting it was he who fent Cortes, it was by the approbation of his Majefty, and by the providence of God; for that any other commander would have failed in an undertaking of fuch danger, and that Cortes was not fent by him to colonize, but to barter; and that his eftablifhment in the country was owing, not to the inftructions of Velafquez, but the inftances of his companions, for the fervice of God, and his Majefty. Alfo that it was well known, that Cortes reported the whole of his proceedings to his Majefty, fending therewith all the gold he had been able to procure, he, and his companions, awaiting his Majefty's further orders, proftrate on the earth. It was alfo reprefented, how the Bifhop of Burgos fuppreffed the faid letters, and feized the prefents, concealing from his Majefty our meritorious fervice; and when our agents wanted to obtain permiffion to wait on his Majefty, he threw one of them, Puertocarrero, into prifon, where he died; and that he forbid the officers of his Majefty at Seville, to furnifh us with what we required. All which was done by the faid bifhop, from a corrupt motive, as he wanted to procure a marriage between either Velafquez or Tapia, and his niece named Donna Petronila de Fonfeca, as he had promifed that his fon-inlaw fhould be governor of Mexico. In fupport of all which accufations they were ready to produce proofs. As to the expedition of Narvaez, our agents replied, that in the firft place Velafquez deferved to fuffer death for difobedience of his Majefty's orders; and alfo, that he applied himfelf folely to the bifhop, neglecting his Majefty, which was a high difrefpect; in confequence therefore of the above mifdemeanors and crimes, our agents, prayed that the court would be pleafed to award punifhment; to which the court replied that they would take it into confideration.

In reply to the charges brought againft Cortes by Narvaez it was reprefented, that on his coming to New Spain he fent word to the great
King

King Montezuma, that he came to refcue him, and thereby caufed fuch a difturbance in the country, as produced a dangerous war. That on his arrival at Vera Cruz, Cortes had written to him a friendly letter, defiring to fee his commiffion, to which Narvaez would make no anfwer; but declared war againft Cortes and his companions, notwithftanding that Cortes invited him to, and reprefented the neceffity of, an amicable junction, for the good of his Majefty's fervice, left all fhould be loft. But Cortes finding that all his offers were neglected, and Narvaez not fhewing him his Majefty's commiffion, and knowing the mifconduct of Narvaez in feizing his Majefty's oydor, to bring him to punifhment for fo doing, went to him, determined to fee his authority, and to know the reafon of his conduct, and that Narvaez had then attempted to furprife and feize him, of which he could adduce proofs and witneffes, amongft others Andrez de Duero, who was at that time with Narvaez. In regard to his caufing the failure of Garay, and poifoning him at breakfaft, it was replied that the failure of the expedition was owing to Garay's own mifconduct, and ignorance of the country. That when Garay found his fituation hopelefs, he accepted the friendly offer which Cortes had made him, of an hofpitable reception at Mexico, where an alliance was agreed upon between the families, and Garay was to have had affiftance to eftablifh a colony on the river Palmas; and that if it was God's will to take him from this life, according to the oaths of the phyficians, by a pleurify, it was not in the power of Cortes to prevent it. Cortes alfo proved in anfwer to the charge of having retained his Majefty's fifth, that he had fairly expended it in the fervice, together with fix thoufand crowns of his own property: that the fifth which he deducted for himfelf was according to compact, and in regard to the charge of detaining the foldiers prize money it was replied, that in the capture of Mexico very little gold remained to be divided, inafmuch as the wealth of the place was almoft all fallen into the hands of the Tlafcalan and Tezcucan allies. In regard to burning the feet of Guatimotzin, it was done contrary to the inclination of Cortes, by his Majefty's officers, to force him to difcover where Montezuma's treafure was concealed. In anfwer to the charge of his buildings it was ftated, that they

were

were truly fumptuous, and that the cypreffes and ftones were brought from a great diftance, but that the faid buildings were for the ufe and honor of his Majefty and his fucceffors : that the materials were brought the principal part of the way by water, and that the work was carried on by the general labour of the Indians, under the order of Guatimotzin, as is always the cafe in building the houfes of the great in that country. As to the complaint of Alonzo de Avila forcibly taking the commiffion from Narvaez, it appeared upon infpection that there was no commiffion whatever in thofe papers, the whole of which were receipts for the purchafe of horfes, and other things fimilar; but that Cortes never faw them, nor was it done by his order. In regard to the complaints of the pilots againft Cortes, the feet of Umbria were cut off by the hand of juftice, as a punifhment for running away with his fhip, and Cardenas had refufed to take his fhare in the divifion of the gold, confenting that the whole fhould be fent to his Majefty, but that Cortes had given him out of his own purfe three hundred crowns, which was as much as he deferved, being a perfon of little confideration, and no foldier. In regard to the charge relative to Tapia, it was alledged that had he come to Mexico and produced his Majefty's orders, they fhould have been received by Cortes, proftrate on the ground, with all refpect, and humility; but his incapacity was fo notorious, that it was the univerfal defire, and advice, of the Spaniards then in New Spain, that Cortes fhould remain in the command. Thefe charges and exculpations having been duly weighed by the court for five days, it was determined to lay the whole of the proceedings before his Majefty, together with their decifion, which was accordingly done. The fentence which they gave was entirely in favour of Cortes : the merit and valour of him and the old conquerors of Mexico were highly praifed, and filence was impofed on Velafquez as to his complaints, he being told that if he looked for a remuneration of his expences he muft feek it from Cortes by courfe of law. Cortes was alfo declared governor general of New Spain, according to the orders of his holinefs the Pope. The court alfo approved of the arrangements made by him in that country, and authorized him to make the divifions of the diftricts in fuch a manner as he thought fit.

Narvaez

Narvaez was referred for redress to France, where Avila who had seized his papers was at present prisoner; the pilots Umbria and Cardenas obtained royal cedules, granting to them property in New Spain to the amount of one thousand crowns in rent; and it was ordained, that Cortes's veterans should all have immediate and ample gratifications, in lands and Indians, and should enjoy pre-eminence and precedency, such as their valour deserved. The sentence thus given was taken to Valladolid to be confirmed by his Majesty, who was then on his way to Flanders, and who did confirm and ratify it accordingly. His Majesty also gave orders relative to the banishment of lapsed converts in that country, and forbid the admission of scholars for a term of years. His Majesty and the King of Hungary were also pleased to write to Cortes and to us, thanking us for the services we had rendered. The affair being thus decided in our favour, the documents were intrusted to Rodorigo de Paz, cousin to Cortes, and to another relation of his, named Francisco de las Casas, who arrived at St. Jago in Cuba, the residence of Velasquez the governor, where the sentence being made known to him, and proclaimed by sound of trumpet, he fell ill from vexation, and shortly after died very poor and miserable. Montejo was given by his Majesty the government of Yucatan and Cozumel, with the lordship and title of Don. To Diego de Ordaz he confirmed his possessions in New Spain, and ennobled him giving him for a coat of arms the Volcano of Guaxocingo, and with these honours and emoluments they returned to Mexico, from whence in two or three years De Ordas went back to Castille, to obtain from his Majesty permission to conquer the province of Maranion, in which undertaking he lost his life and all his property. The Bishop of Burgos was reduced to despair when he learned the manner in which the affair had gone, and that all his transactions with Velasquez had come to light.

When Las Casas and Rodrigo de Paz brought the intelligence to Mexico, that Cortes was appointed governor of that country, there was universal rejoicing. The messengers were liberally rewarded, Las Casas being made captain and presented with a good district called Anquitlan,

and

and De Paz obtained other valuable poffeffions, and was appointed by Cortés his major domo and fecretary. To all thofe who came from his country of Medellin, Cortes gave Indians, and . to the captain of the veffel a liberal reward in gold.

Some readers may be curious to learn how thefe matters came to my knowledge; to which I reply, that the conquerors received information of the proceedings of our agents or procuradors, in four or five letters written by them from Caftille; but I ufed then to fay often, that it appeared to me that they procured only for Cortes and themfelves, and during all that time, we who had made Cortes what he was, remained encountering one danger and hardfhip after another. May God grant us his protection, and inftil into the mind of our great Cæfar the determination to caufe his true and juft intentions to be carried into effect.

CHAPTER VI.

Transactions and occurrences in Old and New Spain.
Expedition against the Zapotecans.

IT appeared to us, the most ancient, wise, and experienced conquerors of Mexico, that Cortes ought now to consider duly who were his friends, and stood by him through the whole of his difficulties and dangers, from the first, and to settle his accounts with Pedro, with Sancho, and with Martin, according to their deserts; which was to be done by recalling to him those who were low, and poor, and unfortunate, and by placing them in good situations, according to their deserts, and his Majesty's orders. All this Cortes was bound in duty to do, as also to procure for us and our children all the good offices, and emoluments, that were to be had in this country of New Spain. But, "that " which does not grow from the skin, hangs loosely to it;" and so it appeared, for instead of doing this he procured such for no one but himself, as in the first place the government, and afterwards when he went to Castille, and got his title. But to advert to other matters. In regard to the division of the country, it was decided by many of the most experienced, brave, and sage conquerors thereof, that the proper method would be, to divide it into five parts, one whereof should go to his Majesty, another to be for the establishment and revenues of our holy church, and the other three to be given to Cortes, and the rest of us, the true original conquerors of the country; that each should have a share in perpetuity, and in proportion to his rank and deserts, and that we, for our parts, who had served his Majesty here, without putting him to the least cost, and as one may say without his knowledge, he being in Flanders, would be well satisfied therewith, and contented, and

at

at our eafe, not wandering about the world as is at prefent the cafe, and falling from bad to worfe; for many of us at this moment are without a morfel of bread to eat, and God knows what will become of our children.

I will now relate what Cortes did, and which I call a very unfair diftribution. To the Veedor Chirinos, the Factor Salazar, J. de Ribera and all thofe who came from Medellin, and to the dependents of great men who flattered and told him pleafing things, he refufed nothing. Not that I blame him for being generous, for there was enough for all; but I fay that he ought to have firft confidered thofe who ferved his Majefty, and whofe valour and blood made him what he was. But enough of this, and now to other matters, for it is ufelefs detailing our misfortunes, and how he treated us like vaffals, and how we were obliged to take to our old trade of expeditions and battles; for though he forgot us in his diftribution of property, he never failed to call on us when he wanted our affiftance. However before I take leave of the fubject let me mention, that when Luis Ponce de Leon came to fupercede Cortes, we went to the general, to requeft that he would give us fome part of that property which his Majefty had at that time ordered that he fhould refign. He then told us, and fwore it, that if he returned to his government he would provide for us all, and not do as he had done, for which he was very forry. As if we were to be fatisfied with promifes and fmooth words.

There had lately arrived certain officers of his Majefty from Old Caftille, amongft whom were Alonzo de Eftrada the treafurer, Gonzalo de Salazar the factor, Rodrigo Albornos the contador, (Juan de Alderete being dead,) Pedro Almindes Chirinos the Veedor, and many others.

One Rodrigo Rangel whom I have already mentioned, now came to Cortes, telling him that he had hitherto acquired no fame in the wars, and wifhed to have a command given him, wherewith to go and

conquer

conquer the Zapotecans who were in rebellion, and to take with him Pedro de Ircio as his private counsellor and director. Cortes knew very well this man was not fit for any service, being a poor diseased miserable object, from the effects of his sins; he therefore put him off, telling him that nation was not easily to be conquered on account of the high rugged mountains which they inhabit, and which are always covered with mists and clouds; as also that cavalry could not be brought against them, on account of the bad and narrow roads which it was necessary to climb like ladders, each soldier's head at the heels of his file leader. However at last Cortes agreed to the proposal of this man who was a fellow of a very slanderous tongue, and one whom he would have been glad to have got rid of in this way where he was likely to lose his life. The general in consequence wrote to ten or twelve of us who were in Guacacualco, desiring that we should go with him, and I was one of the number thus selected. These Indians are a light and very active people, and when in the field have a way of whistling and shouting, which makes the hills and woods resound again. Having this man with us it was impossible to effect any thing, and as we advanced under a very heavy rain, we came to a village of scattered houses, some being upon a ridge, and others in the valley. Poor Rangel whined and complained all the way of the pain of his limbs, to our great annoyance, knowing it was entirely useless trouble and danger, and that the Indians who were so nimble would destroy us climbing the rocks in one file, if they made a stand any where. It was at last agreed, as Rangel grew worse and worse, to abandon the black expedition as we used to call it, and return to our homes. His counsellor also as he called him, Pedro de Ircio, was the first to advise him to it, and setting the example by following his own advice, went home to his town of Villa Rica. Rangel however preferred accompanying us to Guacacualco, which was more grief to us than going with him in his expedition. He had hopes that the hot climate of that country, as he said, would relieve him of his pains.

No sooner had we arrived at this place then he took in his head to
go

go upon an expedition againſt the Indians of Cimaton and Tatupatan, who were rebellious, for they thought themſelves ſecure amongſt their great rivers and trembling marſhes. They were alſo formidable warriors, uſing very large and ſtrong bows. Rangel however produced his commiſſion from Cortes, and we dare not but to obey and march with him, to the number of one hundred horſe and foot. We accordingly ſet out, and arrived at a paſs between the marſhes and lakes, where the whole force of the Indians was drawn up to receive us, having made circular barricades of very groſs timber, with ſpike holes to ſhoot through, and palliſadoes. Here they gave us a hearty welcome with a flight of arrows and darts, killing ſeven horſes and wounding Rangel and eight ſoldiers. We had often told him what ſtout warriors theſe Indians were, and as he was a prating fellow he now exclaimed, by heaven, if he had believed us, he would not have been in that jeopardy now, and that in future we the old conquerors of the country ſhould be his captains and not he ours. As ſoon as our wounded men and horſes were dreſſed, he begged I would go forward to reconoitre. I took with me a very fierce greyhound which belonged to him, and ſelecting two other ſoldiers for my comrades, deſired the infantry to follow us cloſe, and for Rangel and the cavalry, that they ſhould keep a good diſtance in the rear. Purſuing our route towards Cimaton, we fell in with another poſt fortified like the preceding one, and defended as ſtrongly, from whence we received a volley, which killed the dog, and wounded me and each of my comrades. I received an arrow in my leg, and ſeven more remained in my cotton armour. I called immediately to ſome of our Indian allies who were a little in rear of us, to go and bring up all the infantry, but to order the cavalry not to advance, as all their horſes would ſurely be killed. When the infantry came up we attacked the barricades, and forced the Indians from them, driving them to their marſhes where it was impoſſible to follow them a ſtep, without danger of ſinking and being ſmothered. We then advanced, and halted at a village. On the next day we proceeded, and were encountered by a large body of Indians, poſted in a marſh. This was an inſtance of the addreſs of the natives, in chuſing to meet us in the plain, hoping that they could draw our

cavalry

cavalry to charge them, in expectation that galloping full fpeed they fhould run into the marfh, and fo it happened; for in fpite of all we could fay to Rangel of their art and ftratagem, and how neceffary it was to be wary, he ran his cavalry full at them, and tumbled in himfelf the firft, head foremoft into the marfh, where the Indians began to clofe upon him, in order to feize him alive for facrifice.

By great exertions, we got him, badly wounded, out of their hands, half drowned, and his poor fore head expofed and broken. As this country is very populous, we found a village hard by, whither we went to take repofe and drefs the wounded. It was abandoned on our approach, but we had hardly been there a quarter of an hour when we were attacked with fuch violence, that in the firft onfet they killed one of our foldiers and two horfes, and we had much to do to drive them off. All this time Rangel was complaining of his wounds and bruifes, and the mufquitos got about him in clouds. The vermin alfo with which that country is infefted, bit him to fuch a degree that his life was infupportable, for he could get no reft day or night, and the rain fell inceffantly. He, and fome of Garay's foldiers whom he had brought with him, feeing that nothing had been got but three very hard fought battles, and that eleven horfes and two foldiers had been killed and many more wounded, began to grow very fick of the bufinefs, and to wifh to be quickly at home. But Rangel did not wifh to have it appear that this retreat was a choice of his, and therefore fummoned a council of fuch as he knew were of his own opinion.

About twenty of us had at this time gone to fee if we could make any prifoners among fome gardens and plantations hard by; we took five, and on my return Rangel called me afide and told me that the council had determined to retreat, defiring me to bring over the reft to it. Having known the man before, I had a kindnefs for him. How fir, faid I to him can you now think of returning? What will Cortes and the world fay of you, when they hear of your retreat without effecting any thing in thefe two expeditions? You furely cannot think of

returning

returning till you have reached the head town of thefe Indians! I will go forward on foot and reconoitre with the infantry, give my horfe to another foldier, and do you follow in the rear with the cavalry. By heavens cries out Rangel, for he was a very loud talker, Bernal Diaz gives good advice; the lot is caft and we will march on. This was accordingly done, contrary to the inclination of feveral, and we advanced in good order to Cimaton, the principal town, where we were faluted as ufual with a flight of arrows, and then, on entry, found it abandoned. We burned it in part, and took feveral Indians whom we difmiffed, defiring them to invite their neighbours to peace and amity; but thofe we fent never returned to us. This enraged Rangel againft me, and he fwore I fhould procure him Indians in the place of thofe who had been liberated. To pacify him I was fain to go with thirty foldiers, and we picked up fome among the marfhes, whom I brought to him and he difmiffed, in hopes of inducing the reft to come in, but without effect. Thus ended the famous expedition againft the Zapotecans, and fuch was all the fame Rangel acquired in the wars. In two years afterwards we effected the conqueft of thefe countries, the natives whereof were converted to our holy faith, through the grace of God, and the exertions of the reverend father Bartholome de Olmedo, who poor man was at that time grown weak and infirm. Pity it was, for he was an excellent minifter of the gofpel.

Cortes had now collected eighty thoufand crowns in gold, and a golden culverin, which he named the Phœnix, and had caufed to be made as a prefent for the Emperor, was finifhed. It was a fuperb piece of workmanfhip. The following motto was engraved on it.

" Efta Ave nacio fin par; Yo en fervir os fin fegundo;
" Y vos fin igual en el Mundo.

The

" The immortal Phœnix peerlefs fweeps the air;
" To Charles is given boundlefs rule to bear;
" Zealous to conquer, at my King's command,
" I in my fervices unrivalled ftand.

This prefent was fent to Europe under the care of Diego de Soto. I am not certain if J. de Ribera, formerly fecretary to Cortes, went with it. I always thought him a bad kind of man, from what I obferved in him at play, either with cards or dice: befides this he had many ill qualities.

He however was fent to Caftille, and took a fum of money with him for the general's father; which money he appropriated to his own ufe, and then, unmindful of the obligations he had received, faid much ill of Cortes; and being very flippant and fluent of fpeech, and having been his fecretary, he obtained credit for what he faid, and combining with the Bifhop of Burgos and others, did him much harm; and would have done more had it not been for the interference of the Duke of Bejar, who protected Cortes on account of a treaty of marriage which was then on foot, between our general and a niece of that Duke, named Donna Juana de Zuniga. This, combined with the feafonable arrival of the prefent, gave a favourable turn to the affairs of Cortes.

In regard to the golden Phœnix, I muft obferve, that the motto gave great offence to many, as they thought it prefumption in Cortes to fay he had no equal in his fervices. But his friends juftly defended him; for who had extended fo far the fame and power of his Majefty, or brought fo many thoufands of fouls to the dominion of our holy church? They alfo did not forget us his affociates, but declared that we alfo were intitled to honours and emoluments, having earned them, as the Caftillian nobility did thofe enjoyed by their defcendants.

Ddd

As

As to the culverin, it went no farther than the city of Seville; his Majesty was pleased to make a present of it to Don Francisco de los Cobos, commendador major of Leon, who melted it down. Its value amounted to twenty thousand ducats.

A suit was commenced by Martin Cortes against Ribera, on account of the money of which the latter had defrauded him. While it was yet pending, and as Ribera was on a journey, he stopped to dine at the town of Cadahalsa, where, eating some broiled meat, he fell down dead suddenly, and without confession. God pardon his sins! Amen.

Cortes continued to rebuild and embellish the city of Mexico. It was now as well peopled by the natives as it had ever been before. He gave them privileges, exempting them from all tribute to his Majesty until their houses were completed, as also the causeways, bridges, public edifices, and aqueducts. In the Spanish quarter churches and hospitals were erected, under the care of the good father Bartholome de Olmedo, as vicar and superior. This reverend father had also established an hospital for the natives, to whom he paid the utmost attention.

In compliance with our petition to his Majesty, as formerly related, Don Francisco de los Angeles, general of the Franciscans, sent twelve of his order under the vicarage of father Martin de Valencia. Amongst them came father Toribio de Motolinea; this sirname, the meaning of which is, the poor brother, was given him by the Mexicans, because all that he got in charity he distributed in the same manner, and was frequently without a morsel to eat. He also always went barefooted, and wore a tattered habit, and constantly preaching to the natives, was very popular among them. As soon as Cortes was informed of their arrival at Villa Rica, he gave directions for the road to Mexico to be put in good order, houses to be built at proper stations for them to refresh in, and the inhabitants of all the towns to go out to receive them

with

with reverence, ringing the bells, bearing crucifixes and lighted wax candles, and the Spaniards to kneel down and kiss their hands. When they approached Mexico, he went out to meet them and as soon as they appeared, Cortes threw himself from his horse to kiss the hands of the reverend vicar. When the natives saw the general on his knees to those reverend fathers, with bare feet and in tattered habits, they were astonished, and considering them as gods, they all followed his example, and have continued to do so ever since.

Cortes at this time thought it necessary to inform his Majesty of his proceedings in the conversion of the natives, the rebuilding of the city, and the expedition which he had sent against the province of Honduras under the command of De Oli, who had deserted, and embraced the party of Velasquez, on which account he had determined to send a force against him. He also complained of the proceedings of Velasquez, and of the injury his Majesty's service had sustained thereby, as also by the partiality of the Bishop of Burgos. He remitted at the same time thirty thousand crowns in gold to his Majesty's treasury, and lamented the unfortunate effects of those abuses, as having prevented him from making an ampler contribution of gold. He at the same time complained of one Rodrigo de Albornos, contador in Mexico, who aspersed him from private motives, because he had refused to give him in marriage the daughter of the Indian lord of Tescuco, adding that he understood that this Albornos was attached to the interest of the Bishop of Burgos, and was accustomed to write to him in cyphers.

At this time the news of the bishop's removal had not reached Mexico. Albornos, before mentioned, sent by the same vessel his accusations against Cortes, charging him with levying excessive contributions of gold for his own use. That he was fortifying castles, and marrying the daughters of great lords to his private soldiers, insinuating that Cortes was endeavouring to set himself up as an independent king, and strongly representing the necessity of sending an officer with a great force, to supercede him. These letters came to the hands of the Bishop

of

of Burgos, who laid them before the whole junto of the enemies of Cortes, and this new matter was immediately brought before his Majesty. They complained of the partiality which they alledged was shewn towards him on former occasions, and his Majesty, deceived by these misrepresentations, which were enforced by the bold and lofty tone of Narvaez, now issued an order for the admiral of St. Domingo to go with fix hundred soldiers to arrest Cortes, and make him answer if he found him culpable, with his head. Also to punish all those of us who had been concerned in the attack upon Narvaez. As an encouragement, this officer was promised the admiralty of New Spain, the right of which was now under litigation in the courts.

The admiral, either from want of money, or being apprehensive of serious consequences from committing himself against so able and so successful a leader as Cortes, delayed setting out upon his expedition so long, that it gave time to the friends and agents of Cortes to make a full explanation of the circumstances, and also of the conduct of Albornos, to the Duke of Bejar, who immediately went to wait upon the Emperor, to represent the true state of the case, and to offer his life as a security for the loyalty and good conduct of Cortes.

His Majesty being upon due consideration convinced of the justice of our cause, determined to send a person of high quality and found judgment, and one who feared the Lord, to hold a supreme court of justice in New Spain. Such a person he found in the licentiate Luis Ponce de Leon, cousin to the count Don Martin de Cordova. To him his Majesty intrusted the business of enquiry into the conduct of Cortes, with full power to inflict the greatest punishment, in case he should find him guilty. It was however two years and an half before this gentleman arrived in New Spain.

I have now gone beyond the date of my narrative two years in advance, to inform the reader of this circumstance; and I may now also mention, that during the viceroyalty of Don Anthonio de Mendoza,

that

that moſt illuſtrious nobleman, worthy of eternal memory and heavenly glory, for his wife and juſt government, this ſame Albornos wrote ſlanderous and malignant letters of him, as he had done before of Cortes. The letters which related to Don Anthonio were all returned from Caſtille, into the hands of that nobleman, and when he had read them, with all the perſonal abuſe of himſelf that they contained, he ſent for Albornos, and ſhewing them to him, ſaid in his mild and ſlow manner of ſpeaking, "whenever you chooſe to make me the ſubject of " your letters to his Majeſty, mind that in future you tell the truth; " and now go about your buſineſs, for a knave as you are." Thus he left the contador, overwhelmed with confuſion.

CHAPTER VII.

Expedition of Cortes to Higueras.

DE OLI I have already mentioned as having revolted. When Cortes received intelligence of this, it made him very penſive; but as he was one not to be trifled with in ſuch caſes, he determined to ſend a gentleman who was his relation, by name Franciſco de las Caſas, with five ſhips, and one hundred well provided ſoldiers, having with them ſome of the original veteran conquerors of Mexico.

Las Caſas ſet out from the port of Vera Cruz, with his good ſhips, and his pennants flying, and with fair winds arrived at the bay named El Triumpho de la Cruz, where De Oli had eſtabliſhed his poſt. Although Las Caſas hoiſted the ſignal of peace, De Oli determined upon making reſiſtance, and embarking a number of ſoldiers in two armed veſſels, he ſent them to oppoſe Las Caſas, who being a brave man was determined to land at all events; he therefore ordered out his boats and arming them with ſwivels and muſquetry, attacked the other party, and ſunk one of their veſſels, killing four ſoldiers and wounding many. When De Oli ſaw this he thought it adviſable to propoſe terms of peace, for a conſiderable part of his ſoldiers were detached up the country, in ſearch of another body of troops which was making conqueſts there, about the river Pechin. This laſt mentioned party was commanded by a Captain Gil Gonzalez de Avila.

De Oli as I have already related being in expectation of the return of his detachment, wiſhed for a truce with Las Caſas, which the latter for his misfortune agreed to, and remained at ſea, partly in the intention

tion of looking out for some other place of disembarkation, and partly induced by letters from the friends of Cortes who were in the troops commanded by De Oli. On that night a hard gale sprung up, by which our vessels were driven on shore and entirely lost, with above thirty of the soldiers. The rest were made prisoners, after being two days without food, and almost dying with cold, being thoroughly soaked in the salt water and with rain which at that season fell very heavily. De Oli was very triumphant on this occasion. He made his prisoners swear fidelity to him against Cortes, releasing them all except Las Casas. The parties he had sent out against Gonzalez de Avila returned about this time. It seems that Avila came there as governor of Golfo Dolce, and had founded a town which he named St. Gil de Buena Vista. De Oli on hearing of it sent his troops against him, who in their first attack had taken Avila prisoner, killed his nephew, and also eight of his soldiers. De Oli was now in great state with two captains as his prisoners, and that all might know his valour which certainly was very great so far as his own person was concerned, he wrote a full account of his exploits to his friend Velasquez. He afterwards marched up the country to a place called Naco, in a very populous district, the whole of which is now destroyed. While De Oli remained here, he sent out troops on different excursions; among others he sent a party under one Captain Briones who was the first to instigate him to revolt. He was a seditious fellow, and the lower parts of his ears had been cut off, as he used to tell us, for refusing, together with other officers, to surrender themselves in a certain fortress. This man was afterwards hanged in Guatimala for mutiny. To return to my narrative, intelligence came to De Oli, that Briones with his whole body had revolted from him, and gone to New Spain, which turned out to be the case.

Las Casas and De Avila being at large, though prisoners, for De Oli was too brave to be under any apprehensions from them, concerted a plan with some soldiers to put him to death, the signal for which was to be the words, "To me, friends of the King and Cortes, kill the ty-" rant!" Las Casas half in jest as it were, and laughing, then asked
him.

him for liberty to return to Cortes; to which De Oli replied, that he was too happy to have fo brave a man for his companion, and did not choofe to part with him. "Then," faid Las Cafas in the fame manner, "take care that one of thefe days I do not kill you." All this the other confidered as a joke; but the meafures were taken, and one night after fupper, when the cloths were taken away, and the fervants and pages had fat down in their apartment, as Juan Nunez de Mercado and other foldiers of the party of Cortes, Las Cafas, and Avila, were converfing with De Oli upon the affairs of Mexico, and the fortune of Cortes, he being entirely unfufpicious of their defigns, the confpirators fuddenly drew out penknives and fell upon him. Las Cafas feizing him by the beard made a cut at his throat, and the others gave him feveral wounds; but fuch was his ftrength and activity of body, that he efcaped out of their hands for the prefent, calling aloud to his people for affiftance, but they were all too bufily employed at their fuppers to hear him. He then fled, and concealed himfelf among fome bufhes, in hopes of affiftance. Many were in the act of coming to him for the purpofe, but were deterred by the cries of Las Cafas not to affift the tyrant, but to rally on the fide of their King, and his general Cortes. They firft hefitated, and then obeyed; and Las Cafas immediately gave notice, that whoever knew where De Oli was, and did not immediately reveal it, fhould fuffer death. Information was foon given, in confequence of which he was made prifoner, and, by fentence of the two captains, beheaded in the town of Naco, thus paying with his life for having followed evil counfels; being a very brave man, but of no forefight. Cortes had conferred many favours on him; he held a commiffion of Maeftre de Campo, had valuable eftates, and was married to Donna Philippa de Aranja, a handfome Portugueze lady, by whom he had one daughter.

Las Cafas and Avila being now free and their enemy dead, joined their troops together, and acted in concert. Las Cafas colonized Truxillo in Eftremadura; Avila fent a meffage to his lieutenant in Buena Vifta, ordering him to remain as he was, and that he fhould fhortly

receive

receive reinforcement, which he was going to requeft from Cortes at Mexico. The two captains having fet out for that city, I will now take my leave of them for the prefent.

Cortes, in fome months after the departure of Las Cafas, began to grow apprehenfive of a difafter; not that he entertained the leaft doubt of the valour or conduct of that officer, but he repented, under the circumftances of the cafe, that he had not taken the command himfelf. He was alfo anxious to examine the ftate of that province, more efpecially its mines, and for thefe reafons now determined to fet out upon his journey thither. He appointed a good garrifon to take charge of the city of Mexico during his abfence, and provided the different pofts with artillery, leaving as his deputies in the government, the treafurer Alonzo de Eftrada, and the contador Albornoz. Cortes did not know the fecret fervices the latter had been rendering him at court, or he probably would not have left him in power, although on the other hand it is poffible, that he could not have avoided it. He appointed the licentiate Zuazo alguazil major of the city, and as alguazil major and agent in his private concerns, Rodrigo de Paz. To thefe he ftrongly infifted on the ftricteft attention, both to the intereft of his Majefty, and the converfion of the natives. This he alfo recommended to the worthy fathers Motolinea and Olmedo, both holy men.

In order to deprive the Mexicans of chiefs, in cafe they fhould attempt to rife, he took with him Guatimotzin the late king, the chief of Tacuba, Velafquez an Indian and captain under Guatimotzin, and feveral others. There came alfo with us Fra Juan de las Varillas, another clergyman, two reverend fathers, Flemings, and good theologians, to preach the faith, and the captains De Sandoval and Luis Marin, with many other cavaliers. The fuite, or officers who attended the perfon of Cortes were as follows; a fteward and paymafter, a keeper of the plate, a major domo, two ftewards of the houfehold, a butler, a confectioner, a chamberlain, a phyfician, a furgeon, a number of pages of his houfehold, amongft whom was D. Francifco de Montejo afterwards captain

E e e

in

in Yucatan, two armour bearers, eight grooms, two falconers, five muficians, a ftage dancer, a jugler and puppet player, a mafter of the horfe, three Spanifh muleteers. The general brought a great fervice of gold and filver plate, and a large drove of fwine for his table followed feeding by the way. Three thoufand Mexican warriors attended their chiefs, befides a numerous train of domeftics.

When the party was on the point of fetting out, the factor Salazar, and the veedor Chirinos, either feeing or affecting to fee much danger likely to refult from Cortes quiting the feat of government, and finding alfo that they had not been left in any ftation during his abfence, remon-ftrated with him, but finding it to be to no purpofe, they then requefted permiffion to accompany him as far as Guacacualco. To this he gave his confent, and they accordingly fet out. Cortes was received in all the places upon his way with fuch pomp and rejoicing as is not in my power to defcribe. Above fifty foldiers and ftraggling travellers newly arrived from Caftille joined him upon the road, and the general divided his troops in two parties, until their arrival at Guacacualco, for the greater convenience of obtaining provifions.

During the journey, the veedor and factor kept themfelves clofe to Cortes, efpecially the latter, playing a hundred tricks of fervility and obfequioufnefs, and every word he fpoke, he was cap in hand, and with his fluent fpeech, and fmooth words, as it were trying to get him back to Mexico, and expreffing his folicitude for his fafety. Some-times when he was riding by the fide of the general he would fing, " Ay tio bolvamonos, ay tio bolvamonos." Then Cortes would laugh at him and reply finging,

" Adelante mi fobrino, adelante mi fobrino,
" Y no creais in agueros, que fera lo que dios quifiere,
" Adelante mi fobrino.

Oh

" Oh good uncle let us return.
" Forward, dear nephew forward,
" Truſt in God and never heed auguries.

Quitting the ſubjeƈt of our faƈtor and his delicate ſpeeches, I have now to mention how a marriage took place on the arrival of the party at the town of Ojeda, which is near that of Orizava, between our linguiſt Donna Marina, and Juan Xaramillo. The next place they came to was Guazpaltepeque, in the diſtriƈt of Sandoval. As ſoon as intelligence reached Guacacualco of the advance of Cortes to Guazpaltepeque, all the Spaniards of that ſettlement came thirty three leagues to receive him. This I mention that the reader may ſee what fear and reſpeƈt he was held in by us. Proceeding beyond the place laſt mentioned, in croſſing a large river, fortune began to frown upon us, for three of our canoes overſet, whereby ſome plate and other valuables were loſt, for that river is ſo full of alligators that there was no recovering any thing. Paſſing Illuta, when we came to the river by Guacacualco we found three hundred canoes faſtened two and two to carry us over; here we were received under triumphal arches, and with various feſtivities repreſenting ſkirmiſhes of Chriſtians and Moors, together with fireworks and other ſhows of that kind.

Here Cortes remained ſix days, during which time the faƈtor was continually ſounding in his ears the burthen of his old ſong. He alſo told him of ſecret praƈtices of the contador and the treaſurer, who boaſted that he was the ſon of his catholic Majeſty, and in ſhort a number of ſtories, the drift of all which was, to induce Cortes to ſupercede the preſent deputies, and put him, and the veedor, in their places. In this he too well ſucceeded; for by his arts he obtained from the general a deputation for himſelf and his aſſociate the veedor, to hold the government of Mexico, in caſe they ſhould judge that the preſent deputies

failed

failed in their duty. These intrigues caused much trouble afterwards in Mexico as I will relate at the proper time. The reverend father blamed Cortes for what he had done, and foresaw the consequences that followed. The veedor and factor now took their leaves, with such tenderness and affection, the latter pretending to sob and cry with sorrow at parting, that it was ridiculous to see it. The fellow had by the tricks of his friend Valiente the secretary, got at that time in his pocket the documents he wanted for the furtherance of his views in Mexico, of which as I before observed I will say no more for the present, but continue the narrative of our painful journey, for I left this place with the general, and attended him throughout.

Cortes now sent orders to one of his major domos, Simon de Cuenca, at Villa Rica, to freight two light vessels with biscuit of maiz, (for at that time there was no wheat in New Spain,) six pipes of wine, oil, vinegar, pork, iron, and other necessary articles, and to proceed with them along the coast, northward, until he should receive further directions. The general then ordered all the settlers of Guacacualco who were fit for service to join his expedition. I have already mentioned how this colony was formed out of the most respectable hidalgos, and ancient conquerors of the country; and now that we had reason to expect to be left in quiet possession of our hard earned properties, our houses and farms, we were obliged to undertake an hostile expedition to the distance of five hundred leagues, and which took up the time of above two years and a half. But we dared not say no, neither would it avail us. We therefore armed ourselves, and mounting our horses, joined the expedition, making in the whole above two hundred and fifty veterans, of whom one hundred and thirty were cavalry, besides many Spaniards newly arrived from Europe.

I was immediately ordered to march at the head of thirty Spaniards and three thousand Mexicans, to a district named Cimatan, which was in rebellion, with directions to quarter my troops on the natives, and if I found them submissive, to do no farther injury, but if refractory,

they

they were to be fummoned intelligibly, three times, in prefence of a
royal notary and proper witneffes, and in cafe they perfifted, I was to
make war on, and compel them to fubmit. The orders which I received from the general I now have in my poffeffion, figned and fealed
by him, and counterfigned by his fecretary, A. Valiente. I found the
people peaceable, but in a few months after, in confequence of the fettlers of Guacacualco being withdrawn, they broke out again. However they being in the ftate that I have mentioned, I made no delay, but
fet out with my detachment to rejoin Cortes at Iquinapa.

The general, with the reft of his troops, leaving Guacacualco,
proceeded to Tonala, croffed a river to Ayaqualulco, croffed another river,
and, feven leagues diftant an arm of the fea, upon a bridge of half a
quarter of a league in length; a moft aftonifhing work in fuch a fituation, and conftructed by the natives of the country under the infpection
of two captains, fettlers of Guacacualco. They then proceeded to a large
river named Mazapa, which flows by Chiapa, and is named by mariners Rio de dos Bocas; this they croffed in double canoes, and proceeding through fome villages, came to Iquinapa, where my detachment
joined them. We then croffed another river on wooden bridges, alfo
an arm of the fea, and came to a great town named Copilco, where the
province of Chontalpa begins, which was very populous, covered with
plantations of cocoa, and perfectly tranquil.

From Copilco we marched to Nicaxuxuica, and to Zagutan, paffing another river, in which the general loft fome articles of his baggage. The laft mentioned town was found by us in a ftate of peace,
but the inhabitants fled during the night. Cortes ordered parties out
to fearch the woods and make prifoners, which was a very inconfiderate
thing, and productive of bad confequences; we found, it is true, after
much trouble, feven chiefs and fome others, but they all made their
efcape from us again during the night, and we were thus left without
guides. At this period arrived at our quarters fifty canoes from Tabafco,
loaded

loaded with provifions, alfo fome from a place named Teapan in my encomienda.

We proceeded on our march to Tepetitan and Iztapa, croffing a great river named Chilapa, at which we were detained four days making barks. I propofed to Cortes, to fend five of our Indian guides to a town of the fame name, which I underftood to be on the banks of this river, to defire the people to affift us with their canoes. Cortes affented, and it was done; we procured fix large canoes, and alfo provifions. We were four days in paffing.

From this we went on to Tepetitan which was depopulated and burnt, in confequence of a civil war. For three days of our march from the river of Chilapa, our horfes were almoft conftantly up to the girths in the marfhy grounds which we had to pafs. We then reached a place named Iztapa, the inhabitants of which had fled. We fent in fearch of them, and feveral chiefs and others were brought in, who being treated kindly, made the general a prefent of fome trifling articles in gold. We halted here for three days on account of the plenty of corn and grafs; Cortes alfo approved of it for the fcite of a colony, it being furrounded by many towns which might be attached to it as dependencies. From the travelling merchants here, Cortes obtained information as to his future route, producing to them a map painted on cloth, whereon was reprefented the way which he was to take to reach Huyacala, which means great Acala; it being fo called to diftinguifh it from another place of that name. They told him that the way he was to take was much interfected by rivers, and that in order to reach a place named Tamaztepeque, three days journey diftant, three rivers and an arm of the fea were to be croffed. The general in confequence gave orders to the chiefs to conftruct bridges at the proper places, and alfo to bring canoes; neither of which was obeyed.

The three days which the natives affured us the journey would take up, turned out to be no lefs than feven; but they fucceeded in
getting

getting rid of us, and we set out, provided only with roasted maiz and roots sufficient for three days. We were obliged to construct bridges of timber, at which all laboured from the general downwards, which detained us three days, during which time we had nothing to eat but a certain wild plant named Quexquexque, which inflames the mouth and tongue. When we had crossed this inlet we found no road whatever, and we were obliged to open our way through the woods, as it were, sword in hand. After labouring thus for two days in hopes of reaching the place which we were in search of, we became totally in despair. The trees were so thick that we could not see the sun, and when we ascended to the top of one we could not discover to any distance. Of our three guides also two had fled, and the third was incapable of rendering any service. Cortes, whose resources were inexhaustible, guided himself by a mariners compass, and by his Indian map, according to which, the town we were in quest of, lay to the east. Cortes himself was however forced to acknowledge, that if we were one day more without discovering it, he did not know what we should do

Fortunately we at this time perceived the remains of trees which had been formerly cut, and also a small lane or path, and Lopez the pilot and I returned to report our discovery to the general. Our news revived the spirits of the army, and we pushed forward to a village on the opposite side of a river, where, though the inhabitants had abandoned it, we found sufficiency of provisions for ourselves and our horses. Parties were immediately sent out in quest of the natives, and they soon returned, bringing with them many chiefs and priests, who being well treated, procured us a plentiful supply of provisions, and pointed out our way to Izguantepeque, which was three days journey, or sixteen leagues distant from this town of Tamaztepeque. During our journey hither we lost our stage dancer by fatigue, as also three of the newly arrived Spaniards, and many of the Mexicans were left to die upon the road. It came also to be discovered that some of their chiefs had seized two or three of the natives of the places through which we passed, and

concealed

concealed them with the baggage, until through hunger they had killed and eaten them, dreffing the bodies in their manner, which is, by a kind of oven made with heated ftones which are put under ground. On enquiry it was alfo found out that they had done the fame with two of our guides who had fled from us, but were retaken. Cortes feverely reprehended all thofe concerned, and one of the reverend father Francifcans preached a holy and wife fermon on the occafion, after which, by way of example, the general caufed one againft whom it was moft clearly proved to be burnt; for though all were equally guilty, yet in the prefent circumftances one example was judged fufficient. As for our poor muficians with their inftruments, their fackbuts, and dulcimers, they felt the lofs of the regales and feafts of Caftille, and now their harmony was ftopt, excepting one only, whom the foldiers ufed to curfe whenever he ftruck up, faying it was maiz and not mufic that they wanted. Some perfons have afked me how it happened that fince neceffity has no law, we did not, rather than ftarve, lay our hands on the herd of pigs which Cortes brought with him. To this I reply that they were not within our fight or reach, and the general's fteward, who was a fly artful fellow, faid that they had all been eaten by the alligators in croffing the river. But in reality they had them four days march behind the army. On our route we made croffes in the living trees, and put infcriptions on them faying, " here paffed Cortes and his army " at fuch a time.

The Indians of Tamaztepeque fent forward to our next ftation, Ciguatepecad, to inform the people of our approach, and remove their apprehenfions. They alfo, to the number of twenty attended us thither, where, being arrived and halted, Cortes was anxious to know the courfe of a large river which flows by that town. Upon enquiry he found that it difcharged itfelf in certain inlets of the fea, near the towns named Gueyatafta, and Xicalango, and thereby he thought that he could conveniently fend two Spaniards to the north coaft, to obtain information relative to his fhips. One of his meffengers was Francifco de Medina, to whom he gave a joint commiffion of captain with Simon de

Cuenca,

Cuenca, his officer whom he had employed to freight and command the ships. De Medina was an able and diligent man, and well acquainted with the country; it would have been better however on the present occasion if he had not been entrusted with such powers; as will appear. De Medina having gone down the river to meet the vessels, and having arrived at Xicalonga where they were at anchor, waiting to hear from Cortes, presented the general's letters to Cuenca, and also produced his own commission as captain. A dispute immediately ensued between these two officers relative to the chief command, and each being supported by a party, they had recourse to arms, and fought until there were not eight Spaniards on both sides left alive. When the neighbouring Indians perceived this they fell upon the survivors, put them to death, and destroyed the two ships, so that we did not, for two years and a half, know what was become of them.

We were informed at our present quarters, that the town of Gueyacala was distant three days march from us, and that our way was across deep rivers and trembling marches. Cortes accordingly sent two soldiers to examine them, who, sounding and trying the rivers, came back and reported that they were passable by constructing wooden bridges across them, but as to the marshes, which lay more distant, and which were the most material, they made no examination at all. Cortes also sent me and one Gonzalo de Mexia forward to Gueyacala, with some guides who offered themselves from our present quarters. We set out accordingly, but in the night our Indians left us, for it seemed that the two nations were at war, and we were now forced to rely entirely on ourselves. When we arrived at the first town belonging to the district of Gueyacala, which is the chief over about twenty others, the inhabitants of it shewed some signs of jealousy, but we soon reconciled them. This district is much interfected by lakes, rivers, and trembling marshes. Some of the dependent towns are in islands, and all the communication is by canoes. We invited the chiefs to go and wait upon Cortes, but this they declined on account of the hostility between the two nations. It seems that on the first day of our arrival they had no idea of our force,

F ff

but

but on the next they had received further intelligence concerning it, and treated us with more deference. They promifed that they would provide every accomodation for our people on their arrival, and while we were engaged in difcourfe with them on thefe fubjects, two Spaniards fent by Cortes brought me letters, wherein he ordered, that I fhould within three days meet him with all the provifions that I could collect, for that he had been deferted by the natives, and was on his way to Guey-acala without any neceffaries whatever. Thefe Spaniards alfo informed me, that four of our foldiers who had been detached by Cortes higher up the river had not returned, and were fuppofed to be murdered, as afterwards appeared to be the cafe.

Cortes purfued his march, and was for four days employed in con-ftructing his bridge acrofs the great river, during which time the army fuffered dreadfully from hunger, having left their laft quarters without any provifions whatever. Some old foldiers cut down trees refembling the palm, and procured nuts which they roafted and eat. A very poor refource for fo many. On the night that the bridge was finifhed I arri-ved with one hundred and thirty loads of corn, honey, fruit, and falt, and eighty fowls. It was dark, and Cortes had made mention of his expectation of my arrival. The confequence was, that the foldiers waited for me, and immediately laid violent hands on every atom of provifions which I had brought, not leaving any thing for Cortes or the other officers. The general's fteward and major domo cried out, " this is for the general," and " do not touch that," but it was to no avail, the foldiers faid that the general and the others had been eating their hogs, while the poor foldiers were famifhing, and neither entrea-ties nor arguments could induce them to leave him fo much as a fingle load of corn. Cortes loft all patience when he heard of it, and fwore that he would make enquiry and punifh thofe who had committed the outrage, and who had talked about the hogs. But he foon found that this was merely crying in the defert. He then blamed me, but I told him that a guard fhould have been appointed to receive the provifions when they were brought in, for that hunger knows no law. As he

faw

faw there was no remedy he returned to me, and, Captain **De Sandoval** being prefent, addreffed me with good words faying, "my dear friend " Del Caftillo I am fure that you have left fomething behind you on " the road for yourfelf and our friend here; do let us go together, and " permit me to fhare it with you." Sandoval alfo faid that he vowed to his God he had not fo much as a handful of maiz. When thus applied to I could not refufe them. "Well," faid I, "when the " foldiers are all afleep, come with me, and take fhares of what I pro- " vided for myfelf and thofe with me;" which was, twelve loads of maiz, twenty fowls, three jars of honey, fruits, and falt; I had alfo fome women to make bread. They both thanked and embraced me, and fo we efcaped famine for this time. Cortes enquired how the reverend fathers had fared, but there was no caufe of apprehenfion for them, as each foldier gave them a portion of what he had obtained. Such are the hardfhips attendant upon expeditions in unexplored countries! our general, feared as he was by the foldiers, had his provifions pillaged, and was in danger of ftarving, and Captain De Sandoval would not truft any one, but went himfelf to get his ration from me. On continuing our march, when we had advanced about a league from the river, we came to thofe defperate trembling marfhes. Here our horfes were near being all fmothered; but as the diftance was not above half a bow fhot between the firm ground on each fide, we contrived to draw them through it by main force, and when we had gotten acrofs, after returning thanks to God, Cortes fent to Gueyacala for a frefh fupply of provifions, of which he took care not to be plundered as on the former occafion, and on the enfuing day the whole of onr party arrived, at an early hour, in the town of Gueyacala, where the chiefs attended, and had made ample preparations for our reception.

Cortes, having done whatever was neceffary to conciliate the good will of thefe people, enquired of them relative to his future march, and alfo, if they had ever received any intelligence of fhips being on the coaft, or of any fettlement of Europeans there. They told him, that at the diftance of eight days journey there were many men with beards

like

like ourſelves, who had horſes, and three ſhips with them. They alſo furniſhed him with a map of his route, and offered their aſſiſtance during the march; but in anſwer to his demand that they would open the way for us, they repreſented to him the diſobedience of ſome of their dependencies, and expreſſed their wiſhes to reduce them to ſubmiſſion by our means. This duty he gave to Diego de Mazariegos, a relation of the treaſurer Alonzo de Eſtrada, as a compliment to him, and calling me aſide, he deſired that I would attend him upon the occaſion as his counſellor, from my experience in the affairs of the country. This I ſhould not now mention, nor do I as a boaſt, but it is my duty as an hiſtorian, and further, it was well known to the whole army, and his Majeſty was informed of it in the letters written to him by Cortes. About eighty of us went with Mazariegos upon this occaſion. When we arrived, we found the diſtrict in the beſt diſpoſition poſſible; the chiefs returned with us to wait on Cortes, and brought with them a moſt plentiful ſupply of proviſions. In about four days after this, all the native chiefs deſerted us, and we were left with only three guides, to purſue our route, which we did, croſſing two rivers, to another town in the diſtrict of Gueyacala, which we found abandoned.

Here was the ſcene of the death of Guatimotzin, laſt native king of the Mexicans. It appeared that a plot had been entered into by this unfortunate man, together with many others of his nobility, to murder the Spaniards, and return to Mexico; and that on their arrival, they intended to make a junction of all their forces, and attack the Spaniſh garriſon. Their treaſon was communicated to the general by two lords named Tapia and Juan Velaſquez, who had commanded under Guatimotzin during the ſiege. As ſoon as Cortes got the knowledge of it he took the informations, not only of theſe two, but alſo of ſeveral others concerned; their confeſſion was, that perceiving we marched without precaution, that diſcontent prevailed, that many of our ſoldiers were ſick, and proviſions ſo ſcarce that ten Spaniards had died of hunger abſolutely, and others had returned to Mexico, conſidering alſo the uncertainty of our fate and deſtination they had decided, that dying at once

was

was preferable to going with us any farther. They had therefore refolved to try their fortunes, and fall upon us at the paffage of fome river or marfh, their numbers being an encouragement to the attempt, as they exceeded three thoufand well armed men. Guatimotzin denied that the whole of the Mexican force was concerned in this plot, or that it would have ever been, to his knowledge, carried into effect. But he admitted that it had been heard though never approved of by him. The prince of Tacuba declared that all which had ever paffed between Guatimotzin and him was, frequent declarations that to lofe their lives at once would be preferable to wafting in the manner they were, in a flow death, by hunger and fatigue, and feeing the diftreffes of their friends fuffering around them. Without any more proofs whatever, Cortes ordered Guatimotzin and his coufin the prince of Tacuba to be hanged immediately, and the preparations for the execution being made, they were brought to the place attended by the reverend fathers. Before he was executed, the king turning round to Cortes faid, "Malintzin! now "I find in what your falfe words and promifes have ended;—in my "death.—Better that I had fallen by my own hands than truft myfelf "in your power in my city of Mexico.—Why do you thus unjuftly "take my life? May God demand of you this innocent blood!" The prince of Tacuba only faid that he was happy to die by the fide of his lawful fovereign. Thus ended the lives of thefe two great men, and I muft fay like good chriftians, and for Indians, moft pioufly; and I heartily pitied Guatimotzin and his coufin, having feen them in fuch great fortune and fituations. They behaved very kindly to me during our march, doing me many fervices, efpecially giving me Indians to carry grafs for my horfe; and I alfo declare that they fuffered their deaths moft undefervingly, and fo it appeared to us all, amongft whom there was but one opinion upon the fubject; that it was a moft unjuft and cruel fentence.

We continued our march afterwards with great caution, from apprehenfions of a mutiny among the Mexicans on account of the execution of their chiefs; but the wretches were fo exhaufted by famine, ficknefs,

ficknefs, and fatigue, that they did not appear even to think about the matter. At night we arrived at a village which was abandoned by the inhabitants, but on fearching we found eight priefts who readily attended us to Cortes. He defired them to call back their neighbours, and that they fhould receive no injury. This the priefts readily promifed, requefting at the fame time, that their idols which were in a temple adjoining the building wherein were the quarters of Cortes, fhould not be touched; which the general agreed to, but took the opportunity of expoftulating with them upon the abfurdity of venerating what was in reality no more than clay and timber. The priefts feemed very willing to embrace the true doctrine, and brought us twenty loads of fowls and maiz. To the queftion put to them by Cortes, how many days journey, or funs, it was, to the place where were the men with beards on their faces and who rode horfes they replied, feven; that the place was named Nito, and they offered to be our guides thither.

Cortes caufed a crofs to be fixed in a large ceiba tree clofe to their temple, which as I have before mentioned joined to the building wherein he had taken his quarters. He was at this time very ill tempered, and fad. He was vexed by the difficulties and misfortunes which had attended his march, and his confcience upbraided him with the death of the unfortunate Guatimotzin. He was fo diftracted by thefe thoughts that he could not reft in his bed at night, and getting up in the dark to walk about, as a relief from his anxieties, he went into a large apartment where fome of the idols were worfhipped. Here, he miffed his way, and fell from the height of twelve feet, to the ground, receiving a defperate wound and contufions in his head. This circumftance he tried to conceal, keeping his fufferings to himfelf, and getting his hurts cured as well as he could.

Quitting this place we arrived in two days at a diftrict the people of which are called the Mazotecas, and found a newly built town, fortified and barricaded, with very ftrong pallifadoes in two circles, one of which was like a barbican, with loop holes, and trenches funk
before

before it. The part which was not fortified in this manner was defended by a perpendicular rock, the top of which was piled with ftones fhaped for the fling. It had alfo a parapet, and there was on one fide of
the town an impaffable marfh. On entry we found every houfe filled
with provifions of whatever kind the country afforded, and a magazine
ftocked with arms of all forts, but not a fingle human being. While
we were expreffing our aftonifhment at thefe circumftances, fifteen Indians came out of the marfh, and addreffing us with great fubmiffion,
informed us that they had been driven to the conftruction of this fortrefs, as a laft refource in an unfuccefsful war, in which they had been
engaged with fome of their neighbours, whom, as well as I recollect,
they called the Lazandones. It feemed to be a warfare of plunder on
each fide. The name of this diftrict means in their language a country
abounding with game, which it was very well intitled to be called.
Two of the Indians attended us from this place, and communicated to
Cortes what they knew of the fettlement of the Spaniards.

We now travelled through a country entirely open, confifting of
vaft plains without a tree. The heat of the fun was exceffive, and the
deer which fed over this extenfive range of champaign were innumerable,
and fo tame as almoft to come to our hands. The horfemen took them
after the fhorteft purfuit, and we had in a very little fpace of time above
twenty killed. Afking our guides the reafon of thefe animals not being
alarmed at the approach of men, we found that it was owing to a fuper-
ftition of the people, who confidered them to be divinities, as they faid
that their gods appeared to them in their forms; and alfo that their idols
had commanded that they fhould be neither killed nor frightened. The
heat of the weather was now fo great, that a relation of the general's,
named Palacios Rubios, loft his horfe by purfuing the game. Purfuing our journey by villages where war had left its deftructive marks,
we met fome Indians on their return from hunting. They had with
them a huge lion which they had juft killed, and fome iguanas, a fpecies of fmall ferpent, very good to eat. They led us to their town, being obliged to wade up to our middles in a lake of frefh water with
which

which it was furrounded. In this town was a large pond of frefh water, which was quite full of fifhes, refembling what we call in Europe the fhad fifh, but enormoufly large, with prickles on their backs. We procured fome nets, and took above a thoufand, which afforded us a plentiful meal. We alfo procured here five Indians, who on our enquiry by defcription for our countrymen, readily undertook to guide us to their fettlement, for they at firft thought that we came to put them to death, and were happy to find that they were likely to be rid of us on fuch eafy terms.

We proceeded towards a place named Tayafal, fituated on an ifland, the white temples, turrets, and houfes of which, gliftened from a diftance. It was the chief town of a diftrict. As the road grew very narrow we thought it beft to halt for the night, four companies of foldiers being detached to the fhore, to fearch for a paffage. Luckily they took two canoes, in which were ten men and two women who were conveying falt and maize. Being brought to Cortes and queftioned, they faid, that they belonged to the town before us, which was diftant about four leagues. Cortes detained one canoe and fome of the people, particularly the women, and fent the others with two Spaniards to the chief, to demand from him canoes to crofs the water. Our whole party then fet out towards the river, and arriving there, we found the cacique waiting for us. He invited the general to his town, and Cortes embarked with thirty crofsbow-men, and arriving there, was prefented with fome trifles of gold much alloyed, and a few mantles. They here informed him that they knew of Spaniards being at two different places, one of which it feems was Nito, the other San Gil de Buena Vifta. He alfo learned that many more were at Naco, which is up the country, and diftant ten days journey from Nito, which laft mentioned place lies on the northern coaft. The general on hearing this obferved to us, that probably De Oli had divided his force, for as yet we knew nothing of Gil Gonzalez de Avila.

Our whole body having croffed the river, we halted at the diftance
of

of two leagues from it, to wait the return of Cortes. Here a Negro, two Indians, and three Spanish soldiers deserted; the latter preferring the taking their chance among enemies, to the repetition of the fatigues they had gone through. This day I was sun struck and fell ill of a calenture. The weather also at this time changed, and for three days and nights it never ceased raining; but we were obliged to continue our journey under it, from the apprehension that our provisions should fall short. After two days march we came to a ridge of rocks, the stones whereof cut like knives; we sent soldiers a league's distance on each side to search for some other road, but to no effect. Our horses fell here at every step, and cut themselves to pieces, and the farther we proceeded on the descent, the worse it was. We left eight horses dead upon the spot, and most of the rest were so wounded as not to be able to keep up with us. Amongst others who received hurts the general's relation Palacios Rubios broke his leg by a fall. We called this place La Sierra de los Pedernales. When we had gotten over it we did not fail to return thanks to God for his mercy in extricating us from that difficulty. We then advanced chearfully towards a town named Taica, which lay before us, and where we hoped to find a sufficiency of every thing; but we were suddenly and unexpectedly stopped by an enormous torrent, which, being swelled by the heavy rains, came tumbling between great precipices with a noise which could be heard at the distance of two leagues. Here we were obliged to halt for three complete days, in order to make a bridge from one precipice to the other, and when at the end of the third day we began to pass over, we found that the people on the other side had taken advantage of our delay, to remove themselves and all their provisions out of our reach.

When we learned that after all our fatigues hunger was to be our portion, we seemed as it were thunder struck. I own I never in my life felt my heart so depressed as when I found nothing to be had for myself or my people; and this too on the eve of our Lord's resurrection! a pretty festival we had of it truly! Cortes, after sending out his servants every where, procured about a bushel of maiz. When he saw

the

the diftrefs which we were in, he called together the colonifts of Gua-cacualco, as the flower of his army, and earneftly folicited us to do our utmoft to procure fome neceffaries. Pedro de Ircio who was prefent afked to be appointed to the command, to which Cortes affented; but I, who knew that De Ircio was more of a talking, than a marching foldier, and that he would lag by the way and retard us, whifpered Cortes and Sandoval to prevent his going, for he being duck legged, could not get through the deep ground and mire like us, and would be obli-ged to fit down. Cortes therefore ordered him to ftay, and five of us fetting out together, with two guides, and croffing rivers and marfhes, came to fome Indian houfes where we found provifions in plenty. Here we alfo took fome prifoners, and with their fruit, fowls, and corn, we celebrated the feaft of the refurrection heartily. On the fame night ar-rived a thoufand Mexicans, whom Cortes had ordered to follow us. We joyfully loaded them with all the corn that we could procure, and twenty fowls for Cortes and Sandoval, and there ftill remained fome corn in the town which we ftaid to guard. On the next day we advan-ced to other villages, where we found fuch a plenty of corn that we wrote a billet to Cortes, with ink which we made, and on a piece of a drum head, defiring him to fend all the Indians that he could, to carry it to our people.

Thirty foldiers and about five hundred Indians in a fhort time ar-rived, and thus, thanks to God, we were amply provided for the re-mainder of the five days, during which we ftaid at Taica. I muft obferve, that the bridges which we conftructed on this march, remained perfectly good for many years, and that the Spaniards, when they paf-fed them ufed to fay, "thefe are the bridges of Cortes," as formerly it ufed to be faid, "here are the pillars of Hercules." We continued our march for two days, to a place named Tania, through a country inter-fected with rivers and rivulets, and where all the towns were abandoned; and during the night, our guides, being intrufted to the care of fome of the newly arrived Spaniards who I fuppofe flept upon their pofts, made their efcape. Thus we were left in a difficult country, and not

knowing

knowing which way to turn. In addition to this, it rained moſt heavily. Cortes was out of humour and ſaid, Pedro de Ircio and many
more being by, that he wiſhed others beſides the ſettlers of Guacacualco would beſtir themſelves, and do ſome good, in ſearching for guides.
De Ircio, Marmolejo a perſon of quality, and Burgales afterwards regidor of Mexico, each offered their ſervices, and taking ſix ſoldiers a
piece, were out three days in ſearch of Indians, and all returned without any ſucceſs, having met with nothing but rivers, and waters, and
obſtructions. Cortes was in deſpair at this, and deſired Sandoval to
apply to me, aſking as a favour that I would take the buſineſs on me.
When addreſſed in this manner I could not refuſe, though very ill; and
taking with me two friends, men capable of enduring hunger and thirſt,
we ſet out together, and following a ſtream, the marks of boughs being cut from the trees pointed out a way to ſome houſes, from whence
we ſaw corn fields and houſes with people about them. We remained
concealed until we ſuppoſed the people to be aſleep, and then, taking
the inhabitants by ſurpriſe, made priſoners three men, two Indian girls
who were very handſome, and an old woman. They had a few fowls
and a little corn. The whole of our capture we brought to our quarters.
Sandoval was overjoyed at our arrival; "now," ſaid he to Pedro de Ircio,
in the preſence of Cortes, "was Del Caſtillo right when he inſiſted on
" having none but active men with him, and not to take people who
" hobble along, telling their old ſtories of the adventures that happened to
" the count De Urena, and his ſon Don Pedro Giron." Theſe ſtories De
Ircio uſed to peſter us with, over and over again, for which reaſon all
who were preſent laughed heartily at what was ſaid by Sandoval who
knew that De Ircio and I were not friends. Cortes returned me thanks,
and paid me many compliments upon my conduct, but I will drop this
ſubject, for what is praiſe but emptineſs and unprofitableneſs, and
what advantage is it to me that people in Mexico ſhould tell what we
endured, or that Cortes ſhould ſay when he wanted to perſuade me to
go on this laſt expedition, that next to God it was me on whom he
placed his reliance to procure guides.

From

From the prisoners whom we had taken we learned, that it was neceffary to defcend the river for two days journey, to a place of above two hundred houfes named Oculiztli; which we accordingly did, paffing on our road fome large buildings where the travelling merchants of the Indians are ufed to ftop. At the clofe of the fecond day we arrived at the place to which we had been directed, where we found plenty of provifions. We alfo found in one of the temples an old red cap, and a fandal, as offerings to their idols. Some of our foldiers brought to Cortes two old men and four women, whom they took in the maiz fields; Cortes afked them what diftance the Spanifh fettlement was from this place; to which they replied that it was two days journey, being clofe by the fea fide, and that no town intervened. Upon this Cortes ordered Sandoval immediately to fet out on foot, with fix foldiers, and get down to the coaft, in order to afcertain what number of men De Oli had with him, for as yet we were entirely ignorant of all that had happened there, and Cortes required this information in order to effect what he had determined, which was, to fall upon, and furprife De Oli and his troops during the night.

Sandoval taking three guides reached the fea fide, and going northwards, foon perceived a canoe, and concealing himfelf where he expected it to anchor for the night, he was fortunate enough to get poffeffion of it, and upon examination, found it to belong to Indian merchants who were bringing falt to Golfo Dolce. Sandoval embarked on board this canoe with a part of his foldiers, and fending the reft by land, he purfued his route for the great river. As fortune would have it, on his voyage he fell in with a canoe in which had come four Spanifh fettlers, who were fearching for fruit near the mouth of the river, being in great diftrefs from the hoftilities of the Indians, and the ravages made by difeafe. Two of thefe being up in a tree, were aftonifhed at the fight of Sandoval and the reft, and reported to their companions what they had feen. When they met, Sandoval was informed by them of their prefent diftrefs, and how they had hanged the officer left there by Avila. Upon this he determined to bring them to Cortes, which having declared

red

red, a foldier named Alonzo Ortiz obtained from him permiffion to fet off with the news, in order to get a reward. He accordingly in a fhort time reached us, and by his intelligence rejoiced us all. Cortes prefented him with an excellent horfe named Moor's-head, and each of us gave him fomething proportionate to our abilities. Sandoval arrived a fhort time after, and informed us that they were preparing to embark for the Ifland of Cuba, and how they had hanged their commanding officer, for oppofing them and alfo becaufe he had hanged a turbulent prieft: as alfo that they had elected one Anthonio Niote in his place.

Cortes iffued an order to march immediately for the fea coaft, which was diftant fix leagues, and we had an inlet of the fea to pafs. We were therefore obliged to wait till low water, and then crofs it, wading and fwimming. Cortes pufhed forwards with his attendants, and croffed the river in the two canoes, fwimming the horfes by the fide of them; but he found it fo dangerous from the violence of the current, that he fent word to us not to attempt to follow him until farther orders.

The place where Avila's fettlers now were, was about two leagues diftant from where Cortes landed. They were greatly furprifed at the appearance of Europeans, and more fo when they found that it was the general fo renowned through all thefe countries. Cortes received their congratulations in the moft gracious manner, and defired them to bring together what canoes they could collect, as alfo the boats belonging to their fhips, and to provide bread for the ufe of his people. Of this laft article only fifty pounds could be procured, for they lived almoft entirely on fapotes, vegetables, and what fifh they caught. We were four days paffing the river, with the greateft danger. One foldier with his horfe went to the bottom, and never appeared afterwards. Two other horfes were alfo loft; one of them belonged to a foldier named Cafquete, who heartily curfed Cortes and his expedition, for the ill fortune he had brought upon him.

The

The general trusted the care of the embarkation to Sandoval. One Saavedra, presuming upon his relationship with Cortes, would not pay respect to the captain's orders, and endeavouring to force his passage, laid his hand to his poniard with disrespectful expressions to Sandoval. The latter made few words, but seizing him instantly, threw him into the water; where he was nearly drowned. Our suffering at this time from hunger was beyond my expression. For these four days we had literally nothing but the few nuts that we could gather, and some wild fruits; and when we arrived on the other side our condition was not bettered.

We found this colony to consist of forty men and six women, all yellow and sickly, and without any thing to eat. Of course we were anxious for the moment of setting out in order to search the country for provisions. About eighty of us went on foot, under the command of Captain Luis Marin, to a town at the distance of eight leagues, where we found provisions of all kinds, cocoa in the greatest quantity, and plenty of corn, and vegetables. This place was exactly on the route of Naco, whither it was the intention of Cortes to go. On receiving our intelligence, he dispatched Sandoval with the principal part of his troops to join us. We sent a plentiful supply of maiz to our wretched colonists, who having been so long starving, eat to such an excess that seven of them died immediately. At this time also a vessel arrived there, with seven horses, forty hogs, eight pipes of salted meat, biscuit, and fifteen passengers, adventurers from the Island of Cuba. All the provisions Cortes bought immediately, and distributed them amongst the colonists, with an equally fatal result. They eat of the salted meat to such an excess that it gave them diarrheas, which in a very few days carried off fourteen.

Cortes now determined to examine this great river, for which purpose he fitted out one of the brigantines of Avila which had been stranded, and with this vessel, a boat, and four double canoes, in which he embarked thirty soldiers, with eight sailors of the vessel which lately

arrived,

arrived, he proceeded up the river to a spacious lake with good anchorage, which extended to the distance of six leagues, and the whole of the adjacent country was liable to be inundated. Proceeding higher he found the current more strong, and at length came to some shallows which his vessels could not pass; he accordingly disembarked, and proceeding by a narrow road, passed through different villages. In the first he took some natives to serve as guides, and in the second he found plenty of corn, and fowls, amongst which were pheasants, pidgeons, and partridges. These last I have frequently observed domesticated among the Indians. Pursuing his route, he came near a large town named Cinacan Tencintle, situated amongst fine cocoa plantations, and in which he heard the sound of music, the Indians being engaged in a drunken festival. Cortes waited until a fit opportunity, concealed in a wood, and then suddenly rushing out, made ten men and fifteen women prisoners. The rest attacked him with arrows and darts, but our people closed with them and cut to pieces eight of their chiefs. When the natives found that the affair was going against them they thought it high time to submit; and accordingly four old men, two of whom were priests, came, apparently very much tamed, to petition Cortes for the prisoners, and brought with them a few trifles of gold. Cortes promised to deliver his prisoners on receiving a good supply of provisions which they assured him of, and he pointed out to them where the ships lay. It appears that a misunderstanding afterwards happened between Cortes and the natives, relative to the delivery of his captives, he wishing to retain three women to make bread. They in consequence proceeded to hostilities again; Cortes received a wound in the face, twelve also of his soldiers were wounded, and a boat destroyed. He then returned after an absence of twenty six days, suffering dreadfully by the mosquitos. He wrote to Sandoval giving him an account of all that had occurred at Cinacan, which is distant from Guatimala seventy leagues, and ordered him to proceed to Naco; Cortes himself intending to establish a settlement at the place which was named Puerto de Cavallos, for which purpose he desired ten of the veterans of Guacacualco without whose assistance nothing was conducted properly.

Cortes

Cortes taking with him all the Spaniards that remained at St. Gil de Buena Vista, embarked in two ships, and after eight days sail arrived at Puerto de Cavallos, in order to plant a colony there, the situation being answerable, and the harbour good. He appointed Diego de Godoy commandant of this settlement, which he named Natividad. He thought that by this time Sandoval had arrived at Naco which was not far distant, and wrote to him there, desiring ten of the soldiers of Guacacualco to reinforce him, as he intended to proceed to the bay of Honduras. This letter reached us in the quarters which I last mentioned, for we had not arrived at Naco. I will say no more of the proceedings of Cortes, nor how the flies bit him day and night, and prevented his rest, so that as we afterwards heard he had like to have died or lost his senses, from want of sleep.

Sandoval on receiving the general's letter pressed forwards towards Naco, but was obliged to halt at a place called Cuyocan, in order to bring up his stragglers who had quitted him in search of provisions. We had also a river to pass, and the natives all round were hostile. As our line of march was so very long by the number of invalids who came straggling after us, especially of the Mexicans, it became necessary to establish a post at the ferry on this river, for which purpose Sandoval left me with the command of eight men.

One night a body of the natives fell upon us, but we were prepared for them. They set fire to the house in which we were, and thought to have brought off our canoe; but we, with the assistance of a few Mexicans, beat them off for that time, and knowing that there were some invalids lodged upon the road behind us, we on the next day brought them over and all together set out to join Sandoval. One man died upon the road; he was a Genoese, had been some time ill, and at length sunk under poverty of diet. I was obliged to leave the body behind, for which Sandoval blamed me when I made my report. I told him we had two invalids on each horse, and my companion Bartholome de Villa Nueva haughtily said, that it was difficult enough for us to

bring

bring ourselves, without carrying dead men. Sandoval immediately ordered me and Villanueva to return and bury him, which we accordingly did, and placed a cross over the grave. We found in his pocket a purse containing a quantity of dice, and a memorandum of his family and effects in Teneriffe. Rest his soul! Amen.

In about two days we arrived at Naco, having passed a place where mines have been since discovered, and also a town named Quiniftan. On arriving at Naco we found it to be a good town, but it was abandoned by its inhabitants; however we obtained plenty of provisions and salt which we much wanted. We took our quarters in some very large quadrangles, the same place where De Oli had been executed, and fixed ourselves as if we had been to remain here for ever. In this place is the finest water that we had met with in New Spain, as also a tree, which at the time of the siesta, let the heat of the sun be as great as it will, has a delightful refreshing coolness in its shade, and there seems to descend from it a kind of dew, of the most delicate nature, which is good for the head. The place is well situated, the neighbourhood fertile and producing both the red and the small sapote, and it was at that time populous.

Sandoval having obtained possession of three of the principal natives of the district, treated them kindly, and we continued in peaceable terms with them, but the inhabitants could not be induced to return to the town. It was now time to send the reinforcement Cortes had required, of ten Spanish settlers of Guacacualco. I was an invalid and unable to go, and Sandoval wished to keep me with him; eight valiant soldiers were however sent, who set out heartily cursing Cortes and his expedition at every step. They had some reason, for they did not know the least of the state of the country through which they were to go. Sandoval took the precaution of sending five principal persons of the natives with them, and gave it to be understood that if any injury was done to them the country should be severely punished. They arrived at the place where Cortes was, in safety, and he immediately embarked

H h h

for

for Truxillo, leaving Godoy in the command at Puerto de Cavallos, with forty Spaniards, which was all that remained of the settlers who came with Avila, and those newly arrived from the Island of Cuba.

For some time Godoy maintained himself in the neighbouring country, but as his men were continually dropping off by disease, the Indians began to despise and neglect them, and in a short time they lost by sickness and famine above half their number, and three of them deserted and joined Sandoval. Such was the result of the colonization of Puerto de Cavallos. Sandoval, by different expeditions to the neighbouring districts, named Cirimongo, Acalaco, Quizmitan, and four others, and by judicious measures, brought the whole of the country to peace and subjection, all around Naco, and as far as Godoy's settlement.

After six days sail Cortes arrived at the port of Truxillo. This place had been colonized by Francisco de las Casas, but there were also amongst them many of the mutineers who had served under De Oli, and who had been banished from Panuco. All these, conscious of their guilt, waited on Cortes upon his arrival, to supplicate his pardon for their offences. This Cortes granted them; he also continued those who had been appointed to offices, and put at the head of all those provinces as captain general, his relation Saavedra. Cortes having now summoned the chiefs and priests of the Indians, made an harangue to them, wherein he told them of the object of his coming thither, which was, to induce them to quit the unnatural and cruel practices of their false religion, and to embrace the true one. He also dwelt upon the power and dignity of his Majesty the Emperor Don Carlos, to whom he required their submission. This together with the holy exhortations of our reverend fathers being explained to these people they readily promised to obey him, in becoming his Majesty's vassals; whereupon Cortes signified to them, that they should provide the settlement with all articles of food, especially fish, of which there was a great plenty in the sea about the Islands of Los Guanajes, and also he desired them

to

to fend labourers to clear the woods in front of the town, and open the view to the fea. All this being readily undertaken by them, Cortes ordered a number of fows in young to be turned out on thefe iflands, to ftock them, which they did in the courfe of a few years. The reverend fathers Francifcans alfo preached to the Indians many holy things very edifying to hear. The natives applied themfelves to labour fo earneftly, that in two days they cleared the woods towards the fea, and built fifteen houfes one of which was for Cortes, and a very good habitation. The renown of our general made him feared through all thefe diftricts, as far as Olancho where are the rich mines; the Indians called him the captain Hue-hue of Marina, that is the old captain who brings Donna Marina, and his prefence reduced the whole country to fubmiffion, two or three diftricts in the mountains only holding out. Againft thefe, the names of which were given to him by the chief of Papayeca, then a populous diftrict but now almoft uninhabited, he fent Captain Saavedra with a party of foldiers who brought moft of them under fubjection, the only one that held out being that people named the Acaltecans.

As many of the fuite of Cortes began now to fall fick from the effects of the climate, he fent them on board a veffel to St. Domingo or Cuba, and by this opportunity he alfo fent letters to the reverend fathers of the order of St. Jerome, and the court of royal audience; informing them of all the events that had happened; of his refigning the government of Mexico into the hands of deputies, to proceed againft De Oli in perfon, and alfo of his future intentions. He requefted from them a reinforcement of foldiers, and, to attach credit to his report, he fent a valuable prefent of gold, taken in reality from his fide board, but in fuch a manner that it fhould appear to them the produce of this fettlement. This bufinefs he entrufted to a relation named Avalos, with orders, on his way, to take up twenty five foldiers, who, he had received intelligence, were left in the Ifland of Cozumel, to kidnap Indians. This veffel was wrecked about feventy leagues from the Havannah; the Captain, Avalos, and many paffengers perifhed, and

Hhh 2

those

thofe few who efcaped, amongft whom was the licentiate Pedro Lopez, were the firft who brought to the iflands intelligence of the exiftence of Cortes and his army, for it had been hitherto univerfally believed that we had all perifhed. As foon as it was known where Cortes then was, two old fhips were freighted with horfes and colts, and fent out to us. Except thefe, and one pipe of wine, all the reft of the cargo confifted of fhirts, caps, and ufelefs trumpery of various kinds.

Some Indians of the iflands called the Guanajes, which are about the diftance of eight leagues from Truxillo, came at this time to complain to Cortes, that it had been a practice of the Spaniards to come to their iflands, and kidnap the natives and their maceguales, or flaves, and that a veffel was now there, as fuppofed for that purpofe. Cortes on hearing this ordered out one of his fhips, which came in view of the veffel, but fhe immediately hoifted fail, and made her efcape. It afterwards appeared that the commander of her was the bachelor Moreno, who had been fent on bufinefs to Nombre de Dios, by the royal court of audience of St. Domingo.

Whilft Sandoval remained at Naco, the chiefs of two diftricts in that vicinity named Quecufpan, and Tanchinalchapa, came to him to complain of a party of Spaniards who maltreated their people, robbing them, and putting them in chains, and who were now at the diftance of about one day's march from his poft. He accordingly fet out againft them with feventy men, and arrived at the place where thefe people were, perfectly at their eafe, and not expecting any attack. They were furprifed at feeing us, and ran to their arms; but we foon feized the captain and feveral more, thus getting the better of them without any blood being drawn on either fide. Sandoval cenfured them in very ftrong terms for their mifconduct, and ordered thofe Indians whom they had made prifoners to be immediately releafed. The captain of this party was one Pedro de Garro; he and his men were marched prifoners to our fettlement. From the manner in which they were mounted and attended, they feemed to be lords, in comparifon of us who were dirty and worn

down

down with fervice. Several of them were perfons of quality or gentlemen, and after they had repofed a day amongft us they grew perfectly contented.

The reafon of their being in thefe countries is as follows. Pedro,
Arias de Avila, who had the government of Tierra Firma, fent a captain named Francifco Hernandez to make conquefts in the province of
Nicaragua and Leon. This he did, reducing the natives to obedience,
and eftablifhing a colony there. When Hernandez found himfelf ad-
vantageoufly fettled, he determined to throw off his dependency upon
Pedro Arias, to which I believe he was incited by the bachelor Moreno,
and the reafon of it to the beft of my judgment was this. Arias had
beheaded V. N. de Balboa, who married his daughter Donna Ifabella
Arias de Penofa. This atrocious ftretch of power he committed
moft unwarrantably, and it was on this occafion that the bachelor
Moreno had been fent hither by the royal court of audience. The
bachelor meeting with Hernandez, advifed him to renounce his connexion with Pedro Arias, who had conducted himfelf fo badly, and to
eftablifh a diftinct government in that province, immediately under his
Majefty; and Hernandez taking his counfel, fent this party to make
their way to the north coaft, thereby to open a communication with
the mother country.

All this being explained to Sandoval, was by him communicated
to Cortes, in expectation of his fupporting the views of Hernandez, by
Captain Luis Marin, whom I attended upon this occafion. Our whole
party confifted of ten foldiers, and a moft defperate journey it was.
the Indians were hoftile and attacked us with large heavy lances, wounding two of our foldiers. The rivers which we croffed were fwollen and
rapid, and fo frequent, that in one day we paffed three of them; one
river named Xagua, ten leagues from Triumpho de la Cruz, detained
us for two days, and the inlets and lagoons were infefted by alligators.
By the fide of the river Xagua we found the fkeletons of feven horfes;
they had belonged to De Oli's troops, and died from eating poifonous
herbs.

herbs. Paffing El Triumpho de la Cruz, and a place named Quemara, at length we arrived in the neighbourhood of Truxillo about the hour of vefpers, and faw five cavaliers riding along the coaft. Thefe were, Cortes and four of his friends, who were taking exercife. When he recognifed us, after the firft furprife at the unexpected meeting, he difmounted from his horfe, and running up, embraced us all with tears in his eyes, fo overjoyed was he to fee us. It made me melancholy to find him fo weak and reduced. Diftrefs and difeafe had worn him down; indeed he expected death, and had gotten a Francifcan habit made to be buried in. He had not at this time received any intelligence from Mexico fince he quitted that city. He walked into the town with us, and we fupped with him, wretchedly enough. I had not my fill even of bread or bifcuit. When he had read over the letters relative to the bufinefs of Hernandez, he promifed that he would do all he could to fupport him. The veffels from St. Domingo had arrived here three days before us. I have already mentioned, that except the horfes and one pipe of wine, their cargoes were nothing but frippery; it would have been much better that they had not come, fince it induced us all to run ourfelves in debt buying their ufelefs trafh.

While we were relating to Cortes the hardfhips we had fuftained during our late journey, a fhip was defcried at a diftance, making for our port. This veffel failed from the Havannah, with letters for the general from the licentiate Zuazo, alcalde major of Mexico. The hidalgo who was captain of the veffel came directly to kifs the hands of Cortes, and prefented his letters, the fubftance of which the reader fhall be informed of. As foon as Cortes read them he was overwhelmed with forrow and diftrefs. He retired to his private apartment, where we could hear that he was fuffering under the greateft agitation. He did not ftir out for an entire day; at night he confeffed and ordered a mafs for the enfuing morning, after which he called us together, and read to us the intelligence he had received, and whereby we learned, that it had been univerfally reported and believed in New Spain that we were all dead, and our properties had in confequence been fold by public auction.

auction. From his father in Castille he was informed, of the death of the Bishop of Burgos, that Albornoz had been laboriously undermining us at court, and also of what I have before related, in regard to his Majesty's orders to the admiral, and the interference of the duke of Bejar; also that Narvaez had been appointed to the government of the river Palmas, and that the government of Panuco had been given to one Nuno de Guzman.

In regard to the affairs of New Spain these letters further added, that in consequence of the powers which Cortes had given to the factor Gonzalo de Salazar, and the veedor Pedro Almindes Chirinos, to supercede the deputies he had left in Mexico, viz. the treasurer Alonzo de Estrada, and the contador Albornoz, and to take the administration upon themselves in case of misconduct on the part of the deputies, these two officers having on their return to Mexico formed a strong party, amongst whom was the licentiate Zuazo alcalde major, Rodrigo de Paz alguazil major, A. de Tapia, Jorge de Alvarado, and the rest of the ancient conquerors, attempted to take the government into their hands by main force, and the consequence of the struggle of the two parties was, much disturbance, and bloodshed. The factor and veedor however carried their point, and had made prisoners the two former deputies and many of their friends. Still however there was fighting every day, the predominating party confiscating the property of their opponents, to distribute it among their own adherents. They had, we learned, completely superceded Zuazo in his office, and had imprisoned Rodrigo de Paz the alguazil major, but that the licentiate Zuazo had effected a temporary reconciliation between the parties. During these disturbances, three districts, viz. the Zapotecans, Minxes, and those in the vicinity of a fortified rock named Coatlan had rebelled, and a force going against them under the veedor Chirinos, instead of attending to their business, the troops thought of nothing but card playing, in consequence of which the natives surprised them in their camp, and did them much mischief. The factor had then sent a veteran captain named Andrez de Monjaraz, to assist the veedor, and advise him; but

this

this officer was unable to exert himself properly, being an invalid. As to the city of Mexico, there was danger every hour of an infurrection.

The letters also informed us that the factor constantly remitted gold to his Majesty's treasurer, Don Francisco de los Cobos, to make an interest for himself at court, reporting that we were all dead at Xicalonga, the belief of which was corroborated by Diego de Ordas who, to get out of the factions and troubles of Mexico had sailed with two vessels to search for us, and arriving at the place called Xicalonga, where the captains Simon de Cuenca and Francisco de Medina had been killed, hearing the account of their misfortunes, and not knowing the particulars, had taken it for granted that it could be no others than Cortes and his party who were thus destroyed, and reported so in his letters to Mexico which he sent by certain passengers, and then, without landing, hoisted sail for Cuba. The factor shewed his letter to our relations, and put on mourning; and a monument was erected, and funeral service performed for the honour of Cortes, in the great church of Mexico. The factor then proclaimed himself governor, and captain general of New Spain, with the sound of kettle drums and trumpets, and issued out an order, that all women who had any regard for their souls, and whose husbands had gone with Cortes, should consider them dead in law, and marry again forthwith. And because a woman named Juana de Mansilla did not chuse to take his advice, but insisted on waiting the return of her husband Alonzo Valiente, saying that we were not people who would let ourselves be so easily beaten as the veedor Chirinos and his party, the factor ordered her to be publicly whipped through the streets of Mexico for a witch.

As there are in all places flattering traitors, one of this description, whom we once expected better from, and whose name I will not mention, solemnly assured the factor, before many witnesses, that going one night by the church of St. Jago, which is built on the scite of the great temple of the Mexicans, and looking into the church yard, he

faw

faw the fouls of Cortes, Donna Marina, and Sandoval, burning in flames of fire; and that he had been fo terrified thereat, as to have remained ill ever fince. Another man of good reputation alfo came to the factor, and told him that the quadrangles of Tefcuco were haunted by evil fpirits, which the natives faid were the fouls of Donna Marina and Cortes. All thofe falfehoods they invented to ingratiate themfelves with the factor.

At this time arrived in Mexico the captains Francifco de las Cafas, and Gil Gonzales de Avila, the fame who beheaded Chriftoval de Oli. Las Cafas on his arrival publicly afferted the exiftence of Cortes, and reprobated the conduct of the factor, but declared that fhould it be the cafe, as then believed, that we were all dead, Alvarado was the only proper man to put in the place of Cortes, until his Majefty's further pleafure fhould be known. Alvarado being written to on the fubject fet out for Mexico, but growing apprehenfive of fome attempt upon his life, he thought it moft prudent to return to his diftrict. The factor had at this time collected what gold he could lay his hands upon, to fupport his negotiations at court. In this he was oppofed by almoft every other officer of the government of New Spain, who determined among themfelves, not to permit him exclufively to make reprefentations of the tranfactions there, but to fend likewife their own ftatements at the fame time, and by the fame opportunity with his. When the factor found that he could not bring over Las Cafas, Gonzalez de Avila, and the licentiate, to fupport his views, he caufed the two former to be arrefted and profecuted for the alleged murder of De Oli; and by his wickednefs, and the preponderance of his power, procuring their condemnation, it was with the greateft difficulty that their immediate execution could be prevented, by appealing to his Majefty. He was obliged however to content himfelf with fending them prifoners to Caftille. He then fell upon the licentiate Zuazo, and fent him off to Vera Cruz, and there embarked him for the Ifland of Cuba, as was alleged, o anfwer for his conduct while he was judge there. He next feized Rodrigo de Paz, and demanded of him an account and furrender of the

treafure

treafure of Cortes, whofe major domo he had been, and becaufe he could not, or would not declare, or make difcovery concerning it, he caufed his feet and part of his legs to be burnt; and not content with giving him the torture, and knowing alfo that if left alive he might complain to his Majefty, he ordered him to be hanged, which was accordingly done. He alfo arrefted moft of the friends of Cortes. Tapia and Jorge de Alvarado, however, took fanctuary with the Francifcan fathers; but feveral of them went over to him, partly becaufe he gave them Indians, and partly becaufe it is natural to wifh to be with the ftrongeft power, or, as the faying is, to cry, "fuccefs to the con-" querors." He emptied the arfenal of arms, and brought them to his palace, in the front of which he alfo planted all the artillery, which was commanded by Captain Don Luis de Guzman, fon in law to the Duke of Medina Sidonia. He next formed a body guard for his own protection, compofed in part of the foldiers of Cortes, to the command of which he appointed one Artiaga.

Zuazo alfo wrote to Cortes to inform him, that he had reported many fcandals of him to his Majefty, fuch as defrauding him of the duty upon gold; and as an inftance to what extent he carried his tyranny, he mentioned a circumftance of a travelling Spaniard having informed a woman, and given her proofs, that her hufband who was gone with Cortes was alive. This coming to the ears of the factor, he caufed him to be feized by four alguazils, and would have hanged him, but that he, to excufe himfelf, declared that what he had faid was all a falfehood, and that he had only invented it to comfort the poor woman, feeing her weeping for the lofs of her hufband. The bufinefs which brought this man to Mexico was, to obtain a plantation, this was immediately fettled to his fatisfaction, and he was difmiffed with a hint to hold his tongue, as he valued his life. This letter alfo informed Cortes of the death of the reverend father Bartholome, a holy man, and much regretted by all the natives of Mexico, who in token of their refpect fafted from the time of his death, until he was buried.

Zuazo

Zuazo concluded by faying, that he feared Mexico was loft, and that he had been fent a prifoner in irons to the place from whence he dated his letter.

This intelligence made us all very fad. It was difficult to fay which of the two, Cortes or the factor, we curfed moft heartily in our own minds. We fecretly gave them ten thoufand maledictions, and our hearts funk within us. Cortes retired to his chamber, and did not appear to us till evening, when we entreated him immediately to haften to Mexico. He replied to us kindly and gently, faying, "dear friends " and companions, this villain of a factor is powerful. If I go and you " accompany me he may lay hands upon us by the road, and murder us " all. It were better that I went privately with three or four of you, and " came to Mexico before he was prepared. Let the reft rejoin Sandoval, " and proceed with him to Mexico." Cortes now wrote to Captain Hernandez, promifing him every fupport; he fent him alfo two mules loaded with prefents of fuch things as he knew he wanted, entrufting them to the care of a gentleman named Cabrera, a brave officer who was on the ftaff under Blafco Nunez Velo, and was killed in the fame battle with the Viceroy. When I faw that Cortes was determined to go to Mexico, I requefted of him that he would permit me, who had been in all difficulties and dangers by his fide, to attend him upou this occafion. He embraced me and faid, "I requeft you my fon to remain with " Sandoval. I promife you, and I fwear by this beard, that I confider " myfelf much beholden to you, and have long done fo." However he would not permit me to attend him.

I remember when we were in the town of Truxillo, a gentleman named Roderigo Manueca, a principal officer in the general's houfehold, to divert Cortes, feeing him diftreffed, as he was with good reafon, laid a wager with fome other cavaliers, that he would climb in his armour to the top of the rock, whereon ftood the houfe which the Indians had built for the head quarters. When he had got a confiderable way up he miffed his hold, and falling to the ground, was killed.

Some

Some of the settlers of this place now began to grow mutinous, on finding that Cortes had omitted to name them to any office. He however found the means to pacify them, by promises not to forget them on his arrival at Mexico. Previous to his departure, he ordered Captain Diego de Godoy with his settlers to quit the colony of Puerto de Cavallos, where it was impossible for them to keep their ground, on account of fleas, musquitos, and other vermin, and to relieve us at the good settlement of Naco. He also ordered us to take the province of Nicaragua in our way to Mexico, as the government of it was an object worth applying for. Accordingly we took our leave of Cortes who was embarked, and set out chearfully upon our journey as Mexico was to be the end of it. It was as usual attended with extreme distress. However we reached Naco, and found that Captain De Garro had before our arrival gone for Nicaragua, to acquaint his chief, Hernandez, of the promise which Cortes had made, and we set out on the ensuing day for Mexico.

Two confidential friends of the governor Arias de Avila, having gotten the knowledge that a private correspondence was going on between Hernandez and Cortes, began to suspect the view of the former to surrender his province, and detach himself from Avila. These soldiers were named Garruito and Zamorrano. The former was urged on particularly by an old enmity to Cortes, on account of a rival-ship about a lady in St. Domingo when they were both youths, and which had ended in a duel. These persons informed Avila of the whole that they knew, and he, immediately on receipt of the intelligence, hastened off to seize the parties concerned. Garro, alarmed in time, made his escape to us; but Hernandez, relying upon their former intimacy and friendship, thought that Avila would not proceed to extremities, and did not attempt to avoid him. He was however sadly undeceived, for after a very summary process he was executed as a traitor to his superior officer, in the town which he was colonizing, and thus ended the negotiation between him and Cortes.

The

The firſt time that Cortes ſailed from Truxillo for Vera Cruz, he was obliged to put back by contrary winds, the ſecond time from an accident which happened to the veſſel. He was diſpirited by ſickneſs, the voyage alſo added to his mental depreſſion, and he was apprehenſive of the power of the factor. On his return he ordered a ſolemn maſs, and prayed fervently to the holy Ghoſt to enlighten him as to his future proceedings. It appears that he became inſpired with an inclination to ſtay and colonize the country where he then was; for he ſent three ex-preſſes as hard as they could poſt to recall us, and bring us back to Truxillo. In his letters he expreſſed his determination, which he attri-buted to the inſpiration of his guardian angel. When we received this meſſage we beſtowed a thouſand maledictions on Cortes and the ill for-tune which attended him, and told Sandoval, that if he choſe to remain it muſt be by himſelf, for that we were determined to proceed to Mex-ico. Sandoval was alſo of our opinion; we therefore returned an an-ſwer to this effect, ſigned by us all, and in a few days received another letter from him, which contained great offers to ſuch as ſhould be indu-ced to remain, and concluded by ſaying, that if we refuſed, there ſtill remained ſoldiers in Caſtille and elſewhere. On receiving this letter we were if poſſible more determined than ever to proceed, but Sandoval earneſtly entreated, and perſuaded us to halt for a few days, until he could ſee Cortes, in the hope of perſuading him to undertake the jour-ney to Mexico. We wrote back in reply, that as he ſaid he could find ſoldiers in Caſtille, ſo could we governors and generals in Mexico, who would give us plantations for our ſervices, and that we had ſuffered misfortunes enough already by him. With this anſwer Sandoval ſet off, attended by a ſoldier named Sauzedo, and a farrier, and mounted on his good horſe Motilla, ſwearing by his beard that he would not return until he had put Cortes on board the ſhip for Mexico.

Now I mention Sandoval's horſe, I muſt obſerve of him, that he was the ſwifteſt, and the beſt dreſſed, and fineſt figure of any horſe in New Spain: he was of a dark cheſnut colour, and ſuch was the fame of Motilla, that it reached the ear of his Majeſty, to whom Sandoval

intended

intended to prefent him. Sandoval applied to me at this time for my horfe, an excellent animal for career, exercife, or road. He coft me fix hundred crowns to one Avalos brother to Saavedra, my former one, which had coft me a greater fum, being killed in an action at a place called Zulaco. However Sandoval exchanged with me one of his, which was killed under me in lefs than two months; after which I remained with nothing better than a vicious colt, which I bought a bad bargain of from amongft thofe brought to Truxillo in the two veffels, as I have before related. Sandoval at parting from us defired us to wait his return at a large Indian town named Acalteca. When he reached Truxillo, his friend Cortes was rejoiced to fee him, but neither our letter, nor the preffing inftances of Sandoval, nor of the reverend father Varillas, could induce him to furmount his averfion to proceed to Mexico.

When Sandoval found it impoffible to induce Cortes to go to Mexico, he prevailed upon him to fend a confidential fervant named Martin de Orantes, with a commiffion to Pedro de Alvarado, and Francifco de las Cafas, to take upon them the government during his abfence, in cafe thofe officers were in Mexico, and fhould they not be found there, the fame power was to be exercifed by the treafurer Alonzo de Eftrada, and the contador Albornoz, conformably to the deputation given by Cortes to them, previous to his departure from Mexico, thofe delegated to the factor and veedor being revoked. Cortes having agreed to this, and given his orders and inftructions, directed Orantes to land in a bay between Vera Cruz and Panuco, and to fuffer no one to go on fhore but himfelf; and the veffel was immediately to hoift fail, and proceed for Panuco. Thefe laft inftructions were given, that the arrival of his officer fhould be kept as private as poffible until the proper time. He alfo fent letters by him to all his friends in New Spain, and to the treafurer and contador, although he knew them in reality not to belong to the number.

The wind and weather being favourable, in a few days the veffel
arrived

arrived at its deftination, and Orantes on landing difguifed himfelf as a labourer. On his journey he avoided the Spaniards, lodging and mixing only with the natives. Thofe who had known him before could not have recognized him, after an abfence of two years and three months. To fuch as queftioned him he faid, that his name was Juan de Flechilla; in this manner, being an active man, he arrived in four days at Mexico, and entering the city after dark, he proceeded directly to the lodgings of the reverend fathers Francifcans. On being admitted, he there found the Alvarados and feveral of the friends of Cortes, concealed. When he had explained who he was, and produced the general's letters, all prefent, the reverend fathers not excepted, danced for joy; they immediately locked the gates of the monaftery, to exclude the obfervation of the traitorous party, and at midnight the intelligence was communicated to the treafurer, the contador, and many of the friends of Cortes, who immediately affembled at the Francifcans.

It was then determined by them, as the firft ftep, to feize on the perfon of the factor in the morning. All the intermediate time was employed in collecting arms and friends, and making other preparations for the purpofe. The veedor was at that period at the rock of Coatlan. At day break the whole party marched to the palace inhabited by the factor, crying, "long live his Majefty, and Hernando Cortes." When this was heard by the citizens, they all took to their arms, thinking it fomething wherein government called for their affiftance, and numbers under that idea joined the treafurer on his march. As to the contador, he played a double part, giving intelligence to the factor to put him on his guard, and Eftrada reproached him ftrongly for his conduct.

When the party of Cortes approached the refidence of the factor, they found that he was already well prepared, owing to the information that he had received. His artillery under Don Luis de Guzman was planted in front of the houfe, and he had a ftrong garrifon within fide. Thofe with the treafurer forcing their way in, fome by the different doors, others by the terraces and wherever they could get accefs, all at

the

the fame time, and fhouting for his Majefty and Cortes, the adherents
of the factor became difmayed, and the artillery-men abandoning the
guns, the other foldiers alfo made off and hid themfelves; one of them,
Gines Nortes, leaping down from a corredor, fo that there only remained with the factor, Pedro Gonzalez Sabiote, and four fervants. When
he found himfelf thus abandoned, he became defperate, and endeavoured himfelf to fire off the guns, in which attempt he was feized, and
made prifoner. A large cage of timber was conftructed to receive him,
and thus terminated his career as governor of New Spain. Circular
notice was fent to all the provinces of this revolution, by which each
individual was pleafed or diffatisfied as his particular intereft fwayed
him. When the veedor heard it he was fo diftreffed that he fell fick.
He left his command with Captain De Monjaraz, and got himfelf conveyed towards Mexico, and reaching the monaftery of St. Francis in
Tezcuco, he there fhut himfelf up, and was fhortly after made prifoner
and fecured in another wooden cage.

Immediate intelligence of all that had happened was forwarded to
Pedro de Alvarado, with directions to him to proceed to Truxillo, and
wait upon Cortes. The next thing that the new deputies did was, to
pay their refpects to Juanna de Manfilla, the woman who had been
whipped for a witch. The treafurer placed her on horfeback behind
him, and thus, attended by all the cavaliers in proceffion, fhe was pa-
raded through the ftreets of Mexico like a Roman matron, and was ever
after called Donna Juanna, in honour of her conftancy, in refufing to
comply with the orders of the factor, to marry again, while fhe was
convinced that her hufband was living.

The fituation of Mexico evidently requiring the prefence of Cortes,
Fray Diego de Altamirano was pitched on by his friends to wait upon
him, and reprefent to him the neceffity of his immediately fetting out.
This father had been in the military profeffion before he entered the
church, and was a man of bufinefs and abilities. The conduct purfued
by the veedor and factor, and efpecially their confifcations and diftribution

tion of property among their greedy fupporters, had gained them many adherents, and, if not friends, at leaft perfons interefted in the main-tenance of their government. Thefe, compofed principally of the low and feditious defcription, but mixed with fome of quality, with the fupport and contrivance of the contador who dreaded the arrival of Cortes, had formed a plan to kill the treafurer, and reinftate the factor and veedor in their offices. For the purpofe of releafing them from prifon, they had recourfe to one Guzman, a white-fmith; a fellow of low character, and a ridiculous affecter of wit. To him they applied to make the keys, giving him a piece of gold whereon was marked the form in which they were to be wrought, and charging him at the fame time to keep the ftricteft fecrecy. All this he readily undertook and promifed, fpeaking as if he had the liberation of the prifoners fincerely at heart. They then told him all the particulars which his inquifitive-nefs induced him to queftion them about, and he proceeded in his work, but flowly and aukwardly, in order to induce them to repeat their vifits, to hurry him on; and he thus obtained from the confpirators the know-ledge that he required. The keys being finifhed, and the party ready to make the attempt, he fuddenly went to the houfe of the treafurer, and gave him an account of the whole. The treafurer, affembling the friends of Cortes on the inftant, proceeded to the place of meeting, where he found twenty confpirators armed, and in waiting for the fig-nal. Thefe he feized, but many others made their efcape. Among thefe apprehended were fome notorious characters; one of them had lately committed violence on a Caftillian woman. They were tried be-fore the bachelor Ortega alcalde major, and being convicted, three were hanged, and feveral whipped.

I muft now make a confiderable digreffion from my narrative, though it comes in properly in point of matter, to mention how the fame veffel which conveyed the letters tranfmitted by the factor to his Majefty in Caftille, conveyed others, fo artfully concealed that he had no fufpicion of them, wherein was given a full and true account of all

Kkk

his

his oppreffions, and unlawful proceedings. Thefe facts had alfo been already reported by the courts of St. Domingo, which contradicted the accounts of the death of Cortes, and informed his Majefty how that officer was employed for his fervice. The Emperor is reported to have declared his indignation at the manner in which Cortes had been treated, and his determination to fupport him.

When Fra Altamirano arrived at Truxillo, and explained his bufi-nefs to Cortes, the latter returned thanks to heaven for having granted peace to that country. He alfo declared his intention of going thither, but that it muft be by land, on account of the contrariety of the currents and his own bad ftate of health. The pilots however reprefented to him that the feafon was favourable, it being then the month of April, and prevailed upon him to give up his firft determination, but ftill he could not leave that place until the return of Sandoval, whom he had detached againft a Captain Roxas, who ferved under Arias, and againft whom complaints had been lodged by the natives of a diftrict named Olancho, which was diftant about fifty five leagues from Truxillo. Sandoval had been detached thither with feventy foldiers; at firft the two parties were upon the brink of hoftilities, but became afterwards reconciled and parted amicably, Roxas and his foldiers quitting that country.

Sandoval was immediately recalled in confequence of the meffage brought by Altamirano. The general appointed Captain Saavedra his lieutenant in that province, and wrote at the fame time to Captain Luis Marin, to march our whole party by the road of Guatimala, and Captain Godoy he ordered to Naco. Thefe letters Saavedra mali-cioufly fuppreffed, for they never came to our hands. Cortes previous to his embarkation confeffed to Fra Juan and received the facrament, for he was fo ill that he thought himfelf at the point of death. The wind favouring his voyage to the Havannah, he foon arrived there,

and

and was joyfully received by his former friends and acquaintances; and a veffel from New Spain which arrived about the fame time, brought intelligence that the country was at peace, for that the Indians hearing that Cortes, and we his conquerors were yet living, had come in and fubmitted.

CHAPTER VIII.

Return of Cortes to Mexico; occurrences there. Return of the author to Mexico.

AFTER five days refreſhment at the Havannah, Cortes embarked, and in twelve days arrived at the Port of Medellin, oppoſite to the Iſland De los Sacrificios, where he diſembarked with twenty ſoldiers, and proceeding to the town of San Juan de Ulua, which was diſtant about half a league, it was his fortune to light upon a ſtring of horſes and mules which had conveyed travellers to the coaſt, and which he engaged to take him to Vera Cruz. He ordered thoſe about him to give no hint to any one, who he was, and two hours before day break arriving at the town, he went directly to the church the doors of which were juſt opened. When the ſacriſtan ſaw the church filled with people whom he did not know, he became alarmed and ran into the ſtreet, calling to the civil power to aſſiſt him. The alcaldes, three alguazils and ſome of the neighbours came with arms in conſequence of the noiſe. Cortes was ſqualid, and the white habit of the reverend father was dirty from the ſea voyage, nor did any one recollect them until Cortes began to ſpeak; but as ſoon as he was recognized by them, they all fell upon their knees, kiſſed his hands, and bid him and his attendants welcome. All his old fellow ſoldiers aſſembled around him, and after maſs, eſcorted him to the quarters of Pedro Moreno Medrano, where he remained for eight days, during which time he was feaſted and entertained by the inhabitants. Intelligence was alſo ſent to Mexico to give the people there the joyful tidings, and Cortes wrote to his friends to the ſame effect. The Indians of the neighbourhood brought him

abundant

abundant prefents, and when he fet out for the city of Mexico every preparation was made for his accommodation. The inhabitants of Mexico, and of all the places round the lake celebrated his return with feftivals, and thofe of Tlafcala did the fame.

When he arrived at Tefcuco, where the contador came to wait upon him, he thought it proper to remain there for that night, and on the next morning but one he entered the city, being met by all the officers, cavaliers, and other inhabitants, in great ftate. The natives in their beft dreffes, and armed as warriors, filled the lake with their canoes; the dancing continued in every ftreet during the day, and at night the city was illuminated with lights at every door. Immediately on his arrival he went to the monaftery of St. Francifco, to return thanks to God for all his mercies to him. From that he went to his magnificent palace, where he was ferved and efteemed, and feared, as a fovereign prince, all the provinces making their fubmiffions, and fending prefents and congratulations to him. The entry of Cortes into Mexico was in the month of June. He immediately ordered the arreft of thofe who had been moft eminent for fedition, and faction, and caufed an enquiry to be inftituted into the conduct of the two great culprits. He alfo arrefted one Ocampo, who had been concerned in defamatory libels, and a perfon of the name of Ocana a fcrivener. This man who was very old was called the body and foul of the factor. He now intended to proceed immediately to bring the veedor and factor to juftice for their crimes, and if he had done fo no one could have faid againft it, and it would have met his Majefty's approbation. This I heard faid by fome members of the royal council of the Indies, the Bifhop de las Cafas being prefent, in the year of our Lord one thoufand five hundred and forty, when I was attending on my own affairs; but in this inftance Cortes may be juftly taxed with feeblenefs of conduct.

The reader has already been informed of the charges brought againft Cortes in Caftille, and of the orders iffued to the admiral of St.
Domingo,

Domingo, of the interpofition of the Duke of Bejar, and the appointment of Luis Ponce de Leon. The licentiate at this period of which I am writing, had arrived at Medellin. The fuddennefs of his coming rather furprifed Cortes, who when he received the intelligence, was performing his devotions in the church of St. Francis. He earneftly prayed to the Lord to guide him as feemed beft to his holy wifdom, and on coming out of the church fent an exprefs to bring him information of all particulars. In two days after, the licentiate fent him his Majefty's orders to receive him as refident judge in Mexico, and Cortes in confequence thereof difpatched a perfon with a meffage of compliment, and defiring to know which of the two roads to the city he intended to take, that he might make fuch preparations as were proper for the reception of a perfon of his rank. The licentiate fent him back an anfwer, thanking him for his polite offers, and declaring his intention to repofe after the fatigues of his voyage for a little time, where he was. This interval was bufily employed by the enemies of Cortes, who reprefented to the licentiate that it was his determination to put the factor and veedor to death, before his arrival, and that it was neceffary for him to take good care as to his own perfon, for as to all thefe civilities of Cortes, they were only intended, by afcertaining the road that he intended to take, under the colour of preparation to do him honour, the more effectually to fucceed in his intention to affaffinate him. They alfo mifreprefented every tranfaction in which Cortes had been concerned.

The perfons whom the licentiate principally confulted were the alcalde major Proano, a native of Cordova, and his brother the alcalde of the citadel, named Salazar de la Pedrada, who fhortly after his arrival died of a pleurify, Marcos de Aguilar a licentiate or bachelor, a foldier named Bocanegra de Cordova, and certain fathers of the order of St. Domingo, the provincial of whom was one Fray Thomas Ortiz. He had been a prior fome where that I do not now recollect, and all thofe who came with him defcribed him to be a man more fit for worldly affairs than thofe which particularly concerned his holy office. With
thefe

thefe perfons the licentiate confulted as to his proceeding to Mexico, which they all were of opinion fhould not be delayed an inftant. Accordingly, the laft meffengers difpatched by Cortes met him on the road at Iztapalapa. A fumptuous banquet was here prepared for them, at which, after feveral abundant and magnificent fervices, fome cheefe-cakes and cuftards were placed upon the table, as great delicacies. They were fo much approved of, and fome of the company eat of them in fuch quantities, that they made them fick; but thofe who eat of them in moderation were not at all affected. However this prior, Fray Thomas Ortiz, afferted that they had been poifoned with arfenic, and that he had not eaten of them from a fufpicion that they were fo; but others who were prefent declared, that he ftuffed himfelf heartily with them, and faid that they were the beft he had ever tafted. This new charge was immediately feized on and circulated by the enemies of Cortes, to throw an odium upon him.

During this time Cortes remained in Mexico; report faid that he had fent a good prefent of gold to the licentiate; this I cannot warrant; but as he had perfons ftationed to bring him intelligence, on his quitting Iztapalapa Cortes fet out to meet him, with a grand and numerous retinue of all the officers and gentlemen of the city. When the two parties met, many civilities paffed between the great men; the licentiate feemed to me to be well acquainted with the rules of politenefs. It was with great difficulty that Cortes could prevail upon him to take the right hand. On his entry into the city he proceeded to the monaftery of St. Francifco, bufinefs being deferred till the enfuing day. Cortes attended the licentiate to the palace prepared for him, where he entertained him moft fumptuoufly, but his politenefs and grandeur of manner was more ftriking than all the reft, infomuch that the licentiate obferved privately to his friends, that Cortes muft have been for a long time paft exercifing himfelf in the manners of a great man.

On the enfuing day, the council of Mexico, and all the civil and military

military officers, and the veteran soldiers, were assembled by order; and in our presence the licentiate Ponce de Leon produced his authority from his Majesty, which Cortes having kissed, and placed upon his head in token of submission, we all declared our obedience to, as in duty bound. The licentiate then received and returned back the rod of justice, in token of the surrender of the government into his hands, saying to Cortes, "General, this government I receive from you by his Majesty's " orders, wherein however it is by no means implied that you are not " most worthy of this, or higher trusts." To which the general replied, that he was always happy in obeying his Majesty's commands, and that it was also a satisfaction to him, that he would be thereby enabled to prove the falsehood and malice of his enemies. The licentiate in answer said, that where were good men, there were also bad, and such was the world; but that to each would be repaid in kind. This was all the material business of the day. On the next, Cortes attended the summon of the new governor, who sent it with much respect, and they had a conference, at which no one was present except the prior Thomas Ortiz; but it is said and believed that the licentiate addressed Cortes to the following effect. He first observed that it had been his Majesty's intention, that those who had most merit in the conquest of this country, should be well provided for in the distribution of planta- tions, considering more especially the soldiers who first came thither from Cuba; and that it had been understood, that this was not the case, for that they had been neglected, while others newly arrived had wealth heaped upon them, without any just pretensions. Cortes, to this, re- plied, that all had got shares, but that some of these it was true turned out much inferior to others; however it was in his power as governor now to rectify that. The governor then asked him how it happened that he had left Luis de Godoy to perish for want in a distant settlement, when the veterans ought to have been suffered to remain and enjoy the comforts of established possessions in Mexico, and the new colonizations have been assigned to new comers. He also enquired how Captain Luis Marin, Bernal Diaz del Castillo, and the others of his approved soldiers

had

had been taken care of. Cortes replied, that for bufinefs of danger it was ufelefs to employ any but his veterans; but that they would foon he expected return to Mexico, being then upon their road thither. The governor next afked him, rather fharply, about his imprudent march againft Chriftoval de Oli, undertaken without his Majefty's orders or permiffion. To which Cortes anfwered, that he confidered it to be neceffary for his Majefty's fervice, as the dangerous effects of fuch example among officers intrufted with feparate commands might be very extenfive, and that he had, previous to fetting out, reported to his Majefty his intention fo to do. He then queftioned Cortes as to the affairs of Narvaéz, Garay, and Tapia, to all which Cortes gave fuch fatisfactory anfwers that the governor feemed to be well contented therewith.

After Cortes had retired, Fray Thomas Ortiz called on three perfons intimate friends of the general, and with great earneftnefs told them the fame which he on the enfuing morning told to Cortes himfelf; for coming to him at that time, and defiring to fpeak to him in private, he then affured him, with many proteftations of friendfhip, and wifhes to ferve him, that the governor had fecret orders from his Majefty, immediately to behead him, and that he had thought it proper, in conformity with the duty of his facred function, as well as from his private regard, to give him early intelligence. This friendly communication it may be fuppofed gave Cortes a good deal to reflect upon; he had been informed of the intriguing and fimulating character of the friar, and was induced to think that this might be done to induce him to give a bribe for his interceffion. Others faid afterwards that Ortiz acted by the directions of the governor. Cortes, however, received his pretended friendly information with many thanks, declaring his hopes that his Majefty had a different opinion of his fervices, than to proceed againft him in that manner, and that he had too high an opinion of the governor, to fuppofe he would do any thing without warrant. When the friar found that his tricks were not attended by the effect

L l l   that

that he had flattered himself with, he remained much confused, and did not know what to say.

The new governor iffued public notice, that all who had complaints to make againft the former adminiftration of the country, fhould bring them forward, whether they were concerning Cortes, the civil, or the military officers. In confequence of this a hoft of accufers, litigants, and claimants, ftarted up. All the general's private enemies brought accufations againft him; others who had really juftice on their fide laid claim to what was due to them. Some alledged that they had not received their proper fhares of gold, others that they had not been fufficiently rewarded, and others demanded remuneration for their horfes killed in the wars, although they had gotten ten times the value in gold; and fome demanded fatisfaction for perfonal injuries. Juft at the period when the governor had opened his court to give a hearing to all the parties, it was God's will, and for our fins and misfortunes, that he fhould be taken fuddenly ill of a fever, and a lethargy coming on him he remained in that ftate four days. His three phyficians then advifed him to confefs and receive the facrament, which he did with great devotion, and appointed as his fucceffor in the government, Marcos de Aguilar who had come with him from Caftille. Some faid that the latter was only a bachelor and not a licentiate, and therefore incapable of acting; however the governor left him orders not to proceed further with the bufinefs of the court, but that all fhould be laid before his Majefty. On the ninth day from the time he was taken ill, the governor gave up his breath to our Lord. The whole city went into mourning on the occafion. The military deplored his lofs with particular reafon, for he certainly intended to redrefs all abufes, and to reward us according to our merits.

I heard an anecdote of him, at the time of his death, and it was this. He was of a gay difpofition and fond of mufic; to divert his lethargy, his attendants brought a lute, and played upon it in his apart-

ment;

ment; and they said that while they played him a favourite air, he beat time to it, and juft as it was finifhed he expired. What malignities and flanders were now circulated againft Cortes, by his enemies in Mexico! they faid that he and Sandoval had poifoned the governor, as he had before done Garay. The moft bufy in this malicious affair was the friar Ortiz. It appeared as if the veffel which brought them had been infected with the difeafe of which the governor died; above a hundred of thofe who came in it having died at fea or after landing. All the friars except a very few were fwept off, and the contagion pervaded the city of Mexico.

It was the wifh of thofe who were enemies to Cortes, that the enquiry fhould be proceeded on in the fame manner as was intended before the death of the late governor. Cortes afferted his readinefs, provided that the new governor Aguilar would take upon him the refponfibility of acting contrary to the teftament of his predeceffor. The council of Mexico however infifted that Aguilar was ineligible to that high fituation, on account of his age, infirmities, and other incapacities, which indeed were pretty evident. They therefore recommended that Cortes fhould be affociated with him, but he infifted on adhering ftrictly to the letter of the teftament of his predeceffor, and Cortes was alfo entirely adverfe to taking any fhare of the authority, for private reafons, fo that the whole weight refted on this poor hectic old man, who was obliged to drink goat's milk, and to be fuckled by a Caftillian woman to keep him alive.

I will now go to a diftance both in time and place, to relate that which happened to us on our journey to Mexico from Naco, where we were waiting to hear from Sandoval, who was to fend us notice of the failing of Cortes, which intelligence we never received, Saavedra, I have already mentioned, malicioufly fuppreffing the letters with which he was intrufted.

When

When our captain Marin and the reſt of us found that we were diſappointed, in the receipt of our expected intelligence, we determined to ſend a party to Truxillo to learn the truth. Accordingly ten of the cavalry, of which I was one, ſet out, and on our arrival at a place named Olancho, we learned from ſome Spaniards that Cortes had ſailed. This intelligence was ſoon after confirmed to us in a communication we had with Saavedra; we therefore returned to our Captain Marin with the good news, and ſoon after we all ſet out with joyful hearts for Mexico. I recollect we threw ſtones at the country we left behind us.

On our way, at a place called Maniani, we met five ſoldiers who had been ſent by Alvarado in ſearch of us. They were commanded by one of our veterans named Diego de Villanueva, a brave ſoldier. As ſoon as we had recognized each other and ſaluted, we enquired for his Captain Alvarado, who, he informed us was not far diſtant, and whom accordingly, after two days march farther, we fell in with. Our meeting took place at the town of Cholulteca Malalaca, and a third party joined us there, compoſed of captains under Pedro Arias de Avila, who met Alvarado's party to adjuſt ſome difference about bounds. We remained here together for three days. Alvarado at this time ſent one Gaſpar Arias de Avila, a confidential friend of his to treat with Captain Pedro Arias, about ſome particular buſineſs, I believe relative to a marriage; for Captain P. A. de Avila ſeemed much devoted to Alvarado.

Continuing our march, we croſſed a hoſtile country where the natives killed one of our ſoldiers, and wounded three others. The want of time prevented our puniſhing them as they deſerved. Further on, in Guatimala, they had alſo manned the paſſes againſt us, and we were detained three days in forcing our way; here I received a wound of an arrow, but it was of little conſequence. We then arrived at the valley where the city of Guatimala is now built, the people of which

were

were all hoftile; I recollect that here we had a number of fhocks of an earthquake, very long in their duration, and fo violent as to throw feveral of the foldiers to the ground.

When we paffed old Guatimala, the natives had affembled to give us an hoftile reception, but we drove them away before us, and took poffeffion of their magnificent dwellings and quadrangles, for that night, and on the enfuing day we hutted ourfelves on the plain, where we halted for ten days; during which time Alvarado fent fummons to the neighbouring Indians, to come in and fubmit. We delayed here to receive their anfwers, which none of them thought proper to fend. We then proceeded on our journey by long marches, until we reached the ftation of Alvarado's main force, at Olintepeque. After halting there for fome days we proceeded on towards Mexico, by Soconuzco, and Teguantepeque. On this march we loft two of our Spaniards, and the Mexican lord Juan Velafquez who had been a chief under Guatimotzin.

When we arrived at Guaxaca, we learned the news of the death of the governor Ponce de Leon. Anxioufly preffing forward for Mexico, we arrived at Chalco, from whence we fent forward meffengers to Cortes to inform him of our approach, and requefting that he would provide us good quarters, which we much required, for it was now two years and three months fince we fet out upon our expedition. As Cortes knew of our approach, he rode out with many cavaliers to meet us on the caufeway, and accompany us into the city. We went on our arrival, to the great church, to return our thanks to God. From thence we attended the general to his palace, where he had a fumptuous entertainment provided for us. Alvarado went to his refidence in the fortrefs, of which he had been appointed alcalde. Luis Marin went to lodge with Sandoval, and I and another friend named Captain Luis Sanchez, were taken by Andrez de Tapia to his houfe. Sandoval

and

and all our friends, and Cortes among the reft, fent us prefents of neceffaries, as alfo gold and cocoa for our expences.

On the next day my friend and I, accompanied by Sandoval and Andres de Tapia, proceeded to wait upon the governor Aguilar, who received us with much politenefs, but declared his inability to make any new arrangements, the whole being left to his Majefty's arbitration; but that if he was authorifed, he would do every thing that lay in his power to give us fatisfaction. At this time arrived from the Ifland of Cuba, Diego de Ordaz whom I have already mentioned as the circulator of the report of our deaths; he was feverely taxed for his impropriety, but moft folemnly denied it to us, averring that he had only written an account of the unfortunate affair at Xicalonga as it really happened, and any mifreprefentation that was made, the factor was accountable for; and for the truth of what he afferted he referred to his letters. Cortes had at this time too much bufinefs on his hands to embarrafs himfelf any further with this; he therefore thought proper to drop it, and endeavour to refcue his property, which had been difpofed of upon the fuppofition of his death. A great part of it had been appropriated to the expences of celebrating his funeral fervice, and to the faying maffes for his foul and ours, to give credit to the report; and thefe perpetual maffes which had been fo purchafed out of the property of Cortes upon the fuppofition of his death, and for the good of his foul, were now that he was found to be alive, and no longer to be in need of them, purchafed by one Juan de Caceres, for the benefit of his own foul, whenever he was to die; fo that Cortes was more removed from the re-attainment of his property than ever.

Ordas who was a wife man and one of experience in worldly affairs, feeing that Cortes was neglected and had fallen in public eftimation fince his being fuperceded by the governor Ponce de Leon, advifed him to affume more confequence and a more ftately appearance than his natural difpofition prompted him to, in order to maintain the refpect that

was

was due to him; but such was his natural plainness of manners, that he never at any time liked to be called otherwise than simply, Cortes, and truly it was a great and noble name in itself, and as much revered as Cæsar's and Pompey's in the time of the Romans, Hannibal's among the Carthaginians, or in our time that of Gonzalo Hernandez, or the most valiant and ever invincible Diego Garcia de Paredes. Ordaz also informed Cortes of the report that was circulated through Mexico, of its being his intention to put the factor to death privately in jail; and he warned him of the man being powerfully patronised.

The treasurer Estrada at this time married off two of his daughters; one to Jorge de Alvarado, another to Don Luis de Guzman son to the Count De Castellar. It was then settled that Pedro de Alvarado should go to Castille to solicit the government of Guatimala, and he in the mean time sent his brother Jorge to that province with a force of our allies of different nations, to reduce it. The governor also about that period sent a force against the province of Chiapa under the command of Don Juan Enriquez de Guzman, a near relation of the duke of Medina Sidonia; an other to the province of Tabasco under Balthasar Ossorio, and a third against the Zapotecan mountaineers under Alonzo de Herrera, one of our veterans.

After lingering for eight months, the governor Marcos de Aguilar gave up the ghost, leaving by testament the treasurer Alonzo de Estrada his successor. At this time, the council of Mexico and many principal Spaniards were solicitous that Cortes should be associated with the treasurer in the government, the latter appearing entirely incompetent at the present juncture, more particularly for the following reason. Nuno de Guzman who had for two years governed the province of Panuco, was a man of a most furious and tyrannical disposition, arbitrarily extending the bounds of his jurisdiction, and putting to death all who dared to oppose his will. Thus Pedro Gonzalez de Truxillo, a person of noble condition, asserting with truth that his district was a dependency of

Mexico,

Mexico, the other without any ceremony ordered him to be immediately hanged, which was accordingly done, contrary to all juftice. He alfo put many other Spaniards to death, apparently for no reafon except to make himfelf feared, and fet the authority of the governor of Mexico at defiance. In order therefore to curb the infolence of Guzman, it was the wifh of many that Cortes fhould take a fhare in the government, but he was utterly adverfe to it, knowing the difficulties, and the dangerous power and more dangerous malignity of his enemies, for as ufual, upon the death of Aguilar the ftory was again induftri-oufly circulated, that it was owing to poifon given him by Cortes.

It was determined on the peremptory refufal of the latter, that Sandoval who was alguazil major, fhould act conjointly with the trea-furer, and he was willingly accepted as an affociate by him. His firft bufinefs on entering into office was, to endeavour to bring to juftice one Ruano, who had fled from Mexico for fome crime. He fince became a rich man, for, efcaping for the prefent, he eluded juftice altogether, though Sandoval did his utmoft to apprehend him.

Certain perfons, the inveterate and active enemies of Cortes, now perfuaded the treafurer to write to Caftille, to reprefent at court, that he had been compelled by the influence of Cortes, to affociate Sandoval with him in the government, contrary to his inclination, and to his Majef-ty's fervice. They by the fame opportunity tranfmitted a volume of malignant falfehoods, which they had raked up againft the general, fuch as that he had poifoned Luis Ponce de Leon, and Marcos de Agui-lar the governors, as alfo the Adelantado Garay, and that he had en-deavoured to adminifter arfenic in cheefecakes to a number of people at a feaft. Alfo that he was plotting the fecret murders of the veedor and factor in jail. All which lies were fupported by the induftry of the contador Albornoz, who was then in Caftille. He was alfo charged ftrongly as to the death of his firft wife, and thefe things being thus urged, Cortes was in part judged unheard, an order being fent to releafe the

the veedor and factor, and an officer named Don Pedro de la Cueva commendador major of Alcantara, was ordered to go with three hundred soldiers, at the cost of Cortes, and in case of his guilt being proved, to inflict the punishment of death upon him, and distribute his property amongst the veteran conquerors of Mexico. This was however to be done under the judgment of a royal court of audience, to be present upon the spot for the purpose. All these preparations however ended in nothing; for neither Don Pedro de la Cueva, nor the court of royal audience ever arrived.

The treasurer was now greatly elevated by the countenance which he received at court, and which he attributed to his being considered a son of the catholic king. He disposed of governments at his pleasure, sending his relation Mazariejos to make enquiry into the conduct of Don Juan Enriquez de Guzman in Chiapa, where they say more pillage and plunder took place than ought to have done. He also sent a force against the Zapotecans and Minxes under one De Barrios, said to be a brave soldier, and who had served in Italy. I do not mean Barrios of Seville, the brother-in-law of Cortes. This officer marched against them with a hundred soldiers, but the natives surprised him one night, and killed him with seven more of the party. Such was the difference between us the veteran conquerors, and these raw half formed soldiers, who did not know the arts and stratagems of the enemy. The governor also sent a hundred of the new soldiers, under the command of a particular friend named Figuero, to the province of Guaxaca. On his route by the Zapotecans, Figuero fell in with a captain left in command there by Marcos de Aguilar, named Alonzo Herrera, and some dispute arising between them, swords were drawn, Herrera wounding Figuero, and three other soldiers who were with him. Figuero finding himself not able to go into the field, and his soldiers not being fit for expeditions in the mountains, thought proper to search for and break open the sepulchres, in which the ancient chiefs of those countries were interred, to make prize of the gold, which according to

M m m   custom cuftom was buried with them. In this manner he collected to the value of above one hundred thoufand crowns, and with this wealth, which was increafed by prefents, he fet off for Mexico, leaving the provinces in a worfe ftate than he found them. From Mexico he went to Vera Cruz, and embarking for Caftille, the veffel in which he failed was loft in a gale of wind, and he and all his wealth went to the bot- ton. The bufinefs of fubjecting thefe Indians was finally left to us, the conquerors of Guacacualco, who at length brought them to peace, for their cuftom was to fubmit during the fummer, and to break into rebel- lion as foon as the torrents made their country inacceffible. I was on three expeditions againft them. The town of St. Alfonfo is now built there, to keep them in fubjection.

When the governor heard how his friend had been maltreated by Figucro, he fent the officers of juftice to apprehend him; he however efcaped to the rocks and woods, but they took a foldier who ufed to accompany him, and brought him prifoner to Mexico, where, without a hearing, the governor ordered his right hand to be ftruck off. His name was Cortejo, and by birth he was a gentleman.

A fervant of Sandoval alfo at this time wounded a fervant of the treafurer, in a quarrel. The treafurer had him arrefted, and command- ed his right hand to be cut off. Cortes and Sandoval were at this time at a place called Quernavaca, partly from motives of prudence. On hearing of this infult they pofted off to Mexico, and it is faid that Cor- tes ufed fuch expreffions to the treafurer upon the fubject, as to put the latter in fear of his life. He called his friends about him to form a guard for his perfon, and immediately releafed the veedor and factor from jail. By their advice the governor was then induced to iffue an order, for the inftant expulfion of Cortes from Mexico. This being reprefented to Cortes, he declared his readinefs to obey, fince it was the will of God, that he who had gained that city, at the expence of his beft blood, by day and by night, fhould be banifhed from it, by the

bafe

bafe and unworthy: and that he would fet out immediately, and de-mand juftice from his Majefty.

Inftantly therefore quitting the city, he went to one of his country refidences at Cuyoacan, from whence in a few days he proceeded to-wards the coaft. At this time the lady of the treafurer, a perfon well worthy of memory for her many virtues, feeing the dangerous confe-quences likely to refult from his abfurd and arbitrary conduct, expoftu-lated with him on it, reminding him of the many favours he had re-ceived from Cortes, the ingratitude with which he had repaid him, and the many friends that Cortes had. Thefe reprefentations are faid to have operated on the mind of the treafurer, fo as to caufe fincere repentance of the fteps that he had taken.

At this time arrived in New Spain Fray Julian Garrios, firft bifhop of Tlafcala, and who in honour to our lord the moft chriftian Emperor was named Carolenfe. When this reverend prelate heard of the pro-ceedings of the governor againft Cortes, he was highly difpleafed with them, and two days after his arrival in Mexico where he was received with great pomp, at the requeft of the governor, he undertook to me-diate betwixt them. Many of thefe feditious perfons fuch as there are in all focieties, knowing the diffatisfaction of Cortes, offered him their fervices if he would fet himfelf up as an independent monarch, in New Spain. Thefe people he immediately arrefted, threatening to put them to death, and he wrote directly to the bifhop of Tlafcala, to inform him of the treafon. He had alfo received fimilar offers from Mexico, which he treated in the fame manner. The reports of what was going on however, fo terrified the veedor and factor, who did not know to what extent Cortes might be induced to go, that they became inceffant in their folicitations to the governor to accelerate the departure of the bifhop of Tlafcala. This prelate having waited upon Cortes, and found every part of his conduct perfectly to his fatisfaction, wrote back to Mexico to inform the government there of the refult of his obfervations;

Mmm 2

the

the unalterable determination of Cortes to go to Old Spain, and a fevere cenfure from himfelf, upon the mifconduct of thofe who had been the caufe of his quitting Mexico. I do not know whether Cortes returned to that city in order to arrange his private concerns, but he appointed feveral agents for that purpofe, the principal of whom was the licenti-ate Altamirano. He brought with him from Mexico many curiofities of the country for his Majefty, fuch as various kinds of birds unknown in Europe, two tigers, many barrels of ambergris and indurated balfam, and another kind that refembled oil, four Indians expert at playing the ftick with their feet, other Indian dancers who had a manner of appear-ing as if they flew in the air, three humpbacked dwarfs of extraordinary deformity, and alfo fome male and female Indians whofe fkins were remarkable for their whitenefs, and who have a natural defect of vifion. He was alfo attended by feveral young chiefs of the Tlafcalan and Mex-ican nations, whom he confented to take to Europe with him, at their own requefts.

CHAPTER IX.

Cortes goes to Europe; is created Marquis of the Valley.
of Guaxaca. Account of various transactions and occurrences.
in Old and New Spain. Death and character of the Marquis
of the Valley.

CORTES now received letters from the president of the Indies, the
Duke of Bejar, and several other of his friends, informing him of the
necessity of his appearance in Castille; to do away the malignant accusations of his enemies. Others also informed him of the death of his father
Martin Cortes. Having performed the funeral obsequies to his father,
he ordered two ships to be purchased, which he stored with such quantities of provisions of every kind, that the overplus when he arrived in
Spain, would have sufficed for a two years voyage.

For making these preparations he employed his major domo who
was named Esquival. This officer crossing the lake of Mexico to Ayotcingo in a large canoe with six Indian rowers and one Negro, and having some ingots of gold in his possession, was way-laid and murdered
somewhere on the lake. The manner of his death never was known,
neither canoe, Indians, or Negro, ever being traced. The body of
Esquival was found four days after in a small island, half eaten by birds
of prey. There were many suspicions entertained about this affair; the
man was said to be a great boaster of the favours he received from the
ladies. There were also other bad stories told of him, which gave rise
to suspicions of such a nature as I cannot relate; no great enquiry was
made

made as to his death, God pardon him his fins! Cortes appointed other officers to complete the preparations for his voyage. He offered by proclamation a free paffage to all fuch Spaniards' as obtained a permiffion from the government to go to Caftille, and a fupply of provifions to them on the voyage.

All things being ready, and having confeffed and comulgated, he embarked in company with Sandoval, Tapia, and other cavaliers, and after a voyage of forty one days arrived in Europe, difembarking near the town of Palos; as foon as he fet his foot on fhore he fell on his knees, to return thanks to God for his mercies. His arrival in Old Spain was in the month of December in the year one thoufand five hundred and twenty feven. To good fortune fucceeded grief, by the death of the brave Captain Sandoval, after a lingering ficknefs, at his lodgings in the houfe of a rope maker at Palos, who, in his prefence, robbed him of thirteen bars of gold. This rogue perceiving his weak fituation, fent his fervants on a pretended meffage from Sandoval to Cortes, who was then at Nueftra Senora de la Ravida, and having the houfe to himfelf, went into Sandoval's room, and breaking open his cheft, took out the gold, while our poor friend lay in bed unable to refift him, and apprehenfive, if he made any outcry, that the fellow would fmother him in the bedclothes. As foon as he had got the gold he made his efcape with it into Portugal, where he could not be purfued. Cortes fhortly after arrived, and was informed of what had happened, but purfuit was too late. Sandoval then grew worfe every hour, and the phyficians recommended confeffion; which being done, and having received the holy facrament, in a fhort time after he gave up the ghoft, but not before he had made a will, whereby he left his property to a fifter who afterwards married a natural fon of the Count de Medelin. Sandoval died univerfally regretted. His funeral was attended by a great train of mourners, among whom was Cortes. God pardon him his fins! amen.

Cortes

Cortes fent an exprefs to his Majefty, and alfo to his patrons at court, informing them of his arrival, and alfo of the death of his friend Sandoval, whofe merits and fervices were known to his Majefty, and for whofe lofs he was pleafed to exprefs great regret. The Duke of Bejar and the Count of Aguilar, on receiving the intelligence, waited on his Majefty, but found him in poffeffion of it by the letter of Cortes. His Majefty feemed to have at prefent a conviction of that officer's loyalty, for which his friend the Duke of Bejar had been three times obliged to engage his life, for he was pleafed to order that in all the cities and towns through which Cortes paffed, he fhould be received with the higheft honour.

When he arrived at Seville he was entertained there by the Duke of Medina Sidonia, who made him a prefent of feveral beautiful horfes. From thence he proceeded, to attend the nine days devotions to our Lady of Guadeloupe. Donna Maria, wife of the commendador Don Francifco de los Cobos, with many other ladies of great rank arrived at the fame time. As foon as Cortes had paid his devotions, given charity to the poor, and ordered mafs to be faid, he went attended by all his retinue of cavaliers to pay his refpects to Donna Maria, the beautiful lady her fifter, and the many others of diftinguifhed rank who were in her company. Here Cortes had an opportunity of exhibiting that politenefs, gallantry, and generofity, in which he furpaffed all men. He made prefents of golden ornaments of great value, to all, but more efpecially to Donna Maria and her fifter: and to each lady he gave a penache of green feathers, richly ornamented with gold. He then produced his Indian dancers who threw the flick from one foot to another, to the aftonifhment of the fpectators, and in addition to all this, underftanding that one of the mules belonging to the fifter of Donna Maria was unable to travel, he caufed to be purchafed for her two of the fineft that could be procured for money. He alfo waited the departure of thofe ladies for the court, attending them upon the journey and providing magnificent entertainments for them, the honours of which he did

with

with a grace peculiar to himſelf, infomuch that Donna Maria de Mendoza began to entertain thoughts of an alliance between her ſiſter and Cortes. However in marriages as in other caſes it is the hand of God which leads us, and therefore no more need be ſaid upon the ſubject. Donna Maria was ſo taken with the politeneſs and generoſity of Cortes, that ſhe wrote to the commendador of Leon ſaying, that the fame of Cortes and his heroic actions was far ſhort of the judgment which muſt be formed of him, by thoſe who had the good fortune of his acquaintance, and brought over her huſband completely to his intereſt.

When our general arrived at court, his Majeſty was pleaſed to appoint the apartments to receive him, and his friends came out in a body to meet him on the road. On the enſuing day he went by permiſſion to throw himſelf at his Majeſty's feet, being attended by the Duke of Bejar, the admiral of the Indies, and the commendador of Leon. His Majeſty commanded him to riſe, and Cortes, after a ſhort enumeration of his ſervices, and vindication of his conduct from the aſperſions of his enemies, preſented a memorial wherein the whole was fully detailed. His Majeſty having received it, commanded him to riſe, and immediately honoured him with the title of Marquis del Valle, and the order of St. Jago. He alſo gave him an eſtate to maintain his new dignity, and confirmed him captain general of New Spain and of the ſouth ſeas. Cortes, thus loaded with honours, retired from the royal preſence to receive in a few days a ſtill greater than all. Shortly after his arrival in Toledo he fell dangerouſly ill; when the Emperor heard it, he did him the honour of paying him a viſit in perſon. He however recovered in a ſhort time, and the particular favour of his Majeſty encouraged him to aſſume a rank and character equal to his high title. One ſunday that his Majeſty was at maſs in the cathedral, and ſeated according to cuſtom with his nobility each in his proper ſtation, Cortes, deſignedly as it is ſaid, came there late, and after all were ſeated; and paſſing before the whole of them, took his place next to the

the Count de Nafao, who was neareft to the Emperor. This gave great offence to many though others faid it was by the Emperor's defire. Indeed Cortes began to feel his elevation fo much, that it made him not hold fome of his former patrons in the eftimation he ought, all his attention being beftowed on the Duke of Bejar, the Count de Nafao, and the admiral. Thinking that now the ball was at his foot with the fupport of fuch great men, he applied to the Emperor for the government of New Spain; this requeft, though fupported by his patrons, did not fucceed, his Majefty thinking he had done fufficiently and that fome of his attention was due to thofe conquerors, by whofe affiftance he had gained that country. From this time Cortes did not feem fo much in favour as before.

His Majefty was then proceeding on his journey to Flanders. After his departure, the marriage took place between the Marquis del Valle, and Donna Juana de Zuniga, on which occafion he prefented his lady with the moft magnificent jewels that ever had been in Caftille. Her Majefty Queen Ifabella, from the account given by the lapidaries, expreffed a wifh to have fome, which Cortes accordingly prefented her with, but it is faid that they were not fo fine or fo valuable as thofe which he gave to his lady.

I will now relate fome other circumftances, fuch as I have heard concerning him while he refided in Caftille. One was, that Queen Ifabella was not his friend on account of the appearances of ingratitude in his conduct to his patrons, and alfo in confequence of the inferiority of the prefents which he made her. However fhe ordered in the Emperor's abfence, that he fhould have every fupport from the council of the Indies. Cortes at this time obtained permiffion to fit out two fhips on a voyage of difcovery to the fouth feas, with a condition that he fhould enjoy certain rights and revenues from whatever lands were acquired to the crown of Spain. Don Pedro de la Cueva was at this time at court; this was the officer who was to have gone to Mexico to try, and

if

if found guilty, to execute Cortes. They were now on the most amicable and intimate footing. Don Pedro told him that even his innocence would have been fufficiently expenfive to him, as the cofts of the expedition, which he muft have paid, amounted to upwards of three hundred thoufand crowns. All thofe, and other particulars we received an account of in private letters, as well from the Marquis del Valle, as from other perfons. He now fent a gentleman to Rome, to kifs the feet of his Holinefs Pope Clement, and with a rich prefent of gold, filver, and jewels. He alfo fent fome of the Indians who played with the ftick, and a full memorial of all circumftances concerning the newly difcovered country. He alfo took this opportunity to fupplicate for a partial remiffion of the tithes of New Spain.

This gentleman, Juan de Herrada, was a brave foldier, who attended Cortes in his expedition to Honduras. After he returned from Europe he went to Peru, where Don Diego de Almagro left him in the office of governor to his fon. He was highly in the confidence of this family, and ferved as Maeftre de Campo to the young Almagro; he was alfo captain of the party which killed Don Francifco Pizarro the elder.

His Holinefs on the receipt of the letters returned thanks to God for the opportunity of making fo many thoufand converts to the holy faith. He alfo praifed the fervices rendered by us, to the church and our monarch, and fent us bulls of indulgence from penalties of our fins, with others for churches and hofpitals. In regard to the tithes, I do not know what was done. The Indians were brought to dance before his Holinefs and the cardinals, who expreffed their high fatisfaction at their performances. After Herrada had concluded his bufinefs at Rome, he returned with a liberal reward from Pope Clement, who gave him the title and rank of count palatine, and wrote by him, ftrongly requefting for him a grant of a confiderable plantation in New Spain, which he never received, and in confequence went to Peru.

While

While Cortes was in Castille, the members of the royal court of audience arrived in Mexico. Nuno de Guzman formerly governor of Panuco was the president. The Oydors were, four licentiates, by name Matienzo, Delgadillo, Maldonado, (I do not mean Alonzo Maldonado the good who was governor of Guatimala) and Parada. These magistrates from their first arrival shewed a determination to do justice. They were armed with greater powers than any officers ever sent by his Majesty to New Spain. They were also intrusted with the management of the final partition of landed property, wherein his Majesty had particularly charged them to take care of the interests of the conquerors. On their arrival, they issued a proclamation, requiring the attendance of an agent from each settlement, with memorials and returns of the several districts. The agents all arrived in the course of a few days. I was then in Mexico on my office of procurador sindico of the town of Guacacualco; I posted off to the last mentioned place, in order to attend at the election of the agents, about which there was a violent contest but plurality of voices decided it in favour of Captain Luis Marin and myself. When we arrived at Mexico we found that two of the oydors were dead of pleurisies, and that the factor Salazar had acquired so complete an ascendency over the others, that they did nothing but as he advised them. It was lucky for Cortes that he was not at Mexico; the death of the two oydors would have been certainly laid to his charge.

The agents now called loudly for a final repartition; but the factor had persuaded the president and oydors, not to agree to that which would be a diminution of their influence, by taking so much patronage out of their hands. It was also settled, that Salazar should go to Europe to solicit the government of New Spain for the president Guzman. He actually sailed, but being overtaken by a storm was shipwrecked on the coast near Guacacualco, from whence he returned to Mexico. The treasurer Estrada died in a short time after his being superseded, which he was more by his own tameness than from any right they could prove

from

from his Majefty's orders, for they were, that he fhould govern folely; nor was any thing faid of affociating Guzman with him; whereas the latter ufurped the government to himfelf entirely, from the time he was appointed prefident of the court. He was much regretted by all, having conducted himfelf in fuch a manner as to give univerfal fatisfaction, nor would he have wanted fupport if he had infifted on maintaining his office.

A commiffion was appointed at Guatimala, where Jorge de Alvarado was eftablifhed, but I do not know the refult of it.

In Mexico they proceeded with great feverity againft the Marquis del Valle. The factor efpecially took the opportunity to revile and flander him in the groffeft manner, and fouleft expreffions. The Marquis's friend the licentiate Altamarano remonftrated with the court upon thefe indecencies, but to no good effect, for the factor, countenanced by Guzman and the reft, became more abufive than before. The court was thereby thrown into confufion; for Altamirano was at laft fo provoked as to draw his poniard, and would have put the factor to death had it not been for the interference of thofe prefent. Altimirano was carried to the fortrefs, the other was fent to his houfe, and the whole city was in an uproar. The licentiate, upon our fupplication, was at the end of three days releafed from confinement, and the prefent matter was made up; but a greater ftorm fucceeded, for at this time there arrived in Mexico one Zavalos, a relation of the Captain Pamfillo de Narvaez, who had been fent by the wife of the latter in queft of her hufband, who had gone as governor to the river of Palmas, and was fuppofed to have been loft or dead. When Zavalos arrived in Mexico, inftigated as is fuppofed by the members of the court, he lodged informations againft all the foldiers of Cortes who had been concerned in the attack upon Narvaez. Of courfe nearly the whole of us who were in the city, and myfelf amongft the reft, amounting in all to about two hundred and fifty, were apprehended, brought to trial, and convicted.

We

We were fentenced to pay a fine of a certain quantity of gold, and to be banifhed to the diftance of five leagues from Mexico. However the fentence was but flightly enforced, the banifhment being remitted and very few paying the fine.

The enemies of the Marquis del Valle now took a new ground of attack againft him, which was, that he had embezzled the treafure of Montezuma and Guatimotzin, and that he was anfwerable to the fol- diers, not only for that which he had appropriated to his own ufe, but alfo for that which he had fent to Europe as a prefent to his Majefty, and which had been captured by the corfair Juan Florin. A long ca- talogue of other demands followed, every one of which he was con- demned upon, and his property fold for the payment. One Juan Xu- ares his brother-in-law was alfo at this time brought forward, to demand juftice in open court for the murder of his fifter Donna Catalina, offer- ing to produce witneffes of the manner of her death. Many of us the friends of the Marquis, feeing the attacks that were made againft him, met by appointment and under the licence of an alcalde, at the houfe of one Garcia Holguin, where we entered into a refolution to renounce all claim to the treafure; but when the oydors heard our bufinefs, they ordered us all to be arrefted, as they alleged, for meeting without per- miffion. We produced to them the licence which we had obtained for the purpofe, but they, to keep up appearances, banifhed us to the diftance of five leagues from Mexico. We were however allowed to re- turn; though we ftill thought ourfelves hardly treated enough.

New matter for confufion was now brought forward; a proclama- tion was iffued that all perfons of Indian defcent, or of that of Moors, who had been burned or *enfanbenited by the holy inquifition, as far as the fourth degree from their anceftors who had thus fuffered, fhould quit New Spain within four months from the date thereof, on pain of lofing one half of their properties. It was moft wonderful to fee what hofts of accufers and informers ftarted up at once on this occafion, and what

* San Benito; a drefs put on criminals.

what slanders and infamies were brought forward. At last it ended in the expulsion of two individuals.

The court was generous in fulfilling his Majesty's commands, in regard to the old conquerors, who were all well provided for; the greatest error it committed was, the excessive licence given to the branding slaves. So many were made in the province of Panuco that it became almost depopulated. The president Guzman, who was of a noble and liberal disposition, made a new year's gift of a whole district named Guazpaltepeque, to Albornoz who was newly returned from Spain. He brought with him his Majesty's patent, under which he erected some sugar works in Cempoal, which went to ruin after a few years. The oydor Delgadillo was censured on account of his free gifts, for it was noticed that some rent was reserved to himself in them, and the consequent extortions and oppressions of those he patronised were excessive. The conduct of Guzman was equally reprehensible; as to the other oydor, Matienzo, he was superannuated. The abuses of this court came at length to such an excess, that it was thought proper by the higher powers in Europe, completely to supercede it, and substitute one composed of persons of more discretion. Old Matienzo who was the least objectionable, was sent to Panuco to enquire into and remedy the abuses which had been committed there. This officer ordered accounts or lists of the slaves to be drawn out, to prevent them from being arbitrarily transported from one province to another, and he revoked the grants which the president and the other oydor had made to their friends and clients, bestowing the plantations upon those persons who were pointed out by his Majesty's instructions. Every one then who had acquired the plantations which they were to deliver up, insisted that they had been granted as a reward of former merits, the proofs of which they endeavoured to adduce, and utterly disclaimed all patronage or protection from the president and oydor. The confusion was extreme. However many if not almost all succeeded in keeping

what

what they had got, the only perfons deprived being Albornoz of his new year's gift, one Villaroel, and Villegas.

As foon as the members of the court heard that they were to be fuperceded, they refolved to difpatch agents to Caftille with plenty of witneffes, fuch as were fit and well prepared for their purpofe, to vouch for the propriety of their conduct. It was determined to proceed to the election of the agents who were to be fent on this occafion, and for this purpofe all the veteran conquerors, with many other perfons of confideration, met in the great church, where the perfon was to be chofen by vote. Guzman and the oydors recommended the factor Salazar, and although they had committed fome improprieties, yet as they had in the main acted fo well by us in the diftribution of property, we were all well inclined to vote for the perfon recommended by them, and which they expected us to do. When we had all affembled for the purpofe in the great church, there was fuch a noife and outcry fet up by perfons who had no bufinefs there, but had crouded in, that it was hardly poffible to proceed to the election. It was ordered that all who had not been fummoned fhould quit the place, but it was to no effect; they would not go, and at laft the queftion was obliged to be put to the whole. Since thofe who had no bufinefs there would neither quit the place nor be filent, it may be judged what kind of an election it was. When we perceived how matters were going, it was agreed amongft us to adjourn until the following day, at the houfe of the prefident of the council, and none were fummoned but perfons of one way of thinking. Of courfe it was amicably decided. In confequence of an adjuftment, two agents were to be chofen, one, Anthonio de Carvajal, on the part of the oydors, and another, Bernardino Vafquez de Tapia, on that of Cortes. However it appeared to me that both were equally devoted to the views of the prefident; and it was natural enough, for the latter had rendered much more fervice to our intereft in his fhort time, than Cortes had done during the long period of his power. But fuch is the natural loyalty of the Spaniards, that we were more attached

to

to Cortes, from his having been our captain, than he was to our interefts, although he had his Majefty's orders to attend to them. Of this a proof now occurred, for the prefident and oydors intrigued for an application to be made to his Majefty, in manner of a petition, againft the appointment or return of Cortes to New Spain, at any future time. The grounds upon which they moved it were, the dangers that would occur from public difturbances and factions, which might end in the lofs of the country. This we oppofed with all our might, and Alvarado, being at this time arrived in Mexico with the office of governor and adelantado of Guatimala, and a commandery of St. Jago, it was agreed between him and the friends of Cortes, to lay before his Majefty a ftatement of the whole affair, with the views of the members of the council; and it hereby appearing to the fupreme court of the Indies, that all thefe meafures were guided by paffion and intereft, it confirmed the original determination to fupercede Guzman and the oydors. The prefence of Cortes in Spain alfo at this period was highly favourable to his interefts, and he now was rapidly proceeding to the pinnacle of his fortune.

When Nuno de Guzman had received certain intelligence from Old Spain of his being fuperceded, he determined to go upon an expedition to the province of Xalifco, now called New Gallicia. For this purpofe he collected the greateft force that he was able in Mexico, partly of volunteers, and partly of fuch as he compelled to join him by the weight of power of which he was not yet deprived. Thofe who did not ferve perfonally he compelled to find, or pay for fubftitutes, and thofe who had horfes were obliged to give them for half their value. He brought with him a number of Mexicans as foldiers, or to convey his baggage, and cruelly oppreffed the provinces through which he paffed. In Mechoacan he obtained a great quantity of gold, which the inhabitants had collected and amaffed for ages paft; it was much lowered in value by a mixture of filver. The unfortunate chief of the province, not being able to gratify his avarice to its full extent, he firft
commanded

commanded him to be put to the torture by burning his feet, and afterwards upon some trifling and false allegations caused him to be hanged, which was one of the wickedest and cruellest actions ever committed by an officer, and as such it was confidered by every Spaniard in his army. He brought from this province also a number of natives loaded with booty, to the city of Compostello, which he founded at a heavy expence to his Majesty and the inhabitants of Mexico. Here Guzman remained until his arrest.

As I have before related, in consequence of the injustice practised by the former court of audience, his Majesty was pleased to suppress it and cancel all its grants. He also appointed a new one, composed of wise and upright members, whereof D. Sebastian Ramirez de Villaescasa bishop of St. Domingo was president, and the licentiates Maldonado de Salamanca, Zainos de Toro, Vasco de Quiroga de Madrigal afterwards bishop of Mechoacan, and Solomon de Madrid were oydors. These officers being arrived, the court opened its sittings, which was notified by a proclamation, in consequence whereof there assembled such crouds of complainants, from city, towns, and country, of all descriptions, settlers, agents, and native chiefs, alledging acts of partiality and oppression against the former court, and demanding justice, that the members were quite astonished. The demands of the agents of Cortes for what had been unjustly alienated from him, if they had been all to be now repaid, would have amounted to above two hundred thousand crowns. Nuno de Guzman being absent, the whole blame was laid upon him by the other members of the old court, who alledged that they were compelled to act as he thought proper to order them. He was accordingly summoned to appear, which he did not think proper to do, and in the present circumstances it was judged most expedient to refer the affair to the supreme court in Europe: which being done, a civil officer named Torre, a licentiate and native of Badajos, was sent with full power, to the province of Xalisco, and with orders to transmit Guzman to Mexico and commit him to the common goal.

O o o   He

He had alfo a commiffion to indemnify us in the cofts which we had been fined upon the affair of Narvaez, and thofe at the time that we were arrefted, as I have already related. But I will now take leave for the prefent of the licentiate Torre, and return to the affairs of the court.

The properties of Delgadillo and Matienzo were fold to pay the damages of thofe who had gained their caufes againft them, and their perfons were imprifoned for the deficiency. A brother of Delgadillo who was alcalde major in Guaxaca, was fined and imprifoned for the fame reafon; he died in jail, as did another who was alcalde amongft the Zapotecans, and certainly the new judges were fo wife and juft, that they confidered nothing but what was in compliance with the will of God and his Majefty. They alfo fhewed a laudable anxiety for the converfion of the Indians to our holy faith, and immediately prohibited the branding them for flaves, and made many other good regulations. After four years thus employed, the oydors Solomon and Zaynos petitioned for leave to retire, being both of an advanced age, and very wealthy, and his Majefty in confideration of their eminent fervices, was pleafed to grant their requeft. The prefident alfo, by command of his Majefty, repaired to Europe, to give an account of the affairs of this country. He was then bifhop of St. Domingo, but was advanced in fucceffion through the fees of Toro, Leon, and Cuenca, with fuch celerity, that the bulls had hardly a day's interval between them. He was alfo prefident of the royal chancery of Valladolid, and while in poffeffion of thefe honours he was feized by death, and placed in glory among the virtuous, according to the promife of our holy faith, for he was a true and upright judge. He had been before his promotion to a bifhopric, inquifitor in Seville. The good conduct of the oydor Maldonado was rewarded with the government of the provinces of Guatimala, Honduras, and Viragua, and with the title of adelantado of Yucatan, and the oydor Quiroga obtained the bifhopric of Mechoacan. Such were the rewards of the good judges! Delgadillo and Matienzo

returned

returned to Caſtille in poverty, where, as I have heard, they died in the courſe of two or three years.

At this time his Majeſty was pleaſed to appoint to the vice-royalty of New Spain, the moſt illuſtrious and worthy cavalier of praiſe worthy memory, D. Anthonio de Mendoza brother to the Marquis of Montejar. There alſo came as oydors the doctor Queſada, the licentiate Tejada de Logrono, and the licentiate Loayſa native of Cuidad Real; he was an old man, and ſtayed three or four years in Mexico; and during that time having collected a good ſum of money, he took his leave of the country at the expiration of it, and returned to his home. There was alſo another licentiate who came out as oydor, who was named Santillana; but the licentiate Maldonado had not then vacated his office. All were excellent magiſtrates. As ſoon as they had opened the court, free enquiry was proclaimed into the conduct of their predeceſſors, which was found to be in every reſpect conformable to juſtice.

The Viceroy, on his arrival, knowing that the licentiate Torre was ſent out with orders to arreſt Nuno de Guzman, to ſave Guzman from that inſult ſent to him to come to Mexico, which he having complied with, the Viceroy aſſigned him apartments in his palace, and treated him with much politeneſs. Juſt about this time Torre arrived with his Majeſty's orders to arreſt Guzman, but with directions to communicate them to the Viceroy. It ſeems that the licentiate did not find the ſupport to his ſtrong meaſures that he expected, and this exaſperating his natural violence, he in conſequence went to the Viceroy's palace, and there furiouſly ſeized, and dragged Guzman to the common jail, ſaying he did it by his Majeſty's order, and that he cared for nothing further. Here Guzman remained for ſeveral days, and was at laſt releaſed on the interceſſion of the Viceroy. It was well known that Torre had ſtrong powers given to him to act diſcretionarily in regard to Guzman.

This licentiate was much addicted to card playing, although he

did

did not game deeply, playing only at triumpho and primero for paſtime. His propenſity being however well known, ſome friend of Guzman's took advantage of it, to mortify and turn him into ridicule, and the method which was taken to do it was as follows. The civilians at that time wore gowns with looſe hanging ſleeves, into one of which ſomebody maliciouſly put a pack of cards, and contrived it in ſuch a manner, that as Torre was walking acroſs the crouded ſquare of Mexico, in company with ſeveral perſons of quality, a dexterous twitch being given, the cards began to drop from his ſleeve, leaving a long trail of them after him as he went on. Thoſe who ſaw it laughed and called the attention of others to the cards coming out of the licentiate's ſleeve; but when he found out what the joke was, and that he was the ſubject of it, being naturally choleric, it enraged him exceedingly, and he went off ſaying he ſaw clearly it was their intention to prevent his doing juſtice, but he would, though he died for it; and that his Majeſty ſhould know the indignity that had been offered to his officer. Either from vexation, or a calenture natural to the climate, with which he was ſeized juſt after this, he died in the courſe of a few days, whereby the affair of Guzman, luckily for him, was reſpited for the preſent.

Cortes having now been a long time in Caſtille, married to the niece of the Duke of Bejar, advanced to the rank of marquis, captain general of New Spain, and admiral of the South Seas, became anxious to return to his eſtates in this country. He now embarked from Old Spain with his family and twelve reverend fathers of the order of mercy, and after a proſperous voyage arrived at the port of Vera Cruz, where he did not experience the kind of reception he formerly met with. From thence he proceeded to Mexico, to preſent his patents to the Viceroy, and enter upon his offices. He alſo at this time made application upon a particular point relative to his Majeſty's grant of lands and towns. This point, which I do not well underſtand, I muſt leave to better judges. The grant ran thus; mentioning the diſtrict, it enumerated the inhabitants, by the word "vecinos," or neighbours, conſidered to belong

belong to it, and who were to be his tributaries. Cortes underſtood
that the head of the family only was conſidered as the vaſſal or "vecino,"
or that one only ſhould be counted for each houſe, but the oydor, doctor
Quezada who was ſent to allot his diſtrict, inſiſted that every male
adult, maſter or head of family, ſon, ſervant, or ſlave, was to be counted
in the number, and as there were frequently twelve or fifteen of thoſe
to one houſe, the Marquis was much diſappointed, and ſeveral lawſuits
enſued. The matter was reported to his Majeſty, but continued in
ſuſpence for ſeveral years, during which time the Marquis received his
full rents, without any moleſtation. He retired to a place upon his
eſtate named Quernavaca, where he eſtabliſhed his reſidence, never
returning to Mexico.

While Marcos de Aguilar had the government of New Spain, the
Marquis del Valle fitted out four ſhips at Zacatula. They were well
provided, loaded with various articles of merchandize, and commanded
by Alvarado de Saavedra, who with two hundred and fifty ſoldiers took
his courſe for the Molucca and Spice Iſlands, and China. This was by
his Majeſty's command, as I can teſtify, the royal letters having been
ſhown to me and many others. He was further ordered to cauſe ſearch
to be made during the courſe of his voyage, for a ſquadron which had
ſailed from Caſtille for China, under the command of Don Garcia de
Loayſa, commander of St. John of Rhodes. At the time that Saavedra was preparing for his expedition, a veſſel arrived belonging to this
fleet, from the pilot and crew of which Saavedra acquired all the information he wanted, and taking one pilot and two ſailors from this veſſel
with him, he ſet ſail in December, of one thouſand five hundred and
twenty ſeven or twenty eight, and ſuſtained many misfortunes, hardſhips, and loſſes, in the way to the Molucca Iſlands. I do not know the
particulars, but in three years afterwards I met with a ſailor who had
been on board this fleet, and who told me many ſtrange and ſurpriſing
things of the cities and nations he had ſeen, during his voyage. Theſe
are the countries to which they are now ſending expeditions from
Mexico.

Mexico. I also heard that the Portugueze had made prisoner Saavedra or some of his people, and brought them to Castille.

In the month of May, one thousand five hundred and thirty two, the Marquis del Valle sent two ships from the port of Acapulco, to make discoveries in the South Seas. They were commanded by a captain named Diego Hurtado de Mendoza, who, without going far to sea, or doing any thing worthy of relating, had the misfortune of a mutiny among the troops, in consequence whereof, one ship, of which the mutineers took possession, as is said, but very improbably, by the approbation of Hurtado himself, returned to New Spain, to the great disappointment of Cortes. As for Hurtado, neither he nor his vessel were ever more heard of.

After this, Cortes sent off two other vessels, one of which was commanded by a gentleman named Diego Bezerra de Mendoza; he was of the Bezerras of Badajos or Merida; the other was commanded by one Hernando de Grijalva. The principal pilot was one Ximenes, a Biscayan, and a great cosmographer. The orders from the Marquis were, first to go in search of Hurtado, and in case of not finding him, to go upon a voyage of discovery of new islands, especially those which were reported to be rich in pearls. The Biscayan pilot, before they sailed, was always telling the others how he would bring them to countries where they should all make their fortunes. Many were weak enough to believe him. The first night after they left the port of Guantepeque, a gale of wind rose and separated the vessels, which never afterwards joined company, Grijalva not choosing to be under the command of Bezerra, who was very haughty. He had also another motive, in wishing to keep the merit of any discoveries he should make, to himself. After sailing two hundred leagues, he came to an island which was uninhabited, and which he named Santo Tome. Bezerro and his pilot Ximines had a quarrel upon their voyage, and the former having made himself very odious by his domineering disposition, the pilot

formed

formed a plot for the assassination of him and several more, which he put in execution one night as the captain and the others were sleeping. The sanguinary views of the conspirators went much farther, but the intercession of two Franciscan friars saved the lives of many who were already bleeding from their treachery, but whom, together with the friars, they determined to land in Xalisco. Ximines taking the command upon the death of Bezerra, and continuing his route, discovered an island to which he gave the name of Santa Cruz. It was said that pearls were found on its coasts. It was inhabited by savages, and here he determined to put the friars and those whose lives had been spared at their intercession on shore, which he accordingly did, and being in want of water, he went to the shore at the same time in search of it; they had been on the island but a very short time when the natives came down upon them, and put every person they found to death, in view of those on board the ship.

This gave the Marquis great vexation. He now determined not to trust any one, but to go in person, having three ships ready to launch in the port of Guantepeque. When the Spaniards of those countries saw that he intended to embark upon a voyage of discovery, they thought success was certain, and numbers prepared to follow him as soldiers, above one hundred and thirty of whom were married men, and brought their wives with them. They were in all above three hundred and twenty, the women included. The Marquis left Mexico accompanied by Andres de Tapia and several other officers, some ecclefiastics, physicians, surgeons, and an apothecary, and having embarked, in the month of May, one thousand five hundred and thirty six, or seven, he set sail for the Island of Santa Cruz, with as many colonists and soldiers as the vessels could contain; and having arrived there after a prosperous voyage, he sent back the ships to bring the remainder of his people. The second voyage was not so fortunate. They met with gales of wind, in which they were separated near the river of St. Peter and St. Paul, one vessel only arriving at the Island of Santa Cruz, where

where the Marquis anxiously expected them, as the provisions, of which he began to be in great want, were on board. Of those vessels which did not join him at Santa Cruz, one was stranded on the coast of Xalisco, and the people on board being tired of the business quitted her there, most of them returning to New Spain. This was the one which contained the provisions. The other came to a bay which they named, from the quantity of guayavas, Guayaval.

During this time the Marquis and those with him were famishing upon this uncultivated island. Twenty three of the soldiers died from absolute distress, and the rest were sinking every day, and cursing his expeditions and discoveries. Their situation and murmurs compelled him at length to go in search of his ships, and he accordingly embarked with fifty soldiers, and judging that they must have been driven on the coast in the storms, he searched in that direction, and after some time found one as before mentioned, stranded on the coast of Xalisco, and abandoned by the people. The other was met with by him amongst some rocks. Having got them repaired and afloat, with much trouble, he brought them to his Island of Santa Cruz, and a quantity of provisions being now served out to the famished soldiers, they eat thereof in such a manner that the half of them died.

The Marquis, in order to avoid such a scene of distress, embarked in pursuit of new discoveries, and during this voyage fell in with the land of California. He was by that time as heartily tired of the business as any one, but he could not bear the thoughts of returning after such expences and losses, without having effected something, lest his misfortunes should be ascribed to the curses of the conquerors of Mexico, his ancient companions.

The Marchioness del Valle, hearing of the loss of one of the vessels on the coast, grew very apprehensive, and accordingly fitted out two ships, which sailed under the command of one Ulloa, in search of
the

the marquis and his squadron, with letters from his lady and the Viceroy earnestly soliciting his return. Ulloa was fortunate enough to light upon him, and the Marquis suffered himself to be prevailed upon, and returned to Mexico by the port of Acapulco, leaving Ulloa in command of the squadron. His return rejoiced the Spaniards, who feared always that the native chiefs, not being awed by him, would break out into revolt. In a short time after his arrival, the people whom he had left in California returned, but I cannot say whether in consequence of orders from the government or not.

After the Marquis had reposed for a few months, he fitted out another expedition of two ships under the command of Francisco de Ulloa, already named by me, who sailed from the port of Natividad in the month of June, of I forget what year, with orders to examine the coast of California, and to search for Captain Hurtado who never had been heard of. Ulloa employed in this voyage about seven months, at the expiration of which he returned to Xalisco, without having effected any thing; and going for a few days on shore to repose, a soldier who bore a malice against him took an opportunity to way-lay and assassinate him, and thus ended the discoveries of the Marquis del Valle, in which he expended, as I have heard him declare, above three hundred thousand crowns.

In order to get some allowance from his Majesty for this loss, he determined to go to Castille; he had also other business which called him there, such as the dispute about his vassals, and the restitution of his property which had been seized by Nuno de Guzman, now prisoner in Old Spain. I will conclude this account by observing, that it appears that the Marquis never prospered from the time of his first conquest of New Spain, and his ill fortune is ascribed to the curses with which he was loaded.

The Viceroy and court of royal audience had sent out a military

force

force commanded by an officer named Francifco Vafquez Coronado, who married the virtuous and fair daughter of the treafurer Eftrada. Coronado left his government of Xalifco to an officer named Onate, and after he had been for fome months in the country to which he was fent, and which was named Celibola or the feven cities, a Francifcan friar named Marcos de Nica, returned from thence to Mexico to give an account of the country to the Viceroy. He defcribed it as confifting of fine plains full of herds of cattle, but which were quite different in their appearance from thofe of Caftille. The houfes he defcribed as having two ftories and ftairs, and the towns as being populous. He alfo reprefented, that as it lay near the Pacific Ocean, a fupply of neceffaries could be fent to the Spanifh force, conveniently, in that direction. It was for this reafon that three fhips were fent thither under the command of Hernando de Alarco, an officer in the Viceroy's houfehold.

I muft not omit to mention the particulars of the great armament prepared by Don Pedro de Alvarado, in the year one thoufand five hundred and thirty feven, in the port of Acaxatla on the Pacific Ocean. This fleet was fitted out by Alvarado in confequence of permiffion obtained from his Majefty, by whom he was granted certain rents and advantages, in fuch countries as he fhould difcover towards the weft; that is to fay China, the Moluca, and Spice Iflands.

Alvarado being always zealous for his Majefty's fervice, as appeared by his conduct in Mexico and Peru, was anxious that this expedition fhould exceed any other that had ever been fitted out. It confifted of thirteen fail, amply provided. The port at which the preparations were made was above two hundred leagues diftant from that of Vera Cruz, from which all the iron, and moft other neceffary articles were to be brought by land carriage. The confequence was, that the money expended would have built eighty fuch fhips in Seville. All the wealth Alvarado brought from Peru, what he got from the mines of Guatimala, with the rents of his eftates and the prefents of his friends and

relations,

relations were infufficient, although the merchandize was taken upon credit. The expence attending the fhips was nothing in comparifon to that of his army, confifting of fix hundred and fifty foldiers with their officers, and a number of horfes, of which latter a good one could not be procured for lefs than three hundred crowns. Alvarado failed fome time in the year one thoufand five hundred and thirty eight, for the harbour of the Purification in the province of Xalifco, where he was to take in water, and embark more foldiers. When the Viceroy heard of this great armament, he became anxious to have a fhare in it, and went with Alvarado to view his fleet, after which they returned to Mexico.

Alvarado wifhed to have a relation of his own, named Juan, (not the Juan de Alvarado of Chiribito) as general, and the Viceroy was anxious that an officer named Villalobos fhould have the command, conjointly with him. Things were in this ftate when Alvarado was obliged to return to his fleet at the port of Natividad; and being there, and juft ready to fet fail, he received a letter from Chriftoval de Onate who was left in command at Xalifco, in the abfence of Francifco Coronado, requefting his immediate affiftance to fave him and the fettlement from the deftruction with which they were threatened, by the force of the neighbouring Indians of Cochitlan. Alvarado fet off with his troops to their relief, and found them in a moft defperate fituation indeed. The infurgents rather decreafed the violence of their attacks upon the appearance of Alvarado's force, but ftill hoftilities were carried on, and one day that Alvarado was purfuing fome of the enemy among the rocks and mountains where they had retreated, a foldier who was on horfe-back at a confiderable height above him on the fide of a mountain, and whofe horfe had loft his footing, came, horfe and all, rolling down the precipice, and ftriking Alvarado, brought him down with them. By this accident he was fo much bruifed, that in confequence thereof, and of being removed too fuddenly to the town of the Pacification, he was feized with fainting fits, and in the courfe of a few days gave up the ghoft. God pardon his fins! fome fay that he made a

will

will previous to his death, but it never appeared. He was buried with as much ceremony as could be beftowed upon his funeral, and his remains were, as I have heard, afterwards removed to the town of Piripito by Juan de Alvarado his relation.

As foon as the news of his death was known to his fleet and army, numbers difcharged themfelves, and returned to their homes with what they had received. In Mexico he was greatly regretted. The Viceroy fent off immediately the licentiate Maldonado, to take proper fteps to prevent any confufion likely to enfue, and fhortly after following in perfon, collected what remained of the foldiers, and marching againft the infurgents in the rocks, after a tedious expedition fucceeded in reducing them. The lofs of Alvarado was feverely felt in his family. As foon as the fatal intelligence arrived in Guatimala, the Bifhop D. Francifco Marroguin of excellent memory, and all the clergy, affifted in rendering him the funeral honours. His majordomo alfo, to fhew his forrow, caufed the walls of his houfe to be painted black, which colour they remained ever after. Many cavaliers waited upon his lady Donna Beatrix de la Cueva and her family, in order to confole them, for their diftrefs was very great. They told her that fhe fhould give thanks to God, fince it was his will to take her hufband, to which fhe as a good chriftian affented, but obferved, that fhe wifhed to be free from this melancholy world, and all its misfortunes.

Thefe circumftances I mention, becaufe the hiftorian Gomara attributes the unfortunate event which fhortly afterwards befell her, to her having fpoken blafphemoufly, in faying that God could do her no more injury than fhe had already fuffered. She met with her death in the following manner. A deluge of water and mud broke from the Volcano which is at the diftance of about half a league from Guatimala, and bringing with it great quantities of large ftones and trees, overwhelmed the houfe of Donna Beatrix, who was at the time praying with her women. As to the words which Gomara afcribes to her, fhe

never

never uttered them, nor was her death a judgment of God in any respect. But I must observe the particularities of the fate of this family. Although Alvarado and his four brothers had served his Majesty so zealously, not any part of his property descended to his children. D. Pedro de Alvarado died as I have related, by an uncommon accident in Cochitlan; his brother George died in the city of Madrid, in the year one thousand five hundred and forty, being then soliciting his Majesty for some reward; Gomez de Alvarado died in Peru, Gonzalo de Alvarado in Mexico or Guaxaca, I forget which, and Juan on his voyage to the Island of Cuba. His eldest son going with his relation Juan de Alvarado the younger to wait on his Majesty, and solicit a recompence for his father's services, the ship wherein they went was lost, and neither they nor it were ever heard of after they set sail. Don Diego the younger son, seeing his fortunes desperate, returned to Peru, where he died in battle, and the lady of Pedro de Alvarado, with the female part of his family, one only excepted, were drowned by a torrent from a Volcano. Now curious readers reflect on what I have related of the fate of this family, and may our Lord Jesus Christ take them into his holy glory! amen. The only survivor, Donna Leonora one of his daughters who was saved from the torrent, has caused to be built two sepulchres in the great church of this city of Guatimala, to receive the bones of her relations.

In about a year after the death of D Pedro de Alvarado, the Viceroy collected the best of the thirteen ships which composed his fleet, and sent them under the command of an officer named Villalobos, to make discoveries to the westward, but what the result was, I never heard. As to the expences incurred by Alvarado he never recovered any part of them, nor his family after him.

The Marquis del Valle being in Spain at the time of the expedition against Algiers, and attending his Majesty in it, with his eldest son, and also Don Martin his son by Donna Marina, the fleet

was

was difperfed in a ftorm. The veffel on board which the Marquis was being ftranded, he, his fons, and the other cavaliers reached the fhore with very great difficulty. His fervants have related, that before he quitted the veffel, he tied round his arm in a handkerchief a quantity of jewels of ineftimable value, which he wore according to the cuftom of great lords, as we fay "para no menefter," or becaufe they are not wanting, but in the confufion of quitting the veffel by fome accident they were all loft. On account of this difafter to the fleet, the council of war were of opinion to raife the fiege immediately. To this council the Marquis was not fummoned, but he is faid to have declared, that had he been prefent at it he would have given his vote for the continuation of the fiege, and that if it had been his fortune to have had fuch brave foldiers as thofe who firft accompanied him to Mexico, he would entertain no doubt of fuccefs.

The Marquis was now grown old, and he was worn down by fatigues; he was therefore very anxious to return to New Spain, but a treaty of marriage was on foot between his eldeft daughter Donna Maria Cortes, for whom he had fent to Mexico, and Don Alvaro Pinez Oforio fon and heir to the Marquis of Aftorga. The lady was to have a fortune of a hundred thoufand ducats, and the Marquis had gone as far as Seville to meet her on her arrival in Spain, but the match was broken off, as it is faid, by the fault of Don Alvaro. The Marquis was greatly difpleafed, and being in a bad ftate of health before, he declined fo rapidly that he found it neceffary to retire from Seville to Caftileja de la Cuefta, to attend to his foul, and make his laft teftament. Having arranged all his affairs for this, and the next world, it was the Lord's will to take him from this troublefome ftate, on the fecond day of December one thoufand five hundred and forty feven. He was buried with great pomp in the chapel of the Dukes of Medina Sidonia, but his remains were afterwards, according to his will, brought to New Spain, and interred in Cuyoacan or Tezcuco, I am uncertain which. In regard to his age, I will give the beft account that I am able. In

the

the year one thoufand five hundred and nineteen, when we went with him from Cuba to New Spain, he ufed to tell us that he was thirty four years of age; from one thoufand five hundred and nineteen, to one thoufand five hundred and forty feven, is a period of twenty eight years, which makes him at the time of his death exactly fixty two years old.

The legitimate children of the Marquis del Valle were, Don Martin the prefent Marquis, Donna Maria before mentioned who married the Count de Luna de Leon. Donna Juana, who married Don Hernando Enriquez heir to the Marquis of Tariffa, and Donna Catalina de Arrellano, who died in Seville. Thefe ladies came with the Marchionefs from Mexico; her brother Fray Anthonio de Zuniga being fent for them. One daughter named Donna Leonora, was married in Mexico, to a rich Bifcayan named Juanes de Tolofa, which alliance gave great offence to the young Marquis. He alfo left two natural fons, one by Donna Marina, named Don Martin, who was commander of the order of St. Jago. The other, Don Luis, who was a commander of the fame order, was the fon of a lady, by name, De Hermofilla. He had alfo three natural daughters, one by an Indian woman of Cuba, was named Donna——Pizarro; the others were by a Mexican woman. Thefe ladies were all left great fortunes. The Marquis alfo having due time, took care of his foul, by difcharging his fins; endowing an hofpital in Mexico, and a monaftery of nuns in his own town of Cuyoacan.

The motto and arms which were granted to him were well adapted to a valiant warrior. The former being in Latin I will fay nothing about, becaufe I do not underftand that language. His arms were the heads of feven kings in a chain, reprefenting Montezuma, Cacamatzin, Guatimotzin, Tulapa, Coadlavaca, and the princes of Tacuba and Cuyoacan.

I will now proceed to defcribe the perfon and difpofition of the Marquis. He was of a good ftature and ftrong built, of a rather pale
complexion,

complexion, and ferious countenance. His features were, if faulty, rather too fmall; his eyes mild and grave. His beard was black, thin, and fcanty; his hair in the fame manner. His breaft and fhoulders were broad, and his body very thin. He was very well limbed, and his legs rather bowed; an excellent horfeman, and dexterous in the ufe of arms. He alfo poffeffed the heart and mind, which is the principal part of the bufinefs. I have heard that when he was a lad in Hifpaniola, he was very wild about women, and that he had feveral duels with able fwordfmen, in which he always came off with victory. He had the fcar of a fword-wound near his under lip, which appeared through his beard if clofely examined, and which he received in fome of thofe affairs. In his appearance, manners, tranfactions, converfation, table, and drefs, every thing bore the appearance of a great lord. His cloaths were according to the fafhion of the time; he was not fond of filks, damafks, or velvets, but every thing plain, and very handfome; nor did he wear large chains of gold, but a fmall one of prime workmanfhip, bearing the image of our Lady the Bleffed Virgin with her precious fon in her arms, and a Latin motto; and on the reverfe, St. John the Baptift with another motto. He wore on his finger a ring with a very fine diamond, and in his cap, which according to the fafhion of that day was of velvet, he bore a medal, the head and motto of which I do not recollect; but latterly he wore a plain cloth cap, without any ornament.

His table was always magnificently attended and ferved, with four major domos or principal officers, a number of pages, and a great quantity of plate both gold and filver. He dined heartily at mid-day, and drank a glafs of wine mixed with water, of about half a pint. He was not nice in his food, nor expenfive, except on particular occafions where he faw the propriety of it. He was very affable with all his captains and foldiers, efpecially thofe who accompanied him in his firft expedition from Cuba. He was a Latinift, and as I have been told, a bachelor in laws. He was alfo fomething of a poet, and a very good

rhetorician;

rhetorician; very devout to our Holy Virgin, and his advocates St. Peter, St. Jago, and St. John the Baptift in particular; and charitable to the poor. When he fwore he ufed to fay, "by my confcience!" and when he was angry with any of us, his friends, he would fay, "oh! may you repent it." When he was very angry, the veins in his throat and forehead ufed to fwell, and when in great wrath, he would not utter a fyllable to any one. He was very patient under infults or injuries; for fome of the foldiers were at times very rude and abufive with him; but he never refented their conduct, although he had often great reafon to do fo. In fuch cafes he ufed only to fay, "be filent," or, "go away " in God's name and take care not to repeat this conduct, or I will have " you punifhed." He was very determined and headftrong in all bu-finefs of war, not attending to any remonftrances on account of danger; an inftance of which he fhewed in the attack of thofe fortreffes called the rocks of the Marquis; which he forced us to fcale, contrary to our opinions, and where neither courage, counfel, or wifdom, could give any rational hope of fuccefs. Another inftance was given by him of his obftinacy in regard to the expedition againft De Oli. I repeatedly advifed him to go by the mountains; but he perfifted in adhering to the coaft, whereas if he had gone in the direction that I propofed he would have found towns the whole way, of which the following route is a proof; Guacacualco, the high road to Chiapa, from that to Guatimala, and from thence to Naco. Where we had to erect a fortrefs, Cortes was the hardeft labourer in the trenches; when we were going into battle, he was as forward as any.

Cortes was very fond of play, both at cards and dice, and while playing he was very affable and good humoured. He ufed frequently at fuch times, thofe cant expreffions which perfons who game are ac-cuftomed to do. In military fervice he practifed the moft ftrict atten-tion to difcipline, conftantly going the rounds in perfon during the night, vifiting the quarters of the foldiers, and feverely reprehend-ing thofe whom he found without their armour and appointments, and

Qqq

not

not ready to turn out; repeating to them the proverb, that "it is a bad "sheep which cannot carry its own wool." On our expedition to Higueras I perceived that he had acquired a habit which I had never before obferved in him, and it was this; after eating, if he did not get his fiefta or fleep, his ftomach was affected, and he fell fick. For this reafon, when on the journey, let the rain be ever fo heavy, or the fun ever fo hot, he always repofed for a fhort time after his repaft, a carpet or cloak being fpread under a tree, on which he lay down, and having flept a fhort time he mounted his horfe and proceeded on his journey. When we were engaged in the wars during the conqueft of New Spain, he was very thin and flender, but after his return from Higueras he grew fat, and acquired a belly. He at this time trimmed his beard which had not begun to grow white, in the fhort fafhion. In his early life he was very liberal, but grew clofe, latterly; fome of his fervants complaining that he did not pay them as he ought, and I have alfo to obferve that in his latter undertakings he never fucceeded. Perhaps fuch was the will of heaven, his reward being referved for another place; for he was a good cavalier, and very devout to the Holy Virgin, and alfo to St. Paul and other Holy Saints. God pardon him his fins; and me mine; and give me a good end which is better than all conquefts and victories over Indians.

CHAPTER X.

*Enumeration and account of the valiant companions who paf-
fed over to the conqueft of New Spain with the moft adventurous and magnanimous Don Hernando Cortes Marquis of
the Valley. Advantages refulting from the conqueft—Tranfactions at court. Concluding obfervations of the author.*

IN the lift of the conquerors of Mexico the firft is the Marquis Don
H. Cortes; with him came the following officers and soldiers. Don
P. de Alvarado, commander of St. Jago, adelantado and governor of
Guatimala, Honduras, and Chiapa; he was about thirty four years
of age when he came to this country, of a handfome perfon, very chearful countenance, and mild look; for which reafon he was called by the
Mexicans, "Tonatio," which fignifies the fun; he was very active, and
a good horfeman; of a generous difpofition, and courteous manners,
very fplendid in his drefs, wearing a gold chain with a medal round
his neck, and a diamond ring on his finger.

F. de Montejo was of the middle ftature, of a chearful countenance, and gay difpofition; at the time of his arrival here he was about
thirty five years of age; he was fitter for bufinefs than war, and of a
liberal turn, expending more than he received; he arrived to the dignity
of adelantado and governor of Yucatan, and died in Caftille.

Captain G. de Sandoval was at the time of his arrival here about
twenty two years of age; he was joint governor of New Spain for about
eleven months; in this officer courage and judgment were combined;

he

he was robuſt in body, his legs rather bowed, and his countenance maſculine; his hair and beard were curled, and of a light brown; his voice was rough, and ſomewhat terrible, and he ſtammered a little; he was a plain man, and one who did not know much of letters, not avaritious of gold, but attentive to his buſineſs like a good officer, ſeeing that his ſoldiers did their duty well, and taking good care of them. He was not fond of rich dreſſes, but went plain and like a ſoldier. He had the beſt horſe that ever was ſeen; he was a cheſtnut, with a ſtar in his forehead, and his near foot white; his name was Motilla; he became a proverb, ſo that when any horſe was extraordinarily good, we uſed to ſay he was as good as Motilla. Sandoval was an officer fit for any ſtation; he was a native of Medellin, and an hidalgo; his father was an alcalde of a caſtle.

Don C. de Oli was a Hector in battle, but his judgment was not equal to his valour, and he required to be kept under command. The captains De Alvarado, De Sandoval, and De Oli, were in high eſtimation with his Majeſty, who was pleaſed to ſay that he had three in New Spain who might be compared with the greateſt the world had produced. Cortes alſo uſed to talk highly of his officers and ſoldiers, but what Bernal Diaz del Caſtillo thinks upon the ſubject is this; that if what Cortes afterwards ſaid in their favour, he had written at firſt to his Majeſty, he would have done right; but at that time he made no mention of our valiant actions, nor even our names; but only ſaid, "this I did; this I ordered to be done;" whereas I think the leaſt he ſhould have done was to make mention of us. I will now return to my enumeration of our officers and ſoldiers.

J. V. de Leon, native of Old Caſtille, was about twenty ſeven years of age, well proportioned, and robuſt; his beard was red and curled, his voice rough and fierce, and he ſtammered a little; he was a cavalier of good manners, and generous, ſharing what he had with his companions; he killed a perſon of conſequence in the Iſland of Hiſ-

paniola,

paniola, for which he was obliged to conceal himself, and the officers of justice never were able to apprehend him, he made such resistance He was most valiant both on horseback and on foot; he died at the bridge.

D. de Ordas, from the neighbourhood of Campos, was about forty years of age; he was captain of the soldiers armed with sword and buckler, not being a horseman; he was very valiant, and wise, strong, and of good stature, of a masculine countenance, and black thin beard. In speaking there were certain words which he could not pronounce; he was generous, and of good manners. He was commander of St. Jago, and governor of Maranion, where he died.

Captain L. Marin was valiant, and stout built; bow legged, with a red beard, and a full and chearful countenance, slightly marked with the small pox. He was about thirty years of age, and a native of St. Lucar, lisping a little, like the Sevillians. He was a good horseman, and of mild manners; he died in Mechoacan.

Captain P. de Ircio was of middle stature, chearful countenance, and duck legged; a great boaster of his exploits, but by what we could perceive in him good for very little; he was always repeating certain stories of the Count de Urena, and Don Pedro Giron; we used to call him Agrages without deeds; he was for a time captain under Sandoval during the siege, and died in Mexico.

A. de Avila was of a good person and countenance, clear and sensible in his conversation, very valiant, and about thirty three years of age. He was free with his companions, but proud, fond of commanding, and impatient of controll, with a considerable share of envy, and turbulence, insomuch that Cortes could not bear to have him near him; he therefore took care that he should be employed in such affairs as would draw him to a distance; he was uncle to the cavaliers the sons of

Benavides,

Benavides, who were beheaded in Mexico; he died in that city or in Yucatan.

A. de Monjarez was of middling stature, and a good countenance; he acted as captain during the siege, but was always an invalid; he was aged about thirty years, and died a natural death.

C. de Olea was a native of Medina Del Campo, and a most valiant soldier; he was about twenty six years of age, of the middle stature, with a masculine but pleasing countenance; his hair and beard a little curled, and a clear voice; this soldier's bravery was such that we all held him in the highest honour; he saved the life of Cortes at Suchimillico, when the enemy had seized and were carrying him off to sacrifice; and a second time upon the causeway of Mexico when he was in a still more desperate situation, being wounded and in the hands of a number of the Indians, the brave De Olea, though mortally wounded, with his sword killed and beat off every one of these who were upon Cortes, thus saving his general's life, and losing his own at the same time. When the person of this valiant soldier recurs to my mind, and the manner he used to fight at our sides, the tears flow from my eyes, for he was my towns-man, and we were related to the same families.

G. Dominguez, and Lares, were soldiers of high renown, and might be put in comparison with Olea; the first died by the fall of his horse, the second at the battle of Otumba.

A. de Tapia was aged about twenty four years, of a pale complexion and grave countenance; he was a valiant captain, and died in Mexico, a natural death.

J. de Escalante was a captain; he died at Villa Rica. F. de Lugo, a brave officer, acted as captain occasionally; he was the natu-

ral

ral son of a wealthy gentleman at Medina del Campo; he died a natural death. Gregorio de Monjaraz; a good soldier; lost his hearing during the siege, and died a natural death. Four brothers of Don P. de Alvarado. J. Xaramillo was an officer of merit; he died a natural death. Christoval Flores, a worthy soldier. Christoval de Gamboa, equerry to Cortes. One Calcedo, a wealthy man. Francisco de Bonal, a good soldier. Maldonado, surnamed "the broad," a good soldier. Francisco Alvarez Chico, a man of business. Francisco de Torrazas, major domo to Cortes, a person of merit. Christoval del Corral, our ensign; an officer of merit. Anthonio de Villaroel, some time ensign. Alonzo de Grado; one fitter for business than war; by his importunities he induced Cortes to give him the daughter of Montezuma in marriage. Francisco Flores, a very noble person. De Solis. There were four of this name; one was surnamed, "casquete," or "rattle-skull;" another called himself "De la Huerta;" but we called him "silk coat," because he prided himself on his dress. Another was named "De atras la Puerta," because he always sat behind the door of his house, observing the passengers in the street. Bernardino Vasquez de Tapia; a person of wealth and consequence. Juan Lopez de Ximena, alcalde major of Vera Cruz. Juan de Cuellar, a good horseman, married the handsome daughter of the Lord of Tezcuco, named Donna Anna. Another Cuellar related to F. Verdugo. Santos Hernandez, whom we used to call " the good old ranger." Pedro Moreno Medrano, alcalde in Vera Cruz, a good soldier, and an upright judge. Roman Lopez, a person of eminence. Juan de Limpias Caravajal, grew deaf during the siege, where he was captain of a vessel. Melchor de Galvez. Villandrando, said to have been related to the Count of Ribadeo. Ossorio, a good soldier. Rodrigo de Castaneda, a good soldier. Juan de Naxara, a good soldier. Ojeda, who lost an eye during the siege. Alonzo Hernandez Puertocarrero, cousin to the Count of Medellin. Hernando Burgueno, a good soldier. Tirado de la Puebla, a man of business. Hernandes de Alanis, a very brave soldier. Navarrete. Juan Flamenco. Francisco del Barco, promoted to be a captain. Juan Perez, who killed

his

his wife, the daughter of La Baguera. Najara, "the hump backed," a moſt valiant ſoldier. Madrid, "the hump backed;" a very valiant ſoldier. Juan de Inhieſta. De Alamilla, a good croſsbow-man. Moron; a fine muſician. De Varela; a good ſoldier. De Villafuerte; a perſon of conſequence, married to a relation of the firſt wife of Cortes. Gutierrez. Pacheço; a perſon of diſtinction. Hernando de Lerma, or de Lema; a captain. Suarez the elder, who killed his wife with a blow of a hand-mill. Laſios, who had a ſuit about his diſtrict. Garci Caro. One Ximenes. Amaya. Two Carmenos, brothers. One Vargas. Polanco. Juan de Aragon. St. Eſtevan. Bernardino de Coria. Rodorigo Rangel. Almodova, his ſon, and nephew. A reverend father of the order of mercy, named Fra Bartholome de Olmedo; a great theologian, a fine ſinger, and a virtuous man. Two nephews of Alonzo Hernandez de Palo. Chriſtoval Diaz; a good croſsbow-man. Juan Siciliano. Diego de Coria. Juan Sedeno. Saragoſſa, father to the ſcrivener in Mexico. Diego Martin de Agamante, a good ſoldier. Diego Hernandez, loſt his ſight; he was an aſſiſtant ſhipwright. Alvaro Lopez. One Yanez who went to Higueras; during his abſence his wife took another huſband with whom he left her. Martin de Alpedrino, Juan Alvarez Rubazo, Gonzalez Sanchez, brave men, all Portugueze. One Avila. One Eſpinoſa, ſurnamed "De la " buena benedicion," from his often uſing the word. Peron de Toledo. One San Juan. Aparicio Martin. Izguierdo; a good ſoldier. Morrales, an old man, lame of a leg, alcalde in ordinary at Villa Rica, and a ſtrict doer of juſtice. Arevalo, Juan Leon, Madrigal; inhabitants of Villa Rica; never were on ſervice. Navarro. Manzanilla, an Indian of the iſlands. Benito Vejel, a drummer who had ſerved in Italy. Alonzo Romero. Pedro Lopez; a good ſoldier. Juan Garcia, Hernan Martin, and another; ſmiths. Alvaro Gallego. Pedro de Tapia. Lorenzo Ginoves. Ochoa; a rich and eminent perſon. Martin Vaſquez, a man of eminence. Sebaſtian Rodriguez, a croſsbow-man and Trumpeter. Penaloſa. Juan Perez Artiaga, ſurnamed "Malintzin;" a rich man. Pedro Gonzalez Sabiote, a good ſoldier. Aguilar whom

we

we found at the point of Cotoche; a good foldier. Pedro Valenciano. One Tariffa. Another of that name called by us "the meritorious," becaufe he was always bragging of what he had done, and that he had not been properly rewarded; a prating fellow. Pedro Sanchez Farfan; a brave foldier; he acted as captain. Efcobar the bachelor, apothecary, furgeon, and phyfician; he went mad. Juan de Caceres the rich. Gonzalo Hurones. Ramirez the elder. Aftorga. Toftado. Pedro Valencia. Fray Juan de las Varillas, of the order of mercy; a good theologian, and a virtuous man. Thofe enumerated above all died naturally. Francifco de Saucedo, called "the gallant." Francifco de Morla, a very brave foldier. De Lares, a good foldier and horfeman. Another of that name. De Solis, an old man. Benitez, a brave man. Juan Ruano, a good foldier. Two nephews of Gonzales de Najara. Gonzalo Dominguez, very brave and an excellent horfeman. One De Mora, a good foldier. Juan Alvarez Chico. A good foldier who had loft one hand in Caftille by the courfe of juftice. One To-billo, lame, as he faid by a wound received while ferving under the great captain. Gonzalo Lopez de Ximena. One Pilar, a good linguift. Alonzo Luis; a good foldier; being very tall he was called "the infant." Alonzo de Monroy, a good foldier, fon of a commander of St. Stephen; he went under the name of Salamanca. Juan Rico de Alanis, a good foldier. Martin de Vendabal. Pedro Gallego. Three foldiers of the name of Truxillo, brave men. De Valladolid. De Angulo. Fran-cifco Gutierrez. Santa Clara. One Ximenes. Two brothers of the name of Florin. One Vargas. One De Cieza, remarkable for pitch-ing a bar. Bartholome Pardo. Arbolanche, a very brave foldier. A nephew of one Almodovar. Two brothers by name Martinez; brave men. Sancho de Avila who is faid to have brought fix thoufand crowns in gold to Caftille from St. Domingo, having had the luck to fall on fome very rich mines there; he loft the whole at play and then joined us. Alonzo Hernandez de Palo, Alonzo de la Mefta, and Rabanal Montanez, good foldiers. Retamales: Gines Nortes, a brave foldier. Luis Alonzo, an excellent fwordfman. Alonzo Catalan, a good foldier.

R r r

Canillas,

Canillas, a drummer, and a good foldier, having ferved in Italy. Hernandez, fecretary to Cortes. Juan Diaz, belonged to the general's houfehold. Balnor. Cardenas, who faid he was fon to a commander, Arguello, a good foldier. Vafquez, a brave foldier. Arroyuelo. Pizarro; a relation of Cortes, acted as captain; his name was not then remarkable, nor had Peru been heard of. Magellanes, a brave foldier, a Portugueze, as was another, a goldfmith. One Avila. Two of the name of Efpinofa. One of the name of San Juan, called "the lofty," from his prefumptuoufnefs. Caceres, a good foldier. Efcanola the younger. Alonzo de Talavera, a good foldier. An Indian of the iflands named Manzanilla. Galleguillo, a very little man. A fmith whofe name I forget. Paredes. Gonzalo Mexia Rapapello, who faid he was defcended from the corfair of that name in the reign of King John. Lucas Ginoves. Cervantes, a buffoon. Plazuela. Alonzo Perez Maite, a brave foldier, married to a handfome Indian of the iflands. Alonzo de Efcobar, a perfon of confideration, formerly page to Velafquez. Ponce. Mendez. An old crofsbow-man a great card player whofe name I forget. The page Orteguilla and his father. Gaona. Luis Farfan. Morillas. One of the Toftados. Porras, a fine finger, with a very fair complexion. Ortiz; he played on the fiddle and taught dancing. Serrano, a good foldier. Quintero. Andres de Mola. Alberza, a good foldier. Moft of thefe loft their lives at the bridge, were facrificed, or fell in battle.

Simon de Cuenca was killed at Xicalonga, with ten more foldiers. Francifco de Medina died in the hands of the Indians with fifteen more. One De la Serna, who difcovered filver mines, I do not know what is become of him. Martin Lopez, the fhip carpenter who rendered fuch eminent fervices; he is now living in Mexico. One Granado is now living in Mexico. Villa Lobos returned rich to Caftille. Juan del Rio returned to Caftille. Juan Gomez returned rich to Caftille. Herman Lopez de Avila, a truftee of the effects of the dead, returned very rich to Caftille. Pedro Efcudiro, Juan Cermeno, and his brother, all good
foldiers.

foldiers. Gonzalo de Umbria a pilot. Francifco de Orozco; had been a foldier in Italy, and acted as captain during the fiege of Mexico; I know nothing more of him. Mefa had been a canonier in Italy; was drowned in croffing a river, after the conqueft. Luis Velafquez, and Martin Valenciano, died in the expedition to Higueras. Alonzo de Barrientos, Juan del Puerto a good foldier, died of difeafe. Pedro de Guzman, a brave foldier; it is faid that on his journey to Peru, he and his whole family, fervants and horfes, were frozen to death. Cardenas; this was he who talked of the two kings; he was very troublefome to Cortes. The Emperor made him a grant of lands worth a thoufand crowns a year, with which he returned to Mexico, but fhortly after, died. Los Villanuevas; two brothers; Portugueze; I do not know what became of them. Villocinda, a brave foldier, put on the Francifcan habit. Alonzo de Herrera, a good foldier, he fought with Captain Figuero, and to avoid the vengeance of the treafurer, fled to the Indians of Maronon, by whom he was killed. Figuero was drowned going to Caftille. Maldonado de Medellin, I do not know what became of him.

Lencero, a good foldier, had an inn on the road to Vera Cruz, turned friar. Sindos de Portillo, poffeffed large eftates, which he fold, giving the money to the poor, and taking orders, led a holy life. Quintero a good foldier, attained great wealth, which he renounced for God's fake, and taking the Francifcan habit, led a holy life. Alonzo de Aguilar owned the inn between Vera Cruz and La Puebla; a rich man; he fold all his property for the fervice of God, and putting on the Dominican habit, led a holy life. Burguillos, a rich man, renounced his property, and entered the order of St. Francis, which he afterwards quitted. Efcalante, a good foldier, of a gay difpofition; he put on the Francifcan habit, but afterwards quitted the monaftery, and entered again into the military fervice; but, in the courfe of a month, refumed his friar's habit, and led a holy life. Gafpar Diaz, a wealthy man, renounced all for God's fake, and retired to the pine woods of Guaxo-

cingo,

cingo, where, in the moſt retired part, he made a hermitage for himſelf; in this courſe of life he reduced his body to a very weak ſtate, by
faſting and penance, and the fame of his auſterities reaching the Biſhop
Juan de Zumarraga, he entreated him not to carry them to ſuch an extreme. Several other perſons alſo joined him, being induced by his
example to lead holy lives; at the end of about four years, it was God's
will to take them all from this world, to his heavenly glory. Lerma;
a very valiant ſoldier; it was he who rendered ſuch eſſential ſervice to
Cortes, in once ſaving his life; Lerma was afterwards obliged to fly,
and ſeek refuge among the Indians from this very Cortes whom he had
preſerved, and who was exaſperated againſt him, for reaſons which,
from regard to his honour, I will not mention; we never knew what
became of him, but our ſuſpicions were very bad. Pinedo, a good
ſoldier, had been educated in the houſe of Velaſquez; on the arrival of
Narvaez, quitting Mexico to join him, he was way-laid and killed on
the road by Indians; Cortes was ſuſpected of having a hand in his
death.

One Lopez, returned to Hiſpaniola. Alaminos and his ſon, Camacho de Triano, Alvarez de Huelva, Sopuerto del Condado, Cardi-
nas, Umbria, Galdin, and ſeveral others, all pilots; Sopuerto, only,
remained in Mexico; the reſt being in dread of Cortes, becauſe they
had offered their ſervices to Garray. Enreque, drowned himſelf, from
deſpair and fatigue on a march. Zemudio, a very brave ſoldier, returned to Old Spain, on account of having wounded ſeveral perſons in
frays; he was there given the command of a company; he died in
Locaſtil with many other Spaniſh cavaliers. Tariffa, the third of that
name, called by us "of the white hands," becauſe he was not fit either for
war or labour; or any thing elſe except to prate about what had happened to him in Seville; he and his horſe were drowned on the march
to Higueras. Eſcobar, a brave man but very turbulent; he was hanged for ſedition and for violating a married woman. St. Jago, returned
rich to Caſtille. Alonzo de Eſcobar, a perſon of eſtimation, formerly

page to Velafquez. Saldanha and two more whofe names I forget were killed in Tabafco. De Rojas, went to Peru. Guillen de la Loa, Andrez Nunez, Maiffe Pedro el de la Harpa, and three more; the firft died by a cannon fhot, the others by the enemy, or courfe of nature. Alonzo Rodriguez, left good mines in Cuba; was killed at the rocks, together with Gafpar Sanchez, a brave man, nephew to the treafurer of Cuba, and fix of the foldiers of Narvaez. Pedro de Palma, firft hufband of Elvira Lopez "the tall," was hanged together with a foldier named Trebejo, and a prieft, for fedition, by Avila or Las Cafas, after the death of De Oli, under whom they ferved; I was fhewn the tree whereon they were executed, when returning from Higueras with Captain Marin. Many fea-faring men alfo came with us, and behaved very bravely in the wars, but not recollecting their names I do not put them down; I fhould run indeed into too great prolixity if I were enumerate and defcribe all the valiant foldiers who paffed over with Cortes; but they were worthy to be recorded in letters of gold.

Laft of all I put down myfelf, having been in this country antecedent to the coming of Cortes twice, and the third time with him, as I have related; and I give thanks and praife to our Lord God, and his Holy Mother the Virgin Mary, who preferved me from being facrificed like the moft of my companions, that I might now relate and make manifeft our heroic actions, and enumerate by name our valiant captains and foldiers, who conquered this new world, thereby to prevent all the honour and merit from being unjuftly afcribed to one perfon.

Of thofe who came with Narvaez, although feveral were very valiant men, I will fay nothing, becaufe my intention in writing this hiftory, was but to record the heroic actions of the foldiers of Cortes. I will therefore only defcribe Narvaez himfelf.

Narvaez was about forty two years of age, of tall ftature and large limbs, a full face, and red beard, and agreeable prefence; very fonorous
and

and lofty in his fpeech, as if the found came out of a vault; a good
horfeman, and faid to be valiant. He was a native of Valladolid, or
Tudela de Duero, and married to a lady named Maria de Valenzuela.
He had a confiderable property in the Ifland of Cuba, where he was a
captain. One of his eyes was beaten out in the attack which we made
upon him. This gentleman was faid to be very clofe in his difpofition.
He went to Caftille to lay his complaints againft us before his Majefty,
and obtained a royal grant of a government in Florida, where he was
loft and all his property. Thofe who read the particulars of fo many
gallant officers and foldiers, fuch as I have now defcribed them, frequently afk me how it happened that I fhould remember them perfectly, after the lapfe of fo many years. To which I reply, that it is
natural enough that I fhould recollect the names of five hundred and
fifty companions who were always together, in expeditions, in watches,
in battles, and in fkirmifhes, and converfing with each other how fuch
a one had been killed at fuch a place, and how others were carried off
to be facrificed. For this was the manner in which we communicated
with each other, efpecially after we had come out of a bloody and
doubtful battle. And there have been generals who knew the foldiers
of their armies perfonally, even when there were as many as thirty
thoufand men; fo fays hiftory of Mithridates king of Pontus, and
another king of the Epirots, and of Alexander, and Hannibal of Car-
thage, and in our times of the valiant Gonzalo de Cordova called the
great captain, and many others. I fay farther, that I have their figures
fo perfectly pourtrayed in my imagination, that I could draw them as
it were to the life, each of them in the manner he entered into battle,
like the great Apelles, and thefe famous modern painters Michael Angelo, or the far celebrated Burgales, who is faid to be another Apelles.
Glory be to God, and the Holy Virgin, who faved me from being
facrificed to idols, to make thofe things known!

Having enumerated the foldiers who paffed with Cortes, and related in what manner they died, I have now to obferve, that we were for
the

the moſt part hidalgos, although ſome were not of ſuch clear lineage as others, for all cannot be alike in this world, either in rank or in virtues. But whatever may have been the dignity of our birth, we made ourſelves much more illuſtrious by our heroic actions in the conqueſt of this country, at our own proper coſt, and without any ſupport ſave that of our Lord Jeſus Chriſt who is the true aid and ſuccour. If we look into the antient hiſtory of our own country, we ſhall then ſee that many cavaliers aroſe to dignity and honours, by valiant and faithful ſervices to their king; and I have obſerved that thoſe who thus obtained theſe titles and dignities, did not go into the field without receiving pay and ſalaries for their ſervice; and yet they were rewarded with houſes and caſtles, and lands, and privileges, to them and their deſcendents in perpetuity. Alſo when his Majeſty Don Jayme won parts of his kingdom from the Moors, he made grants thereof to thoſe cavaliers who had aſſiſted him in the conqueſt, from which period they derive their honours and blazons. Thoſe alſo who ſerved under the great captain and the Prince of Orange were rewarded in like manner, and we, even without his Majeſty's knowledge, by our valour gained him this great country. I have here recalled this to recollection, that the world may conſider and ſee our manifold, and good, and notable, and loyal ſervices, to God and the King, and all Chriſtendom, and let them be put in a ballance and weighed, and let it be decided if we are not as worthy of rewards and remunerations, as thoſe cavaliers whom I have mentioned above. And as amongſt thoſe whom I have enumerated there were many valiant companions, I was held in no inconſiderable degree of eſtimation in my day as a ſoldier.

Now curious reader reflect on my life, and in how many battles and dangers I have been, ſince I firſt came to this country, and how I was twice in the hands of the enemy who were carrying me off to ſacrifice, and God gave me force to eſcape out of their clutches; beſides the diſtreſſes by hunger, thirſt, and fatigue, which occur to all who undertake diſcoveries in unknown countries.

It

It is now proper that I fhould relate the good effects of our exertions for the fervice of God and his Majefty, by our illuftrious conquefts, in which moft of our companions loft their lives, being facrificed to the idols Huitzilopochtli and Tezcatepuca. In the firft place, we purged the land of its wickednefs and evil cuftoms, as for inftance that of human facrifice. By the accounts taken by certain reverend Francifcan fathers, the firft who came here after Fray Bartholome de Olmedo, it appears, that in the city of Mexico, and fome adjacent towns in the lake, they facrificed every year above two thoufand five hundred human beings, young and old. Of courfe in the whole extent of the country the number thus put to death annually, muft have been much greater. Their various horrid practices of this nature exceed the powers of my pen to defcribe. Their curfed adoratories were fo many that I beftow on all of them a hearty malediction; it feems to me that they refembled what we have in Caftille, for as we fee there in every city, holy churches, and hermitages, and chapels, fo they had in this country their houfes of idols, devils, and diabolical figures. Befides thefe, each native, male or female, had two altars, one by the place where he or fhe flept, the other at the door of the houfe, with chefts containing idols large and fmall, ftones, and ftone knives, with books made of the bark of trees, in which were noted down their records of paft times. They were much addicted to abominable practices, efpecially upon the coaft, and in the fultry provinces, where boys wore female attire. They eat human flefh, as we do beef which we buy in the market, and in every town they had wooden cages, wherein they kept and fattened thofe men, women, and children, who were deftined for that purpofe, as was the cafe with all thofe whom they took in their wars. Inceft was common amongft them; and they were drunkards in an extreme. In the province of Panuco in particular, they took the wine into their bodies in the manner a medicine is adminiftered, by means of a hollow cane; an unheard-of beaftlinefs! They had as many wives as they pleafed, and all thefe, and other abominations, it was the will of our Lord Jefus Chrift that we fhould be the inftruments to fweep from the

land,

land, fubftituting in their places, a good policy and the holy doctrine.
It is true that after the lapfe of two years, when the country was fub-
jugated and civilized, certain worthy fathers Francifcans, of good example and doctrine came here, and were followed in three or four years
by fathers of the order of St. Dominic, who completed what others
had begun, but if it is duly confidered it will appear that the meed and
honour of deftroying the evil cuftoms of the land, in juftice belongs to
us the true conquerors, in preference to any other perfons, even though
they fhould be of the holy profeffion.

Since the deftruction of idolatry, by the will of God, and with
his holy aid, and the good fortune and facred chriftianity of the moft
chriftian Emperor Don Carlos of glorious memory, and of our monarch
and moft fortunate fovereign, the invincible King of Spain, our lord
Don Philip his dear and much beloved fon, to whom may God grant
years, and much increafe of dominion, to be enjoyed by him during
his fortunate and holy life, and to be tranfmitted from him to his pof-
terity, there have been baptized in this country, all the natives, whofe
fouls formerly were funk and loft in the infernal pit. At prefent alfo
as there are here many reverend fathers of the different orders, they go
through the country preaching and baptizing, whereby the holy Evan-
gelifts are firmly planted in the hearts of the natives, who confefs every
year, and thofe fufficiently advanced in the knowledge of the faith co-
mulgate. The churches alfo and their altars are richly adorned, with
all requifites for holy worfhip, as, croffes, and candlefticks, wax candles, chalices, cups, plates, and veffels for incenfe, all of filver. The
ornaments of the altars and croffes are of velvet and damafk, and other
rich materials of various colours and workmanfhip, aud embroidered
with gold, filk, and pearls. The funerals alfo are diftinguifhed by their
emblematic reprefentations of fkulls and bones, and with their palls,
fome good, and others not fo. Each town alfo has its bells, according
to its ability. There are choirs alfo in the chapels, of good voices
which fing in concert, tenors, and trebles, and counter-altos. In fome

places

places are organs, and most have flutes, hautbois, sackbuts, dulcimers, with trumpets base and treble, more in this one province of Guatimala than there are in my native country, which is Old Castille. It is a thing worthy to thank God on to see the devotion which the natives exhibit when at holy mass, especially if it is said by fathers of the orders of St. Francis, or of Mercy, who are appointed to the cures of parishes. All the natives also, men, women, and children, are taught the holy orations in their mother tongue, and when they pass a cross, crucifix, or altar, they bow, and falling on their knees say a Pater Noster or Ave Maria. We, the conquerors also taught them to keep wax candles lighted before the holy altars and crosses, for before our arrival they did not know the use of wax in making candles. We also taught them to behave with respect to the reverend fathers, and when they came to their towns, to go out to meet and receive them with lighted wax candles, ringing the bells, and giving them plentifully to eat; and thus they do. They have also other holy and good customs, for on the day of our Lady, or of Corpus Christi, and other solemn feasts, when we make processions, most of the neighbours of this city of Guatimala go in procession with crosses and lighted candles, bearing the image of the saint who is their patron or patroness, as richly dressed as they can afford; and they go singing the litanies, and other holy orations, and sound their flutes and trumpets.

The natives of these countries have also learned the trades used amongst us in Castille, and have their shops, manufactories, and journeymen, and gain their livelihood thereby. The gold and silversmiths work both in cast metal, and by the hammer, and excel, as do the lapidaries and painters. The engravers execute first rate works, with their fine instruments of iron, especially upon emeralds, whereon they represent all the acts of the holy passion of our redeemer and Saviour Jesus Christ, in such a manner that those who had not seen them execute it, would not believe that such works could be done by Indians; insomuch that according to my judgment, that famous painter of ancient times

the

the renowned Apelles, or the modern ones named Michael Angelo and Berruguete, and another a native of Burgos who is in great fame, being as they say a second Apelles, could not with their subtle pencils equal the works which are done by three Mexican artists named Andres de Aquino, Juan de la Cruz, and El Crespillo. In addition to all these things, the sons of the chiefs used to be grammarians, and were learning very well, until they were forbidden by the holy synod, under an order of the most reverend archbishop of Mexico, but many of them are now, notwithstanding, literate. They are also weavers of silk, stuffs, and cloths, and manufacturers thereof, through all the various stages. They have also learned to be hatters and soap boilers. Two trades only could never be acquired by them; one is, that of making glass, the other that of the apothecary; but this is not owing to any defect of natural genius, for they are surgeons, and herbalists, jugglers, and makers of puppets, and of violins. Tillers of land they were before our arrival; and now they rear stock, and break bullocks, and plow, sow wheat, manure, reap, sell, and make bread and biscuit. They have planted their lands and inheritances with the fruit trees of Old Spain, and sell the fruit, cutting down the unwholesome peach trees, and overshading plantains, to make room for quince, apple, and pear trees, which they hold in high estimation. We have taught them also laws and justice, and in consequence, they every year elect their ordinary alcaldes, regidors, notaries, alguazils, fiscals, and major domos. They have their halls of common council, with bailiffs, where they meet two days in the week, judging, and sentencing, and for some offences punishing and whipping; but for murder and higher crimes, they refer them to the governors, if there is no court of royal audience.

I have further been told by persons well informed upon the subject, that in Tlascala, Tezcuco, Cholula, Guaxocingo, Tepeaca, and other great cities, when the natives go to council, gilt maces are borne before the governors and alcaldes, as is done before the viceroys, and they do

justice

justice with as much zeal and activity as is used among us, priding themselves thereon, and being very anxious to obtain a knowledge of our laws.

All the caciques have horses and are rich, and ride, handsomely caparisoned and attended by their pages, through and about their respective towns. In some towns also they exercise with the lance on horseback, run at the ring, and have bull fights, especially on the days of Corpus Christi, St. John, St. James, our Lady in August, or the patron or patroness of the town. Many also of them will face the bulls be they ever so fierce, and are excellent horsemen, especially those of a place named Chiapa de los Indios. Those who are caciques now breed horses, and use them and mules for ordinary purposes, conveying by their means, wood, maiz, and lime for sale. Many of the natives have likewise taken up the trade of arrieros or carriers, as is in practice in Castille. To conclude, they excel in all manufactures, not excepting that of tapestry.

Other advantages and profits are also derived from our illustrious services. By them our mother country has obtained gold, silver, precious stones, grain, wool, sarsaparilla, and hides; all which are annually transmitted thither to the benefit of his Majesty's revenue. I do not include the presents we at various times sent, and that which is exported by merchants and passengers, for since the time that the wise King Solomon built the holy temple of Jerusalem with the gold and silver which he caused to be brought from the Islands of Tarsis, Ofir, and Saba, ancient or modern history do not record such treasures to have been derived from any country, as what have been sent from New Spain; and this I say, because although it is notorious that from Peru many millions in gold and silver have been obtained, yet at the time of the conquest of this country Peru was unknown, nor was it gained until ten years after. We also from the first continued to send to his Majesty most rich presents, for which and other reasons, I rate this

country

country higher in estimation, because we well know that Peru has been involved in cruel civil wars, whereas we have remained, and will continue to do so, our breasts prostrate on the earth in submission and allegiance to our lord the King, and ready to expose and devote our lives and fortunes in his service.

Let the curious reader consider the number of cities of New Spain, which from their being so many, I will not detail; our ten bishoprics, not including the archbishopric of the noble city of Mexico, the three courts of royal audience, together with the succession of governors, archbishops, and bishops, our holy cathedrals and monasteries, Dominican, Franciscan, Mercenarian, and Augustin, our hospitals with the extensive remissions and pardons attached to them, and the Santa Casa of our Lady of Guadeloupe with the holy miracles there performed every day, and let us give thanks to God, and to his blessed mother our Lady, for giving us grace and support to conquer these countries, where so much christianity is now established.

Let it be also remembered, that in Mexico there is a university wherein are studied and learned grammar, theology, rhetoric, logic, philosophy, and other sciences. There is also a printing press for books both in Latin and Romance, and in this college they graduate as licentiates and doctors; to which I might add many other instances to enhance the value of these countries, such as the mines of silver, and other discoveries, whereby prosperity and grandeur redound to the mother country. If all which I have now said does not suffice, let the wise and learned read my history from beginning to end, and they will then confess, that there never existed in the world men who by bold atchievement have gained more for their Lord and King, than we the brave conquerors; amongst the most valiant of whom I was considered as one, and am the most ancient of all. I say again that I,—I myself,—I, am a true conqueror: and the most ancient of all.

I will

I will now propose a few questions by way of dialogue, with the immortal and illustrious goddess of Fame, who has seen, and proclaims through the world, our manifold, great, and remarkable services, to God, his Majesty and all Christendom, and cries with a loud voice, saying, that it is in justice and in reason, that we should have better estates and situations than others who have not served his Majesty here or elsewhere. The goddess also enquires where are our palaces, and mansions, adorned with distinguishing blazons, with sculptures of our coats of arms, and monumental trophies of our heroic actions, in the same manner as those cavaliers have who served their king in Spain, our atchievements being no way inferior to theirs, but on the contrary of most eminent merit, and not exceeded by any. The goddess of Fame also enquires for those conquerors who escaped from cruel deaths, and for the tombs and monuments of those who fell.

To these questions I reply as follows, with much brevity. Oh excellent and illustrious Fame! desired and sought for by the good and virtuous, but shunned and hated by the malicious, why do you not exalt us as our merits deserve? know, goddess, that of five hundred and fifty soldiers who left the Island of Cuba with Cortes, at the moment that I am writing this history in the year one thousand five hundred and sixty eight no more than five are living, the rest having been killed in the wars, sacrificed to idols, or died naturally. In answer to your question concerning their tombs and monuments, I tell you that their tombs are the maws of cannibal Indians, who devoured their limbs, and of tigers, serpents, and birds of prey, which feasted on their mangled bodies. Such were their sepulchres, and such their monuments! but to me it appears that the names of those ought to be written in letters of gold, who died so cruel a death, for the service of God and his Majesty, to give light to those who were in darkness, and to procure wealth which all men desire.

The illustrious goddess next asks me for an account of those who

came

came with Narvaez, and with Garray; to which I reply, that the number of the foldiers who came with the former was one thoufand three hundred exclufive of the mariners, of whom not more than ten or eleven furvive, the reft having fallen in the wars, and being facrificed and devoured. Thofe who came with Garray, according to my account, including the three companies which landed at St. Juan de Ulua previous to the arrival of Garray himfelf, were in all one thoufand two hundred foldiers, moft of whom were facrificed and devoured in the province of Panuco. Fame alfo afks for the fifteen foldiers who accompanied Lucas Vafquez de Aillon who loft his life on the coaft of Florida; to which I reply that they are all dead. I alfo inform you Oh excellent Fame! that there only remain alive at this moment five of the companions of Cortes, and we are very old, and bowed down with infirmities, and very poor, and with a heavy charge of fons to provide for, and of daughters to marry off, and grandchildren to maintain, and little rent to do it withall! and thus we pafs our lives, in pain, in labour, and in forrow.

Having now anfwered your queftions illuftrious Fame relative to our monuments, blazons, and palaces, I requeft of you that henceforward you exalt to more effect your moft virtuous and excellent voice, in order that our high prowefles may be made known to the univerfe, and not be obfcured as they are by the flanders of the malignant. To this my requeft moft virtuous Fame replies, that fhe will do fo moft willingly; and alfo, that fhe is aftonifhed to find that we have not the beft properties allotted to us in that country which we conquered, and which it was his Majefty's orders fhould be given to us, in like manner as the Marquis Cortes was rewarded, not indeed to the fame extent, but moderately. The goddefs alfo fays that the actions of the valiant and magnanimous Cortes are always to be moft highly eftimated, and confidered amongft thofe moft celebrated in hiftory. She alfo at the fame time obferves, that in the hiftories of Gomara and the Doctor Illefcas and others, no mention is made of any of us, but they only fay, "Cortes
"difcovered,"

difcovered," and "Cortes conquered;" the captains and foldiers remaining unnoticed; but fhe has been very happy to find that all which I have narrated in my hiftory is ftrictly conformable to the truth, and that I follow matter of fact clofely and literally, without running into fervile praifes, and that I do not depreciate many valiant captains and foldiers to exalt one, as is the cafe with Gomara and the other hiftorians. The good goddefs alfo promifes me, that fhe will proclaim thefe truths wherever fhe fhall be, and further, that if this my hiftory is publifhed, it fhall be credited, and its authenticity acknowledged wherever it is feen or heard, and that it fhall obfcure and annull all others.

Befides what I have here propofed by way of dialogue, a certain doctor, an oydor of the court of royal audience of Guatimala, afked me how it happened that when Cortes wrote to his Majefty, and alfo when he went the firft time to Caftille, he did not folicit for us, fince we were, under God, the means whereby he acquired his marquifate and government. To this I then replied, and now fay, that when his Majefty gave him the government, he therewith received the better part of this whole country, believing that he was to remain abfolute mafter thereof, and to have unlimited liberty to beftow or deprive as he thought proper; and this, it is fuppofed, was the reafon why he would not and did not write on the fubject. Alfo, at the time his Majefty gave him his marquifate, he folicited the government in the fame manner that he had held it before; but it was then refufed him, and he did not think of afking any thing that might be ferviceable to us, but only to himfelf.

Further, the veedor and factor, together with other cavaliers of Mexico had reprefented to his Majefty, that the Marquis had taken for himfelf the beft provinces and towns of New Spain, and had affigned others to his friends and relations newly come from Caftille, leaving very little for the royal patrimony; whereupon, as we afterwards learned, his Majefty was pleafed to order that all the overplus fhould be divided

amongft

amongft us, the companions of Cortes, but the Emperor was at that time in Barcelona, preparing to embark for Flanders. Had Cortes immediately after the conqueft divided this country into five parts, and affigned one of the richeft and beft of the fifths for his Majefty; allotted one fhare and a half for himfelf, for churches, monafteries, and municipal properties, as alfo for a fund wherefrom his Majefty could reward cavaliers who ferved him in Italy or againft the Turks and Moors; and divided the other two fifths and a half, by grants in perpetuity to us, we fhould have been all fatisfactorily provided for. As our Cæfar was fo chriftian a monarch, and as the conqueft of this country coft him nothing, he would have readily granted us thefe favours. But we at that time did not know how to apply for juftice, nor to whom to reprefent our fervices or our injuries, except to Cortes himfelf, who did in the bufinefs as he thought fit. We therefore remained with the little which had been affigned us, until we faw that Don Francifco de Montejo who went to wait upon his Majefty in Europe obtained the appointments of adelantado and governor of Yucatan, eftates in Mexico, and other rewards. Diego de Ordas alfo, who went to court, obtained an encomienda of St. Jago, and diftricts in New Spain. Then Don Pedro de Alvarado went to kifs his Majefty's feet and was made adelantado and governor of Guatimala and Chiapa, commander of the order of St. Jago, and obtained diftricts of lands. Laft went Cortes, who was created a marquis, and appointed captain general of the South Sea.

When we the conquerors therefore faw, that thofe who did not reach his Majefty's prefence had no one to fpeak in our favour, we fent to petition that whatever lands thenceforward fell vacant, fhould be diftributed in perpetuities amongft us, according as our claims were fubftantiated, as was the cafe before the firft court of royal audience held in Mexico, whereof Nuno de Guzman was prefident. His Majefty's exprefs directions to Nuno de Guzman were, to throw the whole property of New Spain into a mafs, and then to make the divifions more equal, deducting in due proportion from the immoderate grants of

Ttt　　　　　　　　　　　　　　　　　Cortes

Cortes. Alfo, that to us, the true conquerors fhould be given the beft diftricts and of moft rent, leaving the cities and great towns for his Majefty's property. The Emperor alfo ordered that the vaffals of Cortes fhould be counted, leaving no more with him than his patent fpecified; but what was to be done with the furplus I do not recollect. The reafon why Nuno de Guzman and the oydors did not make this repartition in perpetuity was, that they were mifled by bad advifers, whom, not to difhonour, I will not name, but the perfons I have alluded to told them, that if the conquerors once found themfelves provided for, they would ceafe to refpect and be dependent on them, as was the cafe while they were compelled to fupplicate for a fubfiftence. As alfo, by retaining, they kept the power of beftowing the vacant lands at their pleafure, and to the advantage of their own private intereft. It is true that as diftricts fell vacant, Guzman and the oydors conftantly affigned them to conquerors, and colonifts, to their fatisfaction; and if that court was fuperceded, it was on account of the difputes with Cortes, and of marking free Indians for flaves.

In the year one thoufand five hundred and fifty, I being in Old Spain, the licentiate De la Gafca came from Peru, and with him D. Martin el Regente a Dominican friar; and repairing to the court which was then at Valladolid, his Majefty promoted the aforefaid father to the bifhopric of Las Charcas. At this period a council was formed, compofed of D. Fray B. de las Cafas bifhop of Chiapa, D. Vafco de Quiroga bifhop of Mechoacan, and other cavaliers who came as agents from New Spain and Peru, together with fome hidalgos who were brought by bufinefs to the court, and to this council I was alfo called, as being the moft ancient of the conquerors of New Spain.

De la Gafca and the other Peruvians had brought with them great quantities of treafure, as well for their own ufe as for his Majefty, the latter being fent from Seville to Augufta in Germany where the Emperor then was, and in his company our moft happy Don Philip king of

the

the Spains, our lord his dear and much beloved son, whom God guard. At that time certain of the Peruvian cavaliers waited on his Majesty with the treasure, and to petition that he would cause the allotment of lands in perpetuity to be made. It seems also, that previous to this time a petition to the same effect had been presented from New Spain by Gonzalo Lopez, and Alonzo de Villanueva, who had been sent as procuradors or agents from Mexico. It so happened that just then the bishopric of Palencia fell vacant, and was bestowed on the licentiate De la Gasca who was also made Conde de Pernia, on account, as was said at the court, of the services rendered in Peru, which was then at peace.

His Majesty was pleased, in regard to the repartition of lands in perpetuity, to order, that the Marquis de Mondejar president of the royal council of the Indies, the licentiates Gutierre Velasquez, Tello de Sandoval, Gregorio Lopez and Briviesca, and the Doctor Hernan Perez de la Fuente, oydors of that court, together with cavaliers of other royal councils should assemble, to consider, and see how the repartition should be made, as was best for the service of God and for his Majesty's interest.

When these cavaliers were met in the house of Pero Gonzalez de Leon, where was established the royal council of the Indies, it was proposed in that very illustrious assembly, that the perpetual repartition should take place in New Spain and in Peru; I am not certain that Grenada and Bobotan were included, but am inclined to think that they were, and the reasons offered in support of the measure were holy and good. It was argued that if the lands were granted in perpetuity, the proprietors would for their own interests treat the natives better, and pay more attention to the conversion of them to our holy faith. That if they suffered from sickness or misfortune they would be attended to like their children, and the rents alleviated. The proprietors would also go into improvements, planting vines and breeding cattle; disputes

and

and litigations about lands and boundaries would ceafe, and the office of vifitadors or infpectors would be unneceffary. The minds alfo of the foldiers would be tranquillized, in knowing that the prefidents and governors had not the power of beftowing lands when they fell vacant, on their clients and favourites. His Majefty alfo in doing this would exonerate his royal confcience, in recompenfing thofe who had ferved him faithfully. To thefe, many other good reafons were added. It was alfo propofed to deprive the turbulent and rebellious in Peru of their diftricts. After all this had been well debated and confidered in the illuftrious affembly, we proceeded to give our opinions in favour of the perpetual repartition.

It was then oppofed by the Bifhop of Chiapa, his affociate Fray Rodrigo of the order of St. Dominic, the Bifhop of Palencia, the Marquis of Mondejar, and two oydors of the royal council of his Majefty. The Marquis of Mondejar did not however fpeak upon the occafion, but remained as it were on the look out to fee which party was likely to carry the queftion. The arguments ufed by the others againft the repartition were, that many in Peru had now life eftates, who fo far from deferving perpetuities, merited confifcation, and that if peace was once eftablifhed in that country, if the foldiers who were unprovided for faw that there was no fund for that purpofe, they would become mutinous and caufe new troubles. The Bifhop of Mechoacan who was of our party hereupon afked the licentiate De la Gafca, how it had happened that he did not chaftize the mutineers as he very well knew them; whereas on the contrary he had given them lands. To this the other replied, laughing, that he had hanged and quartered many of them, and thought it no fmall atchievement to have efcaped from amongft them fafe and found. More was alfo faid on this fubject.

It was propofed, and approved by many prefent, that the few of the real conquerors of New Spain who now remained, including thofe who came with Cortes, with Narvaez, and with Garray, fhould re-

ceive

ceive perpetuities, referring the other matter to future consideration. As
soon as this proposition was made, the other party moved that all further proceedings should be postponed until the return of his Majesty to
Castille, because in an affair of such importance his presence was neceffary. It was then urged by the Bishop of Mechoacan and other cavaliers, as well as myself, that the perpetuities might be granted in New
Spain, leaving the Peruvian procuradors to act as they thought fit, this
being conformable to his Majesty's declarations and instructions in our
favour. This now brought on much debate; for we insisted that whatever reasons might be against the granting perpetuities in Peru, could
be of no avail against us in New Spain, considering our great services
to his Majesty and all Christendom. But all we said was of no effect
with the members of the royal council of the Indies, the Bishop Fray
Bartholome de las Casas, Fray Rodrigo his associate, and the Bishop of
Las Charcas. They said that on the return of his Majesty from Au-
gusta in Germany every thing should be arranged to the satisfaction of
the conquerors, and thus the affair dropped for the present.

Intelligence of these matters being conveyed by express to Mexico,
the conquerors there proposed to send procuradors, to apply to his Majesty for our interest, exclusively. In consequence, after my return
from the court I was written to, here, in this city of Guatimala, by
Captain Andres de Tapia, P. Moreno Medrano, and J. de Limpias
Caravajal "the deaf," giving me an account of their intention, and of
those conquerors concerned with them, amongst whom I was put down
as one of the most ancient. I accordingly went round with the letter to
the other conquerors settled in this city, to raise a sum by subscription
for the purpose. This project failed from want of money. It was
then determined that the conquerors in Mexico, conjointly with the
whole of the community, should send procuradors to Castille; but neither was this carried into effect. At a subsequent period, our uncon-
quered king and lord Don Philip, whom God preserve, and may he
live many years in augmentation of power, was pleased to command by
his

his royal ordinances that the conquerors and their posterity should be provided for, attending in the first instance to those who were married, as may be seen in the royal cedules.

When I had written out fairly this my history, two licentiates requested me to lend it to them for their perusal, in order that they might know in detail the occurrences which happened in the conquest of New Spain, and also that they might see what difference existed between my account, and those of Gomara and the Doctor Illescas, relative to the heroic actions of the Marquis Del Valle. I accordingly presented this book to them for their perusal, with the respect which is due to scholars from a poor illiterate person like myself, desiring them at the same time to make no alteration whatever herein, as what I had written was the strict truth. As soon as they had read it, one of them who was a great rhetorician, and vain of his knowledge, began to praise the book, and expressed his surprise at my memory, and at my being able to carry in it such a series of matter, from the time I first came to these countries.

The licentiates also observed, that in regard to my stile or language, it was conformable to that in ordinary use in Old Castille, and that as such it was the more agreeable, not being embarrassed with flowery affected phrases, such as are made use of by historians in general. They also observed that it seemed to them as if I praised myself greatly, in the battles which I give an account of, whereas I ought to have left that to be done by others; and that I should have given my witnesses, testimonies, and quotations, as authorities for what I wrote, and not have said drily, "that I did; this I saw;" it not being conformable to the custom of historical writing; for I am not a witness for myself. To these observations I then replied, as I do now, that in the year one thousand five hundred and forty the Marquis Del Valle wrote a letter to his Majesty giving an account of me and my services, how I had come twice to this country on voyages of discovery previous to his expedition,

how

how he had often been an eye witnefs of my conduct as a brave foldier in battle as well in Mexico as in other places, how I accompanied him in his expedition to Honduras and Higueras, and many other particulars which to avoid prolixity I will not relate. The moft illuftrious viceroy alfo, Don Alonzo de Mendoza wrote to his Majefty informing him of what he had learned relative to me from the captains by whofe fide I fought, and his account was in all refpects conformable to that of the Marquis Del Valle. Proofs to the fame purport were alfo prefented on my part to the royal council of the Indies in the year one thoufand five hundred and forty.

Now, faid I, gentlemen licentiates, are not the Marquis Del Valle, the viceroy D. A. de Mendoza, and my proofs, good witneffes? but if they will not fuffice, I will produce you the Emperor our lord Don Carlos the fifth, who by his royal letter, fealed with his royal feal, commanded all viceroys and prefidents, that refpecting the many and good fervices which I had rendered, benefits fhould be conferred upon me and mine. The original letters are now in my poffeffion, and the copies depofited at court in the archives of the fecretary Ochoa de Luyado. Such was my anfwer to the obfervation of the licentiates.

But to return to my fubject, if more teftimony is wanting look at New Spain which is three times larger than our Caftille, and more thickly inhabited by Spaniards, and the great wealth which it fends to Caftille. But I have obferved that the hiftorians Gomara and Illefcas never chofe to relate our heroic actions, leaving all our value and honours in the dark, where they would have remained were it not for this my true hiftory, and affigning fuch great merit to Cortes; in which, although they were right to a certain degree, yet they ought not at the fame time to have forgotten us.

Of the achievements of Cortes a part alfo of the honour falls to me, for I was one of the moft forward in every battle by his fide, as I

was

was in many others when he sent me under different captains to conquer provinces, as is found written in my history, how, when, and where.

Also when Cortes returned to Europe the first time, to kiss his Majesty's feet, he informed him that he had many valiant captains and companions in the Mexican wars, and who he believed did not yield to the most famous in ancient history. Of this praise a proportionate share falls to me. Further, at Algiers, he said much in praise of his companions the conquerors. Of this I come in for my portion, as I was one of them.

As to what the licentiates said, that I praise myself so much, and that I ought to leave it to be done by others, I say, in common life it is the custom of neighbours to speak of each other as each deserves; but he who never was in the wars with us, nor saw them, nor heard of them, how can he speak of us? were the birds which flew over our heads while in battle to give accounts of us? or the clouds? who then was to speak our praises but we ourselves? Indeed gentlemen licentiates said I had you found that I detracted from the honour due to one of our valiant captains or soldiers, and ascribed it to myself, then you might justly blame me. But the fact is that I do not praise myself so much as I ought.

I will now make a comparison, although on one side the subject of it is very high, and on the other a poor soldier like myself. Historians say that the great emperor and warrior Julius Cæsar was in fifty three pitched battles. I say that I was in many more battles than Julius Cæsar, as may be seen in this my history. Historians also say that Julius Cæsar was brave and active in battle, and that when he had time, he at night committed to writing with his own hand, his heroic actions, although he had many historians, not chusing to entrust the office to them. Truly this happened many years ago, and may or may not be the case; whereas what I relate occurred yesterday as it may be said.

It

It is therefore not extraordinary if I relate the battles in which I fought, that in future ages it ſhould be ſaid, "thus did Bernal Diaz del Caſtillo," in order that my ſons and their poſterity ſhould enjoy the praiſes of their anceſtor, in the manner that many cavaliers and lords of vaſſals in the preſent day, do the fames and blazons of their predeceſſors. I will however drop this ſubject leſt the detracting malicious, to whom theſe things are odious, ſhould charge me with digreſſing too much. There are alſo conquerors now living to contradict me if I were in error, and the world is ſo malevolent that any ſuch thing could hardly paſs without animadverſion; but the narrative itſelf is the beſt teſtimony of its veracity.

I will now enumerate and particulariſe the various battles and other matters of warfare in which I was preſent. They are as follows. At the point of Cotoche, with Captain F. H. de Cordova. At Champoton, a battle, wherein half our companions were killed. In Florida, where we landed to procure water. Under Captain J. de Grijalva, a ſecond battle in Champoton. In my third voyage under Cortes, at Tabaſco, two pitched battles. On our arrival in New Spain, the battle of Cingapacinga. Shortly after, three pitched battles with the Tlaſcalans. The affair of Cholula. On our entry into Mexico I was at the ſeizure of Montezuma; I do not mention it as an affair of war, but on account of its great boldneſs. In four months after, the attack upon Narvaez whom we under Cortes defeated with two hundred and ſeventy ſix men, he having one thouſand three hundred. The relief of Alvarado who was beſieged by the Mexicans, when they made war upon us during eight days and nights, and killed above eight hundred and ſeventy ſoldiers; I conſider ſix battles as having happened during this period, at which I was preſent. The battle of Obtumba. A battle at Tepeaca. Under Cortes a battle at Tezcuco. Two field battles, in one of which I was wounded in the throat by a lance. Two actions concerning the fields of maize. In the expedition round the lake when we made that raſh and inconſiderate attack upon the fortreſſes named the

Vvv

rocks

rocks of the marquis. The battle of Cuernavaca. Three battles at Suchimillco. The fiege of Mexico which lafted ninety three days, during which I was engaged, as I find by my account, in above eighty battles and fkirmifhes. After the conqueft when I was fent to pacify the provinces of Guacacualco, Chiapa, and the Zapotecans. In Chamula and Cuitlan, two engagements. In Teapa and Chimatan two engagements; here I was wounded badly in the throat. I forgot to mention in its place, how, after our flight from Mexico we were purfued for nine days, and fought four battles. In the Expedition to Higueras and Honduras, an action at Culacotu, where my horfe which coft me fix hundred crowns was killed. After my return to Mexico I went againft the Zapotecans and Minxes in the mountains. I do not mention numberlefs other engagements and dangers in which I have been, as it would be endlefs to detail them all. Nor do I chufe to fay how I was one of the firft who came to lay fiege to Mexico, three or four days at leaft before Cortes.

I have therefore according to this account been prefent in one hundred and nineteen battles and engagements; and it is not extraordinary if I praife myfelf, as what I fay is the mere truth. Nor are thefe old ftories or hiftories of Romans, of many ages paft; for evident and true are the many and notable fervices which I have rendered; firft to God, then to his Majefty, and all Chriftendom; and I give thanks and praifes to our Lord Jefus Chrift, that I efcaped from all dangers, to make thefe things manifeft; and I alfo fay, and praife myfelf thereon, that I have been in as many battles and engagements as, according to hiftory, the Emperor Henry the fourth.

F I N I S.

Notes and Errata.

or frequently miſtakes dates; it has been therefore judged neceſſary in the heads of chapters according to the moſt correct accounts.

chapter 3. although the appointment of Cortes took place before, the il for the continent until 1519.

Line 19. *inſtead of* "who took Guatimotzin" *read* whom Guatimotzin took.

—— 18. *inſtead of* "got" *read* gone.

—— 8. from the bottom, *inſtead of* "his" *read* this.

—— 7. *between* "to" *and* "which" *inſert*, the flat ſummit of.

—— 3. *from the bottom* "invalids" *note*, ſuffering by the diſeaſe aſcribed to Hiſpaniola.

—— 8. *inſtead of* "hundred" *read* thouſand.

—— 17. *after* "friends" *inſert* to whom they were given by us.

—— 16. *inſtead of* "Guatimotzin now" *read* Coadlavaca, late.

—— 2. *inſtead of* "our" *read* their.

—— 4. *inſtead of* "we" *read* they.

—— 14. *inſtead of* "Figuero" *read* Herrera.

INTED FOR J. WRIGHT, PICCADILLY, BY J. DEAN, CONGLETON.